Latin 101:
Learning a Classical Language

Hans-Friedrich Mueller, Ph.D.

THE
GREAT
COURSES

PUBLISHED BY:

THE GREAT COURSES
Corporate Headquarters
4840 Westfields Boulevard, Suite 500
Chantilly, Virginia 20151-2299
Phone: 1-800-832-2412
Fax: 703-378-3819
www.thegreatcourses.com

Copyright © The Teaching Company, 2013

Hans-Friedrich Mueller, Ph.D.
Thomas B. Lamont Professor of Ancient and Modern Literature and Chair of the Department of Classics
Union College

Professor Hans-Friedrich Mueller serves as the Thomas B. Lamont Professor of Ancient and Modern Literature and Chair of the Department of Classics at Union College in Schenectady, New York. Professor Mueller received his B.A. in Latin from the University of Wisconsin–Milwaukee in 1985 and, for the next six years, taught Latin and German at Countryside High School in Clearwater, Florida. He earned his M.A. from the University of Florida in 1989 and returned to graduate school in 1991, receiving his Ph.D. in 1994 from The University of North Carolina at Chapel Hill. Subsequently, Professor Mueller spent a year at the Bavarian Academy of Sciences in Munich, Germany, where he worked on entries for an encyclopedic Latin dictionary, the *Thesaurus Linguae Latinae*.

Under Professor Mueller's direction, the Union College program in Classics has been noted especially for its interdisciplinary curriculum. Professor Mueller received the American Philological Association's Award for Excellence in the Teaching of Classics at the College Level in 2000, as well as two awards for excellence in teaching at Florida State University. At the University of Florida, he developed a graduate distance-learning program in Classics for high school teachers. In addition to numerous articles, Professor Mueller is the author of *Roman Religion in Valerius Maximus*, the editor of an abridged edition of Gibbon's *Decline and Fall of the Roman Empire*, and the translator of Andreas Mehl's *Roman Historiography: An Introduction to Its Basic Aspects and Development*. He is also the author of *Caesar: Selections from his Commentarii De Bello Gallico* and coauthor of *Caesar: A LEGAMUS Transitional Reader*.

In German, the surname Mueller means "miller." Both the German surname Mueller and the English surname Miller, however, derive from Molinarius, a Latin word for "miller" and the professor's preferred pseudonym. ∎

Table of Contents

Table of Contents

Latin 101: Learning a Classical Language

Scope:

This course provides a thorough introduction to the pronunciation, morphology, and syntax of classical Latin to enable you to read Latin prose and poetry with confidence, precision, and pleasure. No prior experience is required. We begin where the action is, with the Latin verb, and work our way systematically through the formation of nouns, adjectives, participles, infinitives, relatives, interrogatives, and more. All grammatical terms are explained, and all Latin is translated, both literally and idiomatically. Every lecture includes opportunities for participation through repetition, translation, and pop quizzes—the answers to which are always supplied so that you may check your work.

Throughout the lectures, we combine the brass tacks of mastering the grammatical building blocks of Latin with exercises in reading authentic Latin texts, and we do not shy away from challenge. Early and frequent exposure to authentic passages from the works of ancient authors is essential for gaining an understanding of Latin syntax. Learning the forms of individual words is not enough. Without a sound grasp of syntax, we cannot understand how grammatical links allow us, as readers, to re-create and comprehend authors' statements and thoughts. Building these skills requires exposure to a range of syntactical patterns. Practice is essential for nourishing confidence and fostering a love for the seductive beauties of Latin prose and poetry on the solid basis of morphology and syntax.

To learn to read Latin with understanding, we must also adjust our cultural expectations. Ancient Romans were not modern Americans. We thus read authentic texts that help us appreciate ancient Roman attitudes toward war, love, marriage, the gods, death, and the afterlife. How did Julius Caesar justify his invasion of Gaul? Why, according to the late imperial historian Eutropius, did Caesar's fellow senators stab him 33 times? How many kisses, according to Catullus, were enough if young lovers wanted to frustrate gossipy old men? Why did Roman jurists justify a legal ban on the exchange of gifts between husbands and wives? What did ancient Roman law have to say about divorce or debt? What can Jerome's Latin version of the Bible teach us about classical Latin? What can an inscription from a Roman tomb tell us about ancient Roman views on death and the afterlife? Such texts do more than allow us to observe how Latin works as a language. They have much to tell us about ancient expectations, the awareness of which likewise plays a crucial role in reading classical Latin with understanding.

Our approach is always comparative. Whether we study grammar or vocabulary, we use Latin to illuminate English. Almost every Latin word has been productive in shaping the words we use every day. We use these contributions both to acquire Latin vocabulary and to deepen our understanding of English. Our exploration of Latin grammar and syntax and ancient Roman thought sheds comparative and illuminating light, too. The more we study, read, learn, and understand Latin, the better sense we gain of who we are today and why. We inhabit a linguistic and cultural world shaped by the words and thought of ancient Rome. Latin reveals these many secrets and more, but only to those who make the journey in Latin. ■

Pronouncing Classical Latin
Lecture 1

For thousands of years, the Mediterranean, northern Europe, and the world spoke Latin. Even after the fall of the Roman Empire, when the Venerable Bede wrote the history of England, he wrote in Latin, not English, which didn't exist yet—at least not in a form we can understand today. Even today, more than two-thirds of English vocabulary derives from Latin. The aim in this course is to introduce pronunciation, morphology, syntax, vocabulary, and authentic Latin texts in their cultural context. All this will enable you to appreciate the mysteries that lurk in the words we use every day and to unlock the even greater treasures hidden in the original Latin.

Latin all around us

- Latin is the foreign language that lies at the center of our intellectual traditions, and it is the foreign language we speak every day, whether we are aware of it or not. Indeed, original Latin remains all around us. A simple example can be found in university mottoes. For example, the motto of the University of North Carolina at Chapel Hill is *Lūx, lībertās,* "Light, liberty."

  - *Lūx* is now a technical word in English that refers to units of light in photometry, while *lībertās* has emerged in English as "liberty."

  - In English, "freedom" is a substantive or noun form that derives from the adjective "free." *Lībertās* is likewise a substantive that derives from the adjective *līber,* which in Latin, means "free." Thus, a "liberal education" is one fit for a person who enjoys the privilege of personal freedom or liberty, and the "liberal arts" are the skills useful to a person who enjoys the status of a free person.

- Of course, we can also find Latin on a U.S. penny (*Ē plūribus ūnum,* "Out of the many, one") and on the Great Seal of the United States on the back of a dollar bill. Over the eye floating above a pyramid is the phrase *annuit coeptis*. Below the pyramid is *novus ordō seclōrum.*

- ○ These phrases speak to the American Revolution as a turning point. *Annuit coeptis* refers to the eye of good fortune that has approved the undertakings of the revolutionaries.

- ○ *Novus ordō seclōrum* refers to a "new order of the ages" because the revolutionaries believed that their revolution was the dawning of a new age.

- You may have heard some other Latin phrases here and there: *habeās corpus* (literally, "you should have your body"), *tabula rasa* ("blank slate"), *persona nōn grāta* ("a person not pleasing"), and *curriculum vītae* (literally, "the racetrack of life").

- Contrary to whatever reports you may have heard, Latin is hardly dead. It lives on in Italian, French, Spanish, Romanian, Rhaeto-romance, Catalan, Haitian Creole, and of course, English.

The Great Seal of the United States, which appears on the back of the dollar bill, includes Latin phrases that the American revolutionaries believed related to their cause.

Pronunciation of the Latin alphabet
- The Romans adapted a West Greek alphabet, and the Greeks likely got their alphabet from the Phoenicians, a Semitic people inhabiting coastal areas that we now call Lebanon. We don't, however, have to learn a new alphabet to learn Latin, because we already use the Roman alphabet ourselves. We have no new letters

to learn, but we will have to adjust some of the sounds for restored classical pronunciation.

- To make our work simple, we will discuss only letters that have sounds different from their pronunciation in English; these include vowels and the consonants C, G, I, and V.

- Latin vowels are pure; they each have just two sounds, as shown in the following table.

Vowel	Short Sound	Long Sound	Latin Examples	Notes
A	*a* ⁚ *uh* "uh" in *about, long*	*a* ⁚ *ah* "ah" in *father*	ăd, Rōmānus	Latin A is never pronounced as the English A in either *cat* or *Kate*.
E	"eh" in *get*	"ay" in *cake*	sĕd, sēparō	
I	"ih" in *kin*	"ee" in *machine*	in, līber	
O	"ou" in *ought*	"o" in *go*	nox, nōn	
U	as in *book*	as in *food*	mūrŭs	
Y	treat as *Latin "i"* (above)		Polybius	Used only in words deriving from Greek.

- Consonants in Latin have just one sound each, and for the most part, they represent the same sounds as they do in English. The sounds that differ are shown in the following table.

Consonant	Sound	Latin Examples
C	"k" in *car*	Caesar
G	"guh" in *game*	gemma
I	"yuh" in *yum*	iam
V	"wuh" - - - -	Vēnī, vīdī, vīcī

v

- Diphthongs are a combination of two vowels pronounced at the same time so as to produce a single sound. The following table shows the diphthongs found in Latin.

Diphthong	Sound	Latin Examples
ae	"i" in *ice*	Caesar, aeternus
oe	"oi" in *oil*	moenia, coeptis
au	"ow" in *howl*	Paullus, Paulus

Syllable stress

- The rules for stress in Latin are relatively simple. First, if a word has two syllables, always accent the first syllable: *CAE-sar*.

- If a word has three or more syllables, there are only two choices:
  - The accent goes on the second-to-last syllable if the vowel in the second-to-last syllable is long or counts as long. A short vowel counts as long if it is followed by two or more consonants.

  - If the vowel in the second-to-last syllable is short, then the accent falls on the third-to-last syllable.

Example	Explanation
Caesar	*Caesar* has two syllables, so the accent is on the first syllable.
libertas ("freedom")	The *e* in *libertas* is short, but it counts as long because it is followed by two or more consonants; thus, the stress is on the second-to-last syllable: *li-BER-tas*.
amāmus	The *a* in the second-to-last syllable is long, so that syllable gets the accent: *a-MA-mus*.
interficimus ("we kill")	For this type of verb (as we will learn later in the course), the *i* in the second-to-last syllable is short by nature; thus, the stress is on the third-to-last syllable: *interFIcimus*.

1. In the beginning God created the heavens and the earth.
2. The earth was empty, a formless mass cloaked in darkness.

Practice verses from Genesis (1:1–3)

In principiō creāvit Deus caelum et terram.
Terra autem erat inānis et vacua.
Et tenēbrae super faciem abyssī et spīritus Deī ferēbātur super aquās.
Dīxitque Deus fiat lūx et facta est lūx.

Memoranda ("Things to Remember")

Please learn the sounds made by Latin vowels, diphthongs, and consonants. Further information about Latin pronunciation may be found in Appendix §§ (= sections) 1–12.

1. In the beginning God created the heavens and the earth.
2. The earth was empty, a formless mass cloaked in darkness.
*   And the Spirit of God ~~was~~ was hovering over its surface.*
3. Then God said "Let there be light," and there was light.

i. Using the tables above, practice pronouncing the following words. Long vowels are marked with macrons; vowels that are not marked are short.

1. ad

2. pater

3. Caesar

4. sed

5. sēparō

6. gemma

7. in

8. cīvīlis

9. iam

10. bonus

11. nōn

12. mūrus

13. ventus

14. Vesta

15. aetās

16. moenia

17. aut

18. lībertās

19. amāmus

20. spectāmus

21. interficimus

ii. Please listen again to the "restored classical" recitation of Genesis 1:1–3 in the lecture; then practice pronouncing the following words and phrases.

1. in principiō

2. caelum

3. inānis et vacua

4. tenēbrae

5. fiat lūx

6. et vīdit Deus lūcem

7. appellāvitque

8. vespere

Pronouncing Classical Latin
Lecture 1—Transcript

Salvēte! Greetings! *Salvēte, discipulī!* Greetings, male students! *Salvēte, discipulae!* Greetings, female students! *Salvēte, discipulī discipulaeque, linguae Latīnae!* Greetings, students of the Latin language! *Nōmen mihi est Molinārius.* Born a "Mueller," you can call me *Molinārius,* the Latin word from which both "Mueller" and "Miller" derive. Unlike my ancestors, however, I grind not grain, but ancient languages. We aim in this course to introduce ancient Latin, the language of such politicians as Cicero and Caesar; the poets Catullus, Vergil, and Ovid; such church fathers as Augustine, Jerome, and Arnobius of Sicca; not to mention countless other authors ancient, medieval, and early modern.

For thousands of years, the Mediterranean, northern Europe, and the world spoke Latin. Even after the fall of the Roman Empire, when the Venerable Bede wanted to write the history of England, he wrote in Latin, not English—which didn't even exist yet. At least not in a form we can understand today. And when Martin Luther nailed his 95 theses on the church door in Wittenberg, did he use the ephemeral German dialect of his day? *Nein, überhaupt nicht!* He used something more permanent. He used Latin. What about modern physics? Can you say *Philosophiae Naturalis Principia Mathematica?* OK, fair enough, probably not, or you wouldn't be considering this course. But that was the title of the book—the Latin book—in which Isaac Newton laid out his laws of motion and the universal law of gravitation. Even today more than two thirds of English vocabulary derives from Latin. It's the foreign language that lies at the center of our intellectual traditions, and it's the foreign language we speak every day, whether we are aware of it or not.

But Latin remains around us in the original as well; simple example, university mottoes. I did my doctoral work the University of North Carolina at Chapel Hill. Its motto? *Lūx, lībertās.* Light, liberty. Lux is now a technical word in English that refers to units of light in photometry. *Lībertās* has been beaten up a bit over the centuries and has emerged, in English, as "liberty." When Brutus minted a coin to celebrate the assassination of Julius Caesar, what word did he put on his coin? *Lībertās.* When Pope Benedict resigned in 2013, he made his announcement in Latin, and said "I declare of my own free or, more literally, with full freedom -- *plena libertate* -- that I renounce my post" *plēnā lībertāte dēclārō mē ... commissum renuntiāre*. And there it was, liberty, *lībertās*, more than two thousand years later in a live broadcast in all its classical, or ecclesiastical, Latin glory. That's *glōria* for us Latin buffs. Need I mention our famous Statue of *Lībertās*?

Freedom, in English, is a substantive, or noun form, that derives from the adjective free. And *Lībertās* is, likewise, a substantive that derives from the adjective *līber*, which, in Latin, means "free." So liberal, our class smart alec asks—already—he asks, is someone who wants everything for free? I'm not taking the bait. Try this one instead. A *liberal* education is one fit for what kind of person? A person who enjoys the privilege of personal freedom or liberty. That's the kind of "free" we are talking about. And the *liberal* arts? The skills useful to a person who enjoys the status of a free person. The liberal arts and a liberal education are reserved for people in free societies because there is not much point in teaching slaves to think for themselves. Their masters prefer to do the thinking for them.

In the University of North Carolina at Chapel Hill, it's motto, *lux, libertas,* has obviously resonated across the ages. But we can find Latin in plenty of other places too. How about a U.S. penny? *Ē plūribus ūnum?* Out of the many one. Sure, everyone knows it, but who really understands it word for word? You, my friends, are on your way. And the great seal of the United States on the back of a dollar bill? Take a look. There is an eyeball floating above a pyramid. Above the eye: *annuit coeptis*; below the pyramid: *novus ordō seclōrum*. What do those phrases mean? They refer to the American Revolution as a turning point. *Annuit coeptis* refers to the eye of good fortune that has approved the undertakings of the revolutionaries. And the phrase below the pyramid? It refers to a "new order of the ages," *novus ordō seclōrum*, because the revolutionaries believed that their revolution was the dawning of a new age: Goodbye, monarchy, goodbye tyranny, hello, republic! The founding fathers knew their Latin, as did so most great thinkers, writers, poets, and scientists until relatively recent times.

You may have heard some other phrases here and there: *habeās corpus*, literally, you should have your body; *tabula rasa*, a blank slate; *persona nōn grāta*, a person not pleasing; *cv, curriculum vītae*, literally, the racetrack of life, "rat race" would work too. And the Pope? The Pope still publishes in Latin. Why? Stable vocabulary; stable grammar; for more than two thousand years. Seek, and ye shall find. Latin is everywhere. Can you say eternal in Latin? *aeterna*. But you're skeptical. You've heard the old saw that Latin is dead, as dead as dead can be; first it killed the Romans, and now it's killing me.

Please, please allow me to recite the first lines of a short poem in Latin, one we will read together in lesson twelve, and you tell me whether this language sounds dead or alive:

Vīvāmus, mē Lesbia atque amēmus

Rūmōrēsque senum sevēriōrum

ūnīus aestimēmus assis

sōlēs occidere et redīre possunt

nōbīs, cum semel occidit brevis lūx

nox est perpetu ūna dormienda.

Contrary to whatever reports you may have heard, Latin is hardly dead. Latin lives on. Can you think of the languages? Latin lives on in Italian, French, Spanish, Romanian, Rhaeto-Romance, Catalan, and Haitian Creole, but also in English. The only reason people do not clamor for, and demand Latin, is because they do not know what they are missing. But you do, and that's why you're here.

The aim in this course is to introduce pronunciation, morphology, syntax, vocabulary, and authentic Latin texts with their cultural context. All this will enable you to appreciate the mysteries that lurk in the words we use every day and to unlock the even greater treasures hidden in the original Latin. This will involve some work, of course, but with my help and your efforts, the pleasures along the way should be many and instructive. And, hey, pain can be pleasurable too. Would the simple act of drawing breath feel as good if no one had ever held our heads under water until we were convinced that we were about to drown? That didn't happen to you? Well, think of something else, then.

But where to begin? We have to begin at the beginning. God is, or for you pre-Christian Romanists, the gods are, in the details. True understanding is complete understanding. And what represents the beginning for budding Latinists? The letters, the letters we use to represent the sounds that constitute the beautiful and eternal Latin language. And to make Latin sound beautiful, we must know what sounds to make when we see Latin letters. *Incipiāmus*. Let's begin, shall we, with the letters and sounds that make up the Roman alphabet.

The Romans adapted a West Greek alphabet, and the Greeks, of course, likely got their alphabet from the Phoenicians, a Semitic people inhabiting coastal areas that we now call Lebanon. We can still hear Greek and Semitic connections in our own word for alphabet, which derives from the first two letters of the Greek alphabet, "a" and "b," or alpha and beta, corresponding, in their turn, to, for example, aleph and beth in the Hebrew alphabet. But, hey, do not panic. We don't have to learn these rather different alphabets. Because, as a matter of fact, we use the Roman alphabet ourselves, so you have no new letters to learn. But we will have to adjust some of the sounds for restored classical pronunciation. And to make things simple, we are only going to discuss letters that have sounds different from their pronunciation in English. We are going to discuss vowels, because English vowels are a mess. And we will discuss also the consonants C, G, I, and V. And no, I did not make an error. "I" is more than just a vowel; It's also a consonant.

Let's look at the Latin vowels first, and please keep in mind that the sounds of vowels in English are bizarre. Thanks to a phenomenon known as "the great vowel shift," our mapping of sounds to vowels does not correspond to the mapping of sounds to vowels in other European languages, as you will already know if you have ever studied any other European language. I just wanted to put this out there before anyone complains that "e" is pronounced like "a," and "i" like "e." Latin is not the problem. English is the problem.

Latin vowels are pure. They each have just two sounds. English is hard. Latin is easy. The letter A is either short, uh, as the "uh" in about or long, ah, as the "ah" in "father." Latin examples: ăd, Rōmānus. Latin "a" is never pronounced as the English "a" in either cat or Kate. English vowels are bizarre. Latin has two sounds for a, uh or ah. That's it. Two sounds, long and short: uh, ah.

The letter E: is either short, eh, as in "get" or long, ay, as in "cake." Latin examples: short sĕd, which means but, or long, as the first syllable of sēparō. Again, the letter e in Latin has just two sounds: short eh, Long aye.

The letter I is short, ih, as in "kin" or long, ee, as in "machine." Latin examples: short vowel, in; long vowel, like the first syllable of līber. The letter I has just two sounds: short, ĭ; long, ī. (ee).

The letter O is either short Ŏ, which should be pronounced like the "ou" in "ought," but even shorter. Or long, Ō, as in "go." Latin examples: short, nox; long, nōn. The letter O has two sounds: short, ŏ; Long, oh.

The letter U can be short, o˘o, as in "book," or long, o¯o as in "food." Our Latin example is a two-for-one special: mūrŭs, means wall. The letter U has two sounds: short-u: o˘o; long-u: o¯o.

The letter Y is used only in words deriving from Greek. It is pronounced like the letter "i" in Latin. Latin example: Polybius, a Greek historian from Megalopolis brought to Rome as a prisoner of war.

And now for our consonants. Consonants have just one sound each. But which one? Most of them represent the same sounds as they do in English, so we omit them. Two of the problem children are problematic, however, because we, in English, let them get away with making two sounds. Latin is stricter. These consonants only get to represent one sound.

The letter C is always pronounced like a "k," like the "c" in "car." Latin example: Caesar. Not "Siezer." Where do you think the Germans got their KAISER? Yes. They did not change the pronunciation of C.

The letter G is always hard, "guh," as the "g" in "game." Latin example: *gemma*. The word means "gem," but classical Latin the pronunciation is always hard, "guh": *gemma*.

The letter I, as we've seen, is also a vowel, but it can also be used to indicate the sound we represent with the consonant "y," as pronounced, for example, in the word "yummy." The Latin example, the word "*iam*," which means "now." Older editions of Latin texts sometimes represented consonantal "I" with a j. For example, *jam* spelled with a j instead of an i, but this practice has fallen out of favor. And, in general, we find consonantal "i" at the beginning of words in front of other vowels, as in *iam*.

R, r: I doubt the Romans used a hard American "r," so please feel free to trill the "r" if you are so inclined, but it's not necessary. Let's take the word for Roman. Would they have said *Rōmānus*? I can't trill. *Rōmānus*. I can try. I can do a German trill. *Rōmānus*, but I think I prefer the American. So it's probably a good thing the Romans aren't around to make fun of American accents.

V, v: In this course, we will sound the letter v as a "w." And this will take some getting used to. Caesar, for example, famously said "I came, I saw, I conquered." You may know the phrase as Vēnī, vīdī, vīcī? Well, I'm sorry, but Caesar most likely said "Wēnī, Wīdī, Wīcī." By the way, the Romans did not use the letter "w." In fact, the three letters u, v, and w all derive from the letter v.

Is that it? Almost. There is also a class of vowel sounds that arise when two vowels are combined. These are called diphthongs. Not only are diphthongs a combination of two vowels, they are actually a combination of two vowels pronounced at the same time so as to produce a *single* sound that is a combination of *both* sounds. You don't believe me? Let's experiment.

ae: a + e yields the "i" sound we find in the English word "ice." Please say "ah". Now say "aye."

Say ah, aye. Try and say them at the same time: ah-aye = "I." Experiment a bit on your own. Latin example: *Caesar, aeternus*.

oe: o plus e yields the "oi" sound we find "oil." Plese say oh, aye. At the same time: oh... ay, oh-ay, ohay. Result? oi. Latin examples: *moenia* (walls), *coeptis* (undertakings).

au: a plus u yields the "ow" sound we find in "howl;" ah plus oo. Try saying them at the same time: ah-oo, ow. Latin example: *Paullus* (a famous general), or *Paulus* (a famous apostle).

eu: this diphthong only appears in words deriving from Greek and would have originally sounded like the o umlaut in German "schön" (beautiful). In practice, most Americans pronounce it as the "you" sound in Eucalyptus. But if we like, we could also say "Öcalyptus."

Let's review our problem children.

First the consonants:

C: always "kuh." Please repeat after me: *Caesar, carrus, cibus*

G: always hard, guh." Please repeat: *gemma, Genesis, gigno*

I: as a consonant, yuh. Please repeat: *iam, ianitor, Ianuārius.*

V: We pronounce it as a wuh, *vēnī, vīdī, vīcī.*

And the vowels:

A: short uh. Please repeat: ad, *capiō, ab.* Long ah. Please repeat: *māter, frāter.*

E: short "eh." Please repeat: *sed, ex, medulla.* Long "ay." Please repeat: *rēgēs.*

I: short ih. Please repeat in, *videō, bis.* Long i, pronounced ee. Please repeat: *vīnum, senfīre.*

O: a short o, "o." Please repeat: possum, nox. Long oh: *nōn, pōnō.*

U: short o˘o. Please repeat: *nux, cum* (as in *cum laude*). Long U: o¯o. Please repeat: *mūrus, nūtrix, sūdor.*

ae: a + e yields "i": *Caesar.* Please repeat: *Caesar, aeternus, aes*

oe: o + e yields "oi." Please repeat: *moenia, coepit, poena*

au: a + u yields "ow." Please repeat: *aut, causa, Paullus*

This is a manageable list. But when we look at a Latin word and try to pronounce it, where do we put the accent? This is a vexed question. If we observe modern versions of Latin, we find that some forms of modern Latin, French and Catalan, for example, do not have a strong stress accent. Italian and Spanish, on the other hand, like English, do. Where to put the stress?

The rules are relatively simple.
1.   If a word has two syllables, always accent the first syllable: CAEsar.

2.   If a word has three or more syllables, then you only have two choices.
     a.   The accent goes on the second-to-the-last syllable if the vowel in the second-to-last syllable is long or counts as long. A short vowel counts as long if it's followed by two or more consonants.

     b.   If the vowel in the second-to-the-last syllable is short, then the accent falls on the third-to-last syllable.

These are your only two choices.

Let's look at a few examples:

Caesar: Caesar, *Caesar*, has two syllables, so the accent is on the first syllable. Please repeat after me: *Caesar.*

What about this three-syllable word: *Lībertās*, which means freedom. This is a tough one. There are three syllables, so we have to decide. Second to the last or third to the last? By the way, we have fancy Latin term for counting syllables. We could, using traditional Latin terms, call the last syllable the *ultima,* which means last, and the second to last syllable the *penult.* That means almost last, and the third-to-the-last syllable the *antepenult;* that is, before the almost last. And really, why use English when fancy Latin terms are available?

But going back to *Lībertās.* Our choice is simple: second to last (penult) or third from the end (antepenult). Is the "e" in *lībertās* long or short? It's short, actually, but it counts as long. Why? According to the rule I mentioned, vowels followed by two or more consonants count as long. We, therefore, say *lī-BER-tas,* and not *LĪ-ber-tas.* Please try saying it three times: *lī̄BERtās, lī̄BERtās, lī̄BERtās.* That's what Caesar claimed he was defending, by the way, when he destroyed the Roman republic, *lī̄BERtās,* and even if we say "LI-berty," the word still has a certain ring to it in Latin: *lī̄BERtās.* Why? Two consonants after the vowel "e" in the second-to-last syllable, which some of you may already be calling the penult.

Let's try another three-syllable word, a-m-a-m-u-s. What's the pronunciation? *Amamus* or *amamus?* Is the "a" in the penult—the second-to-the-last syllable—long or short? There is only one consonant after it. It's long, but you probably wouldn't know that unless I marked it as long, and we will, in this course, make every effort to mark long syllables with long marks, which we call macrons. There should be a macron, or long mark, over the second "a." amāmus. And, of course, the Romans themselves did not use macrons. We put them in our texts for ourselves. The Romans didn't need them. At any rate, the penult, or second to last syllable, is long, so it gets the accent. Please repeat: a-MAH-mus.

And, you may be wondering, are there words with the accent on the antepenult, that is, the third-to-the-last syllable? Yes, many. Let's take a look at a verb that means "we kill." The word has five syllables: *IN-TER-FI-CI-MUS.* But in Latin the accent can only fall on the penult (second to the last) or the antepenult (third from the end). There are no other choices. So is it *interfiCImus* or *interFIcimus?* The "i" in the second-to-the-last syllable is not long by position because it is followed by only one consonant, an "m." And we are not putting a macron over it, so is it long by nature? No. For this type of verb, the "i" is short by nature, so we correctly say *interFIcimus,* we kill. Shall we? Please repeat: *interFIcimus. interFIcimus. interFIcimus.*

We are killing it indeed, and we should be proud! So let's review. If the word has two syllables, accent the first syllable. If the word has three or more syllables, accent the penult if it is long (aMAmus). Otherwise, accent the antepenult (interFIcimus). A vowel in the penult can be long by position, that is, it's followed by two consonants, as in līBERtās. Or it can be long by nature as in aMAmus.

Practice makes perfect, and we'll be doing a lot of repetition, so please don't worry. And in fact, now that we've learned the basic principles, we can drill, baby, drill. Let's practice with something longer that could well represent an auspicious beginning for our first lecture. Let's practice with day one from the creation of the universe in the first chapter of *Genesis*, verses 1 through 3. We'll use the Latin of Jerome's Vulgate, and you may find that the text sounds familiar, even if you have never studied a word of Latin before in your life. We are going to pronounce the words using the restored classical pronunciation, not the church, or ecclesiastical, Latin pronunciation, which, I freely admit, is also beautiful. And that is, in fact, the pronunciation one generally hears in concerts, and I certainly have no objections to it. In fact, I rather like it, but our course focuses especially on classical Latin, so we'll drill the classical standard, which, I submit, like its ecclesiastical counterpart, is exceptionally beautiful.

Please allow me to recite our practice verses from Genesis:

1.   *In principiō creāvit Deus caelum et terram.*

2.   *Terra autem erat inānis et vacua.*

3.   *Et tenēbrae super faciem abyssi et spīritus Deī ferēbātur super aquās.*

4.   *Dīxitque Deus fiat lūx et facta est lūx.*

And now let us conclude by reading through this text together. I will read a phrase and then pause. When I pause, please repeat the phrase I've just recited.

In principiō

creāvit Deus

caelum et terram.

Terra autem

erat inānis

et vacua

Et tenēbrae

super faciem abyssi

et spīritus Deī

ferēbātur

super aquās.

Dīxitque Deus

fiat lūx

et facta est lūx.

And that, dear students of the Latin language, was day one in the creation of our new Latin world. Just one more thing, however, before you go. You've got some homework in your course guidebook, where you'll find exercises at the end of each lecture summary. These exercises review and drill the content we've covered together. It's crucial to practice. You should feel comfortable with this lecture before going on to the next. So, please, before you join me for Lecture 2, complete the exercises in the guidebook for Lecture 1. Practice your pronunciation of Latin, preferably out loud. Impress your friends and family. Turn up the volume.

Until the next time, then, enjoy your studies and be well. *Valēte!*

Introduction to Third-Conjugation Verbs
Lecture 2

In our first lesson, we admired Latin's beauty, we remarked on its practical utility, and we practiced pronunciation. We will continue to explore all these things and more, but in this lesson, we will proceed directly to the heart of Latin, the Latin verb. Why is the verb so important? Because that's where Latin happens; that's where the action is. In this lecture, we'll look at the principal parts of Latin verbs and discuss the concepts of number, person, tense, voice, and mood.

Grammatical terms

- Verbs express actions, but we can also talk about Latin verbs in more precise terms. Verbs in Latin can be described in terms of their number, person, tense, voice, and mood.

- How does a verb exhibit number? Verbs may be either singular or plural. For example, in English, you might say, "One head of Cerberus barks," but "Cerberus's three heads bark." In these sentences, *barks* is singular and *bark* is plural, inasmuch as each agrees with a singular or plural subject.

- Singular and plural verbs are also limited by time. They can be present, past, or future. We call a verb's relation to time its tense. For example, "Fluffy barks right now," but "Cerberus barked 2,000 years ago." *Barks* is present tense and *barked* is past tense.

Among Caesar's titles was *pontifex maximus* ("chief priest"), a title still used by the pope.

© iStockphoto/Thinkstock.

21

- In addition to number (singular or plural) and tense (past, present, future), verbs can also indicate person. Who does, did, or will do the verb? We indicate person in English with pronouns.
  - The first-person singular pronoun is *I*, and the first-person plural pronoun is *we*.

  - The second-person singular pronoun is *you*; the second-person plural pronoun is also *you* or, colloquially, *y'all*, *you guys*, and so on.

  - The third-person singular is *he*, *she*, or *it*, and the third-person plural is *they*.

- Latin verbs also have voice. They can be active or passive. A subject performs the action of an active verb. The subject of a passive verb has the action of that verb performed upon himself, herself, or itself. Consider the difference between "I pay" and "I am paid."

- Latin verbs also have three moods.
  - Verbs that state facts, that inform, or that indicate are in the indicative mood.

  - Verbs that command ("Wake up!") are in the imperative mood.

  - Verbs that express wishes, uncertainty, fears, and other emotions or attitudes are in the subjunctive mood.

- Verbal forms that satisfy all five characteristics of a Latin verb—number, person, tense, voice, and mood—are called finite. Another verbal form that is not subject to the limits of person, number, or mood, although it does show tense and voice, is the infinitive (meaning "not finite" or "not as defined"). In English, most infinitives are marked with *to*, as in *to bark*, *to command*, *to do*.

Latin as an inflected language
- Latin is a highly inflected language. Think of it as flexible or bendable. We can bend the shape of words in Latin to indicate how

they relate to other words in the sentence. We have some inflection in English but not much.

o   We can make singular nouns plural by adding an *s*; for example: *chariot* (singular) and *chariots* (plural).

o   We add a different kind of *s* to show possession; for example: "the chariot of the sun god" and "the sun god's chariot." The magic of inflection eliminates the preposition *of.*

o   The addition of *ed* can change time; for example: "The dog barks every morning" and "The dog barked a lot yesterday."

•   Latin makes these kinds of changes much more frequently than English. A key to learning Latin is to pay attention to the ends of words. To convey meaning, English uses predictable word order; Latin uses flexible word endings.

Personal endings for Latin verbs, active voice

	Singular	Plural
1	-ō / -m	-mus
2	-s	-tis
3	-t	-nt

English pronoun equivalents for Latin personal endings

	Singular		Plural	
1	-ō / -m	= I	-mus	= we
2	-s	= you (sing.)	-tis	= you (pl.)
3	-t	= he/she/it	-nt	= they

Present active indicative conjugation of *agō*

agō, agere, ēgī, actum: do, drive

	Singular	Plural
1	agō	agimus
2	agis	agitis
3	agit	agunt

Translation of present active indicative, *agō*

	Singular		Plural	
1	agō	= I do	agimus	= we do
2	agis	= you (sing.) do	agitis	= you (pl.) do
3	agit	= he/she/it does	agunt	= they do

Note: *Agō* is the first-person singular form for the present tense, active voice, indicative mood. *Agō* may be translated three ways: "I do," "I am doing," "I do do."

Imperative of *agō*

	Singular		Plural	
1	***		***	
2	age	= do!	agite	= do!
3	***		***	

Sentence practice

- The phrase *bellum agere* literally means "war to do." Latin tends to put the action after the object, but we can reverse the order: "to do war." In English, we would say, "to wage war."

- Let's look at the sentence *Bellum agunt*. The ending *-nt* tells us that "they" are performing the action of the verb. *Agunt* means "they do"; thus, an idiomatic translation of the sentence reads: "They wage war."

- The sentence *Caesar bellum agit* means, of course, "Caesar wages war." Notice that the verb ends in *-t*, which is the third-person singular ending.

- Let's try this sentence: *Gaius Iulius Caesar, imperātor et pontifex maximus, bellum in Galliā agit*. A word-for-word translation reads: "Gaius Julius Caesar, general (*imperātor*) and chief priest (*pontifex maximus*), war (*bellum*) in Gaul (*in Galliā*) he wages (*agit*)." An idiomatic translation reads: "Gaius Julius Caesar, general and chief priest, wages war in Gaul."

- English word order prefers to place the verb after the subject. Latin can put the verb almost anywhere. How do we know, then, who's "doing" the verb? The ending on the verb tells us the person and number of the subject.

- To give Caesar a command, we need to use the imperative mood. "Wage war, Caesar!" would be *Age bellum, Caesar!* To command Caesar's soldiers (more than one person), we would say, *Agite bellum, mīlitēs!*

Verba (Vocabulary)

agō, agere, ēgī, āctum: do, drive, lead

bellum: war (*agere bellum* = to wage war)

bibō, bibere, bibī, bibitum: drink

caedō, caedere, cecīdī, caesum: cut, cut down, slay

Caesar: Gaius Julius Caesar, politician, author, and conquerer of Gaul, famously assassinated on March 15 (the Ides), 44 B.C.E.

cibum: food

dīcō, dīcere, dīxī, dictum: say, speak, tell

discipulī (m.), discipulae (f.): students

edō, edere, ēdī, ēsum: eat

est: is

et: and

flōrēs: flowers

Gallia: Gaul (corresponding geographically to modern France)

mīles/mīlitēs: soldier/soldiers

mulier/mulierēs: woman/women

-ne (enclitic particle): attaches to the first word in the sentence to indicate that what follows is a question

pōnō, pōnere, posuī, positum: put, place, put aside, put away

pontifex/pontificēs: priest/priests (*pontifex maximus* = chief priest)

salvē (sing.), salvēte (pl.): greetings

valē (sing.), valēte (pl.): be well, farewell

vendō, vendere, vendidī, venditum: sell

vincō, vincere, vīcī, victum: conquer

vīnum: wine

Please learn the personal active endings of the Latin verb, the sign of the present active infinitive, and the imperative endings.

i. In the verb chart below, provide the personal endings of the Latin verb in the present tense active voice.

	Singular	Plural
1		
2		
3		

ii. In the verb chart below, conjugate the verb *agō* in the present active indicative.

	Singular	Plural
1		
2		
3		

iii. Create your own verb chart for each of the verbs below and conjugate in the present active indicative.

1. pōnō
2. bibō
3. vincō

iv. Please translate the following into Latin. (Each translation will be a single word.)

1. to say

2. Put away! (singular)

3. Put away! (plural)

4. to drink

5. Eat! (plural)

6. We sell.

7. to drive

8. She is driving.

9. Drive! (singular)

10. to conquer

11. They are conquering.

12. They drink.

13. We are cutting.

14. Are you (singular) cutting?

15. You (plural) eat.

iv. Please translate the following into English.

1. Caesar dīcit.

2. Dīcimus.

3. Dīcite, muliērēs!

4. Caesar bellum agit.

5. Caesar flōrēs caedit.

6. Mīlitēs flōrēs caedunt.

7. Pōnite flōrēs, mīlitēs, et vincite!

8. Mīlitēs cibum edunt.

9. Pontificēs vīnum bibunt.

10. Servum vendō.

11. Vince, Caesar!

12. Agite bellum, mīlitēs!

13. Cibum edimus et vīnum bibimus.

14. Edisne cibum?

15. Bibitisne vīnum?

Introduction to Third-Conjugation Verbs
Lecture 2—Transcript

Salvēte! Greetings! *Salvēte, discipulī!* Greetings, male students! *Salvēte, discipulae!* Greetings, female students! *Salvēte, discipulī discipulaeque linguae Latīnae!* Greetings, students of the Latin language! *Salvēte* is a plural greeting because I include all my students. To greet me in return, you should use the singular, which is *Salvē,* as in, *Salvē, Molinarī!* Please repeat after me: *Salvē, Molinarī!* And again: *Salvē, Molinarī!* And one more time: *Salvē, Molinarī!* Why, thank you, students, and a singular *salvē* to each of you *individually* and *salvēte* to all of you.

In our first lesson, we admired Latin's beauty, we remarked on its practical utility, and we practiced pronunciation. We will continue to explore all these things, and more, but in this lesson we proceed directly to the heart of Latin, the Latin verb. Why is the verb so important? Because that's where Latin happens. That's where the action is. But first, a few words that we will use in today's lesson. We begin with the name of a man born in 100 B.C.E., chief priest, consul, conqueror, and proconsul of Gaul, dictator for life, assassinated in 44 B.C.E., deified by the Roman Senate in 42, and studied for centuries by school children: Caesar. Please repeat: *Gaius Iulius Caesar.*

Note that the diphthongs A-I and A-E are both pronounced "eye." We pronounce the initial I in *Iulius* like a Y—*Iulius.* And we pronounce the C in Caesar like a K—*Caesar.* Can you read Caesar's name out loud in the original Latin? *Gaius Iulius Caesar.* Caesar was a commander of troops. Here is how you say commander or general in Latin. Please repeat: *imperātor.* Our words for emperor and empire derive from this Latin original. Note the long A in the second to last syllable. That is why the accent is on the penult, and not on the antepenult, or third-to-the-last syllable. Please try to say commander in Latin: *imperātor.* Again: *imperātor.* Feels good, doesn't it?

Please try this: *pontifex maximus.* This means chief priest. The pope still uses this title. Please try to pronounce chief priest in Latin: *pontifex maximus.* Were there any vowels in the penults, or second-to-last syllables, that were marked long? No. Were any of the vowels in the penults followed by two or more consonants? No. So where did we place our stress accents? On the antepenults, that is—*id est*—on the third-to-last syllable. Let's try it again. Please repeat: *pontifex maximus*. And, one more time, chief priest: *pontifex maximus*.

Here's the word for war: *bellum*. No worries about accent here; first syllable. Again, war: *bellum*. And the Latin word for Gaul, a territory we now call France: *Gallia*. Three syllables, but the penult is short, so we accent the first syllable. Again, Gaul, please repeat: *Gallia*.

And, finally, let's look at a verb. Verbs, by the way, come in four standard parts. If you have the four parts and a knowledge of how to apply endings, you can generate all other forms for that verb. It's almost magic, and all you have to do is learn the rules. And I'm here to help, to initiate you into all the secret knowledge that the modern world has kept from you. We are on the cusp of a verbal adventure, a tour into the living, beating heart of the Latin language, the Latin verb. Are you ready?

Here are the four principal parts of a crucial Latin verb that means do, drive, lead, and more. Please repeat after me: *agō, agere, ēgī, actum*. The first principal part ends in O. Please repeat: *agō*. We stress the first syllable. Agō means "I do." Second principal part? Please repeat: *agere*. Where was the stress? The E in the second-to-last syllable was short, so, *agere*. Please repeat: *agere*. *Agere* means "to do." Please repeat the third principal part: *ēgī*. *Ēgī* means "I did" or "I have done." Please repeat: *ēgī*, nice long vowels. Please repeat: *ēgī*. And the fourth principal part? Please repeat: *actum*. *Actum* means "having been done." Please repeat: *actum*. And all four. Please repeat: *agō, agere, ēgī, actum*. And one more time quickly: *agō, agere, ēgī, actum*.

The verb *ago* and its parts live in many English words. An agent is the person who does things on your behalf; the agenda are the things we must do in a meeting; an act is something that's been done. There are more, but it is worth noting that the stems we find in the first, second, and fourth principal parts frequently appear in English derivatives. Now, before we put these principal parts to work, we need to review some grammatical terms, because these terms help us discuss verbs more efficiently. Verbs express actions, but we can talk about Latin verbs more precisely than this. Verbs in Latin can be described in terms of their number, person, tense, voice, and mood. Let us examine each of these terms.

How does a verb exhibit number? Well, verbs may be either singular or plural. Let me give you an example in English. One head of Cerberus barks. Cerberus's three heads bark. Barks is singular and bark is plural, inasmuch as each agrees with a singular or plural subject. Singular and plural verbs are also limited by time. They can be present, past, or future. We call a verb's relation to time, its tense. Fluffy barks right now. Cerberus barked two thousand years ago. "Bark" is present tense and "barked" is past. In addition to number (singular or plural) and tense (past, present, or future), verbs can also indicate person. Who does, did, or will do the verb? We indicate person in English with pronouns. Let's review. Who is number one? I am number one—in the singular. In the plural, we are number one. And the second person? Why, that's you. You are number two in the singular. And y'all are number two in the plural. And who might be the third person? He may be, she may be, or it may be the third person singular. And the third person plural? Why, they are.

We are not quite done. Latin verbs also have voice. They can be active or passive. A subject performs the action of an active verb. The subject of a passive verb has the action of that verb performed upon himself, herself, or itself. It's the difference between "I pay" and "I am paid." Voice matters, especially if we're short on cash.

But there is one more aspect to verbs that we must address. Latin verbs have three moods. They can be all matter-of-fact, pointing things out. We call this mood the indicative. Which finger do we use for pointing things out? No, not that finger. We use that finger to point out bad driving. We use the index finger to point out facts. Which of Cerberus's heads barks at you? Why, that one! *Index* is a good Latin word. It means informer. Verbs that state facts, that inform, that indicate, are in the indicative mood. Verbs can also be in a bossy mood. "Wake up!" "Fix my breakfast!" We call commands the imperative mood. Imperative derives from a verb that means "I command," the same verb that gave us commander or *imperātor*. And finally, verbs can also express wishes, uncertainty, fears, and more. The mood for verbs that express such emotions and attitudes is called subjunctive.

We have now reviewed the five characteristics that define a verb in Latin: number, person, tense, voice, and mood. We call verbal forms that satisfy these definitions finite. Why finite? There is another verbal form that is not subject to the limits of person, number, or mood, although this form does show tense and voice. Because this form is not subject to as many limitations, we call it the infinitive, which means not finite, or not as defined. In English, most infinitives are marked with to, as in to bark, to command, to do. We will soon put this knowledge to work. But before we do, I must share some an important observation. Latin is an inflected language. Think flexible. Things that are flexible bend. We can bend the shape of words in Latin to indicate how they relate to other words in the sentence. We have some inflection in English, but not much. We can make singular nouns plural by adding an S. Please observe the magic: a single Chariot becomes, voila, more than one: Chariots. We can add a different kind of S to show possession. Please observe: the chariot of the the sun-god. the sun-god's chariot. Inflection's magic eliminated the preposition "of." And an E-D can change time. I bark every morning. I barked a lot yesterday." Latin does this much more than English. Latin is a highly inflected language. A key to learning Latin is to learn to pay attention to the endings of the words. To convey meaning, English uses predictable word order. Latin uses flexible word endings.

I think you're ready. Let's take the plunge into Latin verbs. The endings of an active Latin verb are: *o* or *m, s, t, mus, tis, nt.* (That's an NT, which I pronounce, nt). These six active verbal endings are your main take-away for this entire lesson. If nothing else in this half hour, please try to remember *o* or *m, s, t, mus, tis,* and *nt.* I will explain, and in doing so, I will deploy the technical language we just reviewed. Before I ask you to repeat these magically powerful endings, however, let us first look at each individually.

The endings *o* or *m* are equivalent to the first person singular pronoun I in English. The ending *s* is equivalent to the second person singular, you. The ending *t* is equivalent to the third person singular pronouns, he, she, or it. The ending *mus* is equivalent to the first person plural pronoun we. The ending *tis* is equivalent to the second person plural pronoun you, y'all, you guys, youse, you'uns. And the ending *nt* is equivalent to the third person plural pronoun they.

Please repeat: *o* or *m, s, t, mus, tis, nt*. Your key to who is doing a Latin verb, again: *o* or *m, s, t, mus, tis, nt*. We can chart the endings, making columns for singular and plural, and rows for the first, second, and third persons, but we cannot really see the endings in action unless we put them on a real verb. We are now going to put *o* or *m, s, t, mus, tis, nt* on the Latin verb *agō, agere, ēgī, actum*, which means, do or drive. Agō, ends in *o*, and means "I do"; *agis* ends in *s*, and means, "you do"; *agit*, ends in *t*, and means "he, she, or it does"; agimus, ends in *mus*, and means "we do"; agitis ends in *tis*, and means "y'all do"; agunt ends in *nt* and means "they do". Our endings are, and please repeat: *o* or *m, s, t, mus, tis, nt*.

I think you're ready to join me. Please repeat: *o* or *m, s, t, mus, tis, nt*. Again: *o* or *m, s, t, mus, tis, nt*. And one more time: *o* or *m, s, t, mus, tis, nt*. Now please repeat: agō, that's "I do". Please repeat: *agis*, "you do;" *agit*, "he, she, or it does;" *agimus*, "we do"; *agitis*, y'all do; *agunt*, "they do." The endings, please repeat: *o* or *m, s, t, mus, tis, nt*. And the verb in the singular, please repeat: agō, *agis, agit*. And in the plural, please repeat: *agimus, agitis, agunt*.

But let's examine what goes in front of those personal endings *o* or *m, s, t, mus, tis, nt*. Let's look more closely. What do we find in front of the *o* in the first person singular form of agō, "I do"? The letters AG. What do we find in front of the S in the second person singular of *agis*—the you form? We find the vowel I. And in front of the T in the third person singular *agit*, the he, she, or it form? Again, the vowel I. And in front of the MUS in the first person plural we form of *agimus*? Again, the vowel I. And in front of the TIS of the second person plural "y'all" form of *agitis*? Again, the vowel I. And in front of the NT of the they form of *agunt*? The vowel U.

Please observe that we insert no vowel in front of the ending o. We then insert a short I before the personal endings, except for the last form, *nt*, where we insert a short U. Please repeat: agō, *agis, agit, agimus, agitis, agunt*. Again: agō, *agis, agit, agimus, agitis, agunt*. And one more time: agō, *agis, agit, agimus, agitis, agunt*.

I think you're ready for a quiz. I will provide a series of phrases in English. A form of the verb do will appear in my English sentence. Please, in the pause provided, supply the corresponding form in Latin, i.e., *id est*, one of the forms of agō, *agis, agit, agimus, agitis, agunt.* After the pause, I, *Molinārius,* will provide the correct response, so that you, *discipulī discupulaeque linguae Latīnae* (students of the Latin language), may check your work. Are you ready?

First problem:

I do. Answer: agō.

I am doing. [pause] agō.

Do I? [pause] agō?

Am I doing? [pause] agō?

Notice that English is more complex than Latin. The English phrases I do, I am doing, and I do do may all be rendered by the same Latin form: agō. Agō is the 1st person, singular form for the present tense, active voice, indicative mood. Agō may be translated three ways: I do, I am doing, I do do.

Let's try the next person, the second person singular. I'll provide the English, and then pause, so you can form the Latin.

Do you? [pause] *agis?*

You are doing. [pause] *agis.*

You do do it. [pause] *agis.*

And let's try the other persons ...

He does. [pause] *agit.*

Does she? [pause] *agit?*

It is doing. [pause] *agit.*

We do. [pause] *agimus*.

Do we? [pause] *agimus*?

Y'all do. [pause] *agitis*.

Are y'all doing? [pause] *agitis*.

Do they? [pause] *agunt*?

They do. [pause] *agunt*.

In the next lesson, we will continue to practice, but let's take our vocabulary and our new knowledge of the verb to examine some Latin sentences.

Bellum means "war." What might *bellum agere* mean? Do you recall what the second principal part of the verb, the one that ends in RE means? It is the infinitive, to do. So what does the phrase *bellum agere* mean word for word? "War to do." That's not exactly English, but Latin tends to put the action after the object. Let's reverse the order: "to do war." That makes a sort of sense, but we may now observe that there is not a word-for-word correspondence between Latin and English. What would be better English for this idea—to do war? We say, "to wage war." On the other hand, we do a job. We don't wage a job, even if we may wish to earn wages for what we do. Ways of saying things that are peculiar to a language and not something we can translate literally, we call idiomatic. To wage war is idiomatic in English. In Latin one does war. Please repeat: *bellum agere*.

Let's try a whole sentence: *Bellum agunt*. How is this a whole sentence? Do we have a verb? Yes. *Agunt*. Can you tell me who is doing the verb? The ending is NT. If you said they, they are doing the verb, you are correct. *Agunt* means "they do." So what do they do? They do war. *Bellum agunt*. Can you translate a little bit more idiomatically? What are they doing? *Bellum agunt*. "They wage war." And so we begin to get to know the Romans.

Let's try this sentence. Please try reading it aloud. *Caesar bellum agit.* How would we translate this sentence? [pause] Right. "Caesar wages war." What is the ending of the verb? [pause] *Agit* ends with T. Why? What is the person? Third. What is the number? Singular. We speak about Caesar in the third person singular. Caesar is the subject. What we say about our subject Caesar is the predicate. What do we say about Caesar? He wages war. The verb agrees with the third person singular subject Caesar.

Let me try a longer version of the sentence. Please repeat after me: *Gaius Iulius Caesar, imperātor et pontifex maximus, bellum in Gallia agit.* Let's translate word for word. Gaius Julius Caesar, general (*imperātor*) and chief priest (*pontifex maximus*), war (*bellum)* in Gaul (*in Gallia*) he wages (*agit*). Can we formulate this sentence in better English? How about, "Gaius Julius Caesar, general and chief priest, wages war in Gaul." English word order prefers to place the verb after the subject. Latin can put the verb almost anywhere. So how do we know then who's doing the verb if the verb can appear anywhere? The ending on the verb tells us the person and number of the subject.

Let's give the general Caesar a command. This will require the imperative mood. In Latin, we form the imperative of *agō, agere, ēgī, actum* by removing the RE from the second principal part. This gives us a singular command for one person: *age!* "Do it!" For a plural command, we add TE, and change the short ĕ to a short ĭ, giving us *agite!* Do it, ya'll! Let's tell Caesar to wage war. "Wage war, Caesar!" Okay, that was English. How do we say it in Latin? Please repeat: *Age bellum, Caesar!* The word for "soldiers" in Latin is *mīlitēs*. Think military. How would we command the soldiers? "Wage war, soldiers!" And in Latin? Please repeat: *Agite bellum, mīlitēs!* Got it? *Age*, when we command one person. *Agite*, when we command more than one person.

That's exciting, but *tempus fugit*—time flies. Let's review what we have learned. We have formed—or conjugated—the present tense indicative of *agō*, i.e. (*id est*), agō, agis, agit, agimus, agitis, agunt. We have examined the infinitive "to do": *agere.* And we have formed the two imperatives or command forms: *age!* for one person and *agite* for more than one person. We also looked at the principal parts of the verb: *agō, agere, ēgī, actum.* What we have done represents our *acta*. What we still must do, we can call our *agenda*. But no matter how you look at it, we've done a lot. We have some extra reading in the guidebook as well as some extra drill.

Please have a look, and please memorize the forms, or conjugation, of agō before moving on to Lecture 3, where we will review, practice, and expand our knowledge of the present tense.

Until the next time, then, enjoy your studies and be well; that's another second person plural imperative: Be well! *Valēte!*

Introduction to the Subjunctive Mood
Lecture 3

In Lecture 2, we learned nine forms, six indicative endings, two imperative endings, and an infinitive ending. In this lecture, we will explore the power of a single vowel: ā. In the last lecture, we also learned the personal endings of the Latin verb, and we put these endings on *agō, agere, ēgī, actum*, which means "to do." In this lecture, we will use the verb *pōnō, pōnere, posuī, positum*, which means "to put or to place."

Review: Personal endings for Latin verbs, active voice

	Singular	Plural
1	-ō / -m	-mus
2	-s	-tis
3	-t	-nt

Imperative of *pōnō*

pōnō, pōnere, posuī, positum: put, place

	Singular	Plural
1	***	***
2	pōne = put!	pōnite = put!
3	***	***

Present active indicative conjugation of *pōnō*

pōnō, pōnere, posuī, positum: **put, place**

	Singular	Plural
1	pōnō	pōnimus
2	pōnis	pōnitis
3	pōnit	pōnunt

Present active subjunctive conjugation of *pōnō*

pōnō, pōnere, posuī, positum: **put, place**

	Singular	Plural
1	pōnam	pōnāmus
2	pōnās	pōnātis
3	pōnat	pōnant

Quiz

In the following sentences, change the English form of the word "put" or "place" to its Latin equivalent.

1. *Let Caesar put* his legions in Gaul!

2. *Let Pompey and Crassus put* Cicero to work for the triumvirate!

3. *Let us put* that knife in Caesar!

These examples represent one use of the subjunctive. We can use the subjunctive to exhort someone to do something. This is called the hortatory subjunctive because we are exhorting and encouraging, not pointing out facts, which is what the indicative mood is used for.

Answers: 1. *pōnat*, 2. *pōnant*, 3. *pōnāmus*.

Review of mood

- The indicative mood of the verb spells out facts. The word *indicative* derives from *index*, which in Latin meant "informer." Think of using your index finger to point out a fact: "Which of your neighbors moved his boundary stone onto your property?" "He did."

- The imperative mood is bossy; it's used to give direct orders: "Put the dinner on the table now, Julius!"

- The subjunctive mood is more subtle and has many uses. As we said, it can be used to exhort. It can also be used with *ut* to express purpose or result:
  - so that he may put: *ut pōnat*

  - with the result that he may put: *ut pōnat*

- The subjunctive mood can be used with *nē* to express negative purpose or with *ut nōn* to express negative result:
  - so that he may not put: *nē pōnat*

  - with the result that he may not put: *ut nōn pōnat*

- Why is the Latin so much terser than the English? Because we're using convoluted English to capture the sense of the Latin subjunctive more precisely. In English, we can express purpose with an infinitive: "Casca attends the Senate to put his dagger in Caesar." Good Latin would use the subjunctive, which we can mimic: "Casca attends the Senate so that he may put his dagger in Caesar."

- Other uses of the subjunctive include expressing doubt about something someone else has said, when reporting an opinion, when reporting an indirect question, when expressing a general characteristic, and more.

Present active indicative conjugation of *vīvō*

vīvō, vīvere, vīxī, vīctum: live

	Singular	Plural
1	vīvō	vīvimus
2	vīvis	vīvitis
3	vīvit	vīvunt

Present active subjunctive conjugation of *vīvō*

vīvō, vīvere, vīxī, vīctum: live

	Singular	Plural
1	vīvam	vīvāmus
2	vīvās	vīvātis
3	vīvat	vīvant

Present active subjunctive conjugation of *bibō*

bibō, bibere, bibī: drink

	Singular	Plural
1	bibam	bibāmus
2	bibās	bibātis
3	bibat	bibant

Note: Depending on the circumstances, "you should drink," "you may drink," "so that you may drink," and "you drink" may be represented by *bibās*. How can this be? In Latin, the subjunctive represents the attitude of the speaker to the action. We represent attitude in English differently, hence, the lack of one-to-one correspondence.

Present subjunctive conjugation of *fīō*

fīō, fierī, factus sum: be made, become, happen

	Singular	Plural
1	fīam	fīāmus
2	fīās	fīātis
3	fīat	fīant

Present active indicative conjugation of *dēsinō*

dēsinō, dēsinere, dēsiī: cease, desist, stop

	Singular	Plural
1	dēsinō	dēsinimus
2	dēsinis	dēsinitis
3	dēsinit	dēsinunt

Present active subjunctive conjugation of *dēsinō*

dēsinō, dēsinere, dēsiī: cease, desist, stop

	Singular	Plural
1	dēsinam	dēsināmus
2	dēsinās	dēsinātis
3	dēsinat	dēsinant

Catullus and Lesbia

- Catullus was a Roman poet in the 1st century B.C.E., whose poems are some of the most famous to survive from the ancient world. One of his poems is a sort of pep talk to himself. It begins with the line: *Miser Catulle, dēsinās ineptīre!*

- The main action here is in the verb, of course, which is *dēsinās*. How do we translate it? If the indicative *dēsinis* means "you cease, desist, or stop," then the subjunctive form means "you should stop," "you should cease." The infinitive gives us more verbal information. It completes the meaning of the verb *cease*, that is, "you should cease to be a fool."

- Thus, the first line translates: "Unhappy Catullus, cease to be a fool!"

Advice to Himself
by Catullus

Catullus, you wretch, cease to be a fool!

And what you see has been lost, reckon it lost!

Once upon a time, bright white suns shone for you,

when, again and again, you went wherever she would lead,

a girl loved more by us than any other will ever be loved.

Those were the days we had so many laughs, so much pleasure,

which you, Catullus, desired nor did she, your mistress, not desire these things.

Bright white suns— truly they shone for you!

But now she no longer desires: so you, too, raving madman, do not desire!

And do not follow when she flees, and do not live a wretch,

but, with a mind made firm, endure! Be strong!

Good-bye, girlfriend. Catullus is strong now,

and he will not ask for you when you are not willing.

But you will suffer, when you will be asked for—by no one.

Woe is you, vile mistress! What life remains for you?

Who will now approach you? To whom will you seem beautiful?

Whom will you now love? Whose will you be said to be?

Whom will you kiss? Whose little lips will you nibble?

But you, Catullus, you've come to a decision—be strong!

Sentence practice

- The verb "learn," *disco, discere, didicī,* is another verb with three principal parts. Together with our other verbs and a few nouns, we can practice reading some sentences:

1. *Linguam Latīnam discō.* I learn the Latin language.

2. *Linguam Latīnam discimus.* We learn the Latin language.

3. *Linguam Latīnam discāmus.* Let us learn the Latin language.

4. *Bibāmus, ut vīvāmus!* Let us drink, so that we may live!

5. *Vīvimus, ut bibāmus.* We live, so that we may drink.

6. *Lesbia bibit, nē Catullus dēsinat ineptīre.* Lesbia drinks, lest Catullus cease to be a fool. (Lesbia drinks so that Catullus will not cease to be a fool.)

7. *Bibite, Catulle et Lesbia, ut vīvātis!* Drink, Catullus and Lesbia, so that you may live!

8. *Bibite.* Drink!

9. *Dēsinātis ineptīre, nē Lesbia bibat.* Y'all should cease to be foolish, lest Lesbia drink.

10. *Linguam Latīnam discunt, ut in Rōmā antīquā vīvant.* They learn the Latin language so that they may live in ancient Rome.

Verba

dēsinō, dēsinere, dēsiī: cease, stop

discō, discere, didicī: learn

45

fīō, fierī, factus sum: to be made, to happen, to become, to come into existence

linguam Latīnam (direct object form): Latin language (*linguae Latīnae* = of the Latin language)

lūx: light

nē: used with subjunctive verbs to express negative purpose (so that … not)

-que: attaches to a word to indicate "and" (*discipulī discipulaeque* = male students **and** female students)

ut: used with subjunctive verbs to express purpose (so that …)

vīvō, vīvere, vīxī, vīctum: live

Memoranda

Please learn the principal parts, the present-tense active indicative, the present-tense active subjunctive, the present-tense active imperatives (or command forms), and the present active infinitive of *pōnō*. All forms of *pōnō* may be found in Appendix §55, but these more complete charts will become more useful later in the course.

Agenda

i. In the verb chart below, provide the personal endings of the Latin verb in the present tense active voice.

	Singular	Plural
1		
2		
3		

ii. In the verb chart below, conjugate the verb *vīvō* in the present active indicative.

	Singular	Plural
1		
2		
3		

iii. In the verb chart below, conjugate the verb *vīvō* in the present active subjunctive.

	Singular	Plural
1		
2		
3		

iv. Create your own verb chart for each of the verbs below and conjugate in the present tense of the mood indicated.

1. pōnō (subjunctive)

2. dēsinō (indicative)

3. discō (indicative)

4. bibō (subjunctive)

v. Please translate the following into English.

1. bibimus

2. bibāmus

3. discunt

4. discant

5. dēsinitis

6. dēsinātis

vi. Please translate the following into Latin.

1. The women learn.

2. The women may learn

3. Let us learn the Latin language.

4. Stop! (addressing one person)

5. Stop! (addressing more than one person)

6. The soldiers are eating so that they may live.

7. Let the soldier eat and drink.

8. Let us drink so that we may live.

9. Caesar is conquering.

10. Caesar may conquer.

11. Let there be light! (Let light come into existence!)

12. Greetings, (male and female) students!

Introduction to the Subjunctive Mood
Lecture 3—Transcript

Salvēte, discipulī discipulaeque linguae Latīnae! Greetings, students of the Latin language! *Mihi valdē placet vōs pulchram linguam Latīnam aeternam docēre.* But what did Molinārius just say? Let's break it down: *Mihi valdē placet,* "it pleases me very much"; *vōs,* "you"; *pulchram linguam Latīnam aeternam,* "the beautiful and eternal Latin language"; *docēre,* "to teach." *Mihi valdē placet vōs pulchram linguam Latīnam aeternam docēre.* I am very happy to have another chance to speak with you and explore with you the beautiful and eternal Latin language.

In lesson two, we learned nine forms, six indicative endings, two imperative endings, and an infinitive ending. Today, we will explore the power of a single vowel. If you can remember the letter A, better, the long vowel A, you can master today's lesson. There are a few conceptual topics as well. But as far as memorization goes, provided you have mastered the forms of lesson two, basically and seriously, today's lesson involves substituting, or inserting, the letter A.

But, before you get too excited, let's see how much of lesson two you remember. Let's review.

What are the personal active endings of the Latin verb? *o* or *m, s, t, mus, tis, nt.* Again: *o* or *m, s, t, mus, tis, nt.* One more time: *o* or *m, s, t, mus, tis, nt.*

OK, you can chant endings by rote. A necessary start, and something we should practice—often. Here's a quiz. I will give you a personal pronoun in English. Please, in the pause provided, supply the corresponding personal ending. After the pause, I, *Molinārius,* will provide the correct response, so that you, *discipulī discupulaeque linguae Latīnae,* "students of the Latin language," may check your work.

they: *nt*

he: *t*

it: *t*

we: *mus*

she: *t*

y'all: *tis*

you guys: *tis*

I'm talking to you, Julius: *s*

thou, O God: *s*

I: *o or m*

Did that go well? I hope so, because the personal endings of the Latin verb are crucial: *o* or *m, s, t, mus, tis, nt.*

In the last lesson, we put these endings on *agō, agere, ēgī, actum,* which means "to do." In this lesson, we will use the verb *pōnō: pōnō, pōnere, posuī, positum,* which means "to put or to place." The first principal part, *pōnō,* which is the present active indicative, means "I place." What about the second principal part, *pōnere*? What part of speech is *pōnere*? *Pōnere* is an infinitive, It means "to place." What part of *pōnere* represents the ending of the infinitive in Latin, the ending that corresponds to the "to" we place in front of a verb in English to make it an infinitive? *Ere,* and please, let me remind you that that is a short E in *ere. Pōnere,* and it means "to place."

And the command forms? How about a pop quiz? In the following sentences you will hear in English a form of the word put. Turn that form of put into its Latin equivalent in the pause provided. *Molinārius* will provide the correct response after the pause. Are you ready?

Hey, Caesar, *put* the legions in Gaul! *pōne!* (Remember, you only have to do the put form; you don't have to do the whole sentence.) Next,

Hey, Casca and Brutus, put the dagger in his heart! *pōnite!*

OK, that's enough of that. The endings for the command forms, or imperative, are *-e* for giving an order to one person, or short *ite* for ordering a bunch of people around. Let's return to the main game. The personal endings, which we put on the verb stem *pōn* to form the present active indicative. Let's say, but in Latin, *I place*; *you place*; *he, she, or it places*; *we place*; *y'all place*; *they place*. Please, give it a try, I'll wait. … OK, is this what you said?

pōnō

pōnis

pōnit

pōnimus

pōnitis

pōnunt

Did you say *pōnō* for the first person singular and then did you put an I before all the personal endings except the last one, inserting a U before the NT of the they form, the third person plural? If so, you nailed it. If not, try to say them with me, on the count of three, *ūnus, duo, ūnus, duo, trēs*:

pōnō

pōnis

pōnit

pōnimus

pōnitis

pōnunt

One more time, together:

pōnō

pōnis

pōnit

pōnimus

pōnitis

pōnunt

And now, we are ready—almost—to transform the indicative mood of the verb into the subjunctive mood of the verb by changing the vowel in front of the personal endings. But let's recite the personal endings one more time: *o* or *m*, *s*, *t*, *mus*, *tis*, *nt*. And today you will discover why I asked you to say "*o...or m*" from the get-go. This is very exciting. I hope you realize just how powerful the insertion of just one vowel is going to be. We are going to change our attitude toward the action from the indicative, i.e., we are so all matter of fact and objective, we are pointing out the obvious, to, we're kind of moody, doubtful, wishful, bossy. But let's form the subjunctive first. Let us compare and let us contrast:

I place: *pōnō*

Let me place: *pōnam*

We inserted an A for the O, and then added our alternative first person singular ending M. Now you understand! The second person is even easier.

You place: *pōnis*

You should place: *pōnās*

To form the subjunctive, all we did was substitute a long A for the short I.

He, she, or it places: *pōnit*

Let him, let her, or let it place: *pōnat*

We place: *pōnimus*

Let us place: *pōnāmus*

Hey, did you notice the shift in the stress accent from the antepenult, third-to-the-last syllable, to the penult, the second-to-the-last syllable? Why? PO-nimus, short I in the second-to-the-last syllable. But *poNAmus*. Long A in the penult, or second-to-the-last syllable. A long vowel in the penult means that that syllable gets the accent.

But where were we? You plural.

Y'all place: *pōnitis*

Y'all should place: *pōnātis*

Again, the accent shifts.

They place: *pōnunt*

Let them place: *pōnant*

Now the translations you have heard of these slightly modified forms of *pōnō* are not the only possible translations. We are still at the beginning. But let's admire the simplicity and efficiency of this new mood of the present tense active, the subjunctive of *pōnō*. Please repeat:

pōnam

pōnās

pōnat

pōnāmus

pōnātis

pōnant

Again in the singular:

pōnam

pōnās

pōnat

And in the plural:

pōnāmus

pōnātis

pōnant

And one more time, together from beginning to end: *ūnus, duo, ūnus, duo, trēs:*

pōnam

pōnās

pōnat

pōnāmus

pōnātis

pōnant

And now some drill. In the following sentences you will hear, in English, a form of the word put or place. Turn that form of put or place into its Latin equivalent in the pause provided. *Molinārius* will, then, provide the correct response after that pause. Are you ready?

Let Caesar put his legions in Gaul! [pause] *pōnat*

Let Pompey and Crassus put Cicero to work for the triumvirate! [pause] *pōnant*

Let us put that knife in Caesar! [pause] *pōnāmus*

Calm down, class. In these examples, we practice but one use of the subjunctive. We can use the subjunctive to exhort someone to do something. This is called the hortatory subjunctive because we are exhorting and encouraging, not pointing out facts, which is what we use the indicative mood for.

Let us review what we mean by mood when talking about verbs. Most of us probably have at least one index finger that we can use to point at things. Again, imagine that you are living in ancient Gaul. The Romans show up, and ask, "Who did it?" You can't speak Latin, but you can point, and because you are an informer, you use your index finger to get rid of that neighbor who moved his boundary stone onto your property. The word *index* meant just that, as you may recall, in Latin. And the indicative mood of the verb is the mood of the verb when it feels like you're just telling people about what's going on. This mood spells out the facts—what's happening, man, what happened, or what will happen.

The imperative mood is bossy. It's the mood we use to give direct orders. "Put the dinner on the table now, Julius, or I'm sending your friends Crassus and Pompey home hungry!" The subjunctive mood is more subtle. It has many uses. We have examined one. We can use it to exhort. It can also be used with the Latin word *ut*, which we spell U, T—*ut*. And when we use the subjunctive mood with this word, ut, it expresses purpose or result. Example:

"so that he may put": *ut pōnat.* "with the result that he may put": *ut, pōnat.* We can also use it with *nē.* This is spelled N, E., to express negative purpose or with *ut nōn* to express negative result: "so that he may not put": *nē pōnat.* "with the result that he may not put": *ut nōn pōnat.*

Why is the Latin so much terser than the English? Because I use convoluted English to capture the sense of the Latin subjunctive more precisely. We can, in English, express purpose with an infinitive. Good Latin prose does not do this. Casca, for example, attends the Senate to put his dagger in Caesar. We use the infinitive "to put" to express the purpose. Good Latin would not use the infinitive, instead it would use the subjunctive, which we can mimic in English: Casca attends the Senate so that he may put his dagger in Caesar."

Other uses of the subjunctive include expressing doubt about something someone else has said when reporting that other person's opinion. The subjunctive can be used when reporting an indirect question, when expressing a general characteristic, and more. But we do not need to learn all of these uses today. The key take-away for us now is that the subjunctive is really easy to form, and having it available makes Latin a lot more fun. Let us look at some examples. The verb for live is *vīvō, vīvere, vīxī, victum.* Let's conjugate live in the present active indicative.

vīvō

vīvis

vīvit

vīvimus

vīvitis

vīvunt

Let's conjugate live, or the verb *vīvō, vīvere, vīxī, victum,* in present active subjunctive. You're just going to insert that long A before M, S, T, MUS, TIS, NT. Are you ready? *ūnus, duo, ūnus, duo, trēs:*

vīvam

vīvās

vīvat

vīvāmus

vīvātis

vīvant

How would we say, "let us live!" *Vīvāmus!* In the first century B.C.E., a poet by the name of Catullus had a girlfriend, whom he called *mea Lesbia* or "my Lesbia." How would we say, "Let us live, my Lesbia!" *Vīvāmus, mea Lesbia!* And that is exactly how Catullus begins one of the most famous love poems to survive from the ancient world. And, as long as we are on the topic of love, we might try drink, *bibō, bibere, bibī*. The verb is defective, so it only has three parts. It means "drink." Please conjugate drink in the present active subjunctive:

bibam

bibās

bibat

bibāmus

bibātis

bibant

In the following sentence you will hear, in English, a form of the verb drink. Turn that form of drink into its subjunctive Latin equivalent in the pause provided. *Molinārius* will provide the correct response after the pause. Are you ready?

Let me drink! [pause] *Bibam*!

You know, Lesbia, you should really drink more! [pause] *Bibās!* Remember, you only have to do the drink.

Lesbia, I brought wine so that you may drink: [pause] *ut bibās.*

You should drink, you may drink, so that you may drink, you drink, depending on the circumstances, all of these may be represented by *bibās*. How can this be? In Latin, the subjunctive represents the attitude of the speaker to the action. We represent attitude in English differently, hence the lack of one-to-one correspondence. But now my attitude is permissive. Please try this one:

Let her drink! [pause] *Bibat!*

Let them drink! [pause] *Bibant!*

Let's drink! [pause] *Bibāmus!*

Okay, that's enough drinking for now. Let's try a more productive verb. The verb *fīō, fierī, factus sum*, which means "to be made," "to happen," "to become," and thus "to come into existence." It's irregular, but it's easy enough to conjugate in the present tense subjunctive. Just take the stem of the first principal part, *fīō*, remove the O, insert A, and then add the personal endings. Let's conjugate it in the present subjunctive:

fīam

fīās

fīat

fīāmus

fīātis

fiant

How would you say "Let them be made, let them come into existence."? *fiant*

The Latin word for light is *lūx*. If you were God, and you spoke Latin, and you wanted to say, "Let there be light!" how would you say this? *Fiat lūx.* And indeed, let's take another a look at the passage from the Bible that we used for pronunciation practice in lecture one. *Dīxitque Deus: "fiat lūx."* And God said, "let light be made" or "let light come into existence!" God, or at least Jerome, who provided the Latin translation, knew his subjunctive. Try this one. "Let it be made!"

Fiat. And so, without God, and without light, we get a car, a Fiat, but that is, I confess, *mea culpa*, a bad joke. *Fiat* comes into English, however, as something done by decree. What is *"fiat* money?" Literally, the phrase means, "Let there be money!" Money that was created by someone's order. The government and God have the power to insist that their will be done, and the Latin subjunctive provides a helping hand.

Here is another verb with just three, rather than four, principal parts, *dēsinō, dēsinere, dēsīī,* which means, "cease," "desist," as in "cease and desist," "stop!" Let's conjugate *dēsinō* in the present tense indicative.

dēsinō

dēsinis

dēsinit

dēsinimus

dēsinitis

dēsinunt

Let's conjugate this verb in the present tense subjunctive.

*dēsin*am

*dēsin*ās

*dēsin*at

*dēsin*āmus

*dēsin*ātis

*dēsin*ant

You will recall that I mentioned the poet Catullus. Did I tell you that Catullus was unhappy? Of course I did. I told you that he had a girlfriend. Catullus wrote another poem, and in the first line he talks to himself. First he calls himself terribly, miserably unhappy. The Latin word is *miser*. But Catullus is trying to cheer himself up, or at least give himself a pep talk, and you already know enough Latin to figure out the first line of this poem, at least you do, if I tell you that *ineptīre* is an infinitive that means "to be a fool." We get the English word inept from this word. At all events, *miser* Catullus talks to himself in this opening line, and says, in Latin, *Miser Catulle, dēsinās ineptīre!* Notice how *Miser Catulle* is set off by a comma, That is because he is talking to himself. It would be as if I were to ignore you, *discipulī discipulaeque linguae Latīnae,* and instead address myself: *Miser Molinārī!* Why do I call myself a wretch? This is just one of the sacrifices I make for my students. But to return to our poet, *Miser Catulle, dēsinās ineptīre!* Where is the main action? It's in the verb, course, which is *dēsinās.* How do we translate it? Well, if the indicative *dēsinis* means "you cease, desist, or stop," what does the subjunctive form mean? "You should stop," "you should cease." The infinitive gives us more information. It completes the meaning of the verb cease, that is, "you should cease to be a fool." *Miser Catulle, dēsinās ineptīre!* Unhappy Catullus, cease, or you should cease, you really should cease to be a fool. Or, if we translate more loosely, *Catullus, you wretch, stop being an idiot!*

We can tell a little story. *Vīvāmus, mea Lesbia!* Let us live, my Lesbia! *Bibāmus!* Let us drink! I reckon you can figure out how Lesbia responded to the poet's invitations. And then after that response, *Miser Catulle, dēsinās ineptīre!*

But we do not want to end on that note. Let us take the verb learn, *disco, discere, didicī,* another verb with three principal parts. Together with our other verbs, and a few nouns, we can practice reading some sentences. *Lingua* means tongue or language. *Linguam Latīnam discō.* The verb ends in "o," and it's indicative, so, translation, "I learn the Latin language." *Linguam Latīnam discimus.* The verb now ends in "mus," so we are the subject. Is the verb indicative or subjunctive? It's indicative, so we are stating a simple fact. We learn the Latin language. *Linguam Latīnam discāmus.* What is the mood of the verb now? That long A is the give away. *Discāmus* is subjunctive. How does this change our translation?

Let us learn the Latin language!

Do you remember that the word *ut* can be used with the subjunctive to express purpose and *nē* with the subjunctive to express negative purpose? *Bibāmus, ut vīvāmus!* Let us drink, so that we may live! *Bibāmus,* let us drink, we call the hortatory subjunctive. We are exhorting, or encouraging, ourselves to drink. Come on, guys, let's just do it, let's drink! *Bibāmus! Ut vīvāmus,* so that we may live. On the other hand, *ut vīvāmus* expresses purpose. Why is *vīvāmus* subjunctive? Well, I just told you, because it expresses purpose, with *ut. Vīvimus, ut bibāmus.* The sentence is slightly different, *vīvāmus ut vīvāmus,* We live, so that we may drink. We add an indicative and then a subjunctive.

Lesbia bibit, nē Catullus dēsinat ineptīre. Lesbia drinks, lest Catullus cease to be a fool. Or, in more modern English, Lesbia drinks so that Catullus will not cease to be a fool. *Bibite, Catulle et Lesbia, ut vīvātis!* Drink, Catullus, that was an imperative, *bibite,* drink Catullus and Lesbia, so that you may live, *ut vīvātis.*

Commands, that *bibite* form, is stronger than the hortatory subjunctive. Here's another sentence, *Dēsinātis inepīre, nē Lesbia bibat.* Y'all should cease to be foolish, lest Lesbia drink.

For the next one, you need to know that *antīqua* means "ancient." *Linguam Latīnam discunt, ut in Rōmā antīquā vīvant.* They learn the Latin language, so that they may live in ancient Rome. Intellectually, that is, as a way to forget about the present troubles, which is actually a pretty good reason to learn Latin. In fact, the Roman historian Livy said something similar. Livy wrote shortly after fall of the Roman republic and its transformation into a monarchy that was, basically, a military dictatorship dressed up as a republic, Livy, in the preface to his great *History of Rome*, tells us that he writes history, *ut mē ā cōnspectū [tempōrum] malōrum... āvertam.* So that (*ut*) I may turn (*avertam*) myself (*mē*) from (*ā*) the view (*cōnspectū*) of evil times (*[tempōrum] malōrum*). Granted, that's a tough sentence for lecture three, but you can already appreciate that *āvertam* is a first person singular present active subjunctive: *ut...āvertam*, so that I may turn away." Subjunctive in a clause of purpose. We can parse the verb.

Alas, it is now time that I turn myself away from you, so that you may learn Latin, *ut linguam Latīnam discātis*, and practice it on your own before we meet again. *Valete.*

The Irregular Verbs *Sum* and *Possum*
Lecture 4

In the last lecture, we studied the subjunctive power of ā. We turned *pōnō*, "I place" or "I put away," into *pōnam*, "let me put away." We will begin this lecture by reviewing the personal active endings of the Latin verb. These endings work not just for regular verbs but for irregular verbs, as well, and in this lesson, we will learn two of them: *sum* ("I am") and *possum* ("I am able").

Review: Personal endings for Latin verbs, active voice

	Singular	Plural
1	-ō / -m	-mus
2	-s	-tis
3	-t	-nt

Present indicative of *sum*

***sum, esse, fuī, futūrum*: be**

	Singular	Plural
1	sum	sumus
2	es	estis
3	est	sunt

- The verb "to be" is irregular. It has four parts: *sum* ("I am"), *esse* ("to be"), *fuī* ("I have been"), *futūrum* ("going to be").

- In the present indicative, note that despite the irregularities of the base (*su-, e-, es-, su-, es-, su-*), the endings are regular.

Translation of present indicative of *sum*

	Singular			Plural		
1	sum	=	I am	sumus	=	we are
2	es	=	you (sing.) are	estis	=	you (pl.) are
3	est	=	he/she/it is	sunt	=	they are

Quiz

The following English sentences include a form of the verb "to be" in the present tense. Supply the corresponding Latin equivalent.

1. Latin *is* a language.

2. *Is* Pompey in love?

3. There *is* a lion in that cage.

4. *We are* students of the Latin language.

5. *Are you*, Julius, a military genius?

6. *You*, Catiline and Cethegus, *are* conspirators!

7. *I am* not a prophet.

8. *There are* many soldiers outside my door.

Answers: 1. *est*, 2. *est*, 3. *est*, 4. *sumus*, 5. *es*, 6. *estis*, 7. *sum*, 8. *sunt*.

Present subjunctive of *sum*

sum, esse, fuī, futūrum: be

	Singular	Plural
1	sim	sīmus
2	sīs	sītis
3	sit	sint

"To be able"

- In ancient Latin, *pot-* plus "being" yields ability, that is, the forms of the irregular verb "to be able." Note that this verb is irregular in English, as well. Compare "I *can* see you" with "I *am able to* see you." *Can* and *to be able to* are not even close, yet they are considered parts of the same irregular English verb. Latin is much more regular. All that's needed is *pot-* or *pos-*.

- Latin *pot-* is related to the same *pot-* we find in the English word *potent*, a word that means "powerful, able." Thus, combining *est* ("is") with *pot-* yields *potest*, which means, quite literally "able is" or, in normal English word order "is able."

- The only other thing we need to know is that *pot-* changes to *pos-* if the initial letter of the form of "to be" is an *s*.

Present indicative of *possum*

possum, posse, potuī: be able, can

1	possum	possumus
2	potes	potestis
3	potest	possunt

Present subjunctive of *possum*

***possum, posse, potuī*: be able, can**

	Singular	Plural
1	possim	possīmus
2	possīs	possītis
3	possit	possint

Imperatives of *sum/possum*

	Singular	Plural
1	***	***
2	es ("be!") / potes ("be able!")	este ("be!") / poteste ("be able!")
3	***	***

Infinitives of *sum/possum*

Sum: esse ("to be")

Possum: posse ("to be able")

Complementary infinitives
- *Possum* is a verb that allows its meaning to be "completed" by other verbs. Simply stating, "I can" or "I am able," for example, does not always tell us enough.

- If we parse "I am able to read," what verb in what part of speech completes the meaning of the main verb "I am able"? The infinitive "to read" completes the meaning of "I am able" by telling what I am able to do.

- Inasmuch as "to read" is an infinitive that "completes" the meaning of the verb, it's called a complementary infinitive. If the verb *legō, legere, lēgī, lēctum* means "read," and *potest* means "she is able," what does *potest legere* mean? "She is able to read" or "she can read."

Sentence practice

1. *Possumus bibere.* We are able to drink. *Or*: We can drink

2. *Possunt ineptīre.* They are able to be foolish. *Or*: They can be foolish.

3. *Potest linguam Latīnam legere.* She is able to read the Latin language. *Or*: She can read the Latin language.

4. *Bibimus, ut possīmus bene* (well) *vīvere.* We drink so that we can live well. Or, more literally: We drink so that we may be able to live well.

5. *Vīta brevis.* Life is short.

6. *Ars longa.* Art is long.

7. *Vīta est brevis, sed ars est longa.* Life is short, but art is long. (*Sed* is a conjunction that contrasts the thought of what follows it with the idea of the main clause. In Latin, *sed* can be dropped altogether. This is a rhetorical trick that makes listeners or readers combine the clauses on their own without the help of a conjunction. In rhetoric, the figure of speech is called *asyndeton*, which means "no connection" in ancient Greek.)

8. *Sit vīta longa!* May life be long!

9. *Ars brevis esse potest.* Art can be short.

10. *Linguam Latīnam legere possumus.* We can read the Latin language.

11. *Potestis ineptīre.* Y'all can be foolish.

12. *Sumus.* We are.

13. *Sīmus.* Let us be.

14. *Est.* It is.

15. *Sit.* Let it be.

16. *Sit, sit.* Let it be, let it be.

17. *Esse an nōn* (or not) *esse?* To be or not to be?

18. *Esse est posse.* To be is to be able.

19. *Pōne metum; valeō.* Put away your fear, (for) I am well. (Ovid)

20. *Pōnāmus metum.* Let us put away our fear. *Or:* Let's not be afraid.

21. *Pōnāmus nimiōs gemitūs!* Let us put away excessive sorrow! (Juvenal)

22. *Caesar populum Rōmānum dēcipit.* Caesar deceives the Roman people.

23. *Caesar populum Rōmānum dēcipere potest.* Caesar is able to deceive the Roman people.

24. *Fiat lūx!* Let there be light! *Or,* more literally: Let light be made!

25. *Sī lūx est, possumus bibere.* If there is light, we are able to drink.

26. *Sī lūx fiat, possīmus bibere.* If light should be made, we would be able to drink. *Or,* in less formal English: If you'd turn on the light, we'd be able to drink.

27. *Sī lūx fiat, possīmus bibere?* If it should become light, would we be able to drink?

Parsing a Latin sentence

- Let's parse the following Latin sentence: *Bibimus, ut possīmus bene vīvere*, which means, "We drink so that we can live well."

- The verb *bibimus* ("we drink") is in the first-person plural present tense. The mood is indicative, because the sentence is stating a fact.

- The word *ut* is a conjunction that joins one phrase to another, allowing us to combine two clauses into one more complex thought. Note, too, that *ut* is a subordinating conjunction. The thought expressed in the clause or phrase introduced by *ut* is combined with the thought of the main clause (*bibimus*) to explain why we're making the statement *bibimus* ("we drink"). In particular, *ut* introduces purpose or result. In this sentence, we find purpose, but barring further context, we could well have chosen result: "We drink with the result that we are able to live well."

- What is the mood of *possīmus* ("we can" or "are able" or "may be able to")? It is a third-person plural present-tense subjunctive verb in a clause of result or purpose.

- The new word *bene* is an adverb that modifies the infinitive *vīvere* ("to live"). Because it completes the meaning of *possīmus*, *vīvere* is a complementary infinitive.

Verba

bene (adverb): well

dēcipiō, dēcipere, dēcēpī, dēceptum: deceive

legō, legere, lēgī, lēctum: read

nōn: not

possum, posse, potuī: be able

sed (conjunction): but

sum, esse, fuī, futūrum: be

Please learn the principal parts, present-tense indicative and subjunctive, the present imperatives, and the infinitive of *sum* ("to be"). Learn the principal parts of *possum* ("to be able") and familiarize yourself with how to apply the prefix *pot-* (or *pos-*) to the forms of *sum* in order to create *possum*. All forms of *sum* may be found in App. §52, but please study only the present-tense forms. Representative forms of *possum* appear in App. §66.

Agenda

i. In the verb chart below, conjugate the verb *legō* in the present active indicative.

	Singular	Plural
1		
2		
3		

ii. In the verb chart below, conjugate the verb *sum* in the present indicative.

	Singular	Plural
1		
2		
3		

iii. Create your own verb chart for each of the verbs below and conjugate in the present tense of the mood indicated.

1. possum (indicative)

Lecture 4: The Irregular Verbs *Sum* and *Possum*

2. sum (subjunctive)

3. legō (subjunctive)

4. possum (subjunctive)

iv. Please translate the following into Latin.

1. She is able.

2. She may be able.

3. They are.

4. Let them be.

5. We are able to read.

6. We may be able to read.

7. The women can learn.

8. Can the soldiers conquer?

9. Are the male and female students able to learn the Latin language?

10. You are soldiers, but we are not soldiers.

11. Are you a soldier?

12. Let it be.

v. Please translate the following into English.

1. Caesar potest populum Rōmānum dēcipere.

2. Cūrāte, ut valeātis!

3. Bibimus et edimus, ut possīmus bene vīvere.

4. Si lūx est, possumus bibere.

5. Mīlitēs possunt vincere sed nōn vincunt.

6. Vīta brevis est.

7. Ars longa esse potest.

8. Esse est posse.

9. Bene legere potestis, discipulae.

10. Mīlitēs nōn sunt.

The Irregular Verbs *Sum* and *Possum*
Lecture 4—Transcript

Salvēte, discipulī discipulaeque linguae Latīnae! Greetings, students of the Latin language! *Mihi valdē placet vōs pulchram linguam Latīnam aeternam docēre.* I am very happy to have another chance to speak with you and explore with you the beautiful and eternal Latin language. In the last lesson, we studied the subjunctive power of the vowel A. We turned *pōnō*, I place or put away, into *pōnam*, let me put away. We will see that regular verb again soon enough. Let us, instead, now review the personal active endings of the Latin verb. Go ahead. I'll wait a moment while you recite them. *o* or *m, s, t, mus, tis, nt.* Again together: *Ūnus, duo, ūnus, duo, trēs: o* or *m, s, t, mus, tis, nt.* And one more time: *o* or *m, s, t, mus, tis, nt.*

These endings work not just for regular verbs, but for irregular verbs as well, and we are going to learn two of them today: *sum* (I am) and *possum* (I am able). The verb to be, or linking verb, is how we explain what it is, whatever that what, may be. Let us examine the forms of the verb to be together. It's irregular, as I mentioned. It has four parts: *sum* (I am), *esse* (to be), *fuī* (I have been), *futūrus* (going to be). Of these four parts, we will, in this lesson, use only the first two. Let us look at the present active indicative and the present active subjunctive forms of the verb *sum* (I am). We will analyze, we'll compare, we'll contrast, and then we'll chant.

sum

es

est

sumus

estis

sunt

I have overemphasized the endings for a reason. Despite the irregularities of the base—*su, e, es, su, es, su*—the endings are regular. Please repeat the Latin after me:

sum (I am)

es (you are)

est (he, she, or it is, but also, there is)

sumus (we are)

estis (y'all are)

sunt (they are or, there are)

Again, without the English translation, in the singular. Please repeat:

sum

es

est

sumus

estis

sunt

One more time, in the singular first:

sum

es

est

And in the plural:

sumus

estis

sunt

It's already time for a quiz. I will make up a sentence in English that includes a form of the verb to be in the present tense. Please, in the pause provided, supply the corresponding Latin equivalent. After the pause, I, *Molinārius*, will provide the correct response, so that you, *discipulī discipulaeque linguae Latīnae*, students of the Latin language, may check your work. Latin is a language.

est, Is Pompey in love? *est*

There is a lion in that cage. *est*

We are students of the Latin language. *sumus*

Are you, Julius, a military genius? *es*

You, Catiline and Cethegus, are conspirators! *estis*

I am not a prophet. *sum*

There are many soldiers outside my door. *sunt*

Let us now compare the indicative of *sum, es, est, sumus, estis, sunt.* Let's compare these forms to the subjunctive. The key vowel will be the letter I, = and every form will begin with S.

sum becomes *sim, es* becomes *sīs, est* becomes *sit, sumus* becomes *sīmus*, *estis* becomes *sītis*, and *sunt* becomes *sint.*

Let's try the present subjunctive of the verb *sum, esse, fui, futurum* (to be). Please repeat the Latin after me:

sim (let me be or I may be)

sīs (you may be)

sit (let him, her, or it be; or he, she, or it, or there may be)

sīmus (let us be or we may be)

sītis (y'all may be)

sint (let them be, or they may be, or there may be)

Please repeat the Latin singular after me:

sim

sīs

sit

And the plural:

sīmus

sītis

sint

Again:

sim

sīs

sit

sīmus

sītis

sint

And stop. We now exist. We are, and with the addition of three letters, we can also have ability in Latin. Those who are, can, so long as they have enough *pot*. P. O. T., *pot*, plus, "being" yields, at least in ancient Latin, ability, which is to say, the forms of the other irregular verb for today, "to be able." This verb is irregular in English as well. For example, compare "I can see you" to "I am able to see you." "Can" and "to be able" are not even close, and yet they are considered parts of the same irregular English verb. Latin is much more regular than that. All you need is enough *pot*. Well, and you also need to remember to change the final T of *pot* to an S, sometimes. But why does P. O. T, *pot*, provide such magical ability in Latin? Latin *pot* is related to the same P. O. T. we find in the English word potent, a word that means powerful, able.

So if *est* means is, which, of course, it does, and I combine it with *pot*, I obtain *potest*, which means, quite literally, "able is," or, in normal English word order, "is able." It's that simple. The only other thing you need to know is that P. O. T. changes to P. O. S. if the initial letter of the form of to be begins with an S. I've checked my supplies, and I have plenty of P. O. T., *pot*, so let's form the indicative and subjunctive present tenses of to be able.

pot + *sum*, remembering that *sum* begins with S, yields *possum* (I am able or I can) *pot* + *es* yields *potes* (you are able or you can)

pot + *est* yields *potest* (he, she, or it is able; or he, she, or it can)

pot + *sumus*, remembering that *sumus* begins with an S, yields *possumus* (we are able or we can)

pot + *estis* yields *potestis* (y'all are able or y'all can)

pot + *sunt*, remembering that *sunt* begins with an S, yields *possunt* (they are able or they can)

I know how much you like to chant, so, please, repeat after me:

possum

potes

potest

possumus

potestis

possunt

Again:

possum

potes

potest

possumus

potestis

possunt

One more time:

possum

potes

potest

possumus

potestis

possunt

Let's review the present tense subjunctive of the verb to be.

sim

sīs

sit

sīmus

sītis

sint

How many of these forms begin with the letter S? All of them. Will we combine these forms with *pot* or *pos* to form "I may be able," "you may be able," "he, she or it may be able," etc.; *pos* is all we need. Let's give it a try.

pos plus *sim* yields *possim*

pos plus *sīs* yields *possīs*

pos plus *sit* yields *possit*

pos plus *sīmus* yields *possīmus*

pos plus *sītis* yields *possītis*

pos plus *sint* yields *possint*

The present subjunctive of the verb "to be able."

Please repeat after me in the singular:

possim

possīs

possit

And in the plural:

possīmus

possītis

possint

And one more time:

possim

possīs

possit

possīmus

possītis

possint

Let's clean up a few stray details and then take a look at our new forms in action. These two irregular verbs have imperative and infinitive forms. The command forms for "be!" as in "Be faithful, Peter!" *Es!* And in the plural, as in "Be faithful, Peter and Judas!" *Este!* And if you want Peter and Judas to be able? Give them some *pot. Potes!* "Be able, Peter!" *Poteste!* "Be able, Peter and Judas!" And the infinitives? *Esse* means "to be." So how do we form the infinitive "to be able"? I wish I could say *potesse*, and that form does occur in extant Latin literature, but the standard form was, and is, *posse*, which tells us two things. The verb is irregular, and the verb was so common that further contraction took place; *potesse* became *posse*.

What have we learned? Have a look at this chart for the verb *possum*. The handiest thing about *possum* is that it is a verb that allows its meaning to be completed by other verbs. Simply stating "I can or I am able," for example, does not always tell us enough. "You can do what?" "I am able to read Latin!" If we parse, that is, examine the grammatical details of "I am able to read," what verb, in English, in what part of speech completes the meaning of the main verb "I am able?" The answer is "to read." The verb "to read" completes the meaning of "I am able" by telling us what I am able to do. And what part of speech is "to read?" It is the infinitive, or to-form. And, in as much as "to read" is an infinitive that completes the meaning of the verb, we call it a complementary infinitive. Note the spelling, not complimentary with an I, as if an infinitive we're telling you something nice, but complementary with an E, as in an infinitive that completes the meaning of the verb.

If the verb *legō, legere, lēgī, lēctum* means "read," and *potest* means "she is able," in this instance, what does *potest legere* mean? "She is able to read" or "she can read." And we note the peculiarity that in English the infinitive loses "to" after "can." The infinitive used to lose the "to" after "dare" as well, as in "Brutus wouldn't dare stab Caesar," but we increasingly hear such sentences as "Dare to go where no man has gone before." What can I say? Languages change over time. But, in this instance, the irregularity is in English, not Latin. Present tense active Latin infinitives always end in *re*. Except, of course, when they end in *se*, but that's only for a couple of irregular verbs like *esse* (to be) and *posse* (to be able).

Let's try a few sentences using vocabulary from lesson three.

Possumus bibere. We are able to drink. Or, We can drink.

Possunt inepfire. They are able to be foolish. Or: They can be foolish.

Potest linguam Lafīnam legere. She is able to read the Latin language. Or: She can read the Latin language.

Bibimus, ut possīmus bene (well) *vīvere.* We drink so that we can live well. Or more literally, We drink so that we may be able to live well.

Please note that it is not always necessary to represent the Latin subjunctive in English. We used to have a robust subjunctive mood. Today? Not so much. Why? Languages change. Except for classical Latin, which is yet another reason why it is worth knowing. Let's look at that sentence again. *Bibimus, ut possīmus bene vīvere.* Let's parse each word, that is, explain the morphology, grammar, and syntax of each word and constituent phrase of this five-word sentence.

Bibimus: we drink. The verb is in the first person plural present tense. What is the mood? Indicative. Why? Because we state a fact. We are drinking. And the word *ut*? It is a conjunction that joins one phrase to another. This allows us to combine two clauses into one more complex thought. *Ut* is also a subordinating conjunction. The thought expressed in the clause, or phrase, introduced by *ut* is combined with the thought of the main clause (*bibimus*) to explain why we make the statement *bibimus* "we drink."

In particular, *ut* introduces purpose or result. Personally, I opted for purpose, but, barring further context, we could well have chosen result. "We drink with the result that we are able to live well." That's the alternative. "There is," as the old, but now pet-friendly, saying goes, "more than one way to bathe a cat." But what is the mood of *possīmus*, "we can, or are able, or may be able to"? It is a first person plural present tense subjunctive verb in a clause of result or purpose. What about *bene*? That new word is an adverb that modifies the infinitive *vīvere* (to live). And what kind of infinitive is *vīvere*? Because it completes the meaning of *possīmus*, it is a complementary infinitive. And there you have it. We have parsed the sentence.

Parsing gets a bad name. But why? If you study human anatomy, does it matter whether you look at an artery or a vein? Aren't they both just blood tubes? Well, no. And those who want to understand language accurately and with precision, parse. But life is short, which you can now read in the original Latin: *vīta* (life) *est brevis* (short, brief). Brief derives from *brevis*, think brevity, or in better Latin word order: *vīta brevis est*; or perhaps *brevis est vīta*; or simply, *vīta brevis*. The Romans were fond of leaving out the *est* altogether on the grounds that it was so obvious as to be unnecessary. And there are varieties of English, granted, non-standard, that do the same thing. Here's an example. You ask, "Why are you not drinking your coffee, Molinārius?" I respond, "The coffee is cold."

So far, so good. Standard English. But would I really say "is." I would, using my upper midwestern-inflected standard American dialect, actually probably respond: "The coffee's cold," attaching an "s" to coffee, because "is" is so obvious and common that it may be left unstressed. We could, and some do, take it a step further. "Why are you not drinking your coffee, sir?" Answer, "The coffee cold." This is perfectly intelligible, and would be considered elegant, if it were in Latin. In English, on the other hand, the construction serves as a social marker. This speaker has not been educated or has not chosen to supply the useless unstressed S of the third person present tense indicative of the irregular verb "to be." And even if we did not consciously parse that sentence in such detail, most would, when we heard it, using our knowledge of English and its various social registers, instantly have arrived at similar results. We may have even drawn conclusions about the person's social class and ethnicity. The tiniest linguistic details can be powerful markers, and the only way to get at them is to parse them.

Embrace your inner linguist, and the pleasures of parsing. *Vīta brevis.* Life is short. *Ars longa.* Art is long. That's a famous saying, which we could write out more fully, but less pithily as

Vīta est brevis, sed ars est longa. Life is short, but art is long. *Sed*, by the way, is a conjunction that contrasts the thought of what follows *sed* with the idea of the main clause. Latin can drop the *sed* altogether. This is a rhetorical trick that makes listeners or readers combine the clauses on their own without the help of a conjunction. For you rhetoricians, that figure of speech is called asyndeton, which means "no connection" in ancient Greek, the inventors of rhetoric, but I'm not here to teach you ancient Greek. Let's enjoy this phrase in the original Latin and then spell out the thought in the more ponderous language of our own times. *Vīta brevis; ars longa.* Life is short; art long. That is, our individual lives are short, but, our creative products, our art, can last much longer.

Let's drill some of our new forms of *sum* (to be) and *possum* (to be able).

Sit vīta longa! May life be long! *Sit* was subjunctive.

Ars brevis esse potest. Art can be short. Art is able to be short.

Linguam Latīnam legere possumus. We can, or we are able, to read the Latin language.

Potestis ineptīre. Y'all can be foolish.

Sumus. We are.

Sīmus. Let us be.

Est. It is.

Sit. Let it be.

Sit, sit. Bad Beatles joke: Let it be, let it be.

As long as we are in that kind of mood, how about a line from *Hamlet*?

Esse an nōn (or not) *esse?* To be or not to be? *Esse an nōn esse?*

How about this one? *Esse est posse.* To be is to be able.

Here's a quote from Ovid. *Pōne metum; valeō. Metum* means fear; *valeō* is from a verb that means "to be well." *Pōne* is the command form of a verb you have learned: pōnō, pōnere, posuī, positum. What does the poet Ovid tell us? Pōne metum; valeō. Put away your fear, (for) I am well. Did you notice the asyndeton, or lack of connection? *Pōne metum; valeō.* We'd probably say something like, Don't be afraid, because I'm well, or for I'm well. Romans loved that rhetorical trick.

How about *Pōnāmus metum.* What does that mean? What does that A in *ponamus* tell us? It tells us that the verb is in the subjunctive mood. Let us put away our fear. Let's not be afraid. I made that sentence up, but Juvenal, another famous poet wrote, *Pōnāmus nimiōs gemitus! Nimiōs* means excessive, and *gemitus* means sorrow. Try translating the whole sentence. *Pōnāmus nimiōs gemitus!* Let us put away excessive sorrow!

If *dēcipiō, dēcipere, dēcēpī, dēceptum* means "deceive," and it does, try this sentence. *Caesar populum Rōmānum dēcipit.* Caesar deceives the Roman people. Slight variation, *Caesar populum Rōmānum dēcipere potest.* Caesar is able to deceive the Roman people. Please parse *dēcipere.*

Decipere is a complementary infinitive, which is to say, that it completes the meaning of *potest.* Do you recall the phrase, *Fiat lūx!* Let there be light, or, more literally, "let light be made." *Sī*, the word *sī*, is another conjunction that means "if" in Latin. What would this sentence mean? *Sī lūx est, possumus bibere.* If there is light, we are able to drink. This is a simple condition. Let's make it subjunctive. *Sī lūx fiat, possīmus bibere.* If light should be made, we would be able to drink. Or, in less formal English. If you'd turn on the light, we'd be able to drink. Let's turn it into a question by adding a question mark. *Sī lūx fiat,* possīmus *bibere?* If it should become light, would we be able to drink? The English was less simple. Latin word order remained the same, but in English we had to change our word order as well as raise our tone in order to make it a question.

At all events, with just a few words and a few forms, we can say relatively complex things. You should pat yourselves on the back, or, as the poet Ovid commanded those who'd learned his lessons in seduction, *Dīcite, "Iō, Paeon!"* Words to celebrate. *Iō*, basically remains unchanged to this day and was used famously by Sylvester Stallone in *Rocky*, as in "Yo, Adrian!" And *Paeon*, another word that basically means "shout-out," as in "Hey, thanks for the shout-out!" or "Yo, thanks for the 'peon!'" But let's not parse the moment. *Dīcite, "Iō, Paeon!* And with that, all of you lovers of the Latin language, *omnēs amātōrēs linguae Latīnae*, you are free to go. Seriously, *exite* (depart), *ut linguam Latīnam discātis*, and practice it on your own before we meet again. *Grātiās vōbis agō!* Many thanks, and until we meet again, take care, so that you may be well; (*cūrāte, ut valeātis*), *id est*, fare well!

Introduction to Third-Declension Nouns
Lecture 5

In the last three lectures, we've concentrated on verbs because the verb is where the action is in a sentence. The personal active endings of the Latin verb (-ō or -m, -s, -t, -mus, -tis, -nt) tell us who is performing the action of the verb, and if we change the vowel in front of the ending from *i* or *u* to *ā*, we change the mood from indicative to subjunctive. For the irregular verbs *sum* and *possum*, we saw that the subjunctive vowel was *i*. Verbs are central, but there is more to the world than action, and there are more parts of speech than verbs, infinitives, and conjunctions. In this lecture, we will dive into nouns.

Defining "declension"
- As we all know, a noun is a person, place, or thing. Nouns can be the subjects or objects of verbs. They can be used with prepositions in adverbial phrases. They can express the means by which an action is accomplished, and they can show possession. Our linguistic world becomes much richer with the addition of nouns, and Latin has an effective system to organize their syntax, that is, their grammatical relations with other words in sentences, phrases, and clauses.

- As you recall, Latin is a highly inflected language. It changes the endings of words to indicate how those words relate to other words in a sentence. When we put endings on verbs, we call the process "conjugation." When we put endings on nouns and adjectives, we call it "declension."

- Third-declension nouns are the largest class of nouns in the Latin language. The 10 endings for these nouns (5 singular and 5 plural) are shown in the following table.

	Singular	Plural
Nominative	***	-ēs
Genitive	-is	-um
Dative	-ī	-ibus
Accusative	-em	-ēs
Ablative	-e	-ibus

Declension of *mīles* (third-declension noun)

mīles, *mīlitis*, m.: soldier

	Singular	Plural
Nominative	mīles	mīlitēs
Genitive	mīlitis	mīlitum
Dative	mīlitī	mīlitibus
Accusative	mīlitem	mīlitēs
Ablative	mīlite	mīlitibus

Parsing *mīles*

- The first form here is *mīles*, which we call nominative. The word *nominative* derives from the Latin word *nōmen*, meaning "name." This is the form (or case) in which we "name" or identify a word. It is also the form a word takes when it serves as the subject or doer of a verb. In order for a Latin speaker to know that a noun was meant to serve as the subject of a verb, the noun had to be in the nominative case.

o   *Mīles potest dīcere.* The soldier is able to speak.

o   We can parse or construe *soldier* as the subject of *potest* because *mīles* is nominative.

- The second form of the noun is called genitive, and the genitive is the most crucial form of the word for applying the other endings correctly.

    o   In the genitive, *mīles* becomes *mīlitis*, or "of the soldier." *Mīles* has no ending, and *mīlitis* has the ending *-is*, which we translate as the equivalent of our preposition "of." *Legiō* means "legion"; thus, *legiō mīlitis* can be translated as "the legion of the soldier" or "the soldier's legion." The *-is* ending on *soldier* tells us that the legion belongs to the soldier. In other words, the genitive ending or case shows possession.

    o   But the genitive also shows us something essential about the noun. It is in the genitive case where we can determine what the stem or base of the noun might be, and we need that base before we can apply the rest of the endings. If we cut off the genitive ending from *mīlitis* (*-is*), we are left with *mīlit-*. This stem is the form that comes into English in such words as *military.*

    o   If we settle for the nominative, we'll get the wrong stem, and every other form will be incorrect. All nouns, when they are listed in a dictionary, are listed first in the nominative and then in the genitive singular. We need both, and we need to be able to identify the genitive ending so that we can remove it to obtain the noun's base or stem.

- The next case is the *dative.* Here, think "donation." This case is used for giving a direct object to an indirect object. In the sentence "Caesar gives the money *to the soldier,*" Caesar is the subject, and the money is the direct object. The soldier is the indirect object because, although Caesar does not perform the action of giving directly upon him—Caesar does not "give the solider"—the soldier is indirectly involved in the action. After Caesar gives, the soldier has money, which he did not have before Caesar gave. We call the soldier's relation to the verb *give* "indirect."

o   In Latin, to signal that a noun serves as an indirect object, we put it in the dative case; that is, we put the dative ending on the base of the noun.

o   The ending for the dative singular is -ī, which is pronounced "ee." Again, first we find the base, which is *mīlit*, then we add ī to that base: *mīlitī*.

*   The next case is the accusative, the case of the direct object. In the sentence "Caesar hates the soldier," the soldier is the direct object because Caesar directs his hatred—he performs the action of hating—on the soldier directly. In Latin, the sentence reads: *Caesar mīlitem ōdit.*

o   We reverse-engineer *mīlitem* and determine the ending for the direct object, the accusative case.

o   The base of the noun is *mīlit*, and the accusative ending is *-em*.

*   The word *ablative* literally means "carried away"; it describes metaphorically the form "carried away" farthest from the original nominative.

o   In our example, we add the letter *e* (pronounced as ĕ) to the stem, *mīlit*, to get *mīlite*, meaning "by, with, or from the solider."

o   In the sentence *Caesar cum mīlite bibit* ("Caesar drinks with the solider"), the solider is ablative. The preposition *cum* ("with") is associated with or governs the ablative case. The ablative is used to indicate who accompanies Caesar and is, thus, called the "ablative of accompaniment" to distinguish it from other uses of the ablative.

Declension of *lūx* (third-declension noun)

lūx, lūcis, f.: light

	Singular	Plural
Nominative	lūx	lūcēs
Genitive	lūcis	lūcum
Dative	lūcī	lūcibus
Accusative	lūcem	lūcēs
Ablative	lūce	lūcibus

Parsing *lūx*

- *Lūx* is a feminine word meaning "light." The genitive of *lūx* is *lūcis*. If we remove the genitive ending, which is the same *-is* we saw earlier, the base of the word *lūx* is *luc-*.

- A quick declension and translation of *lūx* are shown in the following table.

	Singular	Plural
Nominative	*lūx*: the light "verbs"	*lūcēs*: the lights "verb"
Genitive	*lūcis*: of the light	*lūcum*: of the lights
Dative	*lūcī*: to *or* for the light	*lūcibus*: to *or* for the lights
Accusative	*lūcem*: "verb" the light	*lūcēs*: "verb" the lights
Ablative	*lūce*: by, with, *or* from the light	*lūcibus*: by with, *or* from the lights

- How can we tell the nominative *lūcēs* from the accusative *lūcēs* and the dative *lūcibus* from the ablative *lūcibus*, given that they look and sound exactly the same? The answer is context.

o Consider this sentence: *Lūcēs mēnsem faciunt.* The "lights," *lūcēs,* (i.e., "day-lights" or "days") "make," *faciunt,* "a month," *mēnsem.*

o How do we know that the days make a month, and it is not the month that makes the days? There are several clues.

o Parsing the sentence, we find:

• *Lūcēs*: nominative or accusative plural, subject or direct object

• *mēnsem*: accusative singular, direct object

• *faciunt*: third-person plural present-tense indicative verb

o *Faciunt* requires a plural subject. The only available candidate is the word *lūcēs*. *Mēnsem* is accusative, which means that it must be the direct object, thus leaving *lucēs* available to serve as the subject. The easiest path to a meaningful sentence is to read *lūcēs* as the nominative subject: "The days make a month"; *Lūcēs mēnsem faciunt.*

Declension of *vēritās* (third-declension noun)

vēritās, vēritātis, f.: truth

	Singular	Plural
Nominative	vēritās	vēritātēs
Genitive	vēritātis	vēritātum
Dative	vēritātī	vēritātibus
Accusative	vēritātem	vēritātēs
Ablative	vēritāte	vēritātibus

92

- *Vēritās*, Harvard's motto, means "truth." The final codification of Roman law under the emperor Justinian is known as the *Digest of Roman Law*, and it has the following phrase, simplified here for the purpose of illustration: *Vēritās in lūcem ēmergit*; "The truth emerges into light," or "The truth comes to light."

Pontius Pilate reportedly asked a then obscure but now famous defendant: *Quid est vēritās*? "What is truth?"

- Here, *vēritās* is the nominative subject of the verb *ēmergit*, and *lūcem* is accusative after the preposition *in* for reasons we will not discuss in detail, except to note that prepositions can be used with either the accusative or the ablative, and there are reasons for using one or the other.

- In this sentence, we find *light* as a bona fide direct object: *Vēritās lūcem nōn refugit*. "Truth does not flee the light."

Declension of *Caesar* (third-declension noun)

***Caesar*, *Caesaris*, m: Caesar**

	Singular	Plural
Nominative	Caesar	Caesarēs
Genitive	Caesaris	Caesarum
Dative	Caesarī	Caesaribus
Accusative	Caesarem	Caesarēs
Ablative	Caesare	Caesaribus

Note the shift in accent from *Cae* to *sar* in the dative and ablative plural. The accent in Latin cannot stand farther back from the end than the antepenult (third-from-last) syllable.

Quiz

- In this drill, you will hear a series of sentences in English in which the name *Caesar* appears. Your task is to assess how *Caesar* fits into the syntax of the English sentence and then to translate *Caesar* into the corresponding Latin form.

- For example, in the sentence "Brutus stabs Caesar," *Caesar* is the direct object of the verb *stab*, and in Latin, direct objects must appear in the accusative case. Thus, the corresponding Latin form would be *Caesarem*. Note that the examples in the following sentences refer to a variety of Caesars, not just Julius.

1. Caesar ruled Rome.

2. Suetonius wrote graphic biographies of the Caesars.

3. The law that made adultery a crime against the state was proposed by Caesar.

4. Provincial officials built many temples for the deified Caesars.

5. The Jews and, later, the Christians, refused to worship the allegedly divine Caesars.

6. Render unto Caesar ...

7. ... the things that are Caesar's.

Answers: 1. subject of the verb *ruled*, hence, nominative: *Caesar*; 2. *of*, hence, genitive: *Caesarum*; 3. *by*, hence, ablative: *Caesare*; 4. indirect object of the verb *built*, hence, dative: *Caesaribus*; 5. direct object of the verb *worship*, hence, accusative: *Caesarēs*; 6. *to* or *for* and, apparently, *unto*, thus, indirect object, hence, dative: *Caesarī*; 7. the things "belong to Caesar," thus, possession, hence, genitive: *Caesaris*.

Verba

an (conjunction): or

lūx, lūcis, f.: light

magis (adverb): more

mēns, mentis, f.: mind

mēnsis, mēnsis, m.: month

mīles, mīlitis, m.: soldier

prōcēdō, prōcēdere, prōcessī, prōcessum: go forward, advance, prosper

quid: what?

reddō, reddere, reddidī, redditum: give back, render, restore

vēritās, vēritātis, f.: truth

virtūs, virtūtis, f.: strength, courage

Memoranda

Please learn the third-declension endings for masculine and feminine nouns, as well as the declension of *mīles, mīlitis*, m., "soldier" (which may be found also in App. §17, A).

i. Create your own verb chart for each of the verbs below and conjugate in the present tense of the mood indicated.

1. reddō (indicative)

2. prōcēdō (subjunctive)

3. sum (indicative)

4. possum (subjunctive)

ii. In the noun chart below, provide the endings for third-declension nouns.

	Singular	Plural
Nominative		
Genitive		
Dative		
Accusative		
Ablative		

iii. In the noun chart below, decline the third-declension noun *mīles, mīlitis.*

	Singular	Plural
Nominative		
Genitive		
Dative		
Accusative		
Ablative		

Lecture 5: Introduction to Third-Declension Nouns

iv. In the noun chart below, decline the third-declension noun *virtūs, virtūtis*.

	Singular	Plural
Nominative		
Genitive		
Dative		
Accusative		
Ablative		

v. Create your own noun chart and decline the following third-declension nouns.

1. lūx, lūcis

2. vēritās, vēritātis

vi. Give the case and number of the following noun forms and then translate each into English. Some forms have more than one possible case.

1. vēritātis

2. lūce

3. mīlitēs

4. mīlitum

5. Caesaris

6. mēnsibus

7. vēritātī

8. Caesarī

9. lūcum

10. virtūte

vii. Please translate the following into Latin.

1. Caesar's soldiers are conquering.

2. Caesar speaks the truth to the soldier.

3. Let us advance!

4. Let truth be the light of the mind.

5. The soldiers' strength is great (*magna*).

6. The woman is learning by the strength of (her) mind.

7. Render (plural) praise (*laudem*) to Caesar!

8. Let us render praise to the truth!

9. The soldiers cannot deceive Caesar.

10. We are not able to learn the truth.

Introduction to Third-Declension Nouns
Lecture 5—Transcript

Salvēte, discipulī discipulaeque linguae Latīnae! Mihi valdē placet vōs pulchram linguam Latīnam aeternam docēre. I am very happy to have another chance to speak with you, and explore with you the beautiful and eternal Latin language.

In the last three lessons, we concentrated on verbs, and with good reason. Verbs are where sentences happen. By now I'm sure you know the personal active endings of the Latin verb by heart. I'll wait a moment while you recite them. *o* or *m*, *s*, *t*, *mus*, *tis*, *nt*. Yes, *o* or *m*, *s*, *t*, *mus*, *tis*, *nt*. Six simple endings, and we know whether I, you, he, she, it, we, y'all, or they do the verb. And if we change the vowel in front of the ending from I or U to a long A, we change the mood from indicative to subjunctive. And for the irregular verb *sum* and for the irregular verb *possum*, we saw that the subjunctive vowel was an I. Verbs are central, but there is more to the world than action. There are more parts of speech than verbs, infinitives, and conjunctions. I've already introduced a few nouns and adjectives. I just didn't mention that I'd slipped in unfamiliar parts of speech. *Mea culpa! Ignōsce mihi.* Please forgive me. I aim to make amends in this lesson. We are going to dive into nouns and parse them as you have never parsed them before.

What is a noun? A person, a place, a thing. Nouns can be subjects or objects of verbs. They can be used with prepositions in adverbial phrases. They can express the means by which an action is accomplished. They can show possession, i.e., who owns what. Our linguistic world becomes much richer with the addition of nouns, and Latin has an effective system to organize their syntax, that is, their grammatical relations with other words, in sentences, phrases, and clauses. How do Latin nouns do all these things? Is it magic? Well, in a way, yes. If you recall, Latin is a highly inflected language. Latin changes the endings of words to indicate how those words relate to other words in the sentence. When we put endings on verbs, we call the process conjugation. When we put endings on nouns and adjectives, we call it declension. We *conjugate* verbs. We *decline* nouns and adjectives.

And today we will learn the declension of the largest class of nouns in the Latin language. We traditionally call this set of noun endings the third declension, because students traditionally learned the third declension after two other declensions. But, as this declension is the most common of Latin declensions, we're going to start with the third and most important declension. Why wait for the best when you can have it right away? And, if you learn this declension first, the others will be easier. But I delay, and you are eager to get to grips with the third declension. Let me list the endings that you will have to memorize—yes, memorize—and I know you can do it.

The first ending actually doesn't exist. There is no first ending, so we say blank. Blank because the first form of nouns of this class vary, so there is no ending per se. *Crēde mihi*, trust me, please say blank to hold the place. Blank, *is, ī, em, e, es, um, ibus, es, ibus*. If you counted, you will realize that I recited ten endings. The first five were singular, and the second five were plural. Let's take a good Roman example: *mīles*, which means "soldier." *Mīles* is the first form, which we call nominative. The word nominative derives from the Latin word *nōmen*, meaning "name." *nōmen est Molinārius.* This is the form, or case, as we call it, in which we name, or identify, a word. What is the name for a soldier, the *nōmen*? The nominative is *mīles*, in Latin It is also the form a word takes when it serves as the subject or doer of a verb. In order for a Latin speaker to know that a noun was meant to serve as the subject of a verb, the noun had to be in the nominative case. *Mīles potest dīcere.* The soldier is able to speak. I can parse, or construe, soldier as the subject of *potest* because *mīles* is nominative.

The second form of the noun is called genitive, and the genitive is the most crucial form of the word if one aims to apply the other endings correctly. This is true for reasons that will soon become obvious. In the genitive, *mīles* becomes *mīlitis* or "of the soldier." *Mīles* itself has no ending, and *mīlitis* has the ending -*is*, which we translate as the equivalent of our preposition "of." *Legiō*, in Latin, means legion, so I might say something like *legiō mīlitis*, the legion of the soldier, or the soldier's legion. The -*is* ending that is on the end of "soldier" tells me that the legion belongs to the soldier. We say that the genitive ending, or case, shows possession; *mīlitis legiō*, the soldier's legion.

But the genitive also shows us something absolutely essential about the noun. It is the genitive case where we can determine what the stem, or base, of the noun might be, and we need that base before we can apply the rest of the endings. If we take our genitive soldier, which is *mīlitis*, and chop off the *-is*, which, as I've told you, is the genitive ending, can you find base or stem? *Mīlitis* minus *-is* yields? *mīlit-* And *mīlit*, as the stem, is the form that comes into English when we borrow words from Latin. We have, in English, a soldiery, or a military, not a milary If you settle for the nominative, you'll get the wrong stem, and every other form will be incorrect. All nouns, when they are listed in a dictionary, are listed first in the nominative and then in the genitive singular. You'll need both, and you'll need to be able to identify the genitive ending, so that you can remove it to obtain the noun's base or stem. OK, so far so good. Nominative, *Mīles*. Genitive, *Mīlitis*. The word genitive derives from a word meaning "generate." You can think of the genitive as the source, the origin.

The next case is dative. Think donation. It's the case that is used for giving a direct object to an indirect object. Caesar gives the money to the soldier. Caesar is the subject. He does the giving. The money is the direct object. Caesar gives the money. The soldier is the indirect object, because, although Caesar does not perform the action of giving directly upon the soldier, the soldier is indirectly involved in the action, because, after Caesar performs the action of giving upon the money, the soldier has that money, which he did not have before Caesar performed the action. We call the soldier's relation to the verb, indirect. So the soldier is the indirect object of the verb give, and in Latin, how do we signal that a noun serves as an indirect object? We put that noun in the dative case. And, to put that noun in the dative case, we put the ending I on the stem, a long I, which we pronounce "ee." So, again, first we find the base, which still remains *mīlit*, and then we add that long I to that base, *mīlitī*. Let us review: Nominative, soldier: *mīles*; genitive, of the soldier: *mīlitis*; dative, to or for the soldier: *mīlitī*.

And our next case is the accusative, the case of the direct object. "Caesar hates the soldier." In this sentence, "the soldier" is the direct object because Caesar directs his hatred, he performs the action of hating, on the soldier directly. *Caesar mīlitem ōdit.* *Ōdit* is related to the word in English "odious" and means "hate." Again. *Caesar mīlitem ōdit.* Can we reverse engineer *mīlitem* and determine what the ending is for the direct object, i.e., *id est*, the accusative case? What is the base of the noun? *mīlit*. Can you tell me what the accusative ending is? *–em*. Let's take stock. Nominative: *mīles*, the soldier verbs, or performs the action of a verb; genitive: *mīlitis*, of the soldier; dative: *mīliti*, to or for the soldier; accusative: *mīlitem*, verb the soldier, perform the action of a verb upon the soldier.

And, finally, one more case that matters, the ablative. Literally, the word means "carried away" and describes, metaphorically, the form carried away farthest from the original nominative. It's not a great name, but it also helps explain the words case and declension. The word case derives from the verb *cadō, cadere, cecīdī, casus*, which means "fall." A case is how things fall out. The noun is conceived of as falling away from its original form. This is also the metaphor of the word declension. The noun declines, or leans away, from its nominative and then falls into a case. You can see why people fall in love with Latin. It's written into the code! But to return to the ablative, despite its distance from the nominative, it's not hard to form. Take the stem, in this case, again, *mīlit*, and add the letter E, which we pronounce as a short E, *mīlite*, by, with, or from the soldier.

The ablative case has many uses and can, thus, be translated in many ways, hence the prepositions by, with, or from, and that's only a start. *Caesar cum mīlite bibit.* Caesar drinks with the soldier. The soldier is ablative for two reasons. The preposition *cum*, which means with, is associated with, or governs, the ablative case. The ablative is used to indicate who accompanies Caesar, and is, thus, called the ablative of accompaniment, to distinguish it from other uses of the ablative. But don't worry about the technical terminology. We will review these things many times. Let us take stock now, instead, of where we are: nominative: *mīles*, the soldier verbs; genitive: *mīlitis*, of the soldier; dative: *mīlitī*, to or for the soldier; accusative: verb the soldier, *mīlitem*; ablative: *mīlite*, by, with, or from the soldier. So much for the singular, let's take a look at the plural, where we can have the same fun all over again: nominative: *mīlites*, the soldiers verb; *genitive: mīlitum,* of the soldiers; dative: *mīlitibus*, to or for the soldiers; accusative: *mīlitēs*, verb the soldiers; ablative: *mīlitibus*, by, with, or from the soldiers.

Let's decline soldier, form by form. Please repeat after me:

mīles

mīlitis

mīlitī

mīlitem

mīlite

And the now the plural:

mīlitēs

mīlitum

mīlitibus

mīlitēs

mīlitibus

And the endings in the singular were? Please repeat the five singular endings after me:

blank

-is

-i

-em

-e

And now the plural:

-es

-um

-ibus

-es

-ibus

Let's decline another word. *Lūx* is a feminine word that you have seen before. It means "light." We are equal opportunity. The soldier was masculine; light is feminine. By the way, nouns have grammatical gender, not biological sex. Sometimes gender and sex correspond, as for our Roman soldier, but, more often than not, the gender of a Latin noun has nothing to do with sex. Sorry. The genitive of *lūx*, l-u-x, is *lūcis,* l-u-c-i-s. If we remove the genitive ending, which is the same *-is* we saw before, what is the base of the word *lūx*? If you said, *luc*, l-u-c, you were correct. And, again, the nominative, l-u-x, would have led you astray.

Let's decline, and translate.

lūx, the light verbs

lūcis, of the light

lūcī, to or for the light

lūcem, verb the light

lūce by, with, or from the light

And in the plural:

lūcēs, the lights verb

lūcum, of the lights

lūcibus, to or for the lights

lūcēs, verb the lights

lūcibus, by, with, or from the lights.

Now some of you may be wondering how we can tell the nominative *lūcēs* from the accusative *lūcēs*, and the dative *lūcibus* from the ablative *lūcibus* if they look and sound exactly the same. Contexts, *amīcī amīcaeque*. Here is an example. *Lūcēs mēnsem faciunt*. The lights, *lūcēs*, i.e., day lights or days, make, *faciunt*, a month, *mēnsem*. How do we know that the days make a month, and that it is not the month that makes the days? There are several clues. Let us parse the sentence. *Lūcēs*, nominative or accusative plural, subject or direct object; *mēnsem*, accusative singular, direct object—no other choice; *faciunt*, third person plural present tense indicative verb,

faciunt requires a plural subject; it ends in nt. The only available candidate is the word *lūcēs*. *Mēnsem* is accusative, again, so it has to be the direct object, thus leaving *lucēs* available to serve as the subject. The easiest, actually the only, path to a meaningful sentence is to read *lūcēs* as the nominative subject. "The days make a month." *Lūcēs mēnsem faciunt*.

Vēritās, Harvard's motto, means "truth." The final codification of Roman law under the emperor Justinian is known as the *Digest of Roman Law*, and it has the following phrase, which we have simplified here for the purpose of illustration. *Vēritās in lūcem ēmergit*. The truth emerges into light. Or, The truth comes to light in the end. Here, *Vēritās* is the nominative subject of the verb *ēmergit*, which is singular; it ends in a T. And *lūcem* is accusative after the preposition *in*, for reasons that I do not want to explain in detail, except to say, prepositions can be used with either the accusative or ablative, and there are reasons for one or the other. Here, however, is an example where we find light as a bona fide direct object, *Vēritās lūcem nōn refugit.* Truth does not flee the light. Or literally, Truth light not flees. Truth not flees light. Latin is pithy. A decent English translation, however, requires some filling in. The truth does not flee the light. And, please, always, feel free to fill in definite and indefinite articles, the, a, or an, wherever they make sense. We need them; Latin does not, Latin does not use them. They do not exist in Lantin. Latin just says, *Vēritās lūcem nōn refugit.* "Truth light not flees." Great Latin, questionable English.

As long as we are on the topic of truth, you may recall that Pontius Pilate reportedly asked a then-obscure, but now famous, defendant, *Quid* (what) *est vēritās?* "What is truth?" Although Pontius Pilate was a Roman procurator, the philosophical jest is preserved in ancient Greek, the administrative language of the East, as Τί ἐστιν ἀλήθεια; Romans of the ruling class were bilingual, and Latin students will today, thus, encounter a fair bit of Greek in their Roman studies. We will soon conclude with a provincial view of Roman administration, but let us review and drill the masculine endings of the third declension. Your instructor, *Molinārius,* will, in their proper order, name the cases and their uses, pausing after each in succession. In these pauses, you, whether *discipulus* or *discipula*, should pronounce out loud the corresponding third declension ending. Nominative singular, subject, doer of verb: Your answer for an ending: *blank.* Ready for the next one? Genitive singular, shows possession, translated with of: *is*; dative singular, indirect objects, to or for: long I (Ī), pronounced "ee"; Accusative singular, direct object, receives the action of verb: *em*; Ablative singular, many uses, often translated as by, with, or from: *e.* And in the plural? Nominative plural, subject, doers of the verb: *ēs*; Genitive plural, shows possession, translated with, again, of: *um*; Dative plural, indirect objects, to or for: *ibus*; accusative plural, direct object, receives the action of verb: *ēs*; And finally, ablative plural, many uses, often translated as by, with, or from: *ibus.*

It is crucial to memorize these endings. Please take the time to practice them. And choral chant is a time-tested method. Please repeat after me, and take the time to do this again, and again, and again with or without me. Please, feel free, put me on a loop. I never get tired of declining endings. Please repeat after me now.

blank

is

ī

em

e

ēs

um

ibus

ēs

ibus

Again:

blank

is

ī

em

e

ēs

um

ibus

ēs

ibus

And one more time:

blank

is

ī

em

e

ēs

um

ibus

ēs

ibus

Let's decline Caesar, and we can decline him in the plural too, as every emperor after Augustus was called Caesar, so there were certainly more than one. Caesar's genitive is *Caesaris*, so, in this case, the imperial stem is the same as the dictator's nominative, *Caesar*.

nominative, Caesar verbs: *Caesar*

genitive, of Caesar: *Caesaris*

dative, to or for Caesar: *Caesarī*

accusative, verb Caesar, but be careful when doing so: *Caesarem*

ablative, by, with, or from Caesar: *Caesare*

nominative plural, the Caesars verb (and you bet they did): *Caesares*

genitive plural, of the Caesars: *Caesarum*

dative plural, to or for the Caesars: *Caesaribus*

Note the shift in accent from *cae* to *sar*. Why? The accent in Latin cannot stand farther away from the end of the word than third to the last, or antepenult.

accusative plural, verb the *Caesars*: *Caesares*

and, finally, ablative plural, same as the dative, but meaning by, with, or from the Caesars: *Caesaribus*

In the next drill, you will hear a series of sentences in English in which the name Caesar will appear. Your task is to assess how Caesar fits into the syntax of the English sentence, and then translate Caesar into the corresponding Latin form. For example, if I were to say, "Brutus stabs Caesar," Caesar is the direct object of the verb stab, and in Latin direct object must appear in the accusative case. The corresponding Latin form would thus be *Caesarem*. Just a quick disclaimer, the examples will refer to a variety of Caesars, not just Julius. Let's give it a try.

Caesar ruled Rome: subject of the verb "ruled," hence nominative, form: *Caesar.*

Suetonius wrote graphic biographies of the Caesars: *Caesarum*. It was genitive plural.

The law that made adultery a crime against the state was proposed by Caesar: *Caesare.* By, hence ablative.

Provincial officials built many temples for the deified Caesars: *Caesaribus.* Indirect object of the verb, hence, dative.

The Jews, and later the Christians, refused to worship the allegedly divine Caesars: direct object of the verb, hence accusative, also plural, *Caesarēs.*

Render onto Caesar: Unto, to or for, so indirect object, dative: *Caesarī.*

Render onto Caesar the things that are Caesar's. Okay, the things belong to Caesar. Things of Caesar, shows possession, hence genitive: *Caesaris.*

By the way, the Latin translation of the original Greek is within your Latin grasp. *Redde Caesarī quae sunt Caesaris. Redde,* "render," is a singular imperative ending in E. You've already seen this form; *quae* means "which things" or "those things" or "the things which" or even "the things that." And *sunt*—you should remember, so I'm not telling you.

Redde (give or render)

Caesarī (to or unto Caesar)

quae (the things that)

sunt (ok—are)

Caesaris (Caesar's).

Redde Caesarī quae sunt Caesaris. And with that, all of you, *omnēs amātōrēs linguae Latīnae,* all lovers of the Latin language, are free to go so that you may learn Latin (*ut linguam Latīnam discātis*) and practice it on your own before we meet again. *Grātiās vōbis agō!* Many thanks, and until we meet again, take care, so that you may be well (*cūrāte, ut valeātis*)!

Third-Declension Neuter Nouns
Lecture 6

S o far, we have learned a crucial key to Latin verbs, as well as fundamental lessons about Latin nouns. In this lecture, we will review the personal active endings; the verbs *pōnō*, *sum*, and *possum*; and the masculine/feminine endings for third-declension nouns. We'll then turn to neuter nouns and practice parsing some sentences from Cicero and Caesar.

Review: Personal active endings

	Singular	Plural
1	-ō / -m	-mus
2	-s	-tis
3	-t	-nt

Review: Present active indicative conjugation of *pōnō*

pōnō, pōnere, posuī, positum: put, place

	Singular	Plural
1	pōnō	pōnimus
2	pōnis	pōnitis
3	pōnit	pōnunt

Review: Present active subjunctive conjugation of *pōnō*

pōnō, pōnere, posuī, positum: put, place

	Singular	Plural
1	pōnam	pōnāmus
2	pōnās	pōnātis
3	pōnat	pōnant

Review: Imperative of *pōnō*

	Singular	Plural
1	***	***
2	pōne = put!	pōnite = put!
3	***	***

Review: Infinitive of *pōnō*

pōnere

Quiz
The following sentences in English include a form of the verb "to put, place, or put away." Turn just the form of "put" or "place" into its Latin equivalent using the forms of *pōnere*.

1. *She puts away* her dolls.

2. She's already 13. *Let her put away* her dolls and get married.

3. We were able *to put* the scroll in the library.

4. *We put.*

5. *We may put.*

6. *Let us put away.*

Answers: 1. *pōnit*, 2. *pōnat*, 3. *pōnere*, 4. *pōnimus*, 5. *pōnāmus*, 6. *pōnāmus*.

Review: Present indicative of *sum*

sum, esse, fuī, futūrum: be

	Singular			Plural		
1	sum	=	I am	sumus	=	we are
2	es	=	you (sing.) are	estis	=	you (pl.) are
3	est	=	he/she/it is	sunt	=	they are

Review: Present subjunctive of *sum*

sum, esse, fuī, futūrum: be

	Singular	Plural
1	sim	sīmus
2	sīs	sītis
3	sit	sint

Review: Imperative of *sum*

es (singular); este (plural)

Review: Infinitive of *sum*

esse

Quiz
The following sentences in English include a form of the verb "to be" in the present tense. Supply the Latin equivalent of *sum*.

1. *Y'all are* students of the Latin language.

2. *Y'all may be* the smartest bunch yet.

3. Casca, why *are there* daggers in this drawer?

4. *Let them be* assassins!

5. *Be* gentle, O Venus!

6. *Be* faithful, O disciples!

7. I think, therefore *I am*.

Answers: 1. *estis*, 2. *sītis*, 3. *sunt*, 4. *sint*, 5. *Es!*, 6. *Este!*, 7. *sum*.

Review: Present indicative of *possum*

***possum, posse, potuī*: be able, can**

	Singular	Plural
1	possum	possumus
2	potes	potestis
3	potest	possunt

Review: Present subjunctive of *possum*

***possum, posse, potuī*: be able, can**

	Singular	Plural
1	possim	possīmus
2	possīs	possītis
3	possit	possint

Review: Imperative of *possum*

potes (singular); poteste (plural)

Review: Infinitive of *possum*

posse

Quiz
The following sentences in English include a form of the verb "to be able" in the present tense. Supply the Latin equivalent of *possum*.

1. *Y'all are able* to conjugate.

2. *Y'all may be able* to read love poetry.

3. These soldiers *can* execute the senator now.

4. *I can* conjugate irregular verbs.

5. *To be able* to conjugate pleases me.

Answers: 1. *potestis,* 2. *possītis,* 3. *possunt,* 4. *possum,* 5. *posse.*

Review: Third-declension nouns, masculine/feminine endings

	Singular	Plural
Nominative	***	-ēs
Genitive	-is	-um
Dative	-ī	-ibus
Accusative	-em	-ēs
Ablative	-e	-ibus

Declension of *mīles*

mīles, mīlitis, m.: soldier

	Singular	Plural
Nominative	mīles	mīlitēs
Genitive	mīlitis	mīlitum
Dative	mīlitī	mīlitibus
Accusative	mīlitem	mīlitēs
Ablative	mīlite	mīlitibus

Neuter nouns

- As you recall, third-declension nouns of the masculine and feminine genders have the same endings. A masculine soldier, a *mīles*, has the same endings as a feminine *lūx* ("light").

- The neuter, however, differs from the masculine and feminine nouns in three places: the accusative singular and the nominative and accusative plurals. The neuter endings of the third declension are shown in the following table.

	Singular	Plural
Nominative	***	-a
Genitive	-is	-um
Dative	-ī	-ibus
Accusative	***	-a
Ablative	-e	-ibus

- Notice that the nominative form in the singular serves as the accusative singular, as well. In addition, instead of using *-ēs* for the nominative and accusative plurals, we use *-a*.

Declension of *corpus* (third-declension noun)

corpus, *corporis*, n.: body

	Singular	Plural
Nominative	corpus	corpora
Genitive	corporis	corporum
Dative	corporī	corporibus
Accusative	corpus	corpora
Ablative	corpore	corporibus

Note: In Latin, the word "body" is neuter. In the nominative, "body" is *corpus*. We can find the stem by looking at the genitive form, *corporis*, and removing the ending, -*is*; thus, the stem is *corpor*-. Things in English that have bodies are "corporeal."

Through French, we use the word *corpus* to refer to a "body" of men, as in the Marine Corps.

Parsing a sentence from Cicero

- In his *Tusculan Disputations*, Cicero, who lived during the 1st century B.C.E., writes: "*Corpora [nōn] sumus*," "We are not bodies."

- Who is the subject of *sumus*? The *-mus* on *sumus* tells us that we are the first-person plural subjects, but the word *we* does not appear; hence, we are the unexpressed subjects.

- Is the case of *corpora* nominative or accusative? Do we perform the action of being upon bodies? The answer is no. "To be" merely establishes identity. One does not perform the action of being upon an object. Thus, the word *corpora* is nominative because the bodies are equal to or identified with the subject.

- A predicate is a statement about a subject. When we use a linking verb, however, the predicate is nominative because we say that our statement "is" somehow the subject. Subjects, of course, are nominative. We call such statements of identity that use the nominative case "predicate nominatives." In this sentence, however, we do not need to know that the word *corpora* is in the predicate nominative in order to understand the sentence.

- Cicero is telling us that human beings are something more than just flesh. We have bodies, but we are not necessarily just bodies.

Parsing a sentence from Caesar

- Consider another example from Caesar: *Hostēs ex corporibus pugnant*. *Hostis* is a masculine noun meaning "enemy"; *ex* is a preposition that takes or governs the ablative case. It means "out of," "from," or in this case, "from on top of." *Pugnant* means "they fight." Despite the *a*, we don't say, "Let the enemies fight." This verb is actually indicative, but because it ends in *-nt*, we know that the word *they* serves as the subject.

- *Hostēs* could be nominative plural, so we could translate the sentence as "The enemies fight." On the other hand, *hostēs* could be accusative and the subject could be unexpressed, giving us, "They fight the enemies." The context makes it clear that Caesar is making "the enemies" the subject of *pugnant.*

- A translation of the whole sentence reads: "The enemies fight from on top of the bodies."

Verba

corpus, corporis, n.: body

duo: two

ex (prep. + ablative): from, out of

flōs, flōris, m.: flower

hostis, hostis, m.: enemy

liquor, liquōris, m.: liquid, fluid

mulier, mulieris, f.: woman

pugnant: they fight

Memoranda

Please learn the third-declension neuter endings and the declension of *corpus, corporis,* n., "body" (which may also be found in App. §17, A).

Agenda

i. Create your own verb chart for each of the verbs below and conjugate in the present indicative.

1. sum

2. bibō

3. possum

ii. Create your own verb chart for each of the verbs below and conjugate in the present subjunctive.

1. sum

2. bibō

3. possum

iii. Create your own noun chart for each of the nouns below and decline. (Remember that *corpus* is neuter.)

1. mulier

2. corpus

3. flōs

iv. Practice reciting the full declension of the neuter noun *corpus*.

v. Please translate the following into Latin.

1. to/for the bodies of the soldiers

2. by/with/from the woman's strength

3. to/for Caesar's enemies

4. by the light of the mind

5. The women drink the liquid.

6. The enemies fight with (= *cum* + ablative) the soldier.

7. Greetings, (male and female) students of the Latin language!

8. Let the women put away the flowers.

9. Can we cut the flowers?

10. Let us eat so that we may restore (our) strength.

Third-Declension Neuter Nouns
Lecture 6—Transcript

Salvēte, discipulī discipulaeque linguae Latīnae! Mihi valdē placet vōs pulchram linguam Latīnam aeternam docēre. We have so far in our course learned a crucial key to Latin verbs, as well as fundamental lessons about Latin nouns. It's important to safeguard knowledge this important, so let's do just that and take a moment to review, starting with verbs. I'll wait a moment while you recite the personal active endings of the Latin verb: *o* or *m, s, t, mus, tis, nt. Iterum quaesō.* again, please; together, on the count of thee: *ūnus, duo, ūnus, duo, trē*s: -*o* or -*m, -s, -t, -mus, -tis, -nt.*

Our model verb going forward will be *pōnō, pōnere, posuī, positum*; *pōnō, pōnere, posuī, positum*; to put, to place, or to put away. Let us conjugate *pōnō* in the present active indicative, remembering to use an O in the first person, then to insert short I's before the personal, active endings until we arrive at the third person plural where we insert the U. Ready? Let's do this together, on the count of three, *ūnus, duo, ūnus, duo, trē*s: *pōno, pōnis, pōnit, pōnimus, pōnitis, pōnunt.*

Iterumque quaesō, and again, please: *pōno, pōnis, pōnit, pōnimus, pōnitis, pōnunt.*

And to form the subjunctive, we replace the vowel before the personal active endings with a long A. Let's recite the present active subjunctive together. *Ūnus, duo, ūnus, duo, trē*s: *pōnam, pōnās, pōnat, pōnāmus, pōnātis, pōnant. Iterumque,* And again: *pōnam, pōnās, pōnat, pōnāmus, pōnātis, pōnant.*

And the imperative forms? Please command one person. "Put it away, dude!" *pōne!* And the plural: "Hey you guys, put it away!" *pōnite!* And again, both imperatives, singular and plural: *pōne! pōnite!*

And the infinitive, to place: *pōnere. Iterumque (*And again) to place: *ponere.*

Time for a quiz. You will hear a series of sentences in English with a form of the verb to put, to place, or to put away. Please turn just the form of put or place into its Latin equivalent using the appropriate forms of *pōnere.*

Molinārius will pause to give you time. After the pause, *Molinārius* will provide the correct response. She puts away her dolls: *pānit.* She's already thirteen. Let her put away her dolls, and get married. *pōnat.* Why such a horrible example? If the Romans had had Hallmark cards, this would, I'm sorry to say, have been one of their Hallmark moments.

Let's continue the quiz.

We were able to put the scroll in the library: *pōnere*

We put: *pōnimus*

We may put: *pōnāmus*

Let us put away: *pōnāmus*

We have also learned two irregular verbs. *sum, esse, fuī, futūrum* (to be) and *possum, posse, potuī* (to be able). Let us review the forms of the verb to be in the present tense indicative. Please repeat after me: *sum, es, est, sumus, estis, sunt. Iterumque (*and again): *sum, es, est, sumus, estis, sunt.*

And together, on the count of three, *ūnus, duo, ūnus, duo, trēs: sum, es, est, sumus, estis, sunt.* And stop.

Now the subjunctive, taking care to remember that every form begins with an S and that our subjunctive vowel is I. Please repeat after me: *sim, sīs, sit, sīmus, sītis, sint. Iterumque,* and again: *sim, sīs, sit, sīmus, sītis, sint.* And now together: *ūnus, duo, ūnus, duo, trēs: sim, sīs, sit, sīmus, sītis, sint* And stop.

What are the imperative forms? Please command one person: Be, man! *es!* And more than one person? *este!* And again, what are the two command forms of *sum? es! este!*

And what is the infinitive of *sum?* How do we say to be? *esse.* And again, to be in Latin: *esse.*

Time for the quiz. Molinārius will make up a sentence in English that includes a form of the verb to be in the present tense. During the pause provided, please supply the Latin equivalent. After the pause, *Molinārius* will provide the correct response, so that you, *discipulī discipulaeque linguae Latīnae*, may check your work.

Y'all are students of the Latin language: *estis*

Y'all may be the smartest bunch yet: *sītis*

Casca, why are there daggers in this drawer? *sunt*

Let them be assassins! *sint*

Be gentle, Oh Venus! *Es!*

Be faithful, Oh disciples! *Este!*

I think, therefore I am: *sum*

Optimē. Excellent. Now let's change existence into ability. How do we do it? We just need some *pot*, man. And then we add our *pot, p-o-t,* to the front of *sum*, remembering to change the T to an S if the form of *sum* begins with an S. Let's review of the forms of to be able in the present tense indicative. Please repeat after me:

possum, potes, potest, possumus, potestis, possunt.

*Iterumque (*And again):

possum, potes, potest, possumus, potestis, possunt

And one more time together on the count of three, *ūnus, duo, ūnus, duo, trēs*:

possum, potes, potest, possumus, potestis, possunt.

As you will recall, we form the subjunctive by attaching p-o-s to *sim, sīs, sit, sīmus, sītis, sint*. Please repeat after me: *possim, possīs, possit, possīmus, possītis, possint. Iterumque (*and again): *possim, possīs, possit, possīmus, possītis, possint.* And one more time together, *ūnus, duo, ūnus, duo trēs: possim, possīs, possit, possīmus, possītis, possint.* And stop.

And the imperative forms: Be able, oh singular subject! *potes!* Be able, oh plural subjects! *poteste!* And again, what are the command forms of *possum? potes! poteste!*

And the infinitive, to be able: *posse.* And again, the infinitive, to be able: *posse*

Quiz time, my friends! *Molinārius,* your *magister,* will make up a sentence in English that includes a form of the verb to be able in the present tense. He will pause. During that pause, please study the Latin equivalent of *possum,* and after you study it, supply it. After the pause, I, *Magister Molinārius,* will provide the correct response, so that you, *discipulī discipulaeque linguae Latīnae,* may check your work.

Y'all are able to conjugate: *potestis*

Y'all may be able to read love poetry: *possītis*

These soldiers can execute the senator now: *possunt*

I can conjugate irregular verbs: *possum*

To be able to conjugate pleases me: *posse*

Verbs are where the action is. But we have looked at things, too, substantives, nouns, both common and proper. Let us review the endings of third declension masculine and feminine nouns. Please repeat after me in the singular: *blank, is, ī, em, e.*

And in the plural: *ēs, um, ibus ēs, ibus.*

Iterumque, in the singular: *blank, is, ī, em, e.*

And again, in the plural: *ēs, um, ibus ēs, ibus.*

Let us now recite the ten endings from the nominative singular—*blank*—all the way to the ablative plural *ibus* together, on the count of three, *ūnus, duo, ūnus, duo, trēs:*

blank, is, ī, em, e, ēs, um, ibus ēs, ibus

And again together: *blank, is, ī, em, e, ēs, um, ibus ēs, ibus*

Iterumque: *blank, is, ī, em, e, ēs, um, ibus ēs, ibus*

And stop.

Let us decline soldier. As we go, I will review what we know about the use of the cases. First, let's check to make sure we have what we need to do the job right; *mīles* is the word for soldier. What is the genitive form? *mīlitis.* What is the stem? We remove the genitive *is* to reveal, voila, *mīlit.* Okay, we are ready. Please try to provide the appropriate form of soldier in Latin:

nominative, the soldier verbs: *mīles*

genitive, of the soldier: *mīlitis*

dative, to or for the soldier: *mīliti*

accusative, verb the soldier: *mīlitem*

ablative, by, with, or from the soldier: *mīlite*

So much for the singular. Let's take a look at the plural:

nominative, the soldiers verb: *mīlitēs*

genitive, of the soldiers: *mīlitum*

dative, to or for the soldiers: *mīlitibus*

accusative, verb the soldiers: *mīlitēs*

ablative, by, with, or from the soldiers: *mīlitibus*

If you feel comfortable with the personal endings of the verb and these third-declension endings, you are ready for the next step. The final gender. Neither masculine nor feminine. What should we call it? The Romans called it neuter, which, in Latin, means neither. The Romans were clever that way. And today, when we adopt pets, and we no longer want them to act on their biological sex, male or female, what do we do to them? We neuter them. As you will recall, third-declension nouns of the masculine and feminine genders have the same endings. A masculine soldier, *mīles*, has the same endings as a feminine *lūx*. Heck. A soldier has the same endings as a *mulier*, the Latin word for woman. *mulier, mulieris, mulierī, mulierem, muliere; mulierēs, mulierum, mulieribus, mulierēs, mulieribus.* That's equal opportunity.

The neuter, however, differs from the masculine and feminine nouns in three places, the accusative singular and the nominative and accusative plurals. I think it's time for more choral repetition. The neuter endings of the third declension are, and please repeat after me. in the singular: *blank, is, ī, blank, e*; and in the plural: *a, um, ibus, a, ibus.* What just happened? Three things. The nominative form in the singular serves as the accusative singular as well. And, instead of using *ēs* in the nominative and accusative plurals, we use *a*, the letter A. Let us practice these endings in the singular. Please repeat after me:

blank, is, ī, blank, e

And again, in the singular: *blank, is, ī, blank, e*

And again: *blank, is, ī, blank, e*

And stop. And now in the plural:

a, um, ibus, a, ibus

And again: *a, um, ibus, a, ibus*

One more time: *a, um, ibus, a, ibus*

And stop.

Let's try the whole thing. Please repeat after me, but wait until I've done all ten endings, because I'll pause briefly after the singular, but only enough to separate the singular from the plural. Here goes:

blank, is, ī, blank, e, a, um, ibus, a, ibus

And again: *blank, is, ī, blank, e, a, um, ibus, a, ibus*

And one more time: *blank, is, ī, blank, e, a, um, ibus, a, ibus*

And stop. Can we chant these endings together? We can try. On the count of three, please try to say them with me; *ūnus, duo, ūnus, duo, trēs.*

blank, is, ī, blank, e, a, um, ibus, a, ibus.

And again: *blank, is, ī, blank, e, a, um, ibus, a, ibus*

Fun as chanting endings may be, let us now try to decline the word body, which in Latin is neuter. Body in the nominative is *corpus*. What is the stem? We do not know, unless we remove the genitive ending, and the genitive ending of *corpus* is *corporis*. If we remove the ending *is*, voila, the stem, which is thus, *corpor*. And we need to hang on to that stem for the application of the endings. It's also interesting to note that things in English that have bodies are corporeal. Again, English derivatives can help you remember the stems of words, *corpor* in corporeal. Okay, we've chanted the endings. You have the stem, *corpor*. Let us decline, first, the nominative, but we don't need the stem for that, do we? We go back to the original form, *corpus*, the body verbs, *corpus*; genitive, now we need our stem, *corpor*, of the body, *corporis.* I hope you remember to use *corpor*, especially since I gave you many hints; dative, to or for the body, corporī.

For the accusative, there is no ending to attach to the stem. Remember blank: *blank, is, ī, blank, e,* so what happens? The word reverts back to its nominative form. So, verb the body, please, *corpus,* it's *corpus* again. But now, you must remember to bring back the stem for the ablative. Alright, try the ablative, please, by, with, or from the body: *corpore.*

Okay, so much for the singular. Let's take a look at the plural

Nominative, the bodies verb: *corpora*

genitive, of the bodies: *corporum*

dative, to or for the bodies: *corporibus*

accusative, verb the bodies: *corpora*

ablative, by, with, or from the bodies: *corporibus*

Let's decline body again. First we'll do the singular, and then the plural. Please repeat after me: *corpus, corporis, corporī, corpus. corpore.* And now we'll do the plural. Please repeat after me: *corpora, corporum, corporibus, corpora, corporibus.* Again the singular: *corpus, corporis, corporī, corpus. corpore.* And now the plural: *corpora, corporum, corporibus, corpora, corporibus.*

Let's try the whole declension from nominative singular *corpus* all the way to ablative plural *corporibus.* Please repeat after me, but remember that I'll pause briefly after the singular before proceeding to the plural, so don't begin too early. Here goes: c*orpus, corporis, corporī, corpus, corpore, corpora, corporum, corporibus, corpora, corporibus.*

And now together on the count of three: *ūnus, duo, ūnus, duo trēs: corpus, corporis, corporī, corpus,   corpore, corpora, corporum, corporibus, corpora, corporibus.*

Chances are that you will need a lot more practice than this. That would be normal for most mortals. But if you keep at it, you can burn these declensions into your synapses for quick and frequent retrieval. And if your memories fade, as they so frequently do, you can review. Again, as always, free to put me on a loop. I don't mind. I'll chant with you as many times as you like. But, for now, let's put this declension to work and explore some Latin.

Corpus is an interesting word. In English, we use its closest derivative only to refer to dead bodies, corpses. But in Latin *corpora* can be alive as well as dead. On the other hand, through French, we use the word to refer to a body of men, as in sailor men, the Marine Corps, c-o-r-p-s. All that's missing is the U.

And when a group of people get together to act, at least in business activities, as a single body, what do they do? They *incorporate*. They form a body, and that is, perhaps, in part, why the Supreme Court of the United States declared that corporations are persons. They represent a collection of bodies. Etymology is, I confess, probably not a strong argument. On the other hand, there is the right to have possession of one's body. We call this *habeas corpus*. Literally: "You should have body." *Habeās* is a subjunctive. You may have noticed that long A. The verb also ends in S, hence you, singular. And *corpus* is a direct object, hence accusative. *Habeās corpus.* or *habeas corpus*, in English. And, whose body should you have, but your own?

In other words, other people should not be allowed to take your body from you by locking it up somewhere arbitrarily. Your advocate can file a petition to get it back. This particular right was enshrined in 1305 as the "Great Writ." During the American Civil War, Abraham Lincoln famously suspended the Writ of *habeās corpus*. Congress suspended it again in 2006 with the Military Commissions Act, at least for prisoners taken during the War on Terror. The Supreme Court, then, seemed to restore it in 2008, but… but, irrelevant you protest? *Au contraire, mes amis!* The Latin student understands that the subjunctive and neuter third-declension nouns remain as relevant today as they ever were. *Habeās corpus*, you should have the body, especially your own. Let's examine some Latin sentences more ancient than 1305. In his Tusculan Disputations, or philosophical works, written at his villa in Tusculum, Cicero, who lived during the first century B.C.E., writes,

Corpora [nōn] sumus. What does Cicero say? Please see if you can work it out. "We are not bodies." *Corpora [nōn] sumus.* But what does that mean? If we are not bodies, what are we? Spirits? Ah, well, the things we could discuss if we had time, my friends. Let's look, instead, at the grammar. Who is the subject of *sumus*? We are the unexpressed first person plural subjects. The *mus* on *sumus* tells us that we are the first person plural subjects, but the word we does not appear, hence we are unexpressed, even though we are the subjects. We are the unexpressed subjects.

And in what case are the *corpora?* Is the case nominative or accusative? *Corpora [nōn] sumus.* "We are not bodies." Well, think about it. Do we perform the action of being upon bodies? No. "To be" merely establishes identity. One thing equals another. One does not perform the action of being upon an object. So *corpora* are nominative because they are equal to or identified with the subject. When we make a statement about a subject, we call that statement the predicate. That's a technical term. A predicate is a statement about a subject. When we use a linking verb, however, the predicate is nominative because we say that our statement is somehow the subject. Subjects, of course, are nominative. We call such statements of identity that use the nominative case predicate nominatives.

But did you really need to know that the word *corpora* was the predicate nominative in order to understand the sentence? Not really, however, grammatical precision can assist us. It's nice to know that the case of *corpora* is nominative. However, even saying that, grammatical precision is certainly not sufficient for understanding. Knowing what the words mean can offer even more help. *Corpora nōn sumus.* We are not bodies. In other words, human beings are something more than flesh. We have bodies, but we are not, necessarily, just bodies. Unless, of course, we are dead. Here's an example from Caesar: *hostēs* ex *corporibus pugnant; hostis, hostis,* third declension masculine, word for enemy; *ex* is a preposition that takes or governs the ablative case; ex means out of, from, or here, from on top of. *Pugnant* means "they fight." But there is an a, one of you protests, an a, *pona, pugnant.* Should we not say "let the enemies fight?" *Pugnant,* is it subjunctive? No, because it's a different kind of verb. It's actually indicative. Sorry, language is a messy business. But look on the bright side, it ends in *nt,* so you know that they are the subject.

So who fights? *Hostēs* could be nominative plural, so we could translate "the enemies fight," *hostēs pugnant*. On the other hand, could *hostēs* be accusative, and the subject unexpressed, giving us, "they fight the enemies:" Touché, my clever students. But the context, which I did not give you, makes it clear that Caesar makes the enemies the subject of *pugnant*, so we will translate, "the enemies fight." Can you translate the whole sentence? *Hostēs ex corporibus pugnant.* "The enemies fight from on top of the bodies." Nice.

And with that, all of you, *omnēs linguae Latīnae amātōrēs,* all lovers of the Latin language, are free to go so that you may learn Latin (*ut linguam Latīnam discātis*), and practice it on your own before we meet again. *Grātiās vōbis agō! Cūrāte, ut valeātis!*

First- and Second-Declension Adjectives
Lecture 7

What we examine next may appear daunting at first glance, but once you have mastered this set of endings, you will be in a position to handle most Latin nouns and adjectives. We will begin by examining adjective endings for first-declension (feminine) and second-declension (masculine and neuter) endings. Although we will focus primarily on adjectives in this lecture, note that these endings also work for all first- and second-declension nouns. For this reason, we will include third-declension noun endings in this lecture for the sake of comparison.

Endings for first, second, and third declensions

Case	1st Feminine	2nd Masculine	2nd Neuter	3rd Masc. & Fem.	3rd Neuter
Singular					
Nominative	-a	-us / -er	-um	***	***
Genitive	-ae	-ī	-ī	-is	-is
Dative	-ae	-ō	-ō	-ī	-ī
Accusative	-am	-um	-um	-em	***
Ablative	-ā	-ō	-ō	-e	-e
Plural					
Nominative	-ae	-ī	-a	-ēs	-a
Genitive	-ārum	-ōrum	-ōrum	-um	-um
Dative	-īs	-īs	-īs	-ibus	-ibus
Accusative	-ās	-ōs	-a	-ēs	-a
Ablative	-īs	-īs	-īs	-ibus	-ibus

Comparing singular forms across cases

Case	1st Feminine	2nd Masculine	2nd Neuter	3rd Masc. & Fem.	3rd Neuter
Nominative	-a	-us / -er	-um	***	***

- Notice that nominative forms do not show many similarities. It's also important to remember that the first-declension feminine singular can look like a neuter plural and vice versa. Similarly, the second-declension neuter singular ending can look like the genitive plural ending of the third declension.

- Because the third declension has such a wide variety of endings in the nominative singular, we don't know what may turn up and, thus, call it a "blank." The ending *-us*, for example, which generally serves as the second-declension masculine ending, is a real possibility for third-declension neuter nouns. The word *corpus* ("body"), for example, is neuter and belongs to the third declension.

- The lesson here is to beware the nominative. We must always check the genitive to know the declension of a noun! The genitive case reveals the declension and, if we remove it, the word's true base.

Case	1st Feminine	2nd Masculine	2nd Neuter	3rd Masc. & Fem.	3rd Neuter
Genitive	-ae	-ī	-ī	-is	-is

- Notice that declensions share genitive singular endings:
  - Only the *first* declension has a genitive singular ending in *-ae*.

  - Only the *second* declension has a genitive ending in -ī.

  - And only the *third* declension has a genitive ending in *-is*.

- The genitive is the key that unlocks the mystery of what declension a noun or adjective belongs to. That's why nouns are listed first in their nominative forms and then in their genitive forms.

Case	1st Feminine	2nd Masculine	2nd Neuter	3rd Masc. & Fem.	3rd Neuter
Dative	-ae	-ō	-ō	-ī	-ī
Ablative	-ā	-ō	-ō	-e	-e

- Dative and ablative endings are, in the singular, sometimes but not always the same.

- Except for the first-declension dative singular, -ae, which is a diphthong, dative and ablative singular endings tend to be a single vowel sound.

Case	1st Feminine	2nd Masculine	2nd Neuter	3rd Masc. & Fem.	3rd Neuter
Accusative	-am	-um	-um	-em	***

- The accusative case shows some real similarities in the singular. Every accusative singular except the third-declension neuter ends in -m. That's helpful to know when we look for direct objects.

- Although accusative -um will have to be distinguished from third-declension genitive plurals and neuter nominative singulars, the -m ending will not be confused with a genitive singular and certainly not with any datives or ablatives, singular or plural.

Comparing plural forms across cases

Case	1st Feminine	2nd Masculine	2nd Neuter	3rd Masc. & Fem.	3rd Neuter
Nominative	-ae	-ī	-a	-ēs	-a

- The plural nominative again shows us a mixed picture. Apart from the masculine and feminine nominatives of the third declension, we find vowels.

- One bright spot is that all neuter nominative plurals are the same; they all end in -*a*.

- Unfortunately, neuter plurals look like feminine singulars.

Case	1st Feminine	2nd Masculine	2nd Neuter	3rd Masc. & Fem.	3rd Neuter
Genitive	-ārum	-ōrum	-ōrum	-um	-um

- The genitive plural shows some systemic similarities. All genitive plurals end in -*um*.

- Further, the first- and second-declension genitive plurals precede that -*um* with their theme vowels: *ā* for the first-declension feminine (-*ārum*) and *ō* for the second-declension masculine and neuter (-*ōrum*).

Case	1st Feminine	2nd Masculine	2nd Neuter	3rd Masc. & Fem.	3rd Neuter
Accusative	-ās	-ōs	-a	-ēs	-a

- Again, the accusative plural reveals some patterns. Neuter accusatives repeat their nominative forms, -*a*, and all masculine and feminine accusative plurals, whether first, second, or third declension, end in -*s*.

- The first-declension feminine accusative plural precedes that -*s* with its theme vowel ā: -*ās*.

- The second-declension masculine accusative plural precedes the -*s* with its theme vowel ō: -*ōs*.

- The third-declension masculine and feminine accusative plurals precede the -*s* with ē: -*ēs*.

Case	1ˢᵗ Feminine	2ⁿᵈ Masculine	2ⁿᵈ Neuter	3ʳᵈ Masc. & Fem.	3ʳᵈ Neuter
Dative	-īs	-īs	-īs	-ibus	-ibus
Ablative	-īs	-īs	-īs	-ibus	-ibus

- The ablative and dative plural endings are quite simple. If we count them up, there are only two of them: -*īs* (pronounced "ees") for first- and second-declension words and -*ibus* for third-declension words.

- Note that the first- and second-declension dative and ablative plural, -īs, differs from the genitive singular of the third declension because the *i* in this -īs is long, not short.

Adjectives

- As we know, adjectives modify nouns. In Latin, adjectives take their cue from nouns and agree with them in case, number, and gender but not necessarily ending. Adjectives can change their gender from masculine to feminine to neuter, their number from singular to plural, and their case from nominative to ablative, but they cannot change their declension. Sometimes adjective endings match the endings of the nouns they modify letter for letter, and sometimes they do not, yet adjectives will always agree with the nouns they modify in gender, number, and case.

- The word for "big, large, or great" in Latin is *magna* (feminine), *magnus* (masculine), or *magnum* (neuter). Because "big" appears in these three forms, we know that *magnus, magna, magnum* is a first- and second-declension adjective. A big masculine soldier is *mīles magnus*. A big feminine light is *lux magna*. And a big neuter body is *corpus magnum*. In each instance, we chose the gender of *magnus, magna, magnum* to match the gender of the noun being modified.

- In a dictionary, *magnus, magna, magnum* would likely be listed as follows: "**magn•us, -a, -um,** *adj.*, big." When we see this listing,

137

we're supposed to supply the stem for the truncated -*a*, -*um*, giving us *magnus, magna, magnum*.

- By this logic, "**bon•us, -a, -um,** *adj.*, good" would, when expanded, give us *bonus, bona, bonum*.

- A somewhat tougher one that ends in -*er* in the masculine is "**līber, -a, -um,** *adj.*, free." If we expand it, we get: *līber, lībera, līberum*.

- The takeaway here is that first- and second-declension adjectives appear in the nominative singular for the most part as -*us*, -*a*, -*um* but sometimes as -*er*, -*a*, -*um*.

Declension of *nox perpetua*

***nox, noctis*, f.: night**

***perpetuus, perpetua, perpetuum*: everlasting**

	Singular	Plural
Nominative	nox perpetua	noctēs perpetuae
Genitive	noctis perpetuae	noctium perpetuārum
Dative	noctī perpetuae	noctibus perpetuīs
Accusative	noctem perpetuam	noctēs perpetuās
Ablative	nocte perpetuā	noctibus perpetuīs

Note: In each instance, *perpetua* agrees in case, number, and gender with *nox*, yet their endings never match.

Declension of *senex sevērus*

senex, senis, m.: old man

sevērus, sevēra, sevērum: stern

	Singular	Plural
Nominative	senex sevērus	senēs sevērī
Genitive	senis sevērī	senum sevērōrum
Dative	senī sevērō	senibus sevērīs
Accusative	senem sevērum	senēs sevērōs
Ablative	sene sevērō	senibus sevērīs

Declension of *bāsium fervidum*

bāsium, bāsiī, n.: kiss

fervidus, fervida, fervidum: fiery

	Singular	Plural
Nominative	bāsium fervidum	bāsia fervida
Genitive	bāsiī fervidī	bāsiōrum fervidōrum
Dative	bāsiō fervidō	bāsiīs fervidīs
Accusative	bāsium fervidum	bāsia fervida
Ablative	bāsiō fervidō	bāsiīs fervidīs

Note: The genitive here, *bāsiī*, ends in *-ī*, not *-is*, so this word is not a neuter third declension but a neuter second declension. As mentioned at the beginning of this lecture, first- and second-declension adjective endings work for first- and second-declension nouns, too. If you can decline a neuter adjective, you can decline a neuter noun. Sometimes, the endings on the adjective will match the endings on the noun, as well as agree with them. We will review these declensions again in the next lecture.

bonus, bona, bonum: good

grātissimus, grātissima, grātissimum: most pleasing

līber, lībera, līberum: free

magnus, magna, magnum: big, large, great

miser, misera, miserum: wretched, unfortunate, miserable

nox, noctis, f.: night

perpetuus, perpetua, perpetuum: everlasting, never-ending

pulcher, pulchra, pulchrum: beautiful

senex, senis, m.: old man

sevērus, sevēra, sevērum: stern, severe

Memoranda

Please learn the first- and second-declension endings. Learn the declension of *magnus, magna, magnum*, "big" (which may be found in App. §23).

i. In the noun chart below, provide the first- and second-declension adjective endings.

Case	1st-Declension Feminine	2nd-Declension Masculine	2nd-Declension Neuter
Singular			
Nominative			
Genitive			
Dative			
Accusative			
Ablative			
Plural			
Nominative			
Genitive			
Dative			
Accusative			
Ablative			

ii. In the noun chart below, decline the noun-adjective combination *good soldier*. The nominative and genitive singular forms are done for you.

	Singular	Plural
Nominative	mīles bonus	
Genitive	mīlitis bonī	
Dative		
Accusative		
Ablative		

iii. Create your own noun chart for each of the noun-adjective combinations below and decline. Make sure you check the gender before proceeding.

1. large body

2. beautiful woman

iv. Give the case and number of the following noun forms and then translate each into English. Some forms have more than one possible case.

1. mulieris bonae

2. magnā virtūte

3. lūcī grātissimae

4. noctem perpetuam

5. mentēs pulchrae

6. mīlitēs līberōs

7. mēnsibus perpetuīs

8. hostis sevērus

9. pulchrārum mulierum

10. senem bonum

11. magna corpora

12. flōrēs pulchrī

13. lūcum magnārum

14. vēritātibus sevērīs

15. mīlitī bonō

First- and Second-Declension Adjectives
Lecture 7—Transcript

Salvēte, discipulī discipulaeque linguae Latīnae! Mihi valdē placet vōs pulchram Latīnam aeternam docēre.

What we examine next may appear daunting at first, but, once we have mastered this set of endings, we will be in a position to handle most Latin nouns and adjectives, and we will review. *Ad astra per aspera.* This is a Latin phrase that means "to the stars through difficulties." *Astra* and *aspera* are two good accusative neuter plurals that, whether you know the declensions or not, you can already parse. *Ad astra* (to the stars) *per aspera* (through difficulties). In other words, the path to greatness requires effort. *Ad astra per aspera.* And the view from the stars is great.

Let us examine adjective endings for the first (feminine) and second (masculine and neuter) declension endings. Now, we're going to focus primarily on adjectives in this lesson, but we should note, and this is good news, that these endings also work for all first- and second-declension nouns; they're the same. And for this reason, we will include third-declension noun endings in this lesson for the sake of comparison and review in our rather large chart. Now this complete chart of first- and second-declension adjective endings, and third-declension noun endings is more than most human beings can take in at one glance. So we are going to run through each declension individually, and then compare endings case by case, that's horizontally, looking for points of similarity, as well as potential pitfalls when the cases of one declension look similar to different cases of other declensions.

Let's begin at the beginning with the first declension, which is characterized by the vowel A.

nominative: a, a short a (uh)

the genitive: ae, pronounced (ae)

the dative: ae, pronounced (ae)

the accusative: am, pronounced (um)

and then the ablative, again it's an A, but it's a long ā, which we can mark with a long mark or macron, ā.

And the plural:

the nominative, ae, again pronounced "ae"

the genitive, *ārum*. That's a long a-r-u-m, *ārum*

the dative, it's a long ī followed by an s. We pronounce it "ees"

in the accusative plural, a long a, again, followed by an s, pronounced ās.

the ablative, again, long ī followed by s, īs.

Or, in chanting form for the first declension, and please repeat after me, the singular:

a, ae, ae, am, ā (notice, I always make it a macron)

Again in the singular:

a, ae, ae, am, ā

And in the plural:

ae, ārum, īs, ās, īs

Again, in the plural:

ae, ārum, īs, ās, īs

Let's do the feminine first declension endings again. First the singular:

a, ae, ae, am, ā

And the plural:

ae, ārum, īs, ās, īs

One more time:

a, ae, ae, am, ā, ae, ārum, īs, ās, īs

The masculine and neuter second-declension forms are characterized by the vowel O, although we also find U and I.

The nominative for the masculine is u-s; we can pronounce it "us." It's also, frequently enough e-r, *er*. So it's actually *us* or *er*.

The genitive is a long *ī*, pronounced "ee"

The dative, a long *ō*, pronounced ō

The accusative, u-m, pronounced "um"

And the ablative, again a long *ō*, pronounced ō

Note please that in the singular, the neuter differs from the masculine only in the nominative, and that, as is true for the third declension, neuter endings are the same in the nominative and accusative. But let's look first at the masculine plural.

The nominative is a long *ī*, pronounced "ee," and for the neuter the plural is an A, pronounced a.

The genitive for both is *ōrum*. It's a long ō-r-u-m, pronounced *ōrum*.

145

The dative for both the masculine and neuter is a long ī, followed by an s, pronounced īs.

The accusative for the masculine is a long ō followed by s, ōs.

And for the neuter, the nominative form repeats, and again, we get an a, a.

We can actually see some similarities between the neuters of the second declension and the third declension. Neuters are always the same in the nominative and accusative. But let's look, finally, at the ablative plural for both the neuter and masculine second declension. We find a long ī, followed by s, and we pronounce that īs.

Now, it's hard to look at two genders at the same time, so let's focus on the masculine and look at the endings in chanting form. Let's keep in mind we can substitute e-r, the *er* for the *us* in the nominative singular, but we'll just use the *us* ending, which is the more common for our chanting of masculine second-declension endings. Please repeat, in the singular:

us, ī, ō, um, ō. Again, in the singular: *us, ī, ō, um, ō.*

And in the plural:

ī, ōrum, īs, ōs, īs. And again in the plural: *ī, ōrum, īs, ōs, īs*

Okay, one more time for the masculine second declension. First in the singular:

> *us, ī, ō, um, ō*

And in the plural:

> *ī, ōrum, īs, ōs, īs*

And now let's look at our chanting form of the neuter second declension endings. First in the singular:

um, ī, ō, um, ō

And the plural:

a, ōrum, īs, A, īs

And one more time for the neuter second declension:

um, ī, ō, um, ō, a, ōrum, īs, A, īs

What we have chanted so far will not be enough for mastering these forms, absolutely not. You will need to practice, and we will need to review together, but let's proceed for now and compare these endings across cases. We will begin with the nominative singular endings. The first-declension feminine nominative singular ends with a. The second-declension masculine nominative singular generally ends in us, but sometimes er. And the second-declension neuter nominative ends in um. Third-declension nominatives, no matter what the gender, do not have predictable endings; we call them "blank."

What can we say, then, about these nominative forms? Nominative forms do not show many similarities. It is also important to remember that the first declension feminine singular can look like a neuter plural and vice versa. Similarly, the second-declension neuter singular ending can look like the genitive plural ending of the third declension. And, because the third declension has such a wide variety of endings in the nominative, we do not know what may turn up in a third declension nominative singular.

The ending *us*, for example, which can serve as the second-declension masculine ending, is a real possibility for third-declension neuter nouns. The word *corpus*, body, for example, is, as you know, neuter, and belongs to the third declension. The lesson? Beware the nominative. Do not trust nominative forms. We must always check the genitive to know the declension of a noun! The genitive case is our friend. It reveals the declension, and, if we remove the genitive ending, we can find the word's true base.

Let's look at these trustworthy friends, the genitive singular endings in the first-declension genitive feminine singular. First-declension feminine genitive singular we find, *ae*. If you see an *ae* in the genitive, it's first declension. In the second-declension masculine genitive singular we find long ī. In the second declension neuter genitive singular we find, once again, a long ī, and because the masculine and neuter share that long ī, they both belong to the second declension. And in the third declension, what is the genitive singular? In the masculine and feminine singulars we find a short ī-s. And in the third-declension genitive neuter singular? Again. short ī-s. And that is why masculine, feminine, and neuter third declensions belong together; they all share that *is*.

And that is an important observation. Declensions share genitive singular endings. Only the first declension has a genitive singular in ae. Only the second declension has a genitive in long ī, and only the third declension has a genitive in short *is*, and that *is* is a short *is*, pronounced ĬSS. By their genitives thou shalt know them. The genitive is the crucial key that unlocks the mystery of what declension a noun or adjective belongs to, and that is why nouns are listed first in their nominative and then in their genitive.

We will compare, next, the dative and ablative together for reasons that should soon become obvious. In the first-declension feminine singular we find dative *ae* and ablative ā, a long ā. These are not the same endings, so it's not obvious yet. However, when we look at the masculine and neuter second declension dative and ablative endings, we find that both cases share a long ō. They are the same in the second declension. In the third declension singular, if we look at the masculine and feminine, as well as neuter, we find dative and long ī, and an ablative short e. So what are the lessons? Dative and ablative singular endings are, sometimes, but not always, the same. We can also say that, except for the first-declension dative singular, *ae*, which is a diphthong, dative and ablative endings tend to be a single vowel sound. o, a, i, and e.

Let's look at the accusative singular in the first-declension accusative feminine singular, where we find *am*. In the second-declension masculine accusative singular, we find *um*. In the second-declension neuter accusative singular, we find *um*. In the third-declension masculine and feminine singulars, we find *em*. And in the third declension accusative neuter singular? It's a blank slate.

The accusative case shows some real similarities in the singular. Each and every accusative singular, except the third-declension neuter, which is a wild card, ends in an *m*. That's good to know when we look for direct objects. So, although accusative *um*'s will sometimes have to be distinguished from their third-declension genitive plurals and neuter nominative singulars, that *m* ending should not, and it will not, be confused with a genitive singular, and certainly not with the dative or ablative singular, since those are vowels.

Let's look at our nominative plurals. In the first-declension nominative feminine plural, we find *ae*. And in the second-declension masculine nominative plural, we find long ī. In the second-declension neuter nominative plural, we find *a or a*. And in the third-declension nominative masculine and feminine plurals, we find long ēs, ēs. And in the third-declension nominative neuter plural, we find a, again—a. The plural nominative, again, shows a mixed picture. Apart from the masculine and feminine nominatives of the third declension, we find vowels. One bright spot: All neuter nominative plurals are the same. They end in *a*, second or third declension. If only neuter plurals did not look like the feminine singulars! But we can't have everything.

Let's look at our genitive plurals. In the first-declension genitive feminine plural, we find *ārum*. In the second-declension masculine genitive plural, we find *ōrum*. In the second-declension neuter genitive plural, we find *ōrum*. In the third-declension genitive masculine and feminine plurals, we find *um*. And in the third-declension genitive neuter plural, we find *um*. The genitive plural shows us some real systemic similarities. All genitive plurals end in *um*. And the first- and second-declension genitive plurals precede that genitive *um* with their theme vowels. long ā for the first declension, ārum, and long ō for the second-declension masculine *ōrum*.

Let's look at our accusative plurals. In the first-declension accusative feminine plural, we find long *ās*. In the second-declension masculine accusative plural, we find long *ōs, ōs*. In the second-declension neuter accusative plural, we find a, again—a. In the third declension accusative masculine and feminine plurals, long *ēs, ēs*. And in the third-declension accusative neuter plural, we find *a, a*. The accusative plural, likewise, reveals some patterns. Neuter accusative plurals repeat their nominative forms, the letter a, a. And all masculine and feminine accusative plurals, whether first, whether second, or whether third declension, these accusative plurals end in s.

The first-declension feminine accusative plural precedes that s with its long theme vowel ā, ā̲s̲. The second-declension masculine accusative plural precedes that s with its long theme vowel ō, ō̲s̲. And the third-declension masculine and feminine accusative plurals precede that s with a long ē, pronounced "aye," ē̲s̲,̲

We're almost there. Let's look at our dative and ablative plurals. Why have we compared dative and ablative plurals together will now, very quickly, become obvious. In the first-declension feminine plural, we find in the dative, long ī-s, pronounced "ees"; and in the ablative, again, long ī-s, pronounced "ees." I submit, they are the same. In the second-declension masculine plural, we find in the dative, long ī-s, pronounced "ees"; and in the ablative, again, long ī-s, pronounced "ees." I submit, they are the same. In the second declension plural, we find in the dative long ī-s, pronounced "ees;" and, in the ablative, again, long ī-s, pronounced "ees." I think they're the same. In the third declension masculine and feminine plurals, we find in the dative, *ibus*, and in the ablative, *ibus*; I think those are the same. And in the third declension neuter plural, we find in the dative, *ibus*, and in the ablative? You knew it before I even said it, *ibus*. Do I repeat myself? You betchya. They are the same.

The ablative and dative plural endings are friendly, friendly indeed. There are, if we count them up, only two of them, a long ī-s, pronounced "ees," for first and second declension words, and, please note that the first- and second-declension dative and ablative plural *īs* differs from the genitive singular of the third declension because the I of this *īs* is long, not short. And our only ending for dative and ablative plurals of the third declension? *ibus*.

This looks like a lot. But, broken down the similarities help us remember the cases and navigate the syntax, even if words, we may not be able to parse fully. And that is why we must learn and study all these gorgeous endings. But we must distinguish adjectives from nouns.

Adjectives modify nouns. And in Latin, adjectives are <u>agreeable</u>, very agreeable. Adjectives take their cue from nouns and agree with them in three things: <u>case, number, and gender</u>, but not ending. Adjectives can change their gender from masculine to feminine, from feminine to neuter, their number from singular to plural, and their case from nominative to ablative, but adjectives cannot change their declension. Sometimes endings match letter for letter between adjective and noun, sometimes they do not, and yet, adjectives will agree with the nouns they modify in case, number, and gender.

Let's take a look. The word for big, large or great in Latin is *magna* (feminine), *magnus* (masculine), or *magnum* (neuter). Because big appears in these three forms, we know that *magnus* (masculine), *magna* (feminine), *magnum* (neuter) is a first- and second-declension adjective. A big masculine soldier is a mīles magnus. A big feminine light is lux magna. And a big neuter body is corpus magnum. In each instance, we chose the gender of magnus, magna, magnum that would match the gender of the noun we wanted to modify, although none of the endings matched between the two words, but they did agree in case, number, and gender.

Let's take a quick look at how *magnus, magna, magnum* would look as it would be listed in a dictionary. What you would find, often enough would be the letters magn, and then a dot, and then the us ending so that you would know that when you saw ", -a, -um" that you would precede that a and that um with the stem "magn." And there would be followed by its part of speech, adjective, and it's meaning, big. Why do they do this? Lexicographers like to save ink, and paper, and so they abbreviate. (magn•us, -a, -um, *adj.*, big). When we see magn•us, -a, -um, we are supposed to supply the stem for the truncated -a, -um, which gives us, if we spell everything out, magnus, magna, magnum. Try this: "bon•us, -a, -um, *adj.*, good." Can you expand that adjective into its three full forms? bonus, bona, bonum. Here's a somewhat tougher one that ends in er in the masculine: "līber, -a, -um, *adj.*, free." Can you expand it? līber, lībera, līberum. The take away? First and second declension adjectives appear in the nominative singular for the most part as -us, -a, -um, but sometimes as -er, -a, -um.

Let's take a closer look at how we modify nouns with adjectives. *Nox, noctis,* is a feminine noun that means night. What is its declension? The genitive ends in short is, is. Right. Night is third declension. I would like to decline "the everlasting night" or "the never-ending night" in the singular. The adjective that means "everlasting" in Latin gave us our word "perpetual." The Latin adjective is *perpetuus, -a, -um,* or, spelled out more fully, *perpetuus, perpetua, perpetuum,* hence, first and second declension. We need the feminine first declension so that we can modify the feminine night in Latin. So which one do you want? If you said *nox perpetua* or *perpetua nox,* you were spot on.

We'll put the adjective in its normal place in Latin word order—after the noun—and then decline "everlasting night" in the singular. Let's begin with the nominative singular: the everlasting night scares me: *nox perpetua.*

The genitive singular: of the everlasting night: *noctis perpetuae*

dative singular: to or for the everlasting night: *noctī perpetuae*

accusative singular: I fear the everlasting night: *noctem perpetuam*

and the ablative singular: by, with, or from the everlasting night: *nocte perpetuā*

In each instance, *perpetua* agreed in case, number, and gender with *nox,* yet their endings never matched. Let us try modifying the masculine noun *senex, senis,* which means old man, with the adjective stern or severe, *sevērus,* a, um. Now, if we expand *sevērus,* a, um, we get *sevērus, sevēra, sevērum.* What's the declension of the noun, however, XXXX,. Short is. Correct, third declension, stem is sen. So compare sen to a word we have in English, "senile." You'll see that stem there. And the adjective *sevērus, a, um,* again, belongs to the first and second declensions. So how would you say, the stern old man? If you said *senex sevērus,* you were correct.

But we only wanted to decline these crusty old gusters in the plural, beginning with the nominative plural. So how would we say, the stern old men gossip, nominative, plural: *senēs sevērī;* the genitive plural: of the stern old men: *senum,* for our masculine third declension, and then, *sevērōrum, senum sevērōrum;* the dative plural: to or for the stern old men: *senibus sevērīs;*

the accusative plural: I disregard the stern old men: *senēs sevērōs;* and ablative plural: by, with, or from the stern old men: *senibus sevērīs,*

And let us conclude by modifying the neuter noun *bāsium, bāsiī* (kiss) with the adjective "fiery, glowing hot, burning." What better way to conclude than with a fiery kiss? The Latin adjective is *fervidus, a, um,* first and second declension. But take a look at the genitive of *bāsium, bāsiī.* That genitive ends in a long ī, not is, so this word is not a neuter third declension, but a neuter second declension. What does this mean? As I mentioned at the beginning of this lecture, first- and second-declension adjective endings work for first- and second-declension nouns too. If you can decline a neuter adjective, you can decline a neuter noun. There is another interesting phenomenon. The endings on the adjective will match the endings on the noun, as well as agree with them. This happens sometimes too.

Are you ready for some fiery kisses in Latin?

nominative singular: the fiery kiss burns their lips: *bāsium fervidum*

genitive singular: of the fiery kiss: *bāsiī fervidī*

dative singular: to *or* for the fiery kiss: *bāsiō fervidō*

accusative singular: I would like a fiery kiss, please: *bāsium fervidum*

ablative singular: by, with, or from the fiery kiss: *bāsiō fervid*

nominative plural: fiery kisses are dangerous: *bāsia fervida*

genitive plural: of the fiery kisses: *basiōrum fervidōrum*

dative plural: to or for the fiery kisses: *basiīs fervidīs*

accusative plural: Why does he get the fiery kisses?: *basia fervida*

ablative plural: by, with, or from the fiery kisses: *basiīs fervidīs*

I hate to kiss, and run, but *tempus fugit*, as they say, and I think you get the idea. The endings sometimes match, and often they don't, but they always agree. And these endings of the first and second declension were a lot to absorb, so I suggest studying them intensively before moving on to the next lesson. *Ad astra per aspera.* To the neuter plural accusative stars by way of neuter plural difficulties. The journey is worth it, and I have every confidence in you. *Ad astra per aspera.* And again, please, feel free, put me on a loop. I don't mind. I'm happy to practice everlasting night, strict old men, and fiery kisses at any time.

And with that, all of you, *omnēs linguae Latīnae amātōrēs,* all lovers of the Latin language, you are free to go so that you may learn Latin (*ut linguam Latīnam discātis*) and practice it on your own, before we meet again.

Grātiās vōbis agō! And until we meet again, take care, so that you may be well (*cūrāte, ut valeātis*).

First- and Second-Declension Nouns
Lecture 8

In the last lecture, we walked through the challenges of the first- and second-declension adjectives. In this lecture, we will solidify our grasp of first- and second-declension endings by continuing to expand our range with first- and second-declension nouns. The good news is that the endings for second-declension nouns are exactly the same as the endings for first- and second-declension adjectives. The only oddity is that some masculine nouns appear in the first declension and some feminine nouns appear in the second declension. However, we will begin with nouns that conform to type.

Review: First-declension endings

	Singular	Plural
Nominative	-a	-ae
Genitive	-ae	-ārum
Dative	-ae	-īs
Accusative	-am	-ās
Ablative	-ā	-īs

Declension of *puella* (first-declension noun)

puella, puellae, f.: girl

	Singular	Plural
Nominative	puella	puellae
Genitive	puellae	puellārum

Dative	puellae	puellīs
Accusative	puellam	puellās
Ablative	puellā	puellīs

- Remember that the genitive case tells us what declension a noun belongs to. Every noun that has a genitive singular ending in -ae, as *puellae* does, is a first-declension noun. If the genitive singular ends in -*is*, it's a third-declension noun.

- Also remember that to find a noun's stem or base, we go to the genitive singular form and remove the ending. In this instance, if the genitive is *puellae* and we remove the genitive ending -*ae*, we reveal the base: *puell-*.

Declension of *fēmina* (first-declension noun)

fēmina, fēminae, f.: woman

	Singular	Plural
Nominative	fēmina	fēminae
Genitive	fēminae	fēminārum
Dative	fēminae	fēminīs
Accusative	fēminam	fēminās
Ablative	fēminā	fēminīs

The ending -*ae* in the genitive singular form, *fēminae*, tells us that this can only be a first-declension word; thus, we must follow the first-declension pattern.

If we then remove the genitive ending, we find that the base is *fēmin-*.

Declension of *agricola* (first-declension noun)

agricola, agricolae, m.: farmer

	Singular	Plural
Nominative	agricola	agricolae
Genitive	agricolae	agricolārum
Dative	agricolae	agricolīs
Accusative	agricolam	agricolās
Ablative	agricolā	agricolīs

- The overwhelming majority of first-declension nouns are feminine in gender, but there are a few masculine nouns of the first declension, such as the Latin word for "farmer," *agricola, agricolae*.

- The genitive ending *-ae* tells us that this is a first-declension noun. If we remove the genitive ending from *agricolae*, we get the base *agricol-*.

Review: Second-declension masculine endings

	Singular	Plural
Nominative	-us / -er	-ī
Genitive	-ī	-ōrum
Dative	-ō	-īs
Accusative	-um	-ōs
Ablative	-ō	-īs

Declension of *servus* (second-declension noun)

servus, servī, m.: slave

	Singular	Plural
Nominative	servus	servī
Genitive	servī	servōrum
Dative	servō	servīs
Accusative	servum	servōs
Ablative	servō	servīs

- Most second-declension masculine nominative singulars end in -*us*, as *servus* does, but some end in -*r*.

- We know that *servus* belongs to the second declension because the genitive ends in -ī. If we remove the genitive ending, we reveal the base, *serv-*.

Declension of *puer* (second-declension noun)

puer, puerī, m.: boy

	Singular	Plural
Nominative	puer	puerī
Genitive	puerī	puerōrum
Dative	puerō	puerīs
Accusative	puerum	puerōs
Ablative	puerō	puerīs

- We know that *puer, puerī* ("boy") belongs to the second declension because its genitive ends in -ī. By definition, every noun with a genitive singular ending in -ī belongs to the second declension.

- If we remove the genitive ending, we reveal the base: *puer-*.

Declension of *fraxinus* (second-declension noun)

fraxinus, fraxinī, f.: ash tree

	Singular	Plural
Nominative	fraxinus	fraxinī
Genitive	fraxinī	fraxinōrum
Dative	fraxinō	fraxinīs
Accusative	fraxinum	fraxinōs
Ablative	fraxinō	fraxinīs

- Some words in the second declension look masculine but are feminine, such as the word for "ash tree," *fraxinus, fraxinī*. The word is feminine, but you can't tell by looking at it. It declines just like *servus*.

- If we remove the genitive ending -ī, we get the base *fraxin-*.

Review: Second-declension neuter endings

	Singular	Plural
Nominative	-um	-a
Genitive	-ī	-ōrum
Dative	-ō	-īs
Accusative	-um	-a
Ablative	-ō	-īs

Note: The genitive ending -ī tells us that a noun belongs to the second declension. But if a second-declension noun has a nominative that ends in -um, that noun is neuter.

Declension of *bellum* (second-declension noun)

bellum, bellī, n.: war

	Singular	Plural
Nominative	bellum	bella
Genitive	bellī	bellōrum
Dative	bellō	bellīs
Accusative	bellum	bella
Ablative	bellō	bellīs

- In *bellum, bellī,* we see a nominative ending in -um followed by a genitive ending in -ī. The -um tells us that "war" is neuter, and the -ī tells us that it belongs to the second declension.

- If we remove the genitive ending, we reveal the base: *bell-*.

Modifying nouns
- Let's now modify the nouns we just declined with a first- and second-declension adjective: *bonus* (masculine), *bona* (feminine), *bonum* (neuter), which means "good." Recall that adjectives must agree with the nouns they modify in case, number, and gender.

- This first exercise is simple. Provide the Latin equivalent for the following English phrases, in the nominative case:

1. the good girl

2. the good woman

3. the good farmer

4. the good slave

5. the good boy

6. the good ash tree

7. the good war

Answers: 1. *puella bona*, 2. *fēmina bona*, 3. *agricola bonus*, 4. *servus bonus*, 5. *puer bonus*, 6. *fraxinus bona*, 7. *bellum bonum*.

- In the next exercise, you'll hear a noun-adjective combination in English. Translate that phrase into its Latin equivalent.

1. to or for the good girls

2. of the good girls

3. "verb" the good wars

4. by, with, or from the good slave

5. by, with, or from the good farmer

6. of the good slaves

7. of the good farmers

Answers: 1. dative plural, *puellīs bonīs*; 2. genitive plural, *puellārum bonārum*; 3. accusative plural, *bella bona*; 4. ablative singular, *servō bonō*; 5. ablative singular, *agricolā bonō*; 6. genitive plural, *servōrum bonōrum*; 7. genitive plural, *agricolārum bonōrum*.

Parsing a Latin sentence

- Let's consider a sentence adapted from Valerius Maximus's first book of *Memorable Deeds and Sayings*, his *Facta et Dicta Memorabilia*. The sentence gives us some insight into interactions between the chief priest of Rome's state religion and one of the priestesses who acted as guardians of the goddess Vesta's eternal flame.

- The sentence reads as follows: *Publius Licinius pontifex maximus virginem Vestālem, quia nocte ignem aeternum male custōdit, flāgrō admonet.*

- Carefully parsing the sentence, we arrive at this translation: "Publius Licinius, the chief priest, reminds the Vestal priestess with a whip because at night she watches over the eternal flame poorly."

- Using the vocabulary of the original sentence, try to translate the following variations:

1. Virginēs Vestalēs pontificem maximum flāgrīs custōdiunt.

2. Virginēs Vestalēs nocte pontificem maximum custōdiunt.

Answers: 1. The Vestal priestesses guard the chief priest with whips. 2. The Vestal priestesses guard the chief priest at night.

Verba

aeternus, aeterna, aeternum: eternal

agricola, agricolae, m.: farmer

astrum, astrī, n.: star

bāsium, bāsiī, n.: kiss

bellum, bellī, n.: war

cibus, cibī, m.: food

fēmina, fēminae, f.: woman

ignis, ignis, m.: fire

male (adv.): poorly

maximus, maxima, maximum: greatest, chief

pontifex, pontificis, m.: priest

puella, puellae, f.: girl

puer, puerī, m.: boy

quia (conj.): since, because

servus, servī, m.: slave

vīnum, vīnī, n.: wine

virgō, virginis, f.: young woman, maiden (*virgō Vestālis* = Vestal priestess)

Memoranda

Please learn the declensions of *puella, puellae*, f., "girl" (App. §15); *servus, servī*, m., "slave" (App. §16); and *bellum, bellī*, n., "war" (App. §16).

Agenda

i. Create your own noun chart for each of the noun-adjective combinations below and decline. Make sure you check the gender before proceeding.

1. chief priest

2. eternal star

3. miserable woman (use *fēmina)*

4. miserable farmer

ii. Please translate the following into Latin.

1. to/for the beautiful maiden

2. by/with/from the great war

3. of the large fire

4. of the good boys

5. most pleasing kisses (as subject)

6. of the free women

7. to/for the stern slave

8. to/for the eternal fires

9. the good girls (as direct object)

10. of eternal night

iii. Please translate the following into English.

1. Servī fēminārum bene legunt.

2. Puer miser male vīvit.

3. Bibant virginēs miserae.

4. Mīlitēs sevērī bellum magnum agunt.

5. Sit magnus ignis.

6. Possuntne agricolae bonī cibum vendere?

7. Vēritātem pontificī maximō senex bonus dīcat.

8. Caede flōrēs pulchrōs!

First- and Second-Declension Nouns
Lecture 8—Transcript

Salvēte, discipulī discipulaeque linguae Latīnae! Mihi valdē placet vōs pulchram linguam Latīnam aeternam docēre.

In the last lesson, I led you to the stars through the challenges of the first and second declension adjectives, *ad astra per aspera.* Now that we are among the stars, let us enjoy the view. We will in this lesson solidify our grasp of first- and second-declension endings by continuing to expand our range with first- and second-declension nouns. The good news is, of course, that the endings for the second-declension nouns and first-declension nouns, all these endings are exactly the same as the endings for first and second declension adjectives. The only oddity is that some masculine nouns appear in the first declension and some feminine nouns appear in the second declension. Call them cross dressers, if you will. We can have fun with them, but we will begin with nouns, first, that conform to type.

Let us first review our first-declension endings. Please repeat after me in the singular: *a, ae, ae, am, ā*; and in the plural: *ae, ārum, īs, ās, īs.* And one more time: *a, ae, ae, am, ā*, ae, ārum, īs, ās, īs. Chanting is fun. Let's put these, almost always, feminine endings on a girl, then a woman, and then, for fun, a masculine noun. The word for girl in Latin is *puella.* The genitive is *puellae.* And please remember that it's the genitive case that tells us to what declension a noun belongs. Every noun that has a genitive singular in -ae is a first-declension noun.

What if the genitive singular ends in -is? Right, that's a third-declension noun. You also recall that to find a noun stem, we go to the genitive singular form and remove the ending. So in this instance, if the genitive is *puellae* and we remove the genitive ending ae, we reveal the stem, which is *puell.* We can now decline girl in Latin. Shall we?

Nominative: the girl verbs: *puella*

Genitive: of the girl: *puellae*

Dative: to or for the girl: *puellae*

Accusative: verb that girl: *puellam*

Ablative: by, with, or from the girl: *puellā*

And the nominative plural: the girls are verbing: *puellae*

genitive: of the girls: *puellārum*

dative: to or for the girls: *puellīs*

accusative: verb those girls: *puellās*

ablative: by with or from the girls: *puellīs*

You may recall the word for woman, *mulier, mulieris*. *Mulier, mulieris*, belongs to the third the declension. A genitive ending in -is makes that clear enough. But there is another word for woman in Latin, *fēmina, fēmina, fēminae*. If we examine the genitive singular form *fēminae*, we see the ending ae. This can only be a first-declension word, so we must follow the first declension pattern. If we, then, remove the genitive ending ae, can you tell me what the stem is? Did you say *fēmin*? If so, you were spot on. I'll give you the English, please try to provide the Latin:

The woman verbs: *fēmina*

of the woman: *fēminae*

to or for the woman: *fēminae*

verb that woman: *fēminam*

by, with, or from the woman: *fēminā*

The women verb: *fēminae*

of the women: *fēminārum*

to or for the women: *fēminīs*

verb those women: *fēminās*

by, with, or from the women: *fēminīs*

Now, the overwhelming majority of first-declension nouns are feminine in gender. But there are a few masculine nouns of the first declension too. Let's look at one. The word for farmer in Latin is *agricola, agricolae*. The genitive in ae screams, screams one thing, first declension. If we remove that genitive ending, ae, from *agricolae*, what is our stem? *Agricol*. Even though the word is masculine, the word declines the same way as girl or woman. Shall we?

nominative singular: *agricola*

genitive: *agricolae*

dative: *agricolae*

accusative: *agricolam*

ablative: *agricolā*

And in the plural:

nominative plural: *agricolae*

genitive: *agricolārum*

dative: *agricolīs*

accusative: *agricolās*

ablative: *agricolīs*

The real fun begins when we modify *agricola* with an adjective. But we still have some more work to do.

Let's review our second-declension masculine endings. First the singular, please repeat after me: us *or* -r, ī, ō, um, ō; and now the plural: ī, ōrum, īs, ōs, īs. Again, in the singular: us, ī, ō, um, ō; and the plural: ī, ōrum, īs, ōs, īs. And one more time in the singular: us, ī, ō, um, ō; and in the plural: ī, ōrum, īs, ōs, īs. Most second-declension masculine nominative singulars end in us, but some end in r. We'll practice both. Let's begin with *servus*, *servī*, the word that means slave. How do we know that this word, this noun, belongs to the second declension? The genitive ends in a long ī, and if we remove that genitive ending, we can also reveal the stem, *serv*. Well, that's hard to pronounce. How do you pronounce a w after an r? *serv*, but we will pronounce the v like a w. Let's decline it:

The nominative singular: the slave performs an action, the slave verbs: *servus*

Genitive: of the slave: *servī*

Dative: to or for the slave: *servō*

Accusative: verb that slave: *servum*

Ablative: by, with, or from the slave: *servō*

And the nominative plural: the slaves are verbing: *servī*

genitive: of the slaves: *servōrum*

dative: to or for the slaves: *servīs*

accusative: verb those slaves: *servōs*

ablative: by, with, or from the slaves: *servīs*

Let's try a second declension masculine that ends in -r. The word *puer*, *puerī* means "boy." How do we know that this word belongs to the second declension? Its genitive ends in long ī. By definition, every noun with a genitive singular ending in long ī belongs to the second declension. If we remove that genitive ending in long ī, we reveal the stem onto which we attach the other endings. What is that stem? *puer*.

Let's decline the little fellow:

The boy verbs: *puer*

of the boy: *puerī*

to or for the boy: *puerō*

verb that boy: *puerum*

by, with, or from the boy: *puerō*

The boys verb: *puerī*

of the boys: *puerōrum*

to or for the boys: *puerīs*

verb those boys: *puerōs*

by, with, or from the boys: *puerīs*

And there are some words in the second declension that look masculine, but are feminine. Trees, for example. The word for ash tree is *fraxinus, fraxinī*. That tree is feminine, but you can't tell by looking at it. *Fraxinus* declines just like *servus*. If we remove the genitive i of *fraxinī*, what is our stem? *Fraxin*. Let's see whether we can decline a feminine second-declension noun.

nominative singular: *fraxinus*

genitive: *fraxinī*

dative: *fraxinō*

accusative: *fraxinum*

ablative: *fraxinō*

nominative plural: *fraxinī*

genitive: *fraxinōrum*

dative: *fraxinīs*

accusative: *fraxinōs*

and ablative: *fraxinīs*

Again, the fun is modifying these cross dressers. They're no harder to decline than their gender-conforming look alikes. But we will delay that fun until after we look at the second-declension neuter nouns, which, by the way, unlike first-declension and second-declension primarily masculine nouns, never engage in any cross dressing. If the noun behaves like a second-declension neuter noun, it is a second declension neuter.

What is the pattern? nominative um, followed by a genitive in long ī. The genitive in long ī tells us that the noun belongs to the second declension. But if a second-declension noun has a nominative that ends in -um, that noun is neuter. Let's review second-declension neuter endings. First the singular, please repeat after me: um, ī, ō, um, ō; and now the plural: a, ōrum, īs, a, īs. Again, the singular: um, ī, ō, um, ō; plural: a, ōrum, īs, a, īs. And one more time: um, ī, ō, um, ō; a, ōrum, īs, a, īs.

In the last lesson, we declined *basium, basiī,* which means kiss. That allowed us to reflect on one aspect of Roman culture. In this lesson, let us decline the word for war, *bellum, bellī,* a second-declension neuter that will allow us to reflect on another aspect of Roman culture. If we look at *Bellum, bellī,* we see a nominative in –um, followed by a genitive in long ī. The um tells us that war is neuter, and the long ī tells that war belongs to the second declension. And if we remove the genitive ending in long Ī, we reveal the stem, which is? Bell. So let's decline:

Nominative: the war is the subject of a verb: *bellum*

Genitive: of the war: *bellī*

Dative: to or for the war: *bellō*

Accusative: verb that war: *bellum*

Ablative: by, with, or from the war: *bellō*

And the nominative plural: the wars are subjects of a verb: *bella*

genitive: of the wars: *bellōrum*

dative: to or for the wars: *bellīs*

accusative: verb those wars: *bella*

and ablative: by, with, or from the wars: *bellīs*

And now we can have some fun modifying these nouns. Let's modify each of these nouns with a good first- and second-declension adjective, *bonus, bonus, bona, bonum,* which means "good." Which form is masculine? Which form is feminine? Which form is neuter? *Bonus* is masculine, *bona* is feminine, and *bonum* is neuter. Adjectives, as you recall, must agree with the nouns they modify in case, number, and gender.

Let's review the first- and second-declension nouns we just declined: *puella, puellae,* feminine, girl; *fēmina, fēminae,* feminine, woman; *agricola, agricolae,* masculine, farmer; *servus, servī,* masculine, slave; *puer, puerī,* masculine, boy. *Fraxinus, fraxinī,* feminine, ash tree; *bellum, bellī,* neuter, war. Our first exercise will be simple. Everything will be nominative; everything will be nominative singular. I'll provide the English, you provide the Latin equivalent in the pause provided. After that pause, I, *Molinārius bonus*, will provide the correct response. Are you ready?

the good girl: *puella bona*

the good woman: *fēmina bona*

the good farmer: *agricola bonus*

Did you say *bona* feminine or *bonus* masculine? *Bonus* is correct because adjectives agree with nouns in case, number, and gender. Adjectives are agreeable to that extent, but they draw the line at cross dressing. Adjectives conform to the standard gender of their declension, even if the nouns have crossed the line. *Agricola bonus*.

How about good slave? *servus bonus*

The good boy: *puer bonus*

And the good ash tree: *fraxinus bona*

The adjective *bona* agrees in case, nominative; number, singular; and gender, feminine. It does not agree in declension. *Fraxinus bona*.

And finally, the good war: *bellum bonum*

Okay, let's mix it up a bit. I will give you a noun-adjective combination in English. Try to translate that phrase into its Latin equivalent in the pause provided. After the pause, you will hear the correct response.

to or for the good girls; that's a dative plural: *puellīs bonīs*

of the good girls; that's a genitive plural: *puellārum bonārum*

accusative, verb the good girls: *puellās bona*

How about accusative verb the good wars? *bella bona*

by, with, or from the good slave; that's an ablative singular: *servō bonō*

by, with, or from the good farmer: *agricolā bonō*.

of the good slaves; it's a genitive plural: *servōrum bonōrum*

of the good farmers; genitive plural, *agricolārum bonōrum*

The endings do not always have to match, but you knew that, because in the last lecture we modified third-declension nouns with first- and second-declension adjectives, and those endings certainly do not match.

We could review the third declension too and verb forms as well, but, enjoyable as these drills are, let's look at some Latin sentences and apply what you know to some ancient turns of thought and phrase. Here's a sentence adapted from Valerius Maximus' first book of memorable deeds and sayings, his *Facta et Dicta Memorabilia,* and this sentence gives us some insight into the interactions between the chief priest of Rome's state religion and one of the vestal priestesses who acted as guardians of the goddess Vesta's eternal flame.

Let's read the sentence aloud slowly. I'll pause after every two words so you can repeat after me: *Publius Licinius pontifex maximus virginem Vestālem, quia nocte ignem aeternum male custōdit, flāgrō admonet.* And now the whole sentence: *Publius Licinius pontifex maximus virginem Vestālem, quia nocte ignem aeternum male custōdit, flāgrō admonet.* There are two verbs. Let's translate them first. They are both present tense indicatives that end in t. So who does such a verb? The answer is he, she, or it. *Custōdit* means he, she, or it guards. Think of the custodian who takes care of a building. The word *admonet* means he, she, or it reminds or instructs. Our English word admonish derives from *admoneō.* We will need to figure out who does each of these verbs.

Let's return to the beginning of the sentence. *Publius Licinius pontifex maximus.* In what cases are all these words? Nominative. Which words modify which other words? This is not easy, unless you know that Publius Licinius is the name of a Roman politician who was chief priest from 212 to 183 B.C.E. *Pontifex* is a noun that means priest. *Maximus* means chief or greatest. Does *maximus* modify Licinius or the priest? It modifies *pontifex* to give us chief priest.

But Publius Licinius and the chief priest are the same person. Can a noun modify a noun? Not exactly, but we can put the two next to each other. This is called apposition. By putting chief priest next to Publius Licinius, the author tells us that Publius Licinius is the chief priest. We do the same thing in English. Publius Licinius, chief priest. And because Licinius is nominative, we know that he is the subject of one or perhaps even both of the two verbs we just identified.

Let's go on. *virginem Vestālem*. The vestal priestess. When we see the ending em, we know that what we see is what, what declension? em. Well, it ends in em, it's an accusative singular, third declension. Shall we review? Please repeat after me: *blank*, is, ī, em, e. I don't need to do the plural. *Virginem Vestālem*, we know that the subject either guards or admonishes the vestal priestess.

Let's forge on. *Quia.* This word introduces a subordinate clause. We are not going to get any verbal satisfaction any time soon. *Quia* means because. *Nocte. Nox, noctis* means night. Let's decline till we get to the form *nocte.* The genitive ends in is, so what is the declension? Third. If we remove the is what is our stem? n-o-c-t, *noct.* Let's decline: *Nox, noctis, noctī, noctem, nocte.* We can stop. *Nocte.* Case? Ablative. By, with, or from the night? "By night" would be the closest, but I don't like that, so let's say "at night," which would be better English. The ablative can also be used to tell us when something takes place. We very creatively call this the "ablative of time when."

And on we go. *Ignem aeternum. Ignis, ignis* is a third-declension masculine. *Aeternus, aeterna, aeternum* is a first- and second-declension adjective. Does *aeternum* agree with *ignem*? You bet it does. They are both masculine accusative singular. Somebody verbs the eternal flame, the eternal flame that was never, ever supposed to go dark on the hearth of Vesta's temple, even at night, *nocte.* I see trouble. The next word is *male,* an adverb which means "badly." And then, finally, that verb, *custōdit,* That's not the main verb, but a verb in the subordinate clause introduced by *quia*. Let's go back and do the whole clause: *quia nocte ignem aeternum male custōdit* "Because at night the eternal flame badly he, she, or it guards." But is the subject he, she, or it? Well, the first part of the sentence gives us our clue, as we know. Who is supposed to guard the flame at night? The vestal priestess. That's one of her main jobs, so we can translate the clause this way: "because she poorly guards the eternal flame at night."

And on we go, back to the main clause with the word *flāgrō*. *Flāgrum, flāgrī*, is a neuter noun that means "whip." What is the case? Let's decline: um, ī, ō, um, ō. There are two ō, so it's either dative or ablative, so we can translate to, for, by, with, or from the whip. Alright, those are possibilities. Let's move on. *Admonet*. He, she, or it reminds. Okay, now let's go back to the beginning. We will ignore the *quia* clause; we're just going to do the main clause. Let's translate *Publius Licinius pontifex maximus virginem Vestālem flāgrō admonet*. Publius Licinius, the chief priest, the Vestal priestess to, for, by, with, or from a whip reminds. That's going word for word. Let's ignore the whip. What does the priest do? The priest reminds the priestess. That's nice. But how does he remind her? *flāgrō,* with a whip. I would call this ablative of means, because the whip is the tool or means by which the priest gets the verb done. The chief priest Publius Licinius reminds, or instructs, the Vestal priestess with a whip. Why? *Quia nocte ignem aeternum male custōdit.* Because she guards the eternal flame poorly at night. Let's try the whole sentence. *Publius Licinius pontifex maximus virginem Vestālem, quia nocte ignem aeternum male custōdit, flāgrō admonet.* Publius Licinius, the chief priest, reminds the vestal priestess with a whip because at night she watches poorly over the eternal flame.

I'm not trying to put the Romans in a bad light. They were actually proud of this story. To them it showed how seriously they took their religious duties. We may draw a few lessons of our own based on which gender wielded the whip, and that would not be inappropriate, as patriarchy, my friends, runs deep in the West, and such stories help us understand why those who seek equity have a lot of history to deal with.

Let's take this sentence, though, and use the vocabulary to make up a few variations of our own. *Virginēs Vestalēs pontificem maximum flāgrīs custōdiunt*. Let's parse. Please tell me the case, number, and gender of *virginēs*; nominative plural feminine. Why nominative? The priestesses are the subjects of the verb *custōdiunt*, which ends in nt. Please parse *pontificem*. Accusative singular masculine. Why? *Pontificem* is the direct object of the verb *custōdiunt*. Why is *maximum* accusative singular masculine? It agrees with *pontificem*. Please parse *flāgrīs*. Ablative plural neuter. And why are *flāgrīs* in the ablative? Ablative of means. The priestesses use the whips as a means to guard the priest. Please parse *custōdiunt*? Third person plural. Why? The verb agrees with the subject *Virginēs*.

So, putting all that together, how would you translate *Virginēs Vestalēs pontificem maximum flāgrīs custōdiunt*. The Vestal priestesses guard the chief priest with whips. Now try this one. *Virginēs Vestalēs nocte pontificem maximum custōdiunt*. The vestal priestesses guard the chief priest at night. Please parse *nocte*. Ablative singular feminine. Why is it ablative? Ablative of time when.

So there you have it. After two thousand years, our knowledge of Latin has allowed us to turn the tables on the chief priest. To change the present, we must know the past—and Latin, of course!

And you, my Latin lovers, *amātōrēs linguae Latīnae*, have today safeguarded our precious language well. You are free to go, so that you may learn Latin (*ut linguam Latīnam discātis*), and practice it on your own, before we meet again. *Grātiās vōbis agō!* and, until we meet again, take care, so that you may be well (*curāte, ut valeātis*).

Introduction to the Passive Voice
Lecture 9

W e begin this lecture by reviewing all the active verb forms we've studied. However, in addition to tense (or time) and mood (i.e., indicative, imperative, subjunctive), verbs have voice. They can be active or passive. The subjects of active verbs "do" their verbs; they perform the action of the verb on objects: "You drive a car." "I love this book." But what if a subject does nothing and lets the verb be performed on it? In that case, the subject is passive: "I am hit." To make the distinction between the active and passive voices in English, we need the helping verb *to be* plus a past passive participle. But in Latin, the distinction is made through personal endings.

Review: Personal endings for Latin verbs, active voice

	Singular	Plural
1	-ō / -m	-mus
2	-s	-tis
3	-t	-nt

Review: Present active indicative conjugation of *agō*

agō, agere, ēgī, actum: do, drive

	Singular	Plural
1	agō	agimus
2	agis	agitis
3	agit	agunt

Present active subjunctive conjugation of *agō*

agō, agere, ēgī, actum: do, drive

	Singular	Plural
1	agam	agāmus
2	agās	agātis
3	agat	agant

Imperative of *agō*

age (singular); agite (plural)

Infinitive of *agō*

agere

Passive personal endings

	Singular	Plural
1	-r	-mur
2	-ris	-minī
3	-tur	-ntur

Comparing active and passive of *agō* (indicative mood)

Active		Passive	
agō	I drive	agor	I am driven
agis	You drive	ageris	You are driven
agit	S/he *or* it drives	agitur	S/he *or* it is driven
agimus	We drive	agimur	We are driven
agitis	Y'all drive	agiminī	Y'all are driven
agunt	They drive	aguntur	They are driven

- To form the present-tense active indicative, we started with the principle parts *agō, agere, ēgī, actum* and added the active personal endings *-ō, -s, -t, -mus, -tis, -nt* to the base *ag-*, inserting either the vowel *i* or *u*.

- The passive endings *-r, -ris, -tur, -mur, -minī, -ntur* are applied similarly to the base *ag-*, but we observe some slight adjustments in the vowel to accommodate Roman pronunciation.
  - In the first-person singular, we use an "o" sound before the *-r*, and in the second-person singular, the short *i* of *agis* becomes even more unstressed—the unstressed "uh" sound we hear in *ageris*.

  - Other than this one exception, the vowel sequence *o, i, u* remains virtually unchanged.

Comparing active and passive of *agō* (subjunctive mood)

Active		Passive	
agam	I may drive	agar	I may be driven
agās	You may drive	agāris	You may be driven
agat	S/he *or* it may drive	agātur	S/he *or* it may be driven
agāmus	We may drive	agāmur	We may be driven
agātis	Y'all may drive	agāminī	Y'all may be driven
agant	They may drive	agantur	They may be driven

- The subjunctive is even more regular. As you recall, for the active, we start with the personal endings *-m, -s, -t, -mus, -tis, -nt* and attach them to the base *ag-*, inserting the vowel *a*.

- For the present passive subjunctive, we similarly apply the personal passive endings *-r, -ris, -tur, -mur, -minī, -ntur* to the base *ag-*, inserting the vowel *a*.

Comparing active and passive of *agō* (infinitive)

- For the infinitive, we start with the second principle part, *agere* ("to drive"), remove the active infinitive ending *-ere*, substitute the present passive infinitive ending *-ī*, and get *agī* ("to be driven").

Comparing active and passive of *agō* (imperative mood)

Active		Passive	
age!	Drive!	agere!	Be driven!
agite!	Drive (y'all)!	agiminī!	Be driven (y'all)!

- Note that the second-person singular command form, *agere*, looks and sounds like the active infinitive "to drive." Note, too, that the second-person plural command form, *agiminī*, looks like the second-person plural indicative.

- These forms can be confusing, but context will help us sort them out.

Present passive indicative of *dūcō*

dūcō, dūcere, dūxī, ductum: lead

	Singular	Plural
1	dūcor	dūcimur
2	dūceris	dūciminī
3	dūcitur	dūcuntur

Present passive subjunctive of *dūcō*

dūcō, dūcere, dūxī, ductum: lead

	Singular	Plural
1	dūcar	dūcāmur

2	dūcāris	dūcāminī
3	dūcātur	dūcantur

Present passive infinitive of *dūcō*

dūcī

Present passive imperative of *dūcō*

dūcere (singular); dūciminī (plural)

Quiz

In each of the following English sentences, a form of the verb "to lead" appears in the passive. Provide the Latin equivalent.

1. The legion *is led* by Caesar.

2. *Let* the legion *be led* by Labienus!

3. *We are being led* into prison.

4. If *we should be led* into prison.

5. *Let them be led* by us!

6. *Are y'all being led* to prison?

7. *You*, my friend, *are being led* to prison.

8. *To be led* to prison, however, is better than to be crucified.

9. Listen well, my friend, and *be led* to glory!

10. Sorry, my friends, *be led* to prison!

Answers: 1. *dūcitur*, indicative, statement of fact; 2. *dūcātur*, hortatory subjunctive; 3. *dūcimur*, indicative; 4. *dūcāmur*, subjunctive in a condition; 5. *dūcantur*, hortatory subjunctive; 6. *dūciminī*, indicative; 7. *dūceris*, indicative; 8. *dūcī*, infinitive; 9. *dūcere*, singular imperative; 10. *dūciminī*, plural imperative.

The agent of a passive verb

- In English, we use the preposition "by" to indicate the performer or agent of a passive verb: "The legion is led by Caesar." Latin likewise uses a preposition, *ab* or *ā* (the "b" can fall off before consonants), together with the ablative.

- Here's an example: *Legiō ab Caesare dūcitur*, "The legion (nominative subject) is led (present passive indicative) by (preposition) Caesar (ablative of personal agent)," or "The legion is being led by Caesar."

- Let's compare two somewhat similar sentences: (1) *Caesar pugiōne interficitur*; "Caesar (nominative subject) is killed (*interficitur*) by an ablative dagger (*pugiōne*)." (2) *Caesar ā Brūtō interficitur*; "Caesar (nominative subject) is killed (*interficitur*) by an ablative Brutus (*Brūtō*)."
  - o Notice that with the person, Brutus, we inserted the preposition ā, but for the dagger, we did not; we used the ablative by itself. A dagger is merely the means or tool that a thinking agent (i.e., a person) employs.

  - o Caesar is killed by means of a dagger by the personal agent Brutus. Personal agents must be indicated by deploying the preposition *ab* or *ā*. By contrast, the means, tool, or instrument by which an action is accomplished should be expressed by the ablative without a preposition.

Translating Cicero and Vergil

- In a speech delivered in defense of the Greek poet Archias, Cicero writes, "*Optimus quisque glōriā dūcitur*," meaning "Each or every best person (*optimus quisque*) by means of glory or fame (*glōriā*) is led (*dūcitur*)," or "Every best person is led by fame." *Glōriā* here is the fame that derives from great accomplishments, such as winning a major battle.

o   In other words, Cicero suggests that glory, fame, or honor is the means by which each best person is led or, to use a more modern concept, motivated.

o   The best among us are motivated by fame or the honor that derives from accomplishment.

• In another speech, Cicero took a less kindly view of someone's motivation: "*Favōre populī dūcitur*," meaning "He is being led—or motivated—by the favor of the people." Each or every best person is motivated by *glōriā*, the fame that comes from accomplishment or honor, not by means of the favor of the unruly mob.

• In his story of *pius Aeneas* ("god-fearing Aeneas"), Vergil expressed how the Romans understood themselves: "*Auguriīs agimur dīvum*," meaning "We are driven or led by the divine signs of the gods."

Verba

ab (preposition + ablative): by, from (the *b* can be omitted when *ab* is coupled with a word that begins with a consonant: *a Caesare* = by Caesar)

colō, colere, coluī, cultum: worship

dūcō, dūcere, dūxī, ductum: lead; consider, regard

legiō, legiōnis, f.: legion

Memoranda

Please learn the personal passive endings of the Latin verb. Learn the present tense passive in the indicative and subjunctive, the present passive infinitive, and the present passive imperatives of *pōnō* (which may also be found in App. §55).

i. In the verb chart below, give the active personal endings of Latin verbs.

	Singular	Plural
1		
2		
3		

ii. In the verb chart below, give the passive personal endings of Latin verbs.

	Singular	Plural
1		
2		
3		

iii. Create your own verb chart for each of the following verbs and conjugate in the mood and voice indicated.

1. colō (indicative passive)

2. dēsinō (subjunctive passive)

3. legō (subjunctive active)

4. dūcō (indicative active)

5. mittō (subjunctive passive)

iv. Translate the following into Latin. (Each answer will be a single word.)

1. I am sent.

2. I may be sent.

3. We send.

4. Let us lead.

5. Lead! (addressing one person)

6. Let them be led.

7. to be sold

8. You (plural) are selling.

9. It is being sold.

10. Be driven! (addressing more than one person)

11. to drive

12. I may drive.

v. Describe the difference between the ablative of means and the ablative of agent.

vi. Please translate the following into Latin.

1. The soldiers are being led by Caesar.

2. He is able to be led by truth.

Introduction to the Passive Voice
Lecture 9—Transcript

Salvēte, discipulī discipulaeque linguae Latīnae! Mihi valdē placet vōs pulchram linguam Latīnam aeternam docēre.

Let us review the personal active endings of the Latin verb. Please repeat after me: *-o* or *-m, -s, -t, -mus, -tis, -nt.*

Let us conjugate *agō, agere, ēgī, actum* (do or drive) in the present tense indicative on the count of three, *unus, duo, unus, duo, tres: agō, agis, agit, agimus, agitis, agunt.* And again: *agō, agis, agit, agimus, agitis, agunt.* And in the subjunctive, inserting a long ā before the endings. Please join me, *unus, duo, unus, duo tres: agam, agās, agat, agāmus, agātis, agant. Iterumque,* and again: *agam, agās, agat, agāmus, agātis, agant.* And in the imperative: *age! agite! Iterumque: age! agite!* And the infinitive: *agere. Iterumque: agere.*

These, my friends, *amīcī et amīcae,* are all active forms, they are all the active forms we have studied. Verbs, however, in addition to tense. or time, and mood, *id. est.,* indicative, imperative, subjunctive, have <u>voice</u>. Verbs can be active or passive. The subjects of active verbs do their verbs, they perform the action of the verb upon their objects. *Molinārius carrum agit. Molinārius* drives a car. He performs the action of driving upon the car. I lift this book. I love this book. I actively perform the actions of lifting and loving upon this book. But what if a subject does nothing and lets the verb be performed upon him? That subject is passive. Allow me to demonstrate, and please, ladies and gentlemen, please do not try this at home.

I hit the book. Again, I hit the book. I am the subject; I actively perform the action of hitting upon this object, this book! I'm a pretty darn active subject of an active verb! Thank you very much, *amīcī et amīcae!* But now, for a little grammatical and syntactical magic. I am going to become a passive subject, first in English, and then in Latin. I, *Molinārius,* am a nominative subject. I am the subject of the verb. But watch, I am going to change the voice. "I, *Molinārius,* am hit." I submit that there is a difference between

"I hit," and "I am hitting," and "I am hit," and "I am being hit." Can I get a witness? My head can testify!

How do we make the distinction between the active and passive voices in English? English is complex. We need the helping verb "to be" plus a past passive participle. The compound verb is actually rather hideous in English: "I am being hit." Hence, the admonitions of English teachers to avoid the passive voice, despite the great utility of the passive voice. The passive voice is truly useful for avoiding responsibility. Why? You don't have to say who does or did the verb. It's a favorite of administrators everywhere. What would you rather say? "I made a mistake" or, "Mistakes were made." Yes, mistakes were made. By whom? I don't know, not necessarily me. The Romans loved the passive voice, and with good reason. In Latin, the passive voice is as simple as the active voice. Why? How could this be? The magic of personal endings. Instead of *o* or *m*, "I verb," we add -*r*, "I am "verbed." Instead of *s*, "you verb," we add -*ris*, "you are verbed." Instead of *t*, "he, she, or it verbs," we add -*tur*, "he, she, or it is verbed." Instead of *mus*, "we verb," we add -*mur*, "we are verbed." Instead of *tis*, "y'all verb," we add -*minī*, "y'all are verbed." Instead of *nt*, "they verb," we add -*ntur*, "they are verbed." Six more endings to learn. These are the personal passive endings of the Latin verb: *r, ris, tur, mur, minī, ntur.* Please, please memorize them. Shall we chant them once or twice? It will only take a moment. Please repeat after me, first in the singular, *r, ris, tur;* and now in the plural: *mur, minī, ntur. Iterumque*, and again: *r, ris, tur mur, minī, ntur.* And one more time: *r, ris, tur, mur, minī, ntur.*

Now let us compare, *agō* active, to *agor* passive. We will compare active and passive, person by person, form for form. To form the present tense active indicative, we took the principle parts agō, agere, ēgī, actum, a verb that means to do, and then we added the active personal endings *o, s, t, mus, tis, nt* to the stem *ag*, inserting, as you will recall, either the vowel i or u. *Agō,* I drive; *agis,* you drive; *agit,* he, she, or it drives; *agimus,* we drive; *agitis,* y'all drive; *agunt,* they drive.

The passive endings *r, ris, tur, mur, minī, ntur* are applied similarly to the stem *ag*, but we will observe a slight adjustment in the vowel to accommodate Roman pronunciation at one point. Let's compare form by form. *Agō,* I drive; *agor,* I am driven; *agis,* you drive; *ageris,* you are driven; *agit,* he, she, or it drives; *agitur,* he, she, or it is driven; *agimus,* we drive; *agimur,* we are driven; *agitis,* y'all drive; *agiminī,* y'all are driven; *agunt,* they drive; *aguntur,* they are driven.

In the first person singular, we use an o before the r. And in the second person singular, that's where the difference was. The short i of *agis* becomes, in the second person singular passive, even more unstressed. We call the unstressed uh sound we hear in *ageris* a schwa. To the Roman ear, that uh sound sounded more like a short e, ĕ, than a short i, ĭ, so they spelled it *ageris,* not *agiris.* We don't hear the difference, but, you will see that slight spelling change. Other than that one exception, you see that the vowel sequence: o, i, u remains virtually unchanged.

The subjunctive is even more regular. As you will recall, for the active, we take the personal endings *m, s, t, mus, tis, nt,* and attach them to the stem *ag,* inserting the long vowel a. *Agam,* I may drive, I should drive; *agās,* you may drive; *agat,* he, she, or it may drive; *agāmus,* we may drive; *agātis,* y'all may drive; *agant,* they may drive.

For the present passive subjunctive, we similarly apply our personal passive endings *r, ris, tur, mur, minī, ntur* to the stem *ag,* inserting the vowel a. Let's compare present active and present passive subjunctive forms, person by person, form for form. *Agam,* I may drive or I should drive; *agar,* I may be driven or I should be driven; *agās,* you may drive; *agāris,* you may be driven; *agat,* he, she, or it may drive; *agātur,* he, she, or it may be driven; *agāmus,* we may drive; *agāmur,* we may be driven; *agātis,* y'all may drive; *agāminī,* y'all may be driven; *agant,* they may drive; *agantur,* they may be driven.

And the infinitive? We take the second principle part, *agere,* which means "to drive," remove the active infinitive ending, short *ere,* the ere, and then we substitute the present passive infinitive ending, which is just a long ī, ee, and voila, *agere,* "to drive," becomes *agī,* "to be driven." And the imperative forms? The singular active command is *age!* You've seen it before. Drive! age! The singular passive imperative is *agere!* Be driven! *agere!* Be driven! The plural active command, again, as you may recall, is *agite!* Drive, y'all! And the plural passive command, *agiminī*! Be driven, y'all! Be driven! *agiminī*!

Two points to ponder, the second person singular command form *agere,* be driven!, looks and sounds like the present active infinitive to drive, *agere.* And the second person plural command looks like the second person plural indicative passive form. *Agimini*; they're both *agimini.* Is that confusing? Well, yes, it can be, although, as always, context will help sort things out. In other words, I don't think we need to worry about it until, of course, we do. The important thing is to know that these forms exist and that you know how to apply the basic endings to the verb. So let's practice the endings one more time, put them on another verb, and then take a quiz. What are the personal passive endings of the Latin verb? *r, ris, tur, mur, minī, ntur.* Again, please repeat after me: *r, ris, tur, mur, minī, ntur.* And one more time: *r, ris, tur, mur, minī, ntur.*

And the ending for present passive infinitive? A long ī. And the endings for the imperatives, the command forms? *-ere* in the singular, *-minī* in the plural.

Let's conjugate and translate *dūcō, dūcere, dūxī, ductum,* which means "to lead." Let's conjugate it in the present passive indicative.

dūcor: I am led

Next form, *dūceris:* you are led

Next form, *dūcitur:* he, she, or it is led

dūcimur: we are led

dūciminī: y'all are led

dūcuntur: they are led

Let's conjugate this time but not translate, *dūcō, dūcere, dūxī, ductum* (lead) in the present passive indicative. One, two, one, two, three: *dūcor, dūceris, dūcitur, dūcimur, dūciminī, dūcuntur.* Let's turn the present passive indicative into the present passive subjunctive. All we need to do is change the vowel in front of the endings. We're going to change the o, e, i, or u to an a. Are you ready? *Unus, duo, unus, duo, tres*: *dūcar, dūcāris, dūcātur, dūcāmur, dūcāminī, dūcantur.* If *dūcere*, the present active infinitive, means "to lead," how do I make it passive, how do I change it to "to be led"? *Dūcere* becomes *dūcī, dūcī.* "to be led." How do I command one person, "Be led!" *Dūcere!* It sounds like the infinitive. *Dūcere!* Be led! And more than one person? "Be led, y'all!" *Dūciminī! Dūciminī!*

Time for the quiz. I, *Molinārius*, will make up a series of sentences in English. A form of the verb "to lead" will appear in my sentence, in English, in the passive voice. After each sentence, I will pause. During this pause, please provide the Latin equivalent. Your instructor, *ego, Molinārius Magnus*, will then provide the correct response, so that you, *vōs, discipulī et discipulae*, may check your work. Ready? *Parātī?*

The legion is led by Caesar: *dūcitur*, indicative, statement of fact

Let the legion be led by Labienus! *dūcātur*, subjunctive, let it be led, hortatory

We are being led into prison: *dūcimur*, indicative statement of fact

If we should be led into prison: *dūcāmur*, subjunctive in a condition

Let them be led by us! *dūcantur*, again, subjunctive, hortatory

Are y'all being led to prison? *dūciminī*, indicative

You, my friend, are being led to prison. *dūceris*, again, indicative, this time singular

To be led to prison, however, is better than to be crucified. *dūcī*, infinitive

Listen well, my friend, and be led to glory! *dūcere!* singular imperative

Sorry, my friends, be led to prison! *dūciminī!* plural imperative

The passive voice works in Latin much like the active voice. One applies endings according to number and person. The result is a single, elegant verb form, nothing so hideous our ugly as our ugly English compounds. But an important question remains. How do we indicate who does a passive verb? Is it even possible to express the performer or agent of a passive verb, if the nominative is being hogged by a passive subject? In English, of course, we use the preposition by. The legion is led by Caesar. We use the preposition by to express the personal agent, that is, the person who is the doer, think *agō*, agent. Latin, likewise, uses a preposition, the preposition *ab, a-b,* or *ā*, the b can fall off, this preposition, *ab,* together with the ablative. Here is an example:

Legiō ab Caesare dūcitur. Please repeat after me: *Legiō ab Caesare dūcitur.* We could also drop the b from *ab,* and write: *Legiō ā Caesare dūcitur.* And how do we translate this sentence? "The legion (nominative subject) is led (present passive indicative) by (preposition) Caesar (ablative of personal agent)." "The legion is being led by Caesar."

Please note, once again, that the preposition *ab* commonly drops its *b* before a consonant. But not always, but whether it's *ab* or *ā*, they both mean "by."

Let's compare two somewhat similar sentences. Sentence number one: *Caesar pugiōne interficitur.* Please repeat after me: *Caesar pugiōne interficitur. Pugiō, pugiōnis* is a third declension masculine noun that means "dagger." *Interficio, interficere, interfēcī, interfectum* is a verb that means "kill." How should we translate this sentence? The nominative subject Caesar (*Caesar*) is killed (*interficitur*) by an ablative dagger (*pugiōne*)." Let's read the next sentence. Please repeat after me: *Caesar ā Brūtō interficitur.* In this case, the nominative subject Caesar (*Caesar*) is killed (*interficitur*) by an ablative Brutus (*Brūtō*)."

What is the difference between a dagger and Brutus? With the person, we inserted the preposition *ā*, but for the dagger, we did not. We used the ablative by itself. Was *Molinārius* careless? *Minimē!* A dagger is a mere tool. A dagger cannot think or act. As dagger-loving Romans used to say, "Daggers don't kill; people do!" A dagger is merely the means, or tool, that a thinking agent, that is, a person employs.

Caesar is killed by means of a dagger by the personal agent Brutus. Persons or, better, personal agents, must be indicated by deploying the preposition *ab* or *ā*. By contrast, the means, the tool, or instrument by which an action is accomplished should be expressed by the ablative without a preposition. Why is *Brutus* in the ablative? Ablative of personal agent? Why is dagger in the ablative? Ablative of means or instrument. Grammarians classify uses of the ablative as a way to help us sort out the ablative's many uses. Again, the ablative of agent requires a person capable of thought, the preposition *ab* or *ā*, and the ablative. The ablative of means, on the other hand, requires just the ablative.

Let us turn now to readings from the ancient authors, which you can parse with a little help from your *magister*. In a speech delivered in defense of the Greek poet Archias, Cicero writes *optimus quisque glōriā dūcitur.* Please repeat after me: *optimus quisque glōriā dūcitur.* The adjective *optimus, a, um* means "best," think optimal. *Quisque* is a masculine, and it means each or every. So who is *quisque optimus*? Or *Optimus quisque*? "Each or every best." Latin can say that, because Latin can use adjectives as nouns. This is called the substantive use the adjective. We can do this in English, but we don't like to. We prefer to add the word person or thing just to remind people that we are talking about someone or something corporeal, someone or something substantive. Long story short, we can translate *quisque optimus*, this substantive use of the adjective, as "each or every best person." *Optimus quisque*, for example, *linguam latīnam discit.* Every best person learns Latin.

But let's go back to Cicero. *Glōria, glōriae*, is a feminine noun belonging to the first declension. It means "glory" or "fame." Shall we decline it, just for fun, just for practice? Okay, but just once. Please join me on the count of three, *unus, duo, unus, duo, tres: glōria, glōriae, glōriae, glōriam, glōriā; Plural: glōriae, glōriārum, glōriīs, glōriās, glōriīs.*

Now that you've gotten that out of your system, I think you're ready to identify the case of *gloriā* in *optimus quisque glōriā dūcitur.* Well, yes. You're right, ablative. "by or by means of fame." And *ducitur*? That's a third person singular indicative passive. We were just practicing the forms. You should know that one. So I think you're ready to translate some Cicero: *optimus quisque glōriā dūcitur.* Translation? Each or every best person (*optimus quisque*) by means of glory or fame (*glōriā*) is led (*dūcitur*). "Every best person is led by fame." That *gloria* is the fame that derives from great accomplishments, winning a major battle, for example. In other words, Cicero suggests that glory, fame, or honor is the means by which each best person is led, or to use a more modern concept, motivated. The best among us are motivated by fame or honor that derives from accomplishment. Please repeat after me one more time: *optimus quisque glōriā dūcitur.* No extra charge, by the way, for the ennobling thoughts.

Let's contrast this Ciceronian gem with another gem from a different speech. In this speech, Cicero takes a less kindly view of someone's motivation. Please repeat after me: *Favōre populī dūcitur. Favor, favōris,* is a third-declension noun that means what its English derivative suggests, "favor," "regard." And *populus, populī,* is a masculine noun belonging to the second declension, that means "people." And *ducitur*, you should be able to translate *ducitur*. Yes, "he is being led."

And by what is he being led? *Favōre populī.* By the ablative favor. But to whom does the favor belong? Ah, yes, a genitive is close by to show possession of that favor. Whose favor? The people's favor. He is being led—or motivated—by the favor of the people. Is that favor an ablative of agent or an ablative of means? The answer is means. And if you know how snobby Roman politics were, you will quickly realize that Cicero is disdainful. Each or every best person is motivated by *gloria*, the fame that comes from accomplishment or honor, not by means of the favor of the unruly mob. Let's enjoy this snotty little sentence one more time in Latin. Please repeat after me: *Favōre populī dūcitur.* In other words, what Cicero is saying is, that guy is playing to the lower classes.

I you realize that we are reading Latin composed by a Roman author thousands of year ago for an intelligent and highly educated audience. And in just eight short half-hour lessons, you are reading along with him. This is worth noting, and I hope it motivates you, because you, *discipuli discipulaeque linguae Latinae,* are doing a great job. *Io, Paeon!* That, as you may recall, was a little Latin shout-out. *Io, Paeon!*

But don't let it go to your head. Here's something from Vergil, whose story of *pius Aeneas,* god-fearing Aeneas, and his escape from Troy became Rome's canonical epic, because it expressed so perfectly just how the Romans understood themselves, and this sentence may serve as a case in point. *augurīs agimur dīvum.* Please repeat after me: *augurīs agimur dīvum.* Let's begin with the verb. *Agimur* ends in *mur,* so the verb is passive. Who is being driven, or led, or motivated? We are. *Agimur.* But by what? *Augurium, augurī,* is a neuter noun belonging to the second declension. It means "divine sign." Compare the English derivative "augur," as in, that "augurs."

Please parse *augurīs.* A long *īs* can be either dative or ablative plural. If I tell you that it's an ablative of means, can you translate *auguriis?* "By means of divine signs." So "we are driven (or led) by divine signs." But whose divine signs? Can we get a genitive? Indeed, *dīvum,* an alternative genitive plural of *deus, deī,* a word that means god. The regular form is *deōrum,* but it frequently appears as *dīvum.* Can you translate *dīvum?* "of the gods."

Good, and the whole sentence? "We are driven or led by the divine signs of the gods." In other words, we base our decisions on the signs indicated to us by the gods. That's why they called *Aeneas pius* or "god-fearing," and we derive our own word "pious," of course, from the Latin *pius,* although Aeneas obeyed ancient, pre-Christian, gods. And the Romans, they, considered themselves the most religious people on Earth, which may help in understanding why Vergil's *pius Aeneas* resonated. *augurīs agimur dīvum.* We are led by the gods' divine signs.

But what about us? What drives us? That's an easy question to answer: *Linguā agimur Latīnā. Linguā agimur Latīnā.* And with that, all of you, *omnēs linguae Latīnae amātōrēs,* all you lovers of the Latin language, are free to go, so that you may learn Latin (*ut linguam Latīnam discātis*), and practice it on your own, before we meet again. *Grātiās vōbis agō et, curāte, ut valeātis!*

Third -*io* and Fourth-Conjugation Verbs
Lecture 10

I n the last lecture, we studied the passive voice. We'll return to the passive voice in a future lecture, but now, to avoid getting bogged down in too many endings at the same time, we'll focus more exclusively on the active voice. Keep in mind, however, that our knowledge of the model verb *pōnō, pōnere, posuī, positum*, both active and passive, represents an essential basis for understanding some small variations on the pattern of *pōnō* and is, thus, a key to unlocking two more conjugations that follow the pattern of this third conjugation closely: specifically, third -*io* and fourth-conjugation verbs.

Review: Personal endings for Latin verbs, active voice

	Singular	Plural
1	-ō / -m	-mus
2	-s	-tis
3	-t	-nt

Review: Present active indicative conjugation of *pōnō*

pōnō, pōnere, posuī, positum: put, place

	Singular	Plural
1	pōnō	pōnimus
2	pōnis	pōnitis
3	pōnit	pōnunt

Review: Present active subjunctive conjugation of *pōnō*

pōnō, pōnere, posuī, positum: put, place

	Singular	Plural
1	pōnam	pōnāmus
2	pōnās	pōnātis
3	pōnat	pōnant

Review: Imperative of *pōnō*

pōne (singular); pōnite (plural)

Review: Infinitive of *pōnō*

pōnere

Review: Passive personal endings

	Singular	Plural
1	-r	-mur
2	-ris	-minī
3	-tur	-ntur

Present passive indicative conjugation of *pōnō*

pōnō, pōnere, posuī, positum: put, place

	Singular	Plural
1	pōnor	pōnimur
2	pōneris	pōniminī
3	pōnitur	pōnuntur

Comparison of three verbs (indicative)

Present Active Indicative		
pōnō	capiō	sentiō
pōnis	capis	sentīs
pōnit	capit	sentit
pōnimus	capimus	sentīmus
pōnitis	capitis	sentītis
pōnunt	capiunt	sentiunt

- As you can see, there are two minor differences between the present active indicative conjugations of *pōnō* ("I put") and *capiō* ("I take"). With *capiō*, we insert an *i* before the *o* of the first-person singular and another *i* before the *u* of the third-person plural. The verb *capiō* represents a subset of the third conjugation, which we call the "third -*io*."

- The verb in the third column, *sentiō*, demonstrates more than just an *i* before the *o* of the first-person singular and another *i* before the *u* of the third-person plural. The pronunciation of some forms of *sentiō* is, as a result of some long *ī*'s (marked with macrons), rather different in some places. The *i*'s in *sentiō* are long in the second-person singular, the first-person plural, and the second-person plural. This has a major impact on accent.

- In the first-person plural, the accent in *sentīmus* shifts to the second-to-last syllable because the *i* in *sentīmus* is long. The same phenomenon occurs in the second-person plural. *Sentiō* is different enough to represent a separate conjugation, called the fourth conjugation.

Patterns in the three verbs

	Third	Third *-io*	Fourth
	pōnō, pōnere	capiō, capere	sentiō, sentīre
Pattern	-ō, -ĕre	-iō, -ĕre	-iō, -īre
Stem	pōnĕ-	capĕ-	sentī-

- The first two principal parts of a Latin verb determine the conjugation and will help us decide whether to insert an *i* before the *o* of the first-person singular and the *u* of the third-person plural and, if the verb belongs to the fourth conjugation, to make the *i* of the other persons long (i.e., pronounced "ee").

- If we remove the *-re* from the second principal part, we obtain the verb stem. For example, if we remove the *-re* from *pōnere*, we get the stem *pōnĕ-*. Similarly, for the third *-io* verb *capiō, capere*, if we remove the *-re* from *capere*, we get the stem *capĕ-*. But with the fourth-conjugation verb *sentio, sentīre*, if we remove the *-re* from *sentīre*, we get the stem *sentī-*. The ī in the stem is the source of variation in pronunciation, as well as some other differences.

Quiz

You will hear the first two principal parts of a verb in Latin. Decide whether the verb is third conjugation, third *-io*, or fourth.

1. *cēdō, cēdere* (go away or yield)

2. *condūcō, condūcere* (lead)

3. *veniō, venīre* (come, go, or arrive)

4. *fugiō, fugere* (flee)

5. *bibō, bibere* (drink)

6. *cupiō, cupere* (want, desire)

7. *custōdiō, custōdīre* (guard)

8. *amō, amāre* (love)

Answers: 1. third, 2. third, 3. fourth, 4. third *-io*, 5. third, 6. third *-io*, 7. fourth, 8. first (trick question!).

Comparison of three verbs (subjunctive)

Present Active Subjunctive		
pōnam	capiam	sentiam
pōnās	capiās	sentiās
pōnat	capiat	sentiat
pōnāmus	capiāmus	sentiāmus
pōnātis	capiātis	sentiātis
pōnant	capiant	sentiant

- We form the present active subjunctive for *capiō* and *sentiō* in the same manner as we did for *pōnō*. We use the personal active ending *-m* in the first-person singular and insert the vowel *a* before the active personal endings.

- Note, however, that if there is an *i* before the *o* in a verb's first principal part, that *i* will appear before the *a* of the subjunctive, as well.

Comparing active imperative forms

Present Active Imperative		
pōne!	cape!	sentī!
pōnite!	capite!	sentīte!

- If we compare the command forms for these three conjugations, we see that the third -*io* imperatives look the same as the imperatives of the third. *Pōne* and *cape* both end in a short *e*, just like their stems. In the plural, we find *pōnite* and *capite*.

- The fourth conjugation, in contrast, retains the ī that we found in its base. The singular command is *sentī* and the plural is *sentīte*. The ī affects the accent of the second-person plural, as well. *Sentīte* has an accent on the second-to-last syllable, whereas *pónite* and *cápite* have their accents on the third-from-last syllables.

Pliny the Elder

- Pliny the Elder wrote an encyclopedia of natural history, the *Historia Naturālis*, which is a treasure trove of ancient attitudes toward just about everything.

- In his work, Pliny discusses bodies and the pleasures of the body. In particular, he wrote, "*Duo sunt liquōrēs hūmānīs corporibus grātissimī, intus vīnī, forīs oleī*," meaning, "Two are the fluids to human bodies most pleasing, indoors [the fluid] of wine, outdoors [the fluid] of olive oil."

Verba

adsum, adesse, adfuī (compound of *sum*): be present

capiō, capere, cēpī, captum: seize, capture

cupiō, cupere, cupīvī, cupītum: desire, want

custōdiō, custōdīre, custōdīvī, custōdītum: guard, defend, protect

fugiō, fugere, fūgī: flee, run away

laetus, laeta, laetum: happy, joyful

sentiō, sentīre, sēnsī, sēnsum: feel, perceive

urbs, urbis, f.: city

veniō, venīre, vēnī, ventum: come

Please learn the principal parts, the present-tense active indicative and subjunctive, present-tense active infinitive, and imperatives of third -*io* conjugation *capiō* (cf. App. §56) and fourth conjugation *sentiō* (cf. App. §57).

i. Make a verb chart for each of the following verbs and conjugate in the present tense active of the mood indicated.

1. capiō (indicative)

2. fugiō (subjunctive)

3. sentiō (subjunctive)

4. veniō (indicative)

ii. Please translate the following into Latin. (Each answer will be a single word.)

1. They may come.

2. We are coming.

3. Flee! (plural)

4. Let him seize.

5. to desire

6. Be present! (singular)

7. You (plural) are present.

8. Protect! (plural)

9. She is protecting.

10. I may feel.

iii. Make a noun chart and decline *happy woman*.

iv. Please translate the following into English.

1. In Bethlehem venīre nōn possunt.

2. Possumusne in Bethlehem venīre?

3. Veniant in Bethlehem.

4. Urbem legiō magna custōdīre potest.

5. Vēritātem custōdiat senex.

6. Possuntne mīlitēs sevērī hostēs Caesaris vincere?

7. Ex urbe fugiāmus.

8. Fugimus ex urbe.

9. Mīlitēs veniunt, ut urbem custōdiant.

10. Discipulī pulchram linguam Latīnam discere cupiunt, ut laetī sint.

Third -*io* and Fourth-Conjugation Verbs
Lecture 10—Transcript

Salvēte, discipulī discipulaeque linguae Latīnae! Mihi valdē placet vōs pulchram linguam Latīnam aeternam docēre.

Let us review our personal active endings of the Latin verb: -*o* or -*m, -s, -t, -mus, -tis, -nt*

Let us conjugate *pōnō, pōnere, posuī, positum* (put or place) in the present active indicative: *pōnō, pōnis, pōnit,* (Are you joining in?) *pōnimus, pōnitis, pōnunt.* And again: *unus, duo, unos, duo, tres: pōnō, pōnis, pōnit, pōnimus, pōnitis, pōnunt.* What does *pōnitis* mean? Y'all place. Just checking.

Let's conjugate *pōnō* in the present active subjunctive: *pōnam, pōnās, pōnat, pōnāmus, pōnātis, pōnant.* And again: *pōnam, pōnās, pōnat, pōnāmus, pōnātis, pōnant.* And what does *pōnāmus* mean? Let us place, or we should place, or we may place. What are the active imperative forms?

pōne! That's singular, and *pōnite!* plural. And again: *pōne! pōnite!* What does *pōne!* mean? Place! Put it away! And the active infinitive, the form? *pōnere.* Again: *pōnere,* which means "to place."

In the last lecture. we studied the passive voice. Do you remember the personal passive endings of Latin verb? I'll wait. That's right: -*r, -ris, -tur, -mur, -minī, -ntur.* We should probably do those again. Shall we? *r, -ris, -tur, -mur, -minī, -ntur.*

And if I asked you to conjugate *pōnō* in the present indicative passive, how would you answer? Really? What I was hoping you'd say was: *pōnor, pōneris, pōnitur, pōnimur, pōniminī, pōnuntur.* So please repeat after me: *pōnor, pōneris, pōnitur, pōnimur, pōniminī, pōnuntur.* And what does *pōnitur* mean? *Optimē:* "he, she, or it is placed."

We'll return to the passive in a lecture or two, and review it, and drill it again and again, so please don't forget it. But for the moment, in the interest of time, and so as not to bog you down with too many endings at the same time, we are going to focus, again, more exclusively in this lecture on the active voice.

That said, please remember that your knowledge of the model verb *pōno, pōnere, posuī, positum*, both active and passive, represents an essential basis for understanding some small variations on the pattern of *pōnō*, and thus a key unlocking two more conjugations that follow the pattern of this third conjugation rather closely.

Let us compare three verbs in the present active indicative tense: *Pōnō, ponere, posui, positum*. That verb, you know, means "put" or "place." The second verb, *capiō*, capere, cēpī, captum, those are the principal parts, *capiō*, capere, cēpī, captum, that verb means "take, grab, or seize" And our third verb, *sentiō, sentīre, sensī, sensum* means "feel, think, or perceive." We'll talk about their principal parts in a bit. For now, let's compare their present active indicative forms.

In the first column, you see our old friend, good old model verb *pōnō*. In the second column, you will find *capiō*, and you will have already probably noted that there are two minor differences between the present active indicative conjugations of *pōnō*, I put, and *capiō*, I take. We insert an i before the o of the first person singular, and another i the u of the third person plural. This verb represents a subset of the third conjugation, a subset that we call the third -io, cleverly enough, after the io that appears in the first person singular. The verb in the third column, however, demonstrates more than just an i before the o of the first person singular, and another i before the u of the third person plural. The pronunciation of some forms of *sentiō* is, as a result of some long ī's, which you will see marked with macrons, rather different in some places. The i's in *sentiō* are long in the second person singular, the first person plural, and the second person plural. This has a major impact on accent.

Let's compare our first person plural forms: *pónimus*, we place; *cápimus*, we take; but, *sentímus*, we feel. The accent shifts back to the second-to-last syllable—the penult, if you must—because the i in *sentīmus* is long. We find the same phenomenon in the second person plural: *pónitis*, y'all place; *cápitis*, y'all take; *sentītis*, y'all feel. *Sentiō* is different enough to represent a separate conjugation. We call it the fourth conjugation, and this will become clearer when we compare the principal parts of all three verbs: *pōnō, pōnere, posuī, positum*; please repeat: *pōnō, pōnere, posuī, positum; capiō, capere, cēpī, captum*; please repeat: *capiō, capere, cēpī, captum*; *sentiō, sentīre, sēnsī, sēnsum*. And one more time: *entiō, sentīre, sēnsī, sēnsum*.

The first two principal parts, taken together, reveal a verb's conjugation in Latin. What are the patterns? o, just o, and no i before the o, followed by the infinitive ending e-r-e, and that's a short e in e-r-e, equals the third conjugation.

io, followed by the infinitive ending e-r-e, and again, that's a short e-r-e, equals the third *–io,* the third *-io.*

io, however, followed by the infinitive ending i-r-e, and that is a long ī-r-e equals the fourth conjugation.

The first two principal parts of a Latin verb determine the conjugation and will help us decide whether to insert i's before the o of the first person singular and the u of the third person plural, and, if the verb belongs to the fourth conjugation, to make the i of the other persons long, that is, we will pronounce that i as ee, rather than ih.

We're talking about details that will not actually bother you very much in reading Latin, unless, of course, you want to understand all the variations thoroughly and/or pronounce the Latin correctly. And if you're like me, you want the details because you hate error. On the other hand, if you're like me, you also make a lot of errors. But error, *amīcī et amīcae,* can also lead to revelation, insight, correction, understanding. The pain and darkness of morphological, grammatical, and syntactical error, the humiliation of mispronunciation and misunderstanding, can be redeemed by study and reflection. It may hurt, but it also feels good, finally to understand the details. And that, my friends, is what makes us devotees of the Latin language. *Ad astra per aspera.*

Let's test your conjugational mettle. I, *Molinārius, conjugator maximus*, will give you the first two principal parts, and you, *discipuli discipulaeque*, will tell me whether that verb is third conjugation—o followed by short e-r-e; third -*io*—io followed by short e-r-e; or fourth -*io* followed by long e-r-e. Ready? *Parātī et parātae?*

cēdō, cēdere, means go away or yield. What is the conjugation? *cēdō, cēdere;* o followed by a short e-r-e equals third conjugation.

condūcō, condūcere means "lead." *condūcō, condūcere.* Conjugation identification, please. Again, third conjugation: o followed by short e-r-e.

veniō, venīre means "come, go, arrive." *veniō, venīre.* Conjugation identification? Fourth; yes. That's an io followed by a long i-r-e.

fugiō, fugere means flee, run away. *fugiō, fugere.* Conjugation identification? io followed by a short e-r-e. That's the son of a third, the third -io.

bibō, bibere, as you may recall, means "drink." Conjugation? third; o followed by a short e-r-e.

cupiō, cupere, means "want, desire." *cupiō, cupere.* Conjugation identification? io followed by a short e-r-e. That's the son of a third, the third-io.

custōdiō, custōdīre means "guard." *custōdiō, custōdīre.* Conjugation identification? Fourth; io followed by a long i-r-e.

amō, amāre means "love." *amō, amāre.* Conjugation identification? First. But you don't know that one yet. Sorry. *Ignosce mihi. Mea culpa!* We'll get to the first and second conjugations soon enough. We've saved the easier conjugations for later.

So what else can we do with our first two principal parts? They signal to us other adjustments we will need to make in the remaining present tense active forms. Let us take one more look at the information provided by the first two principal parts. If we remove the re from the second principal part, we obtain the verb stem. If were remove the re from *ponere*, we see that our verb stem is a *pone* with a short e. Similarly, for the third io verb *capio, capere*, if we remove the re from *capere*, we again see a stem ending in a short e: *cape*.

But if take our fourth conjugation verb *sentio, sentīre*, and remove the re from *sentīre*, what is our stem? *sentī* with a long i. That stem in long i is the source of our variation in pronunciation, as well as some other differences.

We have already examined the present indicative active, but have not yet recited all the forms for *capiō* and *sentiō*. Let's take a moment to do that. Please repeat after me: *capiō, capis, capit, capimus, capitis, capiunt.* If there's an i before the o, there's an i before the u. Again: *capiō, capis, capit, capimus, capitis, capiunt.* And one more time: *capiō, capis, capit, capimus, capitis, capiunt.*

Let's try *sentio, sentire.* Please repeat after me: *sentiō, sentīs, sentit, sentīmus, sentītis, sentiunt.* Did you hear those long i's? Please, again, repeat after me: *sentiō, sentīs, sentit, sentīmus, sentītis, sentiunt.* An i before the o means that we'll have an i before the u. And one more time: *sentiō, sentīs, sentit, sentīmus, sentītis, sentiunt.*

We are ready for the present active subjunctive, which we form for *capiō* and *sentiō* in the same manner as we did for *pōnō*. We use the personal active ending *m* in the first person singular and insert the vowel a before the active personal endings. We will need to remember one more thing, however, for *capiō* and *sentiō*. Take a look at the chart and see whether you can figure out what that last detail might be! You have probably already figured it out. If there is an i before the o in a verb's first principal part, that i will appear before the a of the subjunctive as well, in every form. Shall we conjugate our new verbs in the present active subjunctive? *Capio, capere* is a third io, so we will keep the i, insert an a, and add the personal active endings.

Please repeat after me: *capiam, capiās, capiat, capiāmus, capiātis, capiant.* And again: *capiam, capiās, capiat, capiāmus, capiātis, capiant.*

Let's do the same for *sentio, sentīre.* We'll keep the i, insert a, and add the personal active endings. Please repeat after me: *sentiam, sentiās, sentiat, sentiāmus, sentiātis, sentiant.* Again: *sentiam, sentiās, sentiat, sentiāmus, sentiātis, sentiant.* And one more time: *sentiam, sentiās, sentiat, sentiāmus, sentiātis, sentiant.*

Are we done? We haven't done the imperative or command forms. If we compare the command forms for these three conjugations, we see that the third -io imperatives look exactly the same as the imperatives of the regular third conjugation. *Pone!* which means "Put, O singular one!" and so *Cape!* means "Take, O singular one!" both end in short e, *Pone! Cape!* just like their stems when we remove the re from *capere* and *ponere*. In the plural, *Ponite!* "Place" and *Capite!* "Take, O plural people!" Again, *ponite* and *capite* look the same. The fourth conjugation, on the other hand, keeps the long i, pronounced ee, that we found in its base. The singular command is *Sentī!* with a long I, "Feel!" *Sentī!* If you command just one person, *Sentī!* and for the plural, if you feel like commanding a group, *Sentīte!* "Feel!" *Sentīte!* That long i affects the sound of the second person plural as well. *Sentīte!* has an accent on the second-to-last syllable, whereas *pónite!* and *cápite!* have their accents on their antepenults, or third-from-the-last syllable.

This knowledge of the fourth conjugation will enable you to understand and appreciate the commands in the original Latin of the famous old—how old remains somewhat disputed—but the famous, old Christmas carol "O Come All Ye Faithful!" But we'll have to get past the first line. Please repeat after me: *Adeste, fidēlēs, laetī, triumphantēs!* Maybe I said it too fast. Try it again. *Adeste, fidēlēs, laetī, triumphantēs!* If you were here to sing with me, I'd give it a try, but I can't, so again, please repeat after me more rapidly: *Adeste, fidēlēs, laetī, triumphantēs! Sum* means "I am." The singular command form of the verb "to be!" is *Es!* That's the singular, can you remember the plural imperative? That's right: *este!* Be! But the verb is not *sum*, it's *adsum*, a compound verb with the principal parts *adsum, adesse, adfuī, adfutūrum*. It means "to be present." So, if the plural imperative of *sum* is *este!*, can you guess what the plural imperative of *adsum* might be? Yes, just put that *ad* in front, *Adeste*, "be present!"

Then come three adjectives: *fidēlēs, laetī, and triumphantēs. Fidēlēs* is a third declension plural. It means "loyal." *Triumphantēs* is also a third declension. It means "marching in a victory parade." And *laetī* is masculine plural, meaning "happy." Can we translate? Well, literally, I suppose we should say, "Be present, loyal, happy, victoriously marching ones!" *Adeste, fidēlēs, laetī, triumphantēs!* Let's hold on to that thought and proceed to the next line, where I'd promised you a fourth conjugation imperative.

Please repeat after me: *Venīte, venīte in Bethlehem!* And again: *Venīte, venīte in Bethlehem!* Yes, *venīte!* We were introduced to that verb just a few minutes ago: *veniō, venīre, vēnī, ventum* is a fourth conjugation verb that means "come." And what form is *venīte?* Yes, plural imperative, something civilians might call a command. And how should we translate it? *Venīte!* "Come, y'all!" But where? *Venīte! venīte in Bethlehem!* "Come, y'all! Come, y'all, to Bethlehem!" So what have we got? *Adeste, fidēlēs, laefī, triumphantēs! Venīte! venīte in Bethlehem!* which we can translate as "Be present, loyal, happy, victoriously marching ones! Come, y'all! Come, y'all, to Bethlehem!"

Are you thinking what I'm thinking? The standard English version obviously takes some liberties with the Latin, and also shows its age in such archaic plural command forms as "come ye." Compare and contrast: "O come all ye faithful, joyful, and triumphant! O come ye, o come ye, to Bethlehem!" Which is better? The original Latin obviously, so please, one more time, repeat after me: *Adeste, fidēlēs, laefī, triumphantēs! Venīte! venīte in Bethlehem!* You have enough Latin now to understand the whole hymn in Latin, but it makes sense to wait, if not until Christmas, at least until we've looked at the first and second conjugations. And we will look at those conjugations in our next lesson, so you will not have long to wait.

But we have a little time left, so let's look at a short passage that will allow us to review our declensions and hone our syntactical acumen. Pliny wrote an encyclopedia of natural history, the *Historia Naturālis*, which is a treasure trove of ancient attitudes toward just about everything. In it, Pliny talks about bodies, and the body's pleasures. Please repeat after me. *Duo sunt liquōrēs hūmānīs corporibus grātissimī, intus vīnī, forīs oleī.* Or, without the pauses: *Duo sunt liquōrēs hūmānīs corporibus grātissimī, intus vīnī, forīs oleī.* You'll need some vocabulary and some help with the forms, buy, hey, that's why you your *magister nomine Molinārius* is here.

The first word *duo*, as in *unus, duo, tres*, means "two." *Sunt*, as you'd better know, means "they are." So far so good: *duo sunt*, "two are." *Liquor, liquōris*, is a masculine noun belonging to the third declension that means "fluid" or "liquid." And you can find fluid stores in most places even today. But the word *liquor* was, in Latin, was more general than our word "liquor," which now generally refers only to strongly alcoholic fluids. At any rate, *duo sunt liquōrēs*, literally, "two are fluids." Hold that thought. Let's continue, *hūmānīs*. This adjective is easy to understand. It means "human." The long īs ending should make you think not of the genitive singular, that's a short is. No. *Humanus, humana, humanum* is a first and second declension adjective that means "human." And the adjective *hūmānīs* modifies the next word, a noun in the dative, which you should be able to understand: *corporibus*, "to or for the bodies." So what kinds of bodies are *humanis corporibus*? Human bodies.

So what do we have so far? *Duo sunt liquōrēs hūmānīs corporibus*, "two are liquids to or for human bodies." Okay. Not completely clear. Let's march on, *grātissimī*. The adjective *gratissimus, -a, -um*, means "most pleasing." And *gratissimī* is a second declension masculine nominative plural. Do you recall any masculine words from earlier in the sentence that this adjective might modify? Yes, fulids or *liquōrēs*. Let's see if we can translate up to the comma: *Duo sunt liquōrēs hūmānīs corporibus grātissimī*. Literally: "Two are liquids to human bodies most pleasing." Can we put that into real English? "There are two fluids most pleasing to human bodies." That's interesting. What might those fluids be? Any guesses?

Onwards, Roman soldiers! *intus* is an adverb. It means "indoors." Think "interior." *Vīnī*. Take a guess. "Wine". Liquid number one. *Vīnum, vīnī*, is a second declension noun, but we'll deal with the case of *vīnī* later. Onwards, *mīlitēs Rōmānī*. The next word is *forīs*. *Forīs* is another adverb. It means "outside." Onwards: *oleī*. *Oleī* is derived from *oleum, oleī*, another second declension neuter noun, means "olive oil." That's bizarre. Both *vīnī* and *oleī* are second declension neuters in the genitive singular for reasons I'll explain, but let's enjoy the full translation: *Duo sunt liquōrēs hūmānīs corporibus grātissimī, intus vīnī, forīs oleī*. Literally: "Two are the fluids to human bodies most pleasing, indoors of wine, outdoors of olive oil." Okay, these odd genitives, Romans loved ellipsis. They assume that their readers are smart enough to repeat obvious words, so they do not repeat them themselves. They were obviously not writing for a modern audience. We like to spell things out. We have to understand "fluid" or "liquor," *liquor*, twice. If Pliny had spelled it out, we would read: *Duo sunt liquōrēs hūmānīs corporibus grātissimī, intus liquor vīnī, forīs liquor oleī*, which would allow us to translate: "Two are the fluids to human bodies most pleasing, indoors the fluid of wine, outdoors the fluid of olive oil." But that's a bit wordy, even in English. How about this? "There are two fluids most pleasing to the human body, indoors, wine, and outdoors olive oil." Wine indoors. I think we can all understand that. But olive oil? I think I'm going to let you ponder that one on your own.

And with that, *omnēs linguae Latīnae amātōrēs,* you are free to go so that you may learn Latin (*ut linguam Latīnam discātis*), and practice it on your own before we meet again.

Grātiās vōbis agō, et curāte, ut valeātis!

First- and Second-Conjugation Verbs
Lecture 11

In the last lecture, we expanded our verbal range by adding two more conjugations, the third -*io* and the fourth. In this lecture, we'll look at the final two conjugations, the first and second. These conjugations are traditionally taught first because they're considered easier—they're more regular—but they tend to condition students to expect regularity. Thus, if you have mastered the vowel variations in the third conjugation, you won't have any difficulty with the first and second conjugations.

Review: Personal endings for Latin verbs, active voice

	Singular	Plural
1	-ō / -m	-mus
2	-s	-tis
3	-t	-nt

Review: Present active indicative conjugation of *capiō*

capiō, capere, cēpī, captum: take, grab, seize

	Singular	Plural
1	capiō	capimus
2	capis	capitis
3	capit	capiunt

Review: Present active subjunctive conjugation of *capiō*

capiō, capere, cēpī, captum: take, grab, seize

	Singular	Plural
1	capiam	capiāmus
2	capiās	capiātis
3	capiat	capiant

Review: Imperative of *capiō*

cape (singular); capite (plural)

Review: Infinitive of *capiō*

capere

Comparison of three verbs

Present Active Indicative		
1st Conj.	**2nd Conj.**	**3rd Conj. -*io***
-ō, -āre	-eō, -ēre	-iō, -ĕre
amō	videō	capiō
amās	vidēs	capis
amat	videt	capit
amāmus	vidēmus	capimus
amātis	vidētis	capitis
amant	vident	capiunt

- For all three verbs, the personal active endings remain -*o* or -*m*, -*s*, -*t*, -*mus*, -*tis*, -*nt*. For *amō*, we find an *a* as the theme vowel, and for *videō*, we find an *e*.

- But the letter *a* is the sign of the subjunctive! That's true for all conjugations except the first. For first-conjugation verbs, the letter *a* is the sign of the indicative.

- We can distinguish the conjugations by their principal parts. We call this "conjugation identification"; all you need to determine the pattern or conjugation are the first two principal parts.

Comparing patterns

	1st Conj.	2nd Conj.	3rd Conj.	3rd -io Conj.	4th Conj.
Pr. Parts	amō, amāre	videō, vidēre	pōnō, pōnere	capiō, capere	sentiō, sentīre
Pattern	-ō, -āre	-eō, -ēre	-ō, -ĕre	-iō, -ĕre	-iō, -īre
Stem	amā-	vidē-	pōnĕ-	capĕ-	sentī-
Theme Vowel	long ā	long ē	short ĕ	short ĕ	long ī

- Beginning with the first conjugation, we see that *amō* ("I love") ends in an ō; the second principal part, *amāre* ("to love"), reveals āre. An ō followed by an āre means that the verb belongs to the first conjugation. If we remove the *-re* from the infinitive, we reveal the verb stem and its theme vowel: *amā-* and a long ā. Note that the ā is what we found in our first table between the base and the personal active endings.

- The second-conjugation verb, *videō, vidēre* ("to see"), differs from the third conjugation in two ways. We see an *e* before the ō in the first principal part, and the second principal part has ēre, which of course, puts the stress accent on the second-to-last syllable. The pattern for second-conjugation verbs is, thus, *eō* in the first principal part, followed by ēre in the second principal part. And if we remove the *-re* from *vidēre*, we get the stem *vidē-*, with long ē as the theme vowel.

- The pattern for the third conjugation is *ō* followed by *ere*. The stem of *pōnere* is *pōne*, and the theme vowel is short ĕ.

- The pattern for the third *-io* is *iō* followed by *ere*. The stem of *capere* is *cape*, and the theme vowel is short *ĕ*.

- Finally, the pattern for the fourth-conjugation verb *sentiō, sentīre* ("to feel") is *iō* followed by *īre*. The stem of *sentīre* is *sentī*, and the theme vowel is long *ī*.

Quiz

Identify the correct conjugation for each of the following Latin verbs.

1. *cupiō, cupere* (desire)

2. *laudō, laudāre* (praise)

3. *habeō, habēre* (have or hold)

4. *audiō, audīre* (hear)

Answers: 1. third *-io*, 2. first, 3. second, 4. fourth.

Comparing present active indicative

Present Active Indicative		
1st Conj.	**2nd Conj.**	**3rd Conj.**
-ō, -āre	**-eō, -ēre**	**-ō, -ĕre**
amō	videō	pōnō
amās	vidēs	pōnis
amat	videt	pōnit
amāmus	vidēmus	pōnimus
amātis	vidētis	pōnitis
amant	vident	pōnunt

Comparing present active subjunctive

Present Active Subjunctive		
1ˢᵗ Conj.	**2ⁿᵈ Conj.**	**3ʳᵈ Conj.**
-ō, -āre	-eō, -ēre	-ō, -ĕre
amem	videam	pōnam
amēs	videās	pōnās
amet	videat	pōnat
amēmus	videāmus	pōnāmus
amētis	videātis	pōnātis
ament	videant	pōnant

Comparing imperative forms

Present Active Imperative				
First	**Second**	**Third**	**Third -io**	**Fourth**
amā!	vidē!	pōne!	cape!	sentī!
amāte!	vidēte!	pōnite!	capite!	sentīte!

O Come, All Ye Faithful

Adeste fidēlēs laetī triumphantēs

Venīte, venīte in Bethlehem.

Nātum vidēte Rēgem angelōrum.

Venīte adōrēmus

Venīte adōrēmus

Venīte adōrēmus

Dominum.

Verba

adōrō, adōrāre, adōrāvī, adōrātum: worship, adore

amō, amāre, amāvī, amātum: love

angelus, angeli, m.: angel, messenger

audiō, audīre, audīvī, audītum: hear, listen to

domina, dominae, f.: mistress

dominus, dominī, m.: master, lord

habeō, habēre, habuī, habitum: have, hold; consider

laudō, laudāre, laudāvī, laudātum: praise

liber, librī, m.: book

rēx, rēgis, m.: king

videō, vidēre, vīdī, vīsum: see, discern

Memoranda

Please learn the principal parts, the present-tense active indicative and subjunctive, present-tense active infinitive, and imperatives of first conjugation *amō* (cf. App. §53) and second conjugation *videō* (cf. App. §54). Additional remarks on conjugation may be found in App. §§49–51.

Agenda

i. Make a noun chart and decline *good king.*

ii. Fill in the blanks.

1. The infinitive of first-conjugation verbs ends in _____ .

2. The infinitive of second-conjugation verbs ends in _____ .

3. The infinitive of third-conjugation verbs ends in _____ .

4. The infinitive of third -*io* conjugation verbs ends in _____ .

5. The infinitive of fourth-conjugation verbs ends in _____ .

iii. Make a verb chart for each of the following verbs and conjugate in the present active of the mood indicated.

1. audiō (indicative)

2. amō (indicative)

3. habeō (subjunctive)

4. videō (indicative)

5. adōrō (subjunctive)

iv. Please translate the following into Latin.

1. We adore the great master.

2. Let her adore the good king.

3. See (singular) the king of angels!

4. She can hear the king's legions.

5. Do you (singular) love the beautiful soldier?

6. You (plural) may praise the great woman's strength.

7. They are praising the truth.

8. Love the truth, Caesar!

9. She is not happy and deceives the Roman people.

10. We do not see the great king but we can perceive the strength of (his) soldiers.

11. We are not able to love the stern master.

12. Let the master read good books, so that he may love the truth.

13. He does not have strength of mind.

14. Let us have food and wine!

15. They come to Bethlehem so that they may adore the king.

First- and Second-Conjugation Verbs
Lecture 11—Transcript

Salvēte, discipulī discipulaeque linguae Latīnae! Mihi valdē placet vōs pulchram linguam Latīnam aeternam docēre.

In the last lecture, we expanded our verbal range by adding two more conjugations, the third -*io* and the fourth. In this lesson, we'll review, and look at the final two conjugations, the first conjugation and the second conjugation. Why, you might ask, did we begin with the third? The first and second conjugations are traditionally taught first because they're easier. They're easier because they're more regular. But they teach students to expect that regularity all the time, so I began with the third, reckoning that if you could master those vowel variations, you'd find the regularity of the first and second a conjugations a piece of proverbial cake. Which, I hasten to add, is not to say that they, too, won't require some work and memorization. They're not that easy! But let's review the personal active endings of the Latin verb: -*o* or -*m, -s, -t, -mus, -tis, -nt*. You've seen them before; you've heard them before, and they will continue to do heavy lifting for us.

Let us review the conjugation of *capiō: capiō, capere, cēpī, captum,* to take, to grab, to seize. What pattern do we see in the first two principal parts? io followed by a short e-r-e. Conjugation identification? Third -io.

Let us conjugate *capiō,* taking care to insert an i where necessary, in the present tense active indicative, on the count of three, *unus, duo, unus, duo, tres*: *capiō, capis, capit, capimus, capitis, capiunt.* And what does *capiō* mean? "I take." And *capiunt*? "They take."

And in the subjunctive, please remember that for third -io verbs we keep the i before all the vowels. Let's conjugate together, *unus, duo, unus, duo, tres*: *capiam, capiās, capiat, capiāmus, capiātis, capiant.*

And how might we translate the hortatory subjunctive, *capiant*? "Let them take." And what are the imperative forms? *cape!* That's singular, "take," and plural? *capite!* "take." And again, just the Latin: *cape! capite!* And the infinitive, how do we say "to take"? *capere;* and again, in Latin: *capere.*

Why do I repeat myself? Because the verb is where it happens, man. And because your knowledge of the third -io, and fourth conjugations provide a solid base for understanding the small variations that we will soon explore in the remaining two patterns, the first and second conjugations.

Let us compare three verbs in the present active indicative. We'll take our third –io *capio*, and we'll compare it to the first conjugation *amō,* which means "I love," and second conjugation *videō*, which means "I see." Please don't panic. Let's just compare these three verbs. What is the same? What is different? Let's begin with what should prove solid comfort. For all three verbs, the personal active endings remain *-o* or *-m, -s, -t, -mus, -tis, -nt.* But for *am*ō we find an a as the theme vowel, and for *vide*ō, we find an e.

But wait. I did say that all three verbs were present active indicative, so why would *am*ō have an a as its theme vowel? The letter a, you might justly protest, is the sign of the subjunctive! Indeed, for the second, third, third -io, and fourth conjugations, in other words, for all conjugations except the first, the letter a is, indeed, the sign of the present active subjunctive. But for first conjugation verbs, the letter a is the sign of the indicative. But how can we tell the conjugations apart? Please don't panic. By their principal parts ye shall know them! We call this conjugation identification, and all you need to determine the pattern or conjugation are the first two principal parts.

Let's have a look at the patterns for all five conjugations, that's the first; the second; the third; the son of the third, that's the third -io; and the fourth. Beginning with the first conjugation, we see that *amo*, "I love," ends in an o. The second principal part, *amāre*, "to love," reveals a long a-r-e. An o followed by an a-r-e means that that verb belongs to the first conjugation. And if we remove the re from the infinitive, we reveal the verb stem and its theme vowel. Go ahead; don't be shy. Please remove the re from *amāre*. What is the stem? *amā*. And what is the theme vowel? A long a, which is what we found in our first table between the base and the personal endings.

Our second-conjugation verb, *videō, vidēre*, means "to see," and differs from the third conjugation in two ways. We see an e before the o in the first principal part, and the second principal part has, not short e-r-e, but a long e-r-e, *ēre*, which, of course, affects the stress accent. Where do we place the accent on *Ponere*, "to place,"? on the third-to-last syllable, the antepenult. Where do we accent the infinitive "to see," *Vidēre*? On the penult, or second-to-the-last syllable. Why? That second-to-last syllable, that penult, is long. The pattern for the second conjugation verbs is, thus, eo in the first principal part, followed by long e-r-e, -*ēre*, in the second. And if we remove the re from *vidēre*, what is our stem? *Vidē* with a long e. And what is our theme vowel? A long e.

We have already done this for the third, the third -io, and the fourth conjugations, but it never hurts to review, especially as we have such a beautiful and illustrative chart. What is the pattern for the third conjugation? o followed by short e-r-e. What is the stem of *ponere*? *Pone*. And the theme vowel? a short e. What is the pattern for *capio, capere,* "to take," our third -io? io, followed by short e-r-e. And what is the stem of *capere*? Remove the re, *cape*. And the theme vowel? Again, short e.

And, finally, what is the pattern for our fourth conjugation verb "to feel," *sentio, sentīre*? io, followed by a long i-r-e. And what is the stem of *sentīre*? We remove the re, and, voila, *senti*. And the theme vowel? A long i.

Let's play our game of conjugation identification. To what conjugation does *cupiō*, "I desire," belong? *Cupio* ends in io, so, actually, it could be either third -io or a fourth-conjugation verb. We need the first two principal parts to play conjugation identification. Here they are: *cupiō, cupere*. Conjugation? io in the first principal part, followed by an infinitive with short e-r-e. Conclusion? third –io.

How about laudō, "I praise"? Sorry, no can do. Plain o in the first principal part could be either first or third conjugation. Always, always insist on the second principal part, my friends! The infinitive is the true test, *laudo, laudāre*; o in the first principal part, followed by an infinitive with long a-r-e. Conclusion? First conjugation.

Try this verb: *habeō, habēre*, which means "have" or "hold," *habeō, habēre*. Conjugation identification? eo in the first principal part, followed by long e-r-e. It's got to be second conjugation.

And one more: *audiō, audīre,* which means "to hear," *audiō, audīre;* io in the first principal part, followed by long i-r-e. The infinitive does not lie. Fourth conjugation!

But how can we possibly know whether a verb has an infinitive that ends in long a-r-e, long e-r-e, short e-r-e, or long i-r-e? If I tell you to buy a dictionary, will you be angry with me? But, seriously, nitty gritty details do require, alas, looking words up in a dictionary and/or memorizing their principal parts. And that's not a bad way to spend one's time. I have spent much of my life chanting principal parts. I enjoy memorizing forms. So let's try all four principal parts of our model verbs just to give you an idea how much fun it can be.

Here's I love, to love, I have loved, having been loved: *amō, amāre, amāvī, amātum.* Please repeat after me: *amō, amāre, amāvī, amātum.* Again, faster: *amō, amāre, amāvī, amātum.* Again: *amō, amāre, amāvī, amātum.* And one more time: *amō, amāre, amāvī, amātum.* You can't tell me that's not fun. It's a very satisfying pattern, and it helps with other first-conjugation verbs. Here's I praise, to praise, I have praised, having been praised: *laudō, laudāre, laudāvī, laudātum.* The first conjugation is really regular that way.

Let's try our second conjugation, I see, to see, I have seen, having been seen. Please repeat: *video, vidēre, vidī, vīsum.* Again: *video, vidēre, vidī, vīsum.* One more time: *video, vidēre, vidī, vīsum.*

And our third conjugation, to place? Please repeat: *ponō, ponere, posui, positum.*

Please repeat the principal parts for our third io "to take": *capio, capere, cepi, captum.*

And please repeat the principal parts for our fourth conjugation verb to feel: *sentio, sentire, sensi, sensum.*

That, I submit, is an instructive and enjoyable way to spend one's time. Then again, for some it may seem like work. And truth be told, the Internet now provides so many clickable Latin texts that one may simply call up such information quite quickly. At the end of the course I'll show you such a site, but there are sites, and some mobile phone apps too, for that matter, where you can highlight a Latin word that you don't know and magically call up an entire dictionary entry. Such texts did not exist in my youth; I had to page through the dictionary after walking uphill to school, through a blizzard. A sign of the times: *O tempora, o mores!* O times, O customs! as Cicero famously put it. And to think that Plato was worried that writing was dangerous because writing things down would induce laziness in memorization. What would Plato have said about clickable texts?

But rather than dream of ease and comfort, now that we have revealed the vowels of our first and second conjugations, let us round out your knowledge of the entire present active tense, indicative and imperative. All this knowledge is within your reach. Let's do this first for the first conjugation, *amō, amāre, amāvī, amātum,* which we will conjugate in the present active indicative. We need two things, our personal active endings and a theme vowel, which we'll insert between the base and the personal active ending. If we look at *amō,* and remove the o, we see that our base is am. If we look at *amare,* and remove the re, we find our theme vowel, a long a. And our endings, *o, s, t, mus, tis, nt,* they're familiar enough. How scary could this be?

I love? *Amo.* You love? *Amas.* He, she, or it loves? *Amat.* We love? *Amamus.* Y'all love? *Amatis.* They love? *Amant.* Same old endings, but with the vowel a. Please repeat after me: *amo, amas, amat, amamus, amatis, amant.* Again: *amo, amas, amat, amamus, amatis, amant.* And one more time: *amo, amas, amat, amamus, amatis, amant.*

What about the subjunctive? What are we going to do? All the other conjugations use a; we've used it. What do we do for the first conjugation? Well, we use an e. Please repeat after me: *Amem,* I may love; *Ames,* You may love; *Amet,* He, she, or it may love; *Amemus,* We may love; *Ametis,* y'all may love; *Ament,* They may love. And without the English translation? *Amem, ames, amet, amemus, ametis, ament.* Again: *Amem, ames, amet, amemus, ametis, ament.* And one more time: *Amem, ames, amet, amemus, ametis, ament.* It's not that bad.

And *video, vidēre, vidi, visum,* to see, it's pretty straightforward. Our theme vowel is a long e, so what do we find in the present indicative before the endings? And e, and that e tends to be long. Please repeat after me: *video,* I see; *vides,* you see; *videt,* he, she, or it sees; *videmus,* we see; *videtis,* y'all see; and *vident,* they see. And now, without the English translation: *video, vides, videt, videmus, videtis, vident.* And again: *video, vides, videt, videmus, videtis, vident.*

And the present active subjunctive of *video* inserts the customary a, but there is one thing to keep in mind. We retain the e that we see before the a. Please repeat the present active subjunctive of *video* with me: *videam,* I may see; *videās,* you may see; *videat,* he, she, or it may see; *videāmus,* we may see, *videātis,* y'all may see; *videant,* they may see. And, without the English translation, the present active subjunctive, please repeat: *videam, videas, videat, videamus, videatis, videant.* And again: *videam, videas, videat, videamus, videatis, videant.*

Let's review by looking at some charts that show us an overview of what we've just done. In the first chart, we compare the present active indicative forms of *amo, video, pono.* You'll note that the endings, *o, s, t, mus, tis, nt* are the same for all of them. What's different? The theme vowels. We find a for the first conjugation, e for the second conjugation, short i or u for the third.

And now let's review the subjunctive with a table that shows the present active subjunctive for *amo,* for *video,* and *pono,* that is, for first conjugation, the second conjugation, and the third conjugation. We could have included *capio;* we could have included *sentio,* but sometimes less is more, and you've seen those subjunctives already.

What do we see? Our active endings remain *m, s, t, mus, tis, nt.* We also see that the vowel a is the theme vowel for the second conjugation, as it was for the third, the third -io, and the fourth. We must remember, however, to retain the theme vowel e before all the a's of the subjunctive of the second conjugation, as we see in this chart of *video.* The first conjugation, however, which uses an a for the indicative, changes this vowel to e to indicate that it's changed its mood from indicative to subjunctive. At the end of the day, it all comes down to *o or m, s, t, mus, tis, nt* and a few vowel changes. And as long as you know what conjugation a verb belongs to, you can sort out those vowel changes. Easy for me to say? We'll see this again in the command forms.

And what, you beg me to tell you, are the imperative or command forms for all the conjugations?

I'm going to let you in on a little secret. The regular method to form all singular imperatives is to remove the re from the second principal part. If *amare* means to love, how do we command one person to love? Remove the re; answer: *ama!* And observe that we have a nice, long a, *ama!*

Videre, second principal part, means to see. How do command one person to see? Remove the re, *vidē*, again, a nice, long e; there's the theme vowel. *Pōnere*, remove the re, *Pōne!* Place! And that ends in a short e. As does *Cape!* Take! And the singular command for *sentire*, Senti! It ends in a long i. To make the plural command form, just add te to the singular imperative. *Ama!* becomes *amate!* *Vide!* becomes *videte!* And *senti* becomes *sentite!* You'll notice that I skipped the third and third -io. Why? This regular method works, but we have to adjust our spelling. *Pōne!* becomes *Pōnite!* but that unstreesed "uh" sound is spelled with a short i And *Cape!* become *Capite!* but that unstressed "uh" sound, again, becomes short i. And that's why I began with the third conjugation rather than the first. Who'd want to learn such fussy details after observing the greater regularity of the first, second, and fourth conjugations? But you've already done the third, so please, enjoy the greater regularity of the first, the second, and the fourth conjugations. You've earned it!

And now, as promised in our last lecture, we can read, if not the entire Christmas carol "O come all ye faithful!" in the original Latin, at least the first verse and chorus. Please repeat after me:

Adeste fidēlēs laefī triumphantēs. Venīte, venīte in Bethlehem. These two lines we translated in the last lesson as, "Be present, loyal happy victoriously marching ones! Come, y'all, come, y'all, to Bethlehem!" The song continues. Please repeat after me: *Nātum vidēte. Rēgem angelōrum.* You can now translate the second conjugation imperative, *vidēte*, and understand why we have a long e.

What is the command? "See!" or "look at!" But look at what? Let's find a direct object. I suggest to you that there are two accusative singular possibilities. There are three words. Which two look accusative and singular? *nātum* and *rēgem*. You do not have to know that morphology of *nātum* includes various details. But you do have enough Latin to figure it out. It's accusative, it's masculine, and it's singular; it's an adjective that means "born." The word is related to such English words natal, as in neo-natal or new-born unit, and nativity, the scene where at Christmas time, the one who was born is put on display. Is this adjective being used as a noun? We could then translate *nātum* as "the one born." The Romans often used it to mean "son." But if we continue past the command, we stumble upon *regem, rēx, rēgis,* is a masculine word that means "king." Its genitive in is makes the word third declension. If we remove the is, we find the stem. rēg.

Okay, let's decline. *Rex, regis, regi, regem.* I think that's enough of that. I think we've found our form and our direct object; *vidēte regem!* See, look at, the king!

And, finally, the last word, *angelōrum. angelus, angelī* is a masculine word that means angel. Its genitive is a long i, so what is the declension? Second. Can we decline angel? Let's! *angelus, angeli, angelo, angelum, angelo, angeli, angelorum.* Okay, we can stop right there. We've found our form, genitive plural, "of the angels." Let's put these lines together.

Nātum vidēte Rēgem angelōrum: "Look, y'all, at (the one) born the king of angels!" And now for the chorus: *Venīte adōrēmus, Venīte adōrēmus, Venīte adōrēmus Dominum. Venīte* is a fourth conjugation command. Come, y'all! And *adoremus*? The principal parts of the verb are *adoro, adorare, adoravi, adoratum.* Conjugation identification? First. The indicative *adoramus,* with an a, would mean, "we worship," but our form has an e, the sign of the subjunctive for the first conjugation. What does *adoremus* mean, then, in the subjunctive, with an e? "Let us worship." And whom? We find our accusative direct object at the end, *dominum,* the master! "Come! Let us worship, come, let us worship, come, let us worship, the master!" Happy holidays, my friends!

And with that, *omnēs linguae Latīnae amātōrēs,* you are free to go, so that you may learn Latin (*ut linguam Latīnam discātis*), and practice it on your own before we meet again. *Grātiās vōbis agō, curāte, ut valeātis!*

Reading a Famous Latin Love Poem
Lecture 12

In this lecture, we will reap the rewards of our work by reading a love poem by Catullus in the original Latin. The poem tells of Catullus's plan to prevent the possibility that "judgmental old men" might cast a spell on him and his lover, Lesbia, if they knew the exact number of kisses the two had exchanged. Catullus will foil the old men by having Lesbia give him an uncountable number of kisses. This poem will not only allow us to review the forms we have studied so far, but it will also enable us to love in Latin.

Catullus (84–54 B.C.E.)

- The Roman poet Catullus lived in the age of Julius Caesar and wrote poems to a woman he called Lesbia. Sources identify her as one of the famous Clodia sisters, all given the feminine form of their father's (masculine) name, Clodius.

- In Catullus's day, women of the ruling class often conducted affairs with younger lovers, especially younger lovers who aimed to rise in politics. Catullus may have fallen into this category. We know that his father was important enough to entertain Caesar in his home. And the young Catullus had to apologize for some satirical verses he had written about the famous proconsul of Gaul. Catullus was a well-educated scion of the ruling class.

- Clodia was the wife of a powerful politician; thus, it is perhaps not surprising that Catullus used a pseudonym for her in his poems. He called her Lesbia, after the island Lesbos that was home to Sappho, the famous Greek female love poet.

Let us live, my Lesbia, and let us love
by Catullus

Vīvāmus, mea Lesbia, atque amēmus,
rūmōrēsque senum sevēriōrum
omnēs ūnīus aestimēmus assis!
Sōlēs occidere et redīre possunt:
nōbis cum semel occidit brevis lūx,
nox est perpetua ūna dormienda.
Dā mī bāsia mīlle, deinde centum,
dein mīlle altera, dein secunda centum,
deinde usque altera mīlle, deinde centum.
Dein, cum mīlia multa fēcerimus,
conturbābimus illa, nē sciāmus,
aut nē quis malus invidēre possit,
cum tantum sciat esse bāsiōrum.

Let us live, my Lesbia, and let us love,
and the rumors of the judgmental old men
all (of them) let us reckon at the value of a single penny!
Suns can set and return:
for us when once the brief light has set,
a single everlasting night must be slept.
Give me a thousand kisses, then a hundred,
then another thousand, then a second hundred,
then up to another thousand, then a hundred.
Then, when many thousands we shall have made,
we will confuse those (kisses), so that we do not know,
or so that someone evil cannot cast a spell,
as he would know how many kisses there were.

aestimō, aestimāre, aestimāvī, aestimātum: estimate, value, rate

alter, altera, alterum: another, the other

atque (conjunction): and

meus, mea, meum: my

occidō, occidere, occidī, occāsum: fall, fall down, go down, set

rūmor, rūmōris, m.: gossip, report

sōl, sōlis, m.: sun

Memoranda

Please memorize as many lines of Catullus 5 (*Vīvāmus, mea Lesbia*) as you care to have on hand for your own personal performances. A collateral benefit of memorizing poetry is that you will then have examples in mind when you search your memory for vocabulary and endings.

Agenda

i. Make a verb chart for each of the following verbs and conjugate in the present tense of the voice and mood indicated.

1. vīvō (active indicative)

2. amō (active subjunctive)

3. aestimō (passive subjunctive)

4. amō (passive indicative)

5. vīvō (active subjunctive)

ii. Make a verb chart for each of the following irregular verbs and conjugate in the present tense of the mood indicated:

1. sum (indicative)

2. possum (subjunctive)

iii. Give the imperative forms, with translations, of the following verbs.

1. discō

2. adōrō

3. habeō

4. possum

5. audiō

iv. Make a noun chart and decline *everlasting light*.

v. Please translate the following into Latin.

1. Let us live.

2. Let them love.

3. They love.

4. We may hear the old man.

5. The old man hears the truth.

6. She is praising the master's wine.

7. Listen to (plural) my king!

8. The sun is setting.

9. Do you (singular) love another woman?

10. The wretched legions do not see the light.

Reading a Famous Latin Love Poem
Lecture 12—Transcript

Salvēte, discipulī discipulaeque linguae Latīnae! Mihi valdē placet vōs iterum vidēre et pulchram linguam Latīnam aeternam docēre.

In this lesson, you reap rewards for your work. You now are in a position to understand a Latin love poem in the original and lovely Latin. As a bonus, we will review the forms we have studied so far. You can now love in Latin. As you can see, I'm wearing red, so I'm ready for love.

Catullus, whom we have mentioned before, lived in the age of Julius Caesar, around 84 to 54 B.C.E. He wrote poems to a woman he called Lesbia. Our sources identify her as one of the famous Clodia sisters. They were, in the Roman fashion, all named Clodia, the feminine form of their father's name, which was Clodius. Only boys received distinctive first names; sisters could be told apart through simple counting: *prīma* (first), *secunda* (second), *tertia* (third). Sexist? What can I say? Patriarchy runs deep.

Despite the patriarchy, however, women of the ruling class in Catullus' day conducted not infrequent affairs with younger lovers, especially younger lovers who aimed to rise in politics. Was Catullus one of them? We do know that Catullus' father was important enough to entertain Caesar in his home. And the young Catullus had to apologize for some satirical verses he wrote about the famous proconsul of Gaul. Catullus was a well-educated scion of the ruling class. And his girlfriend Clodia, she was older and married. Clodia was the wife of a powerful politician, so it is, perhaps, not surprising that he used a pseudonym for her in his poems. He called her Lesbia, after the island Lesbos, which was home to Sappho, the famous Greek female love poet, giving us such terms as Lesbian and Sapphic. Ancient Greek, as so often, helps explain Latin literature.

But you're here for the Latin. Sex, politics, and Latin poetry, could we ask for more? Let's read Catullus's love poem to Clodia, whom he code named Lesbia. If the accents sound odd, it's because I will read the poem metrically. This also requires running some words together. For example, *Lesbia atque amemus* can be read running the vowels together or making, what we call, elisions. We can read those three words as one word, *Lesbiatquamemus*. But after I read the poem metrically, we'll break it all down, clause by clause. Believe you me, *mihi crēdite*, you already know a lot of Latin.

Here is the poem from start to finish:

Vīvāmus, mea Lesbia, atque amēmus,

rūmōrēsque senum sevēriōrum

omnēs ūnīus aestimēmus assis!

sōlēs occidere et redīre possunt:

nōbis cum semel occidit brevis lūx,

nox est perpetua ūna dormienda.

Dā mī bāsia mīlle, deinde centum,

dein mīlle altera, dein secunda centum,

deinde usque altera mīlle, deinde centum.

dein, cum mīlia multa fēcerimus,

conturbābimus illa, nē sciāmus,

aut nē quis malus invidēre possit,

cum tantum sciat esse bāsiōrum.

Let's break it down. Please, repeat after me: *Vīvāmus, mea Lesbia*. Our first verb, *vīvo, vīvere, vīxī, vīctum*, means live. Conjugation identification? o followed by short e-r-e. Third conjugation. Can you parse *Vivāmus*? It ends in mus, so we are the subject, but the vowel is s, so what is the mood? Subjunctive. Translation? "let us live." *meus, mea, meum* is an adjective that means "my or mine," And *Lesbia, Lesbiae* is the poet's code name for Clodia. Can you translate *Vīvāmus, mea Lesbia?* Let us live, my Lesbia!

And next, please repeat: *atque amēmus.* Or, with the with the elision? *atqueamēmus* *Atque* is a *conjunction* that means "and," but *amemus* you should know. What are the principal parts? *amō, amāre, amāvi, amātum.* Conjugation? First, o followed by a-r-e. The indicative uses a, the subjunctive uses e. Please parse *amemus*. First person plural, present active subjunctive. Why? Catullus is exhorting Lesbia. Can you translate *atque amēmus?* "and let us love." Please repeat after me: *Vīvāmus, mea Lesbia, atque amēmus.* Let us live, my Lesbia, and let us love.

The next clause takes up two lines. Please repeat after me:

rūmōrēsque senum sevēriōrum

omnēs ūnīus aestimēmus assis!

Rumor, rumōris, means "gossip" or "rumor." The *que* attached to the end of *Rumores* is a conjunction, and it means "and," but it joins the word to which it's attached to what went before that word, so we say, "and the rumors" or "and the gossip." *Senex, senis* we've seen before. It means old man. So please parse *senum?* And please be careful. What's the declension? *Senex, senis?* Short is, third declension. So *senum?* Genitive plural, shows possession. "The rumors of the old men." But what kinds of old men?

They are *senum sevēriōrum.* This adjective is not quite like *sevērus, sevēra, sevērum,* which we declined in lesson seven. *Sevērus, a, um* means "stern" or "judgmental." *Servērior,* however, means "rather stern" or "excessively judgmental" and is also third declension. The ending *erior* is how Latin turns "severe" into "severer." *Sevērus* to *sevērior.* At all events, now that you know its third declension, can observe that "rather judgmental" is a genitive plural and modifies the likewise third declension and genitive plural *senum.* Please translate *senum sevēriōrum:* "of the rather judgmental old men."

We proceed to the next line and light upon *omnēs. Omnes* means "all." And *omnēs* sports the third declension ending -ēs. Can you figure out which noun it might modify? Go back. Keep going back. How about the third declension noun *rūmōrēs*? We're making progress. Please translate: *rūmōrēsque senum sevēriōrum omnēs*, "and all the gossip of the rather judgmental old men."

Latin can do this because the endings tell us which word goes with which other word; the order is not as important. We haven't even encountered a verb yet, though. So let's review: "the gossip of the really crotchety old men, all of it (the gossip that is)." Or: "all the rumors of the rather severe old men," to use the English derivatives.

Let us continue. Please repeat: *ūnīus aestimēmus assis*. Here you're going to need a little bit of help. *Ūnīus* is a weird genitive singular that ends in -īus. The word means "one" or "single." *as, assis*, is a masculine word of the third declension. It means a small copper coin. We can call it a penny. And the verb: *aestimō, aestimāre, aestimāvī, aestimātum,* it means reckon, count, value. We derive the word "estimate," and, in fact, you could say "estimate at the value of." The verb is performed upon an accusative direct object, but the value of the object is put in the genitive. But before we start counting, or reckoning value, let's pause for a conjugation identification. *Aestimēmo, aestimēmāre,* -ō, followed by āre. Conjugation? Another first conjugation verb.

Can you parse *aestimēmus*? We see an e, not an a, in front of that mus. Yes, another hortatory subjunctive in the first person plural. So how can we translate it? "Let us estimate, or let us reckon at the value of." So please translate the two lines:

rūmōrēsque senum sevēriōrum

omnēs ūnīus aestimēmus assis!

And let us reckon (*aestimemus*) all the gossip of the rather judgmental old men, *unīus assis*, i.e., at the value of one penny! But what does that mean? Catullus is saying, "Who cares what the old men are saying? Don't worry about your reputation, Clodia!" Easy for Catullus to say.

rūmōrēsque senum sevēriōrum

omnēs ūnīus aestimēmus assis!

Let's proceed to the next line: *sōlēs occidere et redīre possunt.* Please repeat: *sōlēs occidere et redīre possunt. sōlēs?* Suns. Think solar power. Can you translate *possunt?* "They are able to." In this sentence *sōlēs*, "suns," are in the nominative plural, and hence the subject of the third person plural present indicative form of *possunt*, "they are able." "Suns are able." "Suns can." What can the suns do? *Sōlēs possunt occidere et redīre.* Suns can *occidere* and suns can *redīre*. To what part of speech do *occidere* and *redire* belong? They both end in re. They are infinitives; they complete the meaning of *possunt*. What do we call infinitives that complete the meaning of other verbs? *Complementary.* They are complementary infinitives. *Occidere* means to set. And *Redire* means to return. Can you translate *sōlēs occidere et redīre possunt?* "Suns are able to set and to return."

What is the poet saying? The sun rises, the sun sets. This is how it goes, day after day. And the contrast with the next line will make the poet's meaning somewhat clearer. But you may ask, why is the subject plural? Is there more than one sun? Well, I ask you, how do we know it's the same sun every morning? Every day is a new day, a new sun, The sun rises and the sun sets, but if take the days individually and put them together, suns can rise and set. *sōlēs occidere et redīre possunt.*

Onwards. Please repeat after me: *nōbis cum semel occidit brevis lūx, nox est perpetua ūna dormienda. nōbis*: This is a pronoun that means "for us." *Cum* means "when," and *semel*, "once." *Lux* you should know, "light." And *brevis?* It means "brief." And *occidit?* I just told you that the infinitive *occidere* meant "to set." So can you translate *occidit?* He, she, or it sets.

nōbis cum semel occidit brevis lūx. Translation? "For us when once the brief light sets (or has set)" Then what? Answer: *nox est perpetua ūna dormienda.* Again, you know what *nox* means, night. And what is the gender? Feminine. This will become important in a moment. And you've also seen the adjective *perpetuus, perpetua, perpetuum.* Heck, we declined it in lesson seven. It means continuous, everlasting, perpetual. And our verb? *dormiō, dormīre, dormīvī, dormītum*. It means sleep, compare "dormant, dormitory."

The nominative singular feminine *nox* drives all the first-declension nominative feminine singular endings in -a. Night is everlasting. Night is single, or one, and, it is *dormienda*. *-enda* is a verb ending that means "must be verbed." *agō*, as you know, means "do," so an agenda literally means the "things (neuter plural) that must be done." A *comparandum* is a "thing (neuter singular) that must be compared." So a *nox* that is *dormienda* is a night that "must be slept." That's not very good English, but we are after the Latin, not a grade in an English class.

Let's try the whole line: *nox est perpetua ūna dormienda*. "Night (*nox*) is (*est*) everlasting (*perpetua*), single (*una*), must be slept (*dormienda*)." That makes little sense, so let's try adjusting. *Est* can also mean "there is." How about, "There is one everlasting night (that) must be slept." The art of translation requires constant adjustment. Please repeat once again: *nōbis cum semel occidit brevis lūx, nox est perpetua ūna dormienda*. For us, when once this brief light has set, there is a single everlasting night that must be slept by us. In other words, in these lines, "light" signifies the "sunlight" of this world as we experience it, that is, life, which, when it sets, "for us," means a "night" that is "everlasting," a "night that we will have to sleep through forever" when we are dead. This is rather dramatic. So what could our poet possibly want?

Please repeat after me: *Dā mī bāsia mīlle*. Do that again: *Dā mī bāsia mīlle*. Our verb, *dō, dare, dedi, datum* means "give." Conjugation identification? o, followed by a-r-e. First. Can you parse the form? *dā*! That is a singular imperative. The naked verbal stem. What would the plural command form be? *Date*! But how do we translate the singular, *dā*! "Give!" *mī?* That's not too hard. It means me. Actually, it means "to me." It's dative. We'll study the pronouns later. *bāsium, bāsiī*, is a neuter noun. It means, "kiss." *Dā mī bāsia!* Can you translate? Give me kisses! How many? *mīlle*. It's an indeclinable word in the singular. It means one thousand.

Dā mī bāsia mīlle. What command does Catullus issue to Lesbia? *Dā mī bāsia mīlle*. "Give me a thousand kisses!" The same old line. In other words, Catullus writes in the *carpe diem* genre, that's second person singular imperative *carpe*, seize, plus direct object accusative *diem*, *carpe diem*. What genre is that? It's the genre of the love-sick poet who argues that we are all going to die, so let's make love while we still can!

Robert Herrick wrote a famous poem in English that falls squarely in this genre:

Gather ye rosebuds while ye may,

Old Time is still a-flying;

And this same flower that smiles today,

Tomorrow will be dying.

And that's not bad, but I think it sounds better in Latin, and you, my friends, *amīcī amīcaeque linguae Latīnae*, know enough Latin to decide for yourselves and, no matter what you decide, to understand the roots of *carpe diem* poetry, in the original. Please repeat after me, line by line:

Vīvāmus, mea Lesbia, atque amēmus,

rūmōrēsque senum sevēriōrum

omnēs ūnīus aestimēmus assis!

sōlēs occidere et redīre possunt:

nōbis cum semel occidit brevis lūx,

nox est perpetua ūna dormienda.

Dā mī bāsia mīlle,

But the poem is not done. Catullus wants more.

Dā mī bāsia mīlle, deinde centum,

241

dein mīlle altera, dein secunda centum,

deinde usque altera mīlle, deinde centum.

Deinde means "then." And *centum*? If *mīlle* means one thousand, what does *centum* mean? Think century, cent, centimeter, centipede. One hundred.

Dā mī bāsia mīlle, deinde centum,

dein mīlle altera, dein secunda centum

dein, that's the same word for "then," just without the de, *dein, deinde*, both mean then. *alterus, altera, alterum*, it's an adjective that means "another." What does *altera* end with? It ends with an a. So what might it agree with? Catullus wants another thousand... If you said *bāsia*, you are correct. Catullus wants another thousand kisses. *dein secunda centum*. And then? s*ecundus, secunda, secundum*, is an adjective that means second. And what is the ending of *secunda*? It's an a. What is it agreeing with? Catullus wants a second hundred... If you said *bāsia* again, you are, again, correct. He wants a second hundred kisses. *deinde usque altera mīlle, deinde centum. usque* means "all the way up to." "then (deinde) all the way up to (usque) another thousand (altera mille), then a hundred (deinde centum).

Does Catullus repeat himself? Yes and no. Yes, he wants more kisses, but he keeps leaving out the word *bāsia*. On the other hand, the endings on *bāsia*, that a, is picked up by the ending on *altera*, and it's picked up again by the ending on secunda. And so this makes everything clear, at lest to Romans, so let's try reading this section again in Latin:

Dā mī bāsia mīlle, deinde centum,

dein mīlle altera, dein secunda centum,

deinde usque altera mīlle, deinde centum.

Give me a thousand kisses, then a hundred, then another thousand, then a second hundred. No matter how you count it, that's a lot of kisses.

Let's review what we've done so far, line by line. I'll ask you to repeat the Latin, and then I'll provide a translation, which you don't have to repeat unless you want to. But please do repeat the Latin. Please repeat after me:

Vīvāmus, mea Lesbia, atque amēmus,

Let us live, my Lesbia, and let us love

Please repeat:

rūmōrēsque senum sevēriōrum

and the rumors of the judgmental old men

omnēs ūnīus aestimēmus assis!

all (of them) let us reckon at the value of a single penny

sōlēs occidere et redīre possunt

suns can set and return

nōbis cum semel occidit brevis lūx,

for us when once the brief light has set

nox est perpetua ūna dormienda.

A single everlasting night must be slept

Dā mī bāsia mīlle, deinde centum

Give me a thousand kisses, then a hundred

dein mīlle altera, dein secunda centum

then another thousand, then a second hundred

deinde usque altera mīlle, deinde centum

then up to another thousand, then a hundred

That's not quite the end of the poem. Please allow me to translate line by line. Catullus concludes as follows:

dein, cum mīlia multa fēcerimus,

then, when many thousands we shall have made

conturbābimus illa, nē sciāmus,

we will confuse those (kisses), so that we do not know

aut nē quis malus invidēre possit,

or so that someone evil cannot cast a spell

cum tantum sciat esse bāsiōrum.

as he would know how many kisses there were.

Here is the general idea. If you are a judgmental and evil old man, a *sevērus et malus senex*, and you stare (*invidēre*) at Catullus and Lesbia kissing, what might you do? You could cast the evil eye or a spell, an evil spell, provided you knew what? The exact number of kisses. How did Catullus plan to prevent this possibility? Lesbia will give him so many kisses that the old men will never be able to count them, and because the judgmental old men will not know the exact number, they won't be able to cast a spell. Now, none of this is obvious from the literal translation, which is why Latin must be enjoyed slowly. We drink soft drinks and watch television or surf the internet. Ancient Romans stared at each other, counted kisses, and cast the evil eye. We live in different worlds.

If you are ambitious, I suggest memorizing this poem. Not only is it beautiful, the poem can come in handy. You can use it to remind yourself of forms and constructions. Personally, I recite it when people ask me to speak Latin. I've also recited it at closing time, but that's all I'm going to say about that because you, my Latin friends, have tarried with me yet again until closing time, and all I have time for is one more rendition. And although small children now call me grandpa when they see me riding my bicycle, I can remember, with the help of Catullus, those fires of youth:

Vīvāmus, mea Lesbia, atque amēmus,

rūmōrēsque senum sevēriōrum

omnēs ūnīus aestimēmus assis!

sōlēs occidere et redīre possunt:

nōbis cum semel occidit brevis lūx,

nox est perpetua ūna dormienda.

Dā mī bāsia mīlle, deinde centum,

dein mīlle altera, dein secunda centum,

deinde usque altera mīlle, deinde centum.

dein, cum mīlia multa fēcerimus,

conturbābimus illa, nē sciāmus,

aut nē quis malus invidēre possit,

cum tantum sciat esse bāsiōrum.

And with that, all of you, *omnēs linguae Latīnae amātōrēs,* you are all free to go, so that you may learn Latin (*ut linguam Latīnam discātis*), and practice it on your own, before we meet again. *Grātiās vōbis agō, curāte, ut valeātis!*

The Present Passive of All Conjugations
Lecture 13

Catullus, Lesbia, life, death, love, and countless kisses—those were our topics in the last lecture, and we explored them all in the original Latin. In this lecture, our topic is almost as exciting: the present passive in the first, second, third -*io*, and fourth conjugations. We will first review the personal endings for Latin verbs in the passive voice and then walk through the conjugations of our model verbs. We'll close by parsing a quote from Genesis and the opening of a prayer to the emperor Tiberius.

Review: Personal endings for Latin verbs, active voice

	Singular	Plural
1	-ō / -m	-mus
2	-s	-tis
3	-t	-nt

Review: Personal endings for Latin verbs, passive voice

	Singular	Plural
1	-r	-mur
2	-ris	-minī
3	-tur	-ntur

Principal parts: *capiō*

- The principal parts of the verb *capiō* are *capiō, capere, cēpī, captum*.

- The pattern in the first two principal parts is -*io* followed by short -*ere*; thus, the conjugation is third -*io*.

Review: Present active indicative conjugation of *capiō*

capiō, capere, cēpī, captum: take, grab, seize

	Singular	Plural
1	capiō	capimus
2	capis	capitis
3	capit	capiunt

Present passive indicative conjugation of *capiō*

capiō, capere, cēpī, captum: take, grab, seize

	Singular	Plural
1	capior	capimur
2	caperis	capiminī
3	capitur	capiuntur

Present passive subjunctive conjugation of *capiō*

capiō, capere, cēpī, captum: take, grab, seize

	Singular	Plural
1	capiar	capiāmur
2	capiāris	capiāminī
3	capiātur	capiantur

Passive imperative of *capiō*

capere (singular); capiminī (plural)

Passive infinitive of *capiō*

capī

Review: Verb stems

	1st Conj.	2nd Conj.	3rd Conj.	3rd -*io* Conj.	4th Conj.
	amō, amāre	videō, vidēre	pōnō, pōnere	capiō, capere	sentiō, sentīre
Pattern	-ō, -āre	-eō, -ēre	-ō, -ere	-iō, -ere	-iō, -īre
Stem	amā-	vidē-	pōne-	cape-	sentī-
Theme Vowel	long ā	long ē	short ĕ	short ĕ	long ī

Present passive indicative conjugations

Present Passive Indicative				
1st Conj.	2nd Conj.	3rd Conj.	3rd -*io* Conj.	4th Conj.
amor	videor	pōnor	capior	sentior
amāris	vidēris	pōneris	caperis	sentīris
amātur	vidētur	pōnitur	capitur	sentītur
amāmur	vidēmur	pōnimur	capimur	sentīmur
amāminī	vidēminī	pōniminī	capiminī	sentīminī
amantur	videntur	pōnuntur	capiuntur	sentiuntur

Present passive subjunctive conjugations

Present Passive Subjunctive				
1ˢᵗ Conj.	**2ⁿᵈ Conj.**	**3ʳᵈ Conj.**	**3ʳᵈ -*io* Conj.**	**4ᵗʰ Conj.**
amer	videar	pōnar	capiar	sentiar
amēris	videāris	pōnāris	capiāris	sentiāris
amētur	videātur	pōnātur	capiātur	sentiātur
amēmur	videāmur	pōnāmur	capiāmur	sentiāmur
amēminī	videāminī	pōnāminī	capiāminī	sentiāminī
amentur	videantur	pōnantur	capiantur	sentiantur

Parsing Genesis 1:9 and a prayer to Tiberius

- The first part of Genesis 1:9 reads, in "vulgar Latin," as follows: *dīxit vērō Deus: congregentur aquae ... in locum ūnum.* Parsing this quote, we arrive at the following translation: "In truth God said: let the waters be gathered together into one place!"

- Valerius Maximus opens his *Memorable Deeds and Sayings*, his *Facta et Dicta Memorabilia*, with a prayer to the Caesar whom we know as the Roman emperor Tiberius: *Tē, Caesar, invocō, cuius caelestī prōvidentiā virtūtēs ... benignissimē foventur, vitia sevērissimē vindicantur.*
  - The first phrase, *Tē, Caesar, invocō*, means, "I invoke you, O Caesar." An ancient prayer always required invocation of the correct deity.

  - As a whole, the prayer can be translated as: "You, Caesar, I invoke, by whose heavenly foresight virtues are fostered most kindly; vices are punished most severely."

aqua, aquae, f.: water

benignissimē, adv.: most kindly

caelestis, caeleste, third-declension adj.: heavenly

caelum, caelī, n.: sky, heaven

congregō, congregāre, congregāvī, congregātum: gather together, assemble

deus, deī, m.: god

foveō, fovēre, fōvī, fōtum: cherish, foster, nourish

imperātor, imperātōris, m.: commander, emperor

in (prep. + ablative): in, on

in (prep. + accusative): into

invocō, invocāre, invocāvī, invocātum: call upon, invoke

locus, locī, m.: place

multus, multa, multum: much, many

prōvidentia, prōvidentiae, f.: foresight, providence

sevērissimē, adv.: most severely

sub (prep. + ablative): under

tū, tuī, tibi, tē, tē (personal pronoun; App. §40): you (sing.)

ūnus, ūna, ūnum: one

vindicō, vindicāre, vindicāvī, vindicātum: punish, avenge

vitium, vitii, n.: vice

Memoranda

Please learn the present passive indicative and subjunctive, present passive
infinitive, and present passive imperatives of the model verbs *amō* (App.
§53), *video* (App. §54), *pōnō* (App. §55), *capiō* (App. §56), and *sentiō*
(App. §57).

Agenda

i. Conjugate the following verbs in the present tense, using the voice and
mood indicated.

1. laudō (active indicative)

2. video (passive subjunctive)

3. sentiō (passive indicative)

4. congregō (active subjunctive)

5. habeō (active indicative)

6. audiō (passive subjunctive)

ii. Please translate the following sentences into Latin.

1. The girl loves one boy.

2. Many girls are loved by the boy.

3. Let the wretched maiden cease to love the beautiful boy.

4. Let the good old men be heard by Caesar.

5. Caesar is not heard by (his) soldiers.

6. The joyful farmers are assembling in the city.

7. Assemble, slaves!

8. We are being gathered together under the large elm tree.

9. Let the cities be guarded by the commander's legions.

10. Are you (singular) seen by the woman?

11. Do you (plural) see the other boy in the water?

12. Can the enemies be captured?

13. I cannot be heard by the students.

14. May the gods be praised!

15. The light of truth is not perceived by the king.

The Present Passive of All Conjunctions
Lecture 13—Transcript

Salvēte, discipulī discipulaeque linguae Latīnae! Mihi valdē placet vōs pulchram linguam Latīnam aeternam docēre.

Vivamus, mea Lesbia, atque amemus. "Let us live, my Lesbia, and let us love." Catullus, Lesbia, life, death, love, and countless kisses. Those were our topics in the last lecture, all in the original Latin. Today our topic is almost as exciting—present passive conjugation in the first, second, third -io, and fourth conjugations. We know how to live, my friends, and love.

Let us review the personal active endings of the verb. On the count of three, *unus, duo, unus, duo, tres -o* or *-m, -s, -t, -mus, -tis, -nt*

Let us review the personal passive endings of the verb. *Unus, duo, unus, duo, tres: -r, -ris, -tur, -mur, -minī, -ntur.* We are going to need these passive endings, again and again today, so let's recite them again: *-r, -ris, -tur, -mur, -minī, -ntur. Iterumque: -r, -ris, -tur, -mur, -minī, -ntur.* And one more time: *-r, -ris, -tur, -mur, -minī, -ntur.*

We are going to put these endings on our model verb *capio*, to take, so let's review *capio*. *Capio's* principal parts are *capiō, capere, cēpī, captum*. What pattern do we find in the first two principal parts, *capiō, capere*? -io followed by short e-r-e. Conjugation? Third -io. As you may or may not recall, in the present tense indicative, we conjugate *capiō* in the same way we conjugate good old *pōnō* with two exceptions. We must take care to insert an i before the o, which is easy enough, as it's already there in the first principal part. And we must also insert an i before the u in the third person plural. We've done this already in the active. Now we will do it the passive. Bring along *r, ris, tur, mur, mini, ntur*, and I'll guide you through the paradigm.

First person singular, passive indicative: I am taken. *capio* + r yields: *capior;* second person singular: you are taken. In the active, we used cap- short-i, but then we add ris, and say *caperis*, you are taken, we make a slight spelling adjustment and represent that unstressed "uh" with a short e, *caperis*. Let's move to the third person singular; he, she, or it is taken, we take *cap* again, and we have our *tur*, and we insert our customary short i, *capitur*, no spelling adjustments required. First person plural, we are taken: *capimur*, short I, *capimur;* second person plural, y'all are you are taken, *capiminī;* and finally, the third person plural, they are taken, *capiuntur*. And here we inserted an i before the u. Why? Third -io. And again, just in Latin, please repeat after me: *capior, caperis, capitur, capimur, capiminī, capiuntur.* And one more time: *capior, caperis, capitur, capimur, capiminī, capiuntur.*

Let us turn to the present passive subjunctive. As you may recall, in the active, we retained the i that we find before the o of *capio* between our subjunctive vowel a as well. We also retained this i before the a and our personal passive endings *r, ris, tur, mur, mini, ntur*. I think we are ready to conjugate *capio* in the present passive subjunctive. Let me be taken, should I be taken, I may be taken. There are many ways to translate the subjunctive. Form, *capiar*, I may be taken; second person singular, you may be taken, *capiāris;* he, she, or it may be taken *capiātur*, we may be taken: *capiāmur*, y'all may be taken: *capiāminī;* they may be taken: *capiantur.*

Let's conjugate the present passive subjunctive again, but just in Latin this time. Please repeat after me: *capiar, capiāris, capiātur, capiāmur, capiāminī, capiantur*. And the passive imperative, the command form, is formed in same way for *capio capere*, as it was for *pono, ponere*. Be taken, oh singular person; the command form? *capere!* Plural? Be taken, y'all! or, be ye taken! *capiminī!* And again, in Latin, please repeat after me, singular, *capere!* Plural, *capiminī!* And the infinitive? To form the present passive infinitive "to be taken," we take the present active infinitive, the second principal part, "to take," *capere*, we remove the short ĕ-r-e, and then take a long ī, attach it to the *cap*, yielding, *capī*, to be taken. And again, in Latin, to be taken, *capī*.

This present knowledge, together with your new knowledge of verb stems from lesson 11, will help you navigate the present passive forms of all the conjugations. Your knowledge of verb stems is a little rusty? Well, let's review. Let's review our verb stems, and then explore! Please have a look at this chart; o followed by ā-r-e gives us the first conjugation and a theme vowel of long ā; ēo followed by long ē-r-e gives us the second conjugation and a theme vowel of long ē; ō followed by short e-r-e gives us the third conjugation and a theme vowel of short e; iō followed by short e-r-e gives us the third -io conjugation, again, and a theme vowel of short e. But we will have to keep track of some extra i's. And finally, iō, followed by long ī-r-e, gives us the fourth conjugation and a theme vowel of long ī. Please keep these theme vowels in mind, and let's have some passive fun!

Our next chart shows the present tense indicative mood of verbs in the passive voice for the first, second, third, third -io, and fourth conjugations. In the present passive indicative, we see that our passive endings, *r, ris, tur, mur, minī, ntur*, appear with comforting regularity through all the conjugations. What we have to adjust are the theme vowels that appear before those endings, and these, the theme vowels, we find also with comforting regularity; long ā in the first conjugation, long ē in the second conjugation, short ĕ, or "uh," variably spelled i, e, or u, in the third and third -io conjugations. And, finally, long ī in the fourth conjugation.

Let's practice these conjugations. Let us conjugate our first conjugation verb *amō, amāre* in the present passive indicative. Please repeat after me: *amor, amāris, amātur, amāmur, amāminī, amantur*. What vowel appears before the endings? Long a. Let's do it again: *amor, amāris, amātur, amāmur, amāminī, amantur.*

Let's conjugate our second conjugation verb, *video, vidēre,* in the present passive indicative: *videor, vidēris, vidētur, vidēmur, vidēminī, videntur.* What vowel appears before the endings? Long e. Let's do it again: *videor, vidēris, vidētur, vidēmur, vidēminī, videntur.*

Let's conjugate our fourth conjugation verb, I'm skipping the third. Our fourth conjugation verb: *sentiō, sentīre,* in the present passive indicative: *sentior, sentīris, sentītur, sentīmur, sentīminī, sentiuntur.* What vowel appears before the endings? Long ī. Let's do it again: *sentior, sentīris, sentītur, sentīmur, sentīminī, sentiuntur.*

The first, second, and fourth conjugations, whose theme vowels are long, carry their theme vowels throughout their conjugations consistently. The third conjugation, however, characterized by a short e is, as you know, a little fussier. Let's conjugate our third conjugation verb, *pono, ponere,* in the present passive indicative: *pōnor, pōneris, pōnitur, pōnimur, pōniminī, pōnuntur.* What vowel appears before the endings? An "uh" sound, variously represented as short ī, a short e, or a u. Let's do it again: *pōnor, pōneris, pōnitur, pōnimur, pōniminī, pōnuntur.*

And, finally, let's conjugate our third -io verb, *capio, capere,* in the present passive indicative: *capior, caperis, capitur, capimur, capiminī, capiuntur.* What vowel appears before the endings? Again, an "uh" sound, variously represented as a short i, a short e, or a u. Let's do it again: *capior, caperis, capitur, capimur, capiminī, capiuntur.*

I have good news. The subjunctive is even more regular. Please have a look at the chart. Again, our six endings, *r, ris, tur, mur, minī, ntur.* They appear with comforting consistency. On the other hand, whereas we observed four theme vowels in the indicative, here we find just two. First conjugation verbs change the indicative theme vowel a to a subjunctive e. And all the rest of the conjugations? They all use the vowel a.

You don't believe me? Okay, Let's go through them all, starting with the indicative, I am loved: *amor.* Compare the subjunctive I may be loved: *amer.* What vowel do we find in the subjunctive? e. Indicative, you are loved: *amāris*; subjunctive, you may be loved: *amēris.* Indicative a was changed to subjunctive e. Indicative, he, she, or it is loved: *amātur*; subjunctive, He, she, or it may be loved: *amētur.* Again, a changes to e. Indicative, We are loved: *amāmur*; subjunctive, we may be loved: *amēmur.* Indicative a changes to subjunctive e. Indicative, y'all are loved: *amāminī*; subjunctive, y'all may be loved: *amēminī.* A changes to e. Indicative, they are loved: *amantur*; subjunctive, they may be loved: *amentur.* What was an a shows up as e. And that, I submit, is the power of a single vowel. From indicative to subjunctive. And passive to boot. After all that work, it's time to enjoy. Please repeat the present tense passive subjunctive of *amo* after me: *amer, ameris, ametur, amemur, amemini, amentur.*

And the fun does not have to stop at the first conjugation. All the other conjugations use a to signal the subjunctive mood. Let's check it out. Second conjugation: *videor, videre* becomes *videor.* Let's not forget to retain that e we see before the o of the first principal part *videō.* Indicative *vidēris* becomes the subjunctive *videāris.* Indicative *vidētur* becomes subjunctive *videātur*. Indicative *vidēmur* becomes subjunctive *videāmur*. Indicative *vidēminī* becomes subjunctive *videāminī*. And indicative *videntur* becomes subjunctive videantur. What were our endings? *r, ris, tur, mur, minī, ntur*. And our subjunctive theme vowel? an a. Again, it's time to enjoy. Please repeat the present tense passive subjunctive of video after me: *videar, videaris, videatur, videamur, videamini, videantur*.

The third conjugation verb, *pōnō*, you should know very well by now. Just note the familiar passive endings: *r, ris, tur, mur, minī, ntur*, and note also that one, that powerful, that single, subjunctive theme vowel—a. Third -io *capior* becomes... in the first person singular? *capiar*. And please, please don't forget that we retain the i that we find before the o in the first principal part for the third -io verbs. So, in the second person singular, indicative, where we found *caperis*, it becomes the subjunctive, retaining that i, *capiāris*; *capitur*, retaining that i, becomes *capiātur*. *capimur*, an indicative, becomes, in the subjunctive, *capiāmur*. *Capiminī* in the indicative becomes, in the subjunctive, *capiāminī*. And *capiuntur* becomes *capiantur*. Did our endings change? No. They remained *r, ris, tur, mur, minī, ntur*. And what changed our mood from indicative to subjunctive? The single, the powerful, the subjunctive theme vowel a.

Shall we conjugate the present passive subjunctive of *capiō* together? Yes! On the count of three, *unus, duo, unus, duo, tres: capiar, capiaris, capiatur, capiamur, capiamini, capiantur*. And the fourth conjugation? Again, please, please, don't forget to retain the i that we find before the o of the first principal part. The indicative *sentior* becomes the subjunctive *sentiar*; *sentīris* becomes *sentiāris*; *sentītur*, it's indicative, becomes subjunctive *sentiātur*; *sentīmur* becomes *sentiāmur*; *sentīminī* becomes *sentiāminī*; *sentiuntur* becomes *sentiantur*. And our personal endings remained? *r, ris, tur, mur, minī, ntur*. What vowel changed the mood from all matter of fact to all pointing things out, all indicative to conditional; hesitating, doubt, subjunctive? The vowel a.

On the count of three let's conjugate this fourth conjugation verb in the present passive subjunctive, *unus, duo, unus, duo, tres: sentiar, sentiaris, sentiatur, sentiamur, sentiamini, sentiantur*. You have chanted, oh skeptical ones. You have seen, but do you believe? Can I get a witness? What vowel changes the mood of the verb from indicative to subjunctive for the second, the third, the son of a third (that's the third -io), and the fourth conjugations? Yes, the vowel a, the subjunctive vowel par excellence. It's really that simple, my friends. Latin follows its own rules.

Now, as much pure pleasure as Latin morphology offers, these endings can also help us make sense of authentic Latin texts, so let's explore some particularly passive examples. We may start at the beginning in Genesis, oddly enough, in the midst of creation, to find a passive verb, but it's all how we view the action. Here is the first part of Genesis 1:9: *dīxit vērō Deus: congregentur aquae ... in locum ūnum.* That's not classical Latin. This is late antique Latin that mimics the speech of the *vulgus*, or crowd, hence the term "vulgar Latin." And for this translation of the Bible, we call it the Vulgate. *Dīxit* we may gloss as he, she, or it spoke, but look a little further and you will find a subject, *Deus*, a word that you may recall signifies God. God said *vērō*. *Vērō* derives from *vērus, vēra, vērum*, an adjective meaning "true." If we use it as a noun, which we can, it means "the true thing," and we can translate it as "truth." *vērō* is an ablative that means "in truth." We might translate "truly." You may find it interesting that our own adverb "very" derives from the Latin *vērē*, truly. We can try it out. Compare "Latin is truly interesting" to "Latin is very interesting." And, as is so often the case, English bleaches some of the original meaning. "Very" does not sound as "true" as truly.

At all events, so much for the first three words, "And God said in truth." But what did God say? *congregentur aquae.* You will need some vocabulary. *congregō, congregāre, congregavi, congregatum*, it's a verb that means gather together. We can compare our own English congregate. Conjugation identification? *congregō, congregāre*, o, followed by a-r-e? First. Let's parse the verb. Person? Third. Number: plural. Mood? It's first conjugation. Subjunctive, characterized by an e. Voice? Passive. Translation? they may or should be gathered together, but what if God were exhorting, giving some suggestions about the organization of the universe, as it were? Could we read this as a hortatory subjunctive? Yes, I think we might. How would we express that? "Let them be gathered together."

I wonder who they might be. Let's look at the next word: *aqua, aquae*, is a feminine word that means "water." To what declension does *aqua* belong? The genitive is in ae, so, yes, first declension. Let's decline: *unus, duo, unus, duo, tres, aqua, aquae, aquae, aquam, aqua, aquae, aquarum, aquīs, aquās, aquīs*. Three forms end in ae. The genitive singular, the dative singular, and the nominative plural. Let's try them out. Let them be gathered together "of the water." That does not make sense. Let's try the dative singular: Let them be gathered together "for the water." Possible, I suppose. Let's try the nominative plural, which means that we will have to read the waters (the *aquae*) as the subject of *congregentur:* "Let the waters (subject) be gathered together!" Could waters be the subject? Yes, indeed. *Ita vērō*: thus in truth. *Aquae* makes the most sense, so we'll call it nominative plural. In truth, God said, let the waters be gathered together! But where? *In unum locum.*

In is a preposition that, with the accusative case, means "into." *Locus, locī*, is a masculine noun that means place. What is the case of *locum?* I don't know what you decided, but I'm going with accusative singular—*in locum*, "into place." But into which place? *ūnus, a, um* means "one," so *in unum locum* means "into one place." Shall we put it together? Let's read it again in Latin first. Please repeat after me: *dīxit vērō Deus: congregentur aquae ... in locum ūnum.* "In truth God said: let the waters be gathered together into one place!" But who did the work? God said that the waters should be gathered together. And according to the story, the waters were, indeed, gathered together. But who actually did the gathering? That, my friends, is the beauty of the passive. The agent, or doer, is not always expressed. The passive voice helps God to work in mysterious ways.

Later, God populates the planet, and eventually, the Romans arrive. The arrival of the Romans takes place outside the Old Testament, but, if you read the New Testament, you can find quite a few Romans.

Now we took our first passage very slowly, parsing everything along the way. In our concluding passage, I would like to push you a bit through some authentic and relatively complex Latin. Why? To show you just how skilled you are, whether you know it or not. And, as long as we began with a divine topic, let's turn to a Roman god, Julius Caesar. Caesar was, as you may recall, legally deified after his assassination. Temples were build. Romans worshipped him. Greeks worshipped him. Jews, and later Christians, refused to worship him. And then, as time went by, many of the subsequent Caesars were likewise worshipped as gods. How could anyone have ever believed in such a god? We don't have time to pursue that topic, but let's look at a prayer to a Caesar named Tiberius, the Caesar who happened to be in power when the, then obscure, but famous Judean provincial Jesus was crucified by command of a Roman procurator.

Valerius Maximus opens his *Memorable Deeds and Sayings,* his *Facta et Dicta Memorabilia,* with a prayer to this Caesar, whom we call Tiberius. Please repeat after me: *Tē, Caesar, invocō, cuius caelestī prōvidentiā virtūtēs…benignissimē foventur, vitia sevērissimē vindicantur. Tē,* means "you. It is accusative. *Invocō, invocāre,* means "call upon, invoke." Can you translate *Tē, Caesar, invocō?* "I invoke you, oh Caesar." An ancient prayer always required invocation of the correct deity because there were so many possibilities.

Let's go through the rest of the sentence word for word before putting everything together; *cuius* is a word you don't know and can't yet decline. It means "whose," and it is in the genitive case, showing possession of *caelestī providentiā,* celestial providence, if we just use our simple English derivatives, but, to use native English we can call it "heavenly foresight." You, however, *discipulī et discipulae,* should be able to tell me the case of *providentiā.* There's a macron over that a; it gives it away. Yes, ablative. How can we translate *caelestī providentiā* if it's ablative? "by, with, or from heavenly foresight." *Virtutes* are "virtues" or "moral qualities." If you think that *virtutes* looks third declension and plural, you are correct. *Benignissimē*; it means "most kindly." If a benign tumor is a nice tumor, and *begnissime,* which means most kindly, is even nicer.

Our next verb *foveō, fovēre,* means "cherish, foster, nourish." What is the conjugation? eo followed by long e-r-e, so second conjugation. Can you translate *foventur?* "They are cherished, they are fostered, or they are nourished." In our next word, *vitium, vitiī,* we see a neuter that means "vice." *Vitia,* vices, are the opposite of *virtutes,* virtues. *Sevērissimē* is another adverb. It means "most severely," so we would contrast with *Benignissimē,* "most kindly." And, finally, our last verb, *vindico, vindicare,* which we may translate as "punish," is what conjugation? First, so that a is indicative. Can you translate the form *vindicantur*? "They are punished." I think that you're ready for the whole passage. Let's break it down:

Tē, Caesar, invocō: I call upon you, Caesar.

cuius caelestī prōvidentiā: By whose (i.e., Caesar's) celestial foresight

virtūtēs...benignissimē foventur: Virtues are most kindly fostered

vitia sevērissimē vindicantur?: Vices are punished most severely.

Let's do it again.

Tē, Caesar, invocō,

cuius caelestī prōvidentiā

virtūtēs...benignissimē foventur,

vitia sevērissimē vindicantur.

You, Caesar, I invoke, by whose heavenly foresight virtues are fostered most kindly; vices are punished most severely. Long story short, Caesar is up there watching us. He knows who's been naughty, who's been nice. So be careful, my friends.

And with that, *omnēs linguae Latīnae amātōrēs,* you are free to go, so that you may learn Latin (*ut linguam Latīnam discātis*), and practice it on your own, before we meet again.

Grātiās vōbis agō! Et curāte, ut valeātis!

Third-Declension Adjectives
Lecture 14

In this lecture, we will revisit the third declension. We will review the endings for nouns and then turn our attention to third-declension adjectives, which are similar to, but not always exactly the same as, the endings for third-declension nouns. Compared to learning the third declension from scratch, what we face in this lecture is relatively small scale. As so often in Latin, there are patterns, and we'll identify those helpful patterns in this lecture.

Review: Third-declension masculine and feminine noun endings

	Singular	Plural
Nominative	***	-ēs
Genitive	-is	-um
Dative	-ī	-ibus
Accusative	-em	-ēs
Ablative	-e	-ibus

Review: Declension of *mīles* (third-declension masculine noun)

mīles, mīlitis, m.: soldier

	Singular	Plural
Nominative	mīles	mīlitēs
Genitive	mīlitis	mīlitum
Dative	mīlitī	mīlitibus
Accusative	mīlitem	mīlitēs
Ablative	mīlite	mīlitibus

Review: Neuter endings for third-declension nouns

	Singular	Plural
Nominative	***	-a
Genitive	-is	-um
Dative	-ī	-ibus
Accusative	***	-a
Ablative	-e	-ibus

Review: Declension of *corpus* (third-declension neuter noun)

corpus, *corporis*, n.: body

	Singular	Plural
Nominative	corpus	corpora
Genitive	corporis	corporum
Dative	corporī	corporibus
Accusative	corpus	corpora
Ablative	corpore	corporibus

Comparison: Regular third-declension noun and adjective endings

	3rd-Declension Masc. & Fem. Nouns	3rd-Declension Masc. & Fem. Adjectives	3rd-Declension Neuter Nouns	3rd-Declension Neuter Adjectives
Singular				
Nominative	*	*	*	*
Genitive	-is	-is	-is	-is
Dative	-ī	-ī	-ī	-ī
Accusative	-em	-em	*	*
Ablative	-e	-ī	-e	-ī
Plural				
Nominative	-ēs	-ēs	-a	-ia
Genitive	-um	-ium	-um	-ium
Dative	-ibus	-ibus	-ibus	-ibus
Accusative	-ēs	-ēs	-a	-ia
Ablative	-ibus	-ibus	-ibus	-ibus

- If we compare third-declension noun and adjective endings case by case, we see that nouns and adjectives of the third declension have the same endings in the nominative singular, genitive singular, dative singular, and accusative singular.

- Third-declension nouns and adjectives differ in the ablative singular. Adjectives use long ī, rather than a short ĕ. In truth, however, this confused even the Romans a bit. They would sometimes slip and use ĕ in the ablative singular where they should have used an ī or an ī where they should have used an ĕ, especially in inscriptions.

- Masculine and feminine nouns of the third declension have the same endings as third-declension adjectives in the nominative and accusative plurals: -ēs.

- Neuter nouns have nominative and accusative plurals ending in -*a*, and neuter adjectives have nominative and accusative plurals ending in -*ia*.

- In the genitive plural, third-declension nouns have -*um* as their ending. Adjectives have -*ium*.

- The dative and ablative plurals are the same for all genders of both nouns and adjectives: -*ibus*.

- Apart from the ablative singular, we could easily translate all third-declension adjectives on sight, even if we didn't understand why stray *i*'s appeared here and there.

Quiz

For the following lexical entries, provide the declension. Remember, we know the declensions of nouns by their genitives.

1. *puer, puerī*, m., boy

2. *bellum, bellī*, n., war

3. *servus, servī*, m., slave

4. *vulnus, vulneris*, n., wound

5. *nox, noctis*, f., night

6. *puella, puellae*, f., girl

7. *poeta, poetae*, m., poet

8. *senex, senis*, m., old man

Answers: 1. genitive ends in -ī, second-declension masculine; 2. genitive ends in -ī, second-declension neuter; 3. genitive ends in -ī, second-declension masculine; 4. genitive ends in -*is*, third-declension neuter; 5. genitive ends in -*is*, third-declension feminine; 6. genitive ends in -*ae*, first-declension feminine (the majority of first-declension nouns are feminine); 7. genitive ends in -*ae*, first-declension masculine (there are some first-declension masculine nouns; it is the genitive, not the gender, that dictates declension); 8. genitive ends in -*is*, third-declension masculine.

Declension of adjectives

- Adjectives appear in three genders because they need to be able to modify nouns of all three genders. How, then, do we recognize whether adjectives belong to the first and second declensions or to the third declension?

- If we see the endings -*a*, -*um*, the adjective is first and second declension. Consider the following examples:
  - **bonus, bona, bonum** (or, as it's more likely to appear in a dictionary: **bon•us, a, um,** *adj.*, good).
    Here, we're supposed to know that we put the endings -*a* and -*um* on the stem *bon-* to create the feminine and neuter forms. Note again that these endings are all nominative. Dictionaries generally list adjectives exclusively in the nominative (with some exceptions).

  - **līber, -a, -um,** *adj.*, free
    Sometimes, the masculine ends in -*r* rather than -*us* in the nominative. How would we say "the free girl"? *puella* lībera. "The free body"? *corpus* līberum. "The free soldier"? *mīles* līber. The giveaway is found in the endings -*a*, -*um*. Anytime we see three adjective endings concluding with -*a*, -*um*, the adjective will belong to the first and second declensions.

- Third-declension adjectives come in three varieties: with three endings, two endings, or one ending in the nominative singular. Indeed, the only place where third-declension adjectives sometimes differ from each other is in the nominative singular.

Third-declension adjectives, two endings (the most common variety)

facilis, facile: happy

	Singular		Plural	
	Masc. & Fem.	Neuter	Masc. & Fem.	Neuter
Nominative	facilis	facile	facilēs	facilia
Genitive	facilis	facilis	facilium	facilium
Dative	facilī	facilī	facilibus	facilibus
Accusative	facilem	facile	facilēs	facilia
Ablative	facilī	facilī	facilibus	facilibus

Third-declension adjectives, three endings

ācer, ācris, ācre: sharp, fierce

	Singular			Plural		
	Masc.	Fem.	Neuter	Masc.	Fem.	Neuter
Nominative	ācer	ācris	ācre	ācrēs	ācrēs	ācria
Genitive	ācris	ācris	ācris	ācrium	ācrium	ācrium
Dative	ācrī	ācrī	ācrī	ācribus	ācribus	ācribus
Accusative	ācrem	ācrem	ācre	ācrēs	ācrēs	ācria
Ablative	ācrī	ācrī	ācrī	ācribus	ācribus	ācribus

Third-declension adjectives, one ending

audāx, gen. audācis: bold

	Singular		Plural	
	Masc. & Fem.	**Neuter**	**Masc. & Fem.**	**Neuter**
Nominative	audāx	audāx	audācēs	audācia
Genitive	audācis	audācis	audācium	audācium
Dative	audācī	audācī	audācibus	audācibus
Accusative	audācem	audāx	audācēs	audācia
Ablative	audācī	audācī	audācibus	audācibus

- When we reflect on the patterns of third-declension adjectives, we can conclude that the problems, such as they may be, appear only in the nominative singular. Again, that is why we call the nominative "blank." Once we get past that "blank," the rest of the declension is quite regular.

- Apart from the mysteries of the nominative singular, third-declension adjectives are actually somewhat simpler than first- and second-declension adjectives. The endings are the same for all genders except in the nominative and accusative. Masculine and feminine nouns share the accusative singular ending -*em*, and the nominative and accusative plural share the ending -ēs. Neuters have no endings in particular in the nominative and accusative singular and -*ia* in the nominative and accusative plurals.

Quiz
For the phrase "brief light," provide the Latin in the case indicated.

1. nominative: the brief light sets

2. genitive: of the brief light

3. dative: to or for the brief light

4. accusative: I glimpse the brief light.

5. ablative: by, with, or from the brief light

Answers: 1. *brevis lūx*, 2. *brevis lūcis*, 3. *brevī lūcī*, 4. *brevem lūcem*, 5. *brevī luce.*

For the phrase "brief lights," provide the Latin in the case indicated.

1. nominative: the brief lights set

2. genitive: of the brief lights

3. dative: to or for the brief lights

4. accusative: I glimpse the brief lights.

5. ablative: by, with, or from the brief lights

Answers: 1. *brevēs luces*, 2. *brevium lūcum*, 3. *brevibus lūcibus*, 4. *brevēs luces*, 5. *brevibus lūcibus.*

For the phrase "strong body," provide the Latin in the case indicated.

1. nominative singular: The strong body glistens.

2. genitive: of the strong body

3. dative: to or for the strong body

4. accusative: I glimpse the strong body.

5. ablative: by, with, or from the strong body

Answers: 1. *corpus forte*, 2. *corporis fortis*, 3. *corporī fortī*, 4. *corpus forte*, 5. *corpore fortī.*

For the phrase "strong bodies," provide the Latin in the case indicated.

1. nominative: the strong bodies glisten

2. genitive: of the strong bodies

3. dative: to or for the strong bodies

4. accusative: I glimpse the strong bodies.

5. ablative: by, with, or from the strong bodies

Answers: 1. *corpora fortia*, 2. *corporum fortium*, 3. *corporibus fortibus*, 4. *corpora fortia*, 5. *corporibus fortibus*.

Verba

ācer, ācris, ācre: sharp, keen, fierce

audāx, gen. audācis: daring, bold

brevis, breve: brief, short

dolor, dolōris, m.: pain, grief

et … et: both … and

facilis, facile: easy, agreeable

faciō, facere, fēcī, factum: do, make, cause

fortis, forte: strong, brave

gignō, gignere, genuī, genitum: produce, beget, bring forth

lingua, linguae, f.: language, tongue

poēta, poētae, m.: poet

vir, virī, m.: man

vīta, vītae, f.: life

vulnus, vulneris, n.: wound

Please learn the third-declension adjective endings and the declension of
ācer, ācris, ācre, "sharp" (which may be found in App. §26).

Agenda

i. Decline the following noun-adjective combinations.

1. daring poet

2. strong man

3. sharp wound

ii. Please translate the following phrases into Latin. (Sometimes you will
need to use a preposition.)

1. of the easy language

2. to/for the fierce legions

3. under the beautiful sky

4. in great grief

5. by/with/from strong bodies

6. of the bold girls

7. short months (as subject)

8. by/with/from a strong mind

9. easy wars (direct object)

10. into the enemy's fierce city

iii. Translate the following sentences into English.

1. Vulnus mīlitī dolōrem facit.

2. Virtūtem fēminārum fortium laudēmus.

3. Ē dolōribus ācribus discī potest vēritās.

4. Ācrēs mentēs habent linguae Latīnae discipulī et discipulae.

5. Lūce sōlis flōrēs pulchrī gignuntur.

6. Ācrī in bellō virī fortēs bonīque caeduntur.

7. In locum miserum congregantur servae dominī ācris.

8. Fortēs este, puerī et puellae!

9. Deum aeternum, nōn vītam brevem, colāmus.

10. Vēritātem vidēre facile nōn est.

Third-Declension Adjectives
Lecture 14—Transcript

Salvēte, discipulī discipulaeque linguae Latīnae! Mihi valdē placet vōs pulchram linguam Latīnam aeternam docēre.

In this lesson, we revisit the third declension. We will review the endings for nouns and then turn our attention to third-declension adjectives, which are very similar to, but not always exactly the same, as the endings for third-declension nouns. On the other hand, compared to learning the third declension from scratch, what you face here is relatively small scale. We substitute an i in one place and insert a few other i's here and there, elsewhere. And that's about it. Of course, easy for me to say, yes. But, I will take you through it, and you'll see. As so often in Latin, there are patterns, and patterns are our friends.

Let us first review the third-declension noun endings. Can you recite third-declension endings for masculine and feminine nouns? Please repeat after me in the singular: *blank, is, ī, em, e;* and in the plural: *ēs, um, ibus, ēs, ibus.* Again: *blank, is, ī, em, e, ēs, um, ibus, ēs, ibus.* And all together at one go, from *blank,* all the way to *ibus. Unus duo, unus, duo, tres*: *blank, is, ī, em, e, ēs, um, ibus, ēs, ibus.*

Let us decline our loyal soldier. I will review what we know about the uses of the cases in English. Your job is to provide the appropriate form of soldier in Latin:

nominative, the soldier verbs: *mīles*

genitive, of the soldier: *mīlitis*

What is our stem? We remove the genitive ending -is, and, *voila*, the stem, *mīlit.*

We may continue.

dative, to or for the soldier: *mīlitī*

accusative, verb the soldier: *mīlitem*

ablative, by, with, or from the soldier: *mīlite*

And the plural:

nominative, the soldiers verb: *mīlitēs*

genitive, of the soldiers: *mīlitum*

dative, to or for the soldiers: *mīlitibus*

accusative, verb the soldiers: *mīlitēs*

ablative, by, with, or from the soldiers: *mīlitibus*

And now, let us review the neuter endings for third-declension nouns. Please repeat after me, first the singular: *blank, is, ī, blank, e*; And in the plural: *a, um, ibus, a, ibus*. Again, *blank, is, ī, blank, e*. And: *a, um, ibus, a, ibus*.

Let us decline the neuter word "body," which is neuter in Latin. "Body" in the nominative is *corpus*. What is the stem? We examine the genitive. The genitive of *corpus* is *corporis*. Now we remove the genitive, is, and *voila*, the stem, *corpor*. Let us decline, I'll provide the English; please provide the Latin, as you are willing and able:

nominative, the body verbs: *corpus*

genitive, of the body: *corporis*

dative, to or for the body: *corporī*

accusative, verb the body. There is no ending to attach to the stem, so the word reverts to its nominative form: *corpus*. But don't forget to bring the stem back for the next case, where we do have an ending:

ablative, by, with, or from the body: *corpore*

So much for the singular. Let's take a look at the plural:

nominative, the bodies verb: *corpora*

genitive, of the bodies*: corporum*

dative, to or for the bodies: *corporibus*

accusative, verb the bodies: *corpora*

ablative, by, with, or from the bodies: *corporibus*

Let's decline *corpus* from the nominative singular, *corpus*, to ablative plural, *corporibus*, on the count of three, *unus, duo, unus, duo, tres:*

corpus

corporis

corporī

corpus

corpore

corpora

corporum

corporibus

corpora

corporibus

So much by way of review. Let us now compare regular third-declension noun endings to regular third-declension adjective endings. If we compare third-declension noun and adjective endings case by case, we see that nouns and adjectives of the third declension have the same endings in the nominative singular, the genitive singular, the dative singular, and the accusative singular. They differ, however, in the ablative singular. Adjectives use long ī, pronounced "ee," rather than short e. Truth be told, however, this confused even the Romans a bit. They would sometimes slip, and use e in the ablative singular, especially in inscriptions. Language is not always as regular as we would like, and sometimes we forget to follow the rules. Let's put it this way, if you learn that ablative singulars can sometimes appear as ī, you will not be thrown off by an ablative in e, even if you fail to notice it, so learn the rule, and enjoy the exceptions.

And in the plural? Masculine and feminine nouns of the third declension have the same endings as third-declension adjectives in the nominative and accusative plurals. They all end in ēs. Neuter nouns have nominative and accusative plurals in a, neuter adjectives in i-a. We insert an i before the a. In the genitive plural, third-declension nouns have u-m as their ending. Adjectives, again, have an i, i-u-m. They insert an i before the u-m. The dative and ablative plurals, however, are the same for all genders of both nouns and adjectives. They all have the form *ibus*.

Apart from the ablative singular, you could easily translate all third-declension adjectives on sight, even if you did not understand why stray i's were appearing here and there. In fact, you've already seen examples of third-declension adjectives; I just did not want to tell you; I did not want to burden you with so much knowledge at the time.

But as long as I burden you now with knowledge, let's review how adjectives, as opposed to nouns, are presented as lexical entries in a dictionary. How can one know to what declension a noun or adjective belongs? As you know, nouns come in one gender, except when they come in two, as for example, *canis*, dog, which can refer to a male dog or a female dog. But, apart from such exceptions, nouns come in one gender only, and we know the declension by the genitive. Let's review. I'll give you some lexical entries, and you, you tell me the declension: *puer, puerī,* masculine, boy. The genitive ends in i, so *puer* is what declension? Second.

bellum, bellī, neuter, war. The genitive ends in i. What's the declension? Second.

servus, servī, masculine, slave. The genitive ends in i. So what's the declension? Second.

vulnus, vulneris, neuter, wound. The genitive ends in *is*. So what's the declension? Third. It will remain third no matter how much *vulnus* looks like *servus* in the nominative.

Here's the next:

nox, noctis, feminine, night. The genitive ends in *is,* so *nox* is third declension, third declension feminine.

puella, puellae, feminine, girl. The genitive ends in ae, so *puella* is first declension, first declension feminine. And as you've learned, the vast majority of first-declension nouns are feminine. But, *poeta, poetae,* masculine, poet. The genitive, however, still ends in ae, So *poeta* is what declension? First. Again, there are some first-declension masculine nouns too. But it's the genitive, not the gender, that dictates declension.

senex, senis, masculine, old man. The genitive ends in is. So *senex* is what declension? Third.

Lesson? By their genitives ye shall know them. By their genitives ye shall know the declensions of nouns. Adjectives, however, are different. They appear in three genders. They appear in three genders because in order to remain agreeable, they need to be able to modify nouns of all three genders.

So how do we recognize whether adjectives belong, on the one hand, to the first and second declensions, or, on the other, to the third declension? The answer: *a, um.* If you see *-a, -um* the adjective will be first and second declension. Why do I not say -us -a -um? Because sometimes it's *-r -a –um.* Here are some examples of first- and second-declension adjectives:

bonus, bona, bonum. Or, as it's more likely to appear in a dictionary: **bon•us, a, um,** *adj.,*

good. You, dear dictionary interpreters, are supposed to know that you put the endings a and um on the stem bon to create the feminine and neuter forms. Note again that these endings are all nominative. Dictionaries generally list adjectives exclusively in the nominative, except, of course, when they don't, but not to worry, I will explain all. Here's another adjective: **līber, -a, -um,** *adj.,* free. Sometimes the masculine ends in r rather than us in the nominative. How would you say the free girl? *puella lībera,* the free body; *corpus līberum,* the free soldier; *mīles līber,*

-a, -um is the give-away. Any time you see three adjective endings concluding with *-a, -um,* the adjective will belong to the first and second declensions.

But what about third-declension adjectives? Third-declension adjectives come in three varieties. Three endings, two endings, or one ending. And these numbers refer to the number of endings in the nominative singular. Indeed, the only place where third declension adjectives sometimes differ from each other is in the nominative singular. Why the variety? Can you say "blank"? Can you say "masculine," "feminine," "neuter?" The blank means that the nominative is unpredictable, a wild card. But it's not that wild. There are only three genders, and thus only three possibilities, so it's not as bad as it sounds. Let's look at the three types.

The most common variety of third-declension adjectives has two endings, one for the masculine and feminine, on the one hand, and another for the neuter, on the other. Let's try an easy one. **facil•is, e,** *adj.,* easy. We stare in dismay. We fail to find a comforting and familiar *-a, -um.* We conclude with alarm (that will subside with practice) that this adjective belongs to the third declension. Now what do we do?

Let's begin with the nominative. *Facilis* represents the masculine and feminine singular nominative. An easy or facile boy? *Puer facilis.* An easy or facile girl? *Puella facilis.* What about the neuter? An easy or facile war? *Bellum facile.* And after that? We use regular gender-appropriate third-declension adjective endings. If you examine our chart for the third-declension adjectives of two endings, you can see that the masculine and feminine forms are identical everywhere. We note again that an i appears in the ablative singular, and an i-u-m in the genitive plural. And when we turn to the neuter column, we see these endings plus an additional i-a for the neuter nominative and accusative plurals.

Let's try something sharp, an adjective of three endings: *ācer, ācris, ācre,* adjective, sharp, fierce. Here the information is more subtle; *ācer* is masculine, *ācris* is feminine, and *ācre* is neuter. But what is the genitive for each? The disappearance of the e before the r in the feminine and neuter nominatives tells us that the stem is actually ā-c-r, so the genitive for all three will be *ācris,* ā-c-r-i-s. Let's look at our chart for adjectives of three endings. All the adjective endings have been attached to the base ā-c-r. We can also see that masculine and feminine forms are identical with the exception of one form, the nominative singular. Once again we note, an ī in the ablative singular, an i before the u-m in the genitive plural, and, in the neuter column, an additional i-a in the neuter and nominative accusative plurals.

Finally, let's look at a daring third-declension adjective with just one ending in the nominative, *audāx, genitive, audācis, adjective,* daring, bold. Because it is unusual to provide the genitive of an adjective, the dictionary will generally spell it out. The dictionary is trying to say, "Hey, this is an adjective, but we're giving you the genitive, so you'll know that it's third declension, but you're on your own for the rest of it!" This is where the burden of your knowledge about third-declension genitives comes into play. Genitive in is, check; the declension, third. The stem is *audāc,* a-u-d-a-c, as in audacious. And there's one nominative form.

Let's take a look at our chart for this third-declension adjective of one ending. All the nominatives are *audāx.* A bold boy? *Puer audāx.* A bold girl? *Puella audāx.* A bold war? *Bellum audāx.* And after that? The genitive is *audācis* for all three: of the bold boy, *puerī audācis;* of the bold girl, *puellae audācis;* of the bold war, *bellī audācis.* I think that we're on our way. Please examine the chart more closely. Where do the masculine and feminine forms differ? Nowhere. Do we see an singular ablative in i? Yes. Do we see a genitive plural in i-u-m? Yup. What about the neuter? Do the nominative and accusative plurals have i-a? Yes they do. So what was the big deal? The nominative singular is the same for all three genders. And, as is customary for all neuters, the accusative neuter singular is the same as the nominative neuter singular. Is it a trick? No, not at all. Just use regular third-declension adjective endings, and attach them to the stem *audāc.*

When we reflect on the patterns of third-declension adjectives, we can conclude that the problems, such as they may be, appear only in the nominative singular. And again, that is why we call the nominative *"blank."* I could have called the nominative, "your guess is as good as mine." But, once we get past that *"blank,"* the rest of the declension is quite regular. Yes. it would be nice if the dictionaries gave us the nominatives *and* genitives of adjectives, but space was limited back in the day, so they always aimed to save ink and paper, thus imposing on you, my Latin friends, the burden of knowing how to interpret the mysteries of lexical entries. So why do our electronic dictionaries not provide fuller information? Force of habit, I suppose. There are some websites that do, but we'll talk about those later.

At all events, apart from the mysteries of the nominative singular, third-declension adjectives are actually somewhat simpler than first- and second-declension adjectives. The endings are the same for all genders, except in the nominative and accusative. Masculine and feminine nouns share the accusative singular, em, and nominative and accusative plural endings ēs. Neuters have no endings, in particular in the nominative and accusative singular, and i-a in the nominative and accusative plurals. Let's recite these endings. We will begin with masculine and feminine third-declension adjective endings. Please repeat after me in the singular:

blank, is, ī, em, ī; and now in the plural: *ēs, ium, ibus, ēs, ibus.*

And one more time: *blank, is, ī, em, ī;* And in the plural: *ēs, ium, ibus, ēs, ibus.*

And let us review the third-declension adjective endings for the neuter. Please repeat after me in the singular:

blank, is, ī, blank ī; and now in the plural: *ia, ium, ibus, ia, ibus.*

And where do these neuter adjective endings differ from their third-declension noun counterparts? Rather than an e in the ablative singular, we find long i; and we find an i before a in the nominative and accusative plurals, and an i before um in the genitive plural. It's not that bad. Let's chant the neuter third-declension adjective endings one more time: *blank, is, ī, blank ī.* And in the plural: *ia, ium, ibus, ia, ibus.*

And, after all this abstraction, let's sink our teeth into a real declension, and then, with what time remains, look at some authentic Latin, so you can observe how easily we can sail through these endings. Remember when Catullus talked about a "brief light"? *Cum semel occidit brevis lūx?* "When once this brief light has set?" We can now decline *brevis lūx*! Please, please contain your excitement. "Brief" would be listed in the dictionary something like this: *brevis, breve*, adjective, *brief*. Did you see an a, um? *Minime!* What is the declension? *Brevis* is a third-declension adjective. Of how many endings? There were two forms, so there are two adjective endings in the nominative singular. Which of the two forms is used to modify both masculine feminine nouns? *brevis*. And which of those two forms would modify neuter nouns? *breve*. You are clever, my students.

lūx, lūcis, is a feminine noun. To what declension does *lux* belong? Its genitive ends in is, so lux is a third-declension feminine noun. And what is the stem? *lūc*. I guess it's your lūc-y day.

I'll provide the English. Please provide the Latin. I will begin:

nominative, singular: the brief light sets: And you were supposed to provide the Latin. *brevis lūx*

Let's try the next,

genitive, singular: of the brief light: *brevis lūcis*

dative: to or for the brief light: *brevī lūcī*

accusative: I glimpse the brief light: *brevem lūcem*

So far, so good. All the endings have been the same.

ablative, singular: by, with, or from the brief light: *brevī luce*

Did you put a long i on the adjective *brevi* and a short e on the noun *luce*? Did I not tell you this was exciting?

Let's do the plural. I'll do the English. You try the Latin.

nominative: the brief lights set: *brevēs lūcēs*

genitive: of the brief lights: *brevium lūcum*

Again, total excitement. An i before the um for the adjective *brevium*, and no i before the um for the noun *lūcum. brevium lūcum.* Wow. Gather yourselves together. We're moving on to the dative.

to or for the brief lights: *brevibus lūcibus*

accusative: I glimpse the brief lights: *brevēs lūcēs*

ablative: by, with, or from the brief lights: *brevibus lūcibus*

And because you were so good, I'm going to let you decline a neuter third-declension adjective too. And the neuter is definitely more exciting. Let's try a strong body. But first our vocabulary. *Fortis, forte* is a third-declension adjective of two endings. What is the neuter form? *forte. Corpus, corporis* is a noun with a genitive in is, so it, too, as you know, belongs to the third declension. Its stem is *corpor.* Can we decline? I'll provide the English cues, and you go to town in Latin:

nominative singular: The strong body glistens: *corpus forte* genitive: of the strong body: *coporis fortis*

dative: to or for the strong body: *corporī fortī*

accusative: I glimpse the strong body: *corpus forte*

Neuters are the same, of course, in the accusative and nominative singulars.

ablative: by, with, or from the strong body: *corpore fortī*. Bingo.

ablative noun *corpore* in short e and ablative adjective *forti* in long i.

On to the plural:

nominative: the strong bodies glisten: *corpora fortia*

an i before a for the adjective, *fortia*, but no i before the a for the noun, *corpora*.

genitive: of the strong bodies: *corporum fortium*

Again, i before the um, for the adjective, *fortium*, but no i before the um for the noun, *corporum*.

dative: to or for the strong bodies: *corporibus fortibus*

accusative: I glimpse the strong bodies: *corpora fortia*

Deja vu, anyone?: i before the a for the adjective, *fortia*, but no i before the a for the noun, *corpora*.

And finally, ablative:

by, with, or from the strong bodies: *corporibus fortibus*

Recognition is much easier than composition. It's easier to recognize endings than apply or attach them correctly to stems. That's the good news because the Romans tended to put them on automatically and without much thought. Why? Latin was their native language. So let's look at a few examples. I want to reward you for your third-declension labors.

But wait, alas, *mea culpa, tempus fugit.* We're out of time. *Ignoscite mihi*! *Ita potestis, linguae Latīnae amātōrēs, nunc exīre, ut linguam Latīnam discātis. Grātiās vōbis agō et, dōnec nōs iterum vīderimus,* until we meet again, *cūrāte, ut valeātis!*

Third-Declension *I*-Stem Nouns
Lecture 15

In the last lecture, we looked at third-declension adjectives. This puts us in a good position for learning about another class of third-declension nouns: third-declension *i*-stems. Of course, we call them *i*-stems because the letter *i* appears in some forms where regular third-declension nouns don't have it. In fact, *i*-stem nouns look very much like third-declension adjectives. The question is: How can we tell which third-declension nouns are *i*-stems? We can't tell them apart by their genitives, but in this lecture, we'll learn the secrets of recognizing them.

Comparison: Endings of regular third-declension nouns, third-declension *i*-stem nouns, and third-declension adjectives

	3rd-Declension M&F Nouns	3rd-Declension M&F Adjectives	3rd-Declension M&F I-stem Nouns	3rd-Declension Neuter Nouns	3rd-Declension Neuter Adjectives	3rd-Declension Neuter I-stem Nouns
Singular						
Nominative	*	*	*	*	*	*
Genitive	-is	-is	-is	-is	-is	-is
Dative	-ī	-ī	-ī	-ī	-ī	-ī
Accusative	-em	-em	-em	*	*	*
Ablative	-e	-ī	-e	-e	-ī	-ī
Plural						
Nominative	-ēs	-ēs	-ēs	-a	-ia	-ia
Genitive	-um	-ium	-ium	-um	-ium	-ium
Dative	-ibus	-ibus	-ibus	-ibus	-ibus	-ibus
Accusative	-ēs	-ēs	-ēs	-a	-ia	-ia
Ablative	-ibus	-ibus	-ibus	-ibus	-ibus	-ibus

- The nominative case is a blank in the singular. We can't predict the nominative ending of a third-declension noun or third-declension adjective.

- The genitive case, in contrast, is completely regular in the singular. We find the ending -ĭs across the board. The dative singular is likewise completely regular; we find -ī across the board.

- The accusative singular, too, is completely regular. For masculine and feminine nouns and adjectives, the ending is -*em*. For neuter nouns and adjectives, the accusative is the same as the nominative.

- In the ablative singular, we find either a short -ĕ or a long -ī. All third-declension masculine and feminine nouns, including *i*-stem nouns, have an *e* in the ablative singular. Regular third-declension neuter nouns also have an *e* in the ablative singular. Third-declension adjectives, however, and third-declension *i*-stem neuter nouns have an ī in the ablative singular.

- The points to remember here are that adjectives and neuter *i*-stem nouns have an ī in the ablative singular. In all other respects, regular third-declension nouns, *i*-stem nouns, and third-declension adjectives have identical endings in the singular.

- In the plural, masculine and feminine nouns and adjectives all show -ēs in the nominative and accusative plurals. Dative and ablative plurals all end in -*ibus*.

- We find an *i* in front of the *a* for neuter plural adjectives and an *i* in front of the *a* for neuter plural nominatives and accusative *i*-stem nouns. We also find an *i* in front of the *u* in the genitive plural ending -*um* for third-declension adjectives, and we find an *i* in front of the -*um* for all *i*-stem nouns, whether masculine, feminine, or neuter.

- To summarize, masculine and feminine third-declension *i*-stem nouns insert an *i* in front of the *u* of the genitive plural -*um*. That is the only difference between a regular third-declension noun and an *i*-stem noun of the third declension, at least for masculine and feminine nouns. Neuter nouns of the third declension look like third-declension neuter adjectives. They insert an *i* in the ablative singular, as well as an additional *i* in front of the *a* in the nominative plural, an *i* in front of the -*um* of the genitive plural, and an *i* in front of the -*a* of the accusative plural.

Recognizing *i*-stem nouns

- How can we tell whether a noun belongs to the regular third declension or to the *i*-stem declension? Neuter *i*-stem nouns are easy to identify. If the nominative singular of a third-declension neuter noun ends in *e*, *al*, or *ar*, it is an *i*-stem. Examples include *animal, animalis,* "animal"; *exemplar, exemplāris,* "example"; and *mare, maris,* "sea."

- Below is a sample declension of *animal*, an *i*-stem neuter noun.

animal, animalis, n.: animal

	Singular	Plural
Nominative	animal	animālia
Genitive	animālis	animālium
Dative	animālī	animālibus
Accusative	animal	animālia
Ablative	animālī	animālibus

- The first clue to recognizing masculine and feminine nouns of the third declension *i*-stem is an -*is* or -*es* in the nominative singular, but another condition must also be satisfied. The masculine or feminine noun whose nominative ends in -*is* or -*es* must also have the same number of syllables in the genitive as it does in the nominative. Only then will the noun be a third-declension *i*-stem. Consider these examples:

- ○ *auris, auris,* f., ear

- ○ *hostis, hostis,* m., enemy

- ○ *nāvis, nāvis,* f., ship

- ○ *nūbēs, nūbis,* f., cloud

- All these nouns belong to the third declension because they have a genitive ending in -*is*. They are also *i*-stems because they have -*is* or -*es* in the nominative singular, they have the same number of syllables in the genitive singular, and are masculine or feminine. Where do we find the *i* of the *i*-stem? In the genitive plural. Other than the genitive plural, all the other forms of masculine and feminine *i*-stems look exactly like their regular third-declension counterparts.

- There is one other type of third-declension masculine and feminine *i*-stem noun: third-declension nouns that have one syllable in the nominative singular and end in the letter *s* or *x* and have a stem ending in two consonants in the genitive singular. Consider these examples:
  - ○ *ars, artis,* f., skill

  - ○ *dens, dentis,* m., tooth

  - ○ *nox, noctis,* f., night

  - ○ *urbs, urbis,* f., city

- All of these masculine and feminine nouns are monosyllabic in the nominative, which also ends in *s* or *x*. And all of them have a base in the genitive that ends in two consonants. Again, the genitive plural is the only place where a masculine or feminine *i*-stem differs from a regular third-declension noun.

- Are all monosyllabic nominatives that end in *s* or *x* and belong to the third declension also *i*-stems? Consider these two words:
  - *pax, pācis*, f., peace

  - *rēx, rēgis*, m., king

- Both words have *x* in the nominative singular, and both are monosyllables in the nominative singular. But let's look at the stems. The stem of *pācis* is *pāc-* and the stem of *rēgis* is *rēg-*. These stems end in one, not two, consonants, so they are not *i*-stems but regular third-declension nouns.

Parsing Cato the Elder
- The elder Cato (234–149 B.C.E.) is famous for his advocacy of conservative Roman values and his denunciation of Greek literature and philosophy, which he considered degenerate.
  - His historical works survive only in a few fragments, but we do have his handbook on farming, *Dē Agrī cultūrā*, which is full of advice on how to run a farm, the only fit occupation, in Cato's opinion, for an honest Roman man. Cato tells us: *Ex agricolīs et virī fortissimī et mīlitēs strenuissimī gignuntur.*

  - Parsing this sentence, we find: "From farmers both the bravest men and the most vigorous soldiers are produced."

- Elsewhere in his handbook, Cato advocates taking care of the livestock: *bovēs maximā dīligentiā cūrāte*, meaning "Take care of the cows with the greatest diligence!"

- Another gem from Cato's *Dē Agrīcultūrā* is this: *plostrum vetus, ferrementa vetera, servum senem, servum morbōsum ... vendat pater familiās*, meaning "Let the head of household sell an old plow, old tools, an old slave, and the sick slave."

Verba

animal, animālis, n.: animal

ars, artis, f.: art, skill

auris, auris, f.: ear

dēns, dentis, m.: tooth

exemplar, exemplāris, n.: example

mare, maris, n.: sea

nāvis, nāvis, f.: ship

nūbēs, nūbis, f.: cloud

pāx, pācis, f.: peace (not an *i*-stem)

vōx, vōcis, f.: voice (not an *i*-stem)

Memoranda

Please learn the third-declension *i*-stem noun endings and the declensions of *hostis, hostis,* m., "enemy" (App. §19) and *animal, animālis,* n., "animal" (App. §19).

Agenda

i. Decline the following noun-adjective combinations.

1. great sea

2. large city

ii. Please translate the following sentences into English.

1. Pācem cupiunt fēminae urbis.

2. Hostēs nāvibus trāns (across) mare veniunt, ut bellum magnum agant.

3. Vēritās sentīrī ā virīs miserīs nōn potest.

4. In silvā (forest) sunt animālia ācria, sed nocte ā mīlite Caesaris custōdior.

5. Dolōrem noctium perpetuārum vincāmus!

6. Rūmōrēs ā rēge bonō nōn audiuntur.

iii. Translate the following sentences into Latin.

1. The great poet is praising the skill of the young woman.

2. Let him cease to wage war, and let us live in peace joyfully. (Rather than use an adverb, Latin will make *laetus* agree with the subject of the verb.)

3. Many animals are being sold by the other farmer.

4. The old man cannot hear the master's voice.

5. The slaves are being gathered together in large ships by the commander of the legions.

Third-Declension *I*-Stem Nouns
Lecture 15—Transcript

Salvēte, discipulī discipulaeque linguae Latīnae! Mihi valdē placet vōs iterum vidēre et pulchram linguam Latīnam aeternam docēre.

In the last lesson, we looked at third-declension adjectives. This puts us in a good position for learning about another class of third-declension nouns, third-declension i-stems. Why do we call them i-stems? Well, you guessed it: the letter i appears in some forms where regular third-declension nouns don't have it. In fact, i-stem nouns look very much like third-declension adjectives. The question is, how can we tell which third-declension nouns are i-stems? Can we tell them apart by their genitives? No. I will have to initiate you into other deeper Latin secrets.

But before we learn how to identify an i-stem noun, let's compare the endings of regular third-declension nouns and third-declension i-stem nouns, and we'll compare them with third-declension adjectives too. As always, patterns will be our friends. And a chart can make this clear. Let's read the chart horizontally. The nominative case is a *blank*. We can't predict the nominative ending of a third-declension noun or a third-declension adjective. The genitive case, on the other hand, is completely regular in the singular. We find the short ending is across the board. The dative singular is, likewise, completely regular; we find a long *ī* across the board. The accusative singular, too, is completely regular. For masculine and feminine nouns and adjectives, the ending is em. For neuter nouns and adjectives, the accusative is the same as the nominative.

In the ablative singular, however, we encounter trouble. We find either a short e or a long *ī*. All third-declension masculine and feminine nouns, including i-stem nouns, have an e in the ablative singular. Third-declension adjectives, however, and third-declension i-stem neuter nouns have an *ī* in the ablative singular. The takeaway? Adjectives and neuter i-stem nouns have an *Ī* in the ablative singular. In all other respects, regular third-declension nouns, i-stem nouns, in third-declension adjectives have identical endings in the singular.

Let us proceed to the plural. Masculine and feminine nouns and adjectives are no problem. They all show ēs in the nominative and accusative plurals. Dative and ablative plurals all end in ibus. So where do the i's of the i-stem nouns occur? We find an i in front of the a for the neuter plural adjectives and an i in front of the a for neuter plural nominatives and accusative i-stem nouns. And we find an i in front of the u in the genitive plural ending of um for third-declension adjectives, and we find an i in front of the um for all i-stem nouns, whether masculine, whether feminine, or neuter.

Let us summarize our findings for i-stem nouns of the third-declension. Masculine and feminine third-declension i-stem nouns, insert an i in front of the u of the plural um. That's it. That is the only difference between a regular third-declension noun and an i-stem noun of the third-declension, at least for masculine and feminine nouns. Neuter nouns of the third-declension are a different story. They look like third-declension neuter adjectives. They insert an i in the ablative singular, as well as an additional i in front of the a in the nominative plural, an i in front of the um of the genitive plural, and an i in front of the a of the accusative plural.

It's time for your initiation. I'm going to reveal to you the mysteries of how to recognize an i-stem. How can we tell whether a noun belongs to the regular third-declension or to the i-stem declension? Neuter i-stem nouns are easy to identify. If the nominative singular of a third-declension neuter noun ends in e, an al, or an ar, it's an i-stem. Look at a few examples:

animal, animalis, neuter

exemplar, exemplāris, also neuter; it means example

mare, maris, neuter; it means sea

All three of these words are neuter third-declension. Why? They are neuter because the dictionary told us, so they're neuter, and, they have a genitive in is; that makes them third declension. Now let us examine the nominative form of each: *Animal* ends in al. Exemplar ends in ar. Mare ends in e. Because of these nominative endings: -al, -ar, and -e, we know that these neuter nouns are i-stems.

Let us decline animal. I'll provide the English. Please try to supply the Latin:

nominative, the animal verbs: *animal*

genitive, of the animal: *animālis*

What is our stem? We remove the genitive ending -is, and voila, the stem, *animāl*

We may continue...

dative, to or for the animal: *animālī*

accusative, verb the animal: *animal*

ablative, by, with, or from the animal: *animālī*

We used the alternative long-i ending for the ablative singular.

Things will be more exciting the plural:

nominative, the animals verb: *animālia*

genitive, of the animals: *animālium*

dative, to or for the animals: *animālibus*

accusative, verb the animals: *animālia*

ablative, by, with, or from the animals: *animālibus*

Masculine and feminine nouns of the third-declension i-stem are not nearly so exciting. Here's how to spot them. The first clue is when we see in is or in es in the nominative singular, but another condition must also be satisfied. The masculine or feminine noun whose nominative ends in is or es must also have the same number of syllables in the genitive as it does in the nominative. Only then, only then will the noun will be a third-declension i-stem. Let's look at some examples:

auris, auris, feminine, ear.

hostis, hostis, masculine, enemy

nāvis, nāvis, feminine, ship

nūbēs, nūbis, feminine, cloud

All of these nouns belong to the third-declension. Why? They have a genitive in is. They are also i-stems because they have an is or es in the nominative singular, they have the same number of syllables in the genitive singular, and are masculine or feminine. Where will we find the i of the i-stem? In the genitive plural. How do we say of genitive plural ears? *Aurium.* Did you hear the i before the u? Aurium, of the ears. How about, of the genitive plural enemies? *Hostium.* Of the genitive plural ships? *Nāvium.* Of the clouds? *Nūbium.* Other than the genitive plural, all the other forms of masculine and feminine i-stems look exactly like their regular third-declension counterparts.

But there is one other type of third-declension masculine and feminine i-stem noun. Third-declension nouns that have one syllable in the nominative singular and end in the letter s or x, and have a stem ending in two consonants in the genitive singular. Those nouns will follow the i-stem pattern. Did you get all of that? Well, let's look at some examples.

ars, artis, feminine, skill

dens, dentis, masculine, tooth

nox, noctis, feminine, night

urbs, urbis, feminine, city

All of these masculine and feminine nouns are monosyllabic in the nominative. The nominative case also ends in s or x. And all of them have a base in the genitive that ends in two consonants. We see rt, r is one consonant, t is another, that's two consonants, rt in the genitive of *artis*. We see nt in *dentis*, d-e-n-t. The stem ends in two consonants; ct in *noctis*, and rb in urbis. How, then, do we say of the skills? *Artium*. Of the teeth? *Dentium*. Of the nights? *Noctium*. Of the cities? *Urbium*. And, again, the genitive plural is the only place where a masculine or feminine i-stem differs from a regular old third-declension noun.

Are all monosyllabic nominatives that end in s or x and belong to the third-declension also i-stems? What about these two words?

pax, pācis, feminine, peace

rēx, rēgis, masculine, king

Both words have an x in the nominative singular. Both words are monosyllables in the nominative singular. But let's take a look at their stems. The stem of *pācis* is p-ā-c, and the stem of *rēgis* is r-ē-g. These stems end in one, not two, consonants, so they are not i-stems. They are plain old, regular third-declension nouns. So how do we say "of the kings"? *rēgum*.

This is fun, but as we don't have a lot of endings to drill, let's spend some time reading Latin, reviewing morphology, and expanding our knowledge of syntax. The cases, as we have mentioned, have uses. The ablative, for example, has the basic translations of "by, with, or from," but sometimes we translate "by means of" or "in respect of" or "in the manner of" or simply "in" or "at" or "during." Grammarians have helpfully devised names for these various uses, including, for example, the ablative of means, the ablative of manner, the ablative of agent, ablative of time within which, ablative of place where, ablative of respect or specification. Such terms help us understand how the ablative works. They do not translate Latin for us, however. It is, thus, useful to invoke them when they help us, but they are not always necessary. Most Romans certainly had no idea which ablatives they were using. They simply understood the words as they occurred, just as you understand me as I speak. You do not need to parse every single word I say. At all events, I will introduce such terms as an aid, but they will not be a goal in itself.

The elder Cato lived in the third and second centuries B.C.E., and he's most famous for a single line. First the English: Carthage must be destroyed! He ended every speech by saying, Carthage must be destroyed! The Latin: *Carthāgo dēlenda est.* Try it on for size. *Carthāgo dēlenda est.* This Roman politician is also famous, however, for his advocacy of conservative Roman values and his denunciation of Greek literature and philosophy, which he considered degenerate. His historical works survive only in a few fragments, but we do have his handbook on farming, *Dē Agrī cultūrā*, which is chock full of advice on how to run a farm, the only fit occupation, in Cato's opinion, for an honest Roman man. And he tells us why. Please repeat after me:

Ex agricolīs et virī fortissimī et mīlitēs strenuissimī gignuntur.

Ex is a preposition that takes the ablative. It means "from" or "out of." *Agricola, agricolae,* is a masculine word that means "farmer." You've seen it before. In what case are the farmers after *Ex*? Ablative. Why are they ablative? *Ex* takes the ablative. How would we translate that phrase, *Ex agricolīs*? "From ablative plural farmers." Though we probably wouldn't put "ablative plural" in there; "from farmers." The next word is *et*. One *et* means "and." Two *et*s, however, can coordinate words. So we can translate *et*, followed by something, another *et* as both and.

What are *virī*? *Vir, virī* is a masculine word that means "man," hence our own English "virile" or "manly" in English. And "virtue" too, which originally meant "manliness" in Latin, *virtus*, derives from man. It's actually an interesting bit of linguistic history that turned Roman *virtūs* or "manliness" into English "virtue," a moral quality frequently associated more with female chastity than manliness. Why the change? It has something to do with the conversion of the Roman empire to Christianity. But that's too long a story.

Vir, virī belongs to which declension? The genitive ends in i, so it's second declension. Let's decline *vir* together. On the count of three , *unus, duo, unus, duo, tres*: vir, viri, viro virum, viro, viri, virorum, viris, viros, viris.

What are our possibilities for the word *viri*? *Viri* can mean either "of the singular genitive man" or "the nominative plural men."

Fortissimus, -a, -um, is an adjective that means "most strong" or "most brave." *Fortissimi* modifies *virī*, so this man is, or these men are, most brave, most strong. We then see another *et* and *mīlitēs*. *Mīles, mīlitis*, is a third-declension masculine, and by itself could either be nominative or accusative. But the *mīlitēs are* modified by a second-declension adjective, *strenuissimus*, -a, -um, which means "most vigorous." Now, although *strenuissimi* can only be, if we look at it by itself, genitive singular or nominative plural, *mīlitēs* cannot be genitive singular, and *strenuissimi* cannot be accusative plural. So, by the process of elimination, if you have the charts in your head, the only way for the two words to agree is to read them as nominative plural, which means that we can go back and read the very brave men earlier in the sentence, the *virī fortissimī*, as nominative plural as well. So by having more than one declension, it actually helps the reader determine what indeterminate cases actually are.

Now all we need is a verb, and sure enough, it pops up at the end. *Gignuntur*. A nice third person plural passive that will conveniently agree with all the nominative plurals. If *gignō* means "I produce," and it does, what does *gignuntur* mean? Not "they produce," that would be active. No. we want the passive, "they are produced." Let's try the whole sentence:

Ex agricolīs et virī fortissimī et mīlitēs strenuissimī gignuntur.

From farmers both the bravest men and the most vigorous soldiers are produced. Farmers made the best soldiers in Cato's view. Farmers, citizens, soldiers. The Roman ideal. Cato also provided advice for citizen famers and advocated, for example, taking care of the livestock. Here's an injunction:

bovēs maximā dīligentiā cūrāte!

Please repeat after me: *bovēs maximā dīligentiā cūrāte!*

Our verb *cūrō, cūrāre, curāvī, curātum* means to take care of. To what conjugation does the verb belong? o, followed by a-r-e, so, first conjugation.

And what form is *cūrāte*? It's a plural command. What does Cato tell us to do? Take care of! Care for! What should be the direct object of our concern? The *bovēs*. *Bōs, bovis,* which can be masculine or feminine, means ox, bull, cow. Compare "bovine." *bovēs...cūrāte!* Take care of the oxen! *bovēs...cūrāte!* Take care of the cows! But how? *Dīligentiā maximā. Diligentia, diligentiae,* is a feminine word meaning "care, diligence." And *maximus, a, um,* is an adjective meaning "greatest." What is the case of *diligentiā?* Do you see the macron over the a? Yes, so it's ablative. Can we translate *diligentia maxima?* By or with the greatest diligence, carefulness, attentiveness, earnestness. We have an ablative that describes how we are to care for the cows: "with the greatest attentiveness." *bovēs maximā dīligentiā cūrāte!* Care for the cattle with the greatest attentiveness! *bovēs maximā dīligentiā cūrāte!* Take care of the cows with the greatest diligence! What kind of ablative is that? That's an ablative of manner, the manner in which we are to care for cows.

Now, it's very nice that Cato was concerned about cows. Shall we see what he has to say about the people on his farm? As you may know, Roman agriculture was built on the backs of slaves, whom the Romans captured in great abundance during their wars of conquest. In fact, when Caesar was busy conquering Gaul, he flooded the Roman market with so many Gauls that the whole bottom dropped out of the slave market. But that's another story. Please have a look at this gem from Cato's *Dē Agrīcultūra*:

plostrum vetus, ferrementa vetera, servum senem, servum morbōsum ... vendat pater familiās.

Let's read the sentence aloud in Latin again, looking for a verb and a subject.

plostrum vetus, ferrementa vetera, servum senem, servum morbōsum ... vendat pater familiās.

If you were sharp-eyed or sharp-eared, you spotted *vendat* as our only possible verb. Let's parse it. It ends in t, so it's third person singular. We cannot proceed, however, unless we look at the principal parts: *vendō, vendere, vendidī, venditum.* The verb means "sell." *Vendō* gives us such English words as "vendor, seller, vending machine," both of them rack up sales. What is the conjugation? We find an ō in the *vendo,* the first principal part, followed by a short e-r-e in, *vendere*, the second principal part. The conjugation is thus third.

Can the verb mean "he, she, or it sells"? No. That would be *vendit*. What does the vowel a tell us? This verb is subjunctive and used independently, so it's a hortatory subjunctive. That's our best bet. And how should we translate it? "Let him, let her, or let it sell." Now we need a subject, and we find one in *pater familiās*, literally, the father of the family, but a *familia* in ancient Rome was more than just mom, dad, and two kids. A Roman *familia* was extended, and included the slaves. A better translation is "head of the household" or "big boss" or "lord of the manor." The word may look like "family," but *familia* is actually hard to translate, so we frequently, in English, just say *paterfamiliās* to refer to a traditionally patriarchal and frequently authoritarian head of a household. *Vendat pater familiās*. Let's just call him the head of the household. What should the head of the household sell? *Vendat pater familiās*. Let the head of the household sell. Cato lists all the direct objects first.

Plostrum vetus. Plostrum, plostrī, is a neuter noun that means "plow." *Vetus* is a third-declension adjective with one ending in the nominative, namely *vetus*, and it means old. Its genitive is *veteris*. We have a few derivatives in English. Old soldiers are "veterans." An old problem is "inveterate." At any rate, what is a *plostrum vetus*? An old plow. And *ferrementa vetera?* If a *ferrementum* is a neuter singular tool, and it is, what are *ferrementa*? Correct: neuter plural tools, so *ferrementa vetera* are "old tools."

S*ervus, servī,* is a masculine second-declension noun that means "slave." Can you parse *servum*? *Servum* is accusative singular. Why? *Servum* is a direct object. And a *servum senem*? *Senex, senis,* which can mean "old man," can also be used as an adjective that means "old." We can compare our word "senile." *Senem* agrees with *servum*, so we have an "old slave" or a "senile slave."

And a *servum morbōsum*? *Morbōsus, a, um,* is a first- and second-declension adjective, an adjective that means sick. The word for disease in Latin is *morbus*, so *morbōsus*, means full of *morbus* or full of disease. We can compare "morbid," as in English, "morbidly obese," a not infrequent result, alas, from a body mass index calculation. But let's try the whole sentence. *plostrum vetus, ferrementa vetera, servum senem, servum morbōsum* ... *vendat pater familiās.* Let the head of household sell, in other words, the head of the household should sell an old plow, old tools, an old slave, and a sick slave. Why? It's cheaper. And, in the end, it's all about the bottom line, even in good, old Rome. *plostrum vetus, ferrementa vetera, servum senem, servum morbōsum* ... *vendat paterfamiliās.*

And the elder Cato was renowned in antiquity for representing good old-fashioned Roman values. And his thoughts on why farmers make the best citizens influenced the thinking of such early American gentleman farmers as Thomas Jefferson and George Washington. Of course, these early American gentleman-farmers, citizens and patriots that they were, also, we may note, like Cato, were slave owners. And, it is actually an unfortunate fact that Roman thinking about slavery, as well as Roman slave law represent additional inheritances from the ancient world. Truth be told, the influences of Roman antiquity run deep, both for good and for ill, and those who would see clearly, should study Latin. But you, as lovers of the Latin language, already know that. And I'm sure that you plan to go forth and study third-declension i-stem nouns on your own.

Et nunc, linguae Latīnae amātōrēs, potestis omnēs exire, ut linguam Latīnam discātis. Grātiās vōbis agō et, dōnec nōs iterum vīderimus (id. est., until we meet again)*, cūrāte, ut valeātis!*

The Relative Pronoun
Lecture 16

In the last lecture, we looked at third-declension *i*-stems, which did not require us to memorize much in the way of new forms. In this lecture, we will exercise our memories a bit more, but the strain won't be too great. The declension of the relative pronoun combines elements of the first, second, and third declensions, as well as its own forms; thus, we treat it separately. In this lecture, we'll learn to identify relative pronouns, and we'll work on translating some sample sentences from the historian Sallust.

Identifying relative pronouns

- A pronoun takes the place of a noun. *Prō*, in Latin, is a preposition meaning "on behalf of." Thus, a *pronoun* serves "on behalf of a noun." A relative pronoun takes the place of a noun and relates one clause to another.

- Consider these two sentences: Caesar wages war. He is in Gaul. In the second sentence, the pronoun *he* served to take the place of the proper noun *Caesar*.

- Now consider another sentence: Caesar, who is in Gaul, wages war. This sentence has two clauses: a main clause, "Caesar wages war," and a subordinate clause, "who is in Gaul." Subordinate clauses generally cannot stand on their own as independent sentences. But the advantage of having such clauses is that they can provide nuance and further information about the main clause and signal that this information is subordinate to the main thought.

- We use subordination in English all the time, but we're not consistent in our use of relative pronouns. Consider the following examples, all of which are perfectly intelligible although not all are technically correct:
  o The girl, who you see on the corner, is my daughter.

- The girl, whom you see on the corner, is my daughter.

- The girl that you see on the corner is my daughter.

- The girl you see on the corner is my daughter.

- The girl, which you see on the corner, is my daughter.

- In other words, in English, we have, in reference to people, an array of possible relative pronouns, some better than others but all intelligible: who, that, which, or nothing at all. In reference to things, we simply eliminate *who* as a possibility.

The relative pronoun in Latin

	Masculine	Feminine	Neuter	Translation
Singular				
Nominative	quī	quae	quod	who, which, that (masc. & fem.); which, that (neuter)
Genitive	cuius	cuius	cuius	whose, of which
Dative	cui	cui	cui	to *or* for whom; to *or* for which
Accusative	quem	quam	quod	whom, which, that
Ablative	quō	quā	quō	by, with, *or* from whom; by, with, *or* from which
Plural				
Nominative	quī	quae	quae	who, which, that (masc. & fem.); which, that (neuter)
Genitive	quōrum	quārum	quōrum	whose, of which
Dative	quibus	quibus	quibus	to *or* for whom; to *or* for which
Accusative	quōs	quās	quae	whom, which, that
Ablative	quibus	quibus	quibus	by, with, *or* from whom; by, with, *or* from which

Note: The translations remain the same in the plural and the singular. In English, we can't make the relative pronoun plural, but plural forms exist in Latin.

Translating Sallust

- The historian Sallust was born in 86 B.C.E. and was a partisan of Julius Caesar. One of his surviving works describes a conspiracy that was suppressed during the consulship of Cicero in 63 B.C.E. The work is interesting for many reasons, but one of them is that Sallust gives Cicero, who considered himself the hero of the story, such a small role. Instead, in Sallust's account, Julius Caesar and his nemesis, the younger Cato, emerge as the two pole stars of a politically divided society. Sallust's portrait of the conspirator Catiline is also compelling.

   o In the following sentence, Sallust describes Aurelia Orestilla: *Catilīna amat Aurēliam Orestillam, cuius praeter fōrmam nihil umquam bonus laudat.* Catiline allegedly murdered his first wife and son so that he could marry Aurelia, and the relative pronoun helps us understand why.

   o The sentence translates literally as: "Catiline loves Aurelia Orestilla, of whom except for the beauty not at all ever a good person praises." In more readable English, the last phrase reads: "except for whose beauty a good person never praises."

   o The sentence captures some of Sallust's pithiness. What he's saying is that Aurelia was good-looking but morally bankrupt. A good person could say nothing good about her character but, when speaking truthfully, could praise her good looks.

- Here's a more straightforward example from Sallust: *Coniūrant paucī contrā rem pūblicam, in quibus Catilīna est.* In English, it reads: "A few people conspire against the Republic, among whom Catiline is," or "A few people conspire against the Republic, among whom is Catiline."

- Note that relative pronouns agree with their antecedents in number and gender, but their case depends on their use in their own clause.
  - Returning to our first sentence, Aurelia Orestilla is in the accusative feminine singular because she is the direct object of the verb *loves*.

  - The relative pronoun *cuius*, however, is in the genitive because it shows possession of the *fōrmam* ("beauty"). The relative pronoun *cuius* is in the feminine singular because it refers back to Aurelia Orestilla, but unlike accusative Aurelia Orestilla, *cuius* is in the genitive to show possession.

  - All words, including the relative pronoun, take their case from their use in their own clauses, but pronouns can refer to other words in a sentence through their gender and number.

Verba

ager, agrī, m.: field

coniūrō, coniūrāre, coniūrāvī, coniūrātum: conspire

contrā (prep. + accusative): against

dē (prep. + ablative): about, concerning, from

dō, dare, dedī, datum: give, offer

fīlia, fīliae, f.: daughter (the dative and ablative plural are *fīliābus* to distinguish the forms from the dative/ablative *fīliīs*, for "sons")

fīlius, fīliī, m.: son

fōrma, fōrmae, f.: form, shape, beauty

immortālis, immortāle (adj.): immortal

ita (adv.): so, thus

māter, mātris, f.: mother

nihil: nothing, not at all

pater, patris, m.: father

paucī, paucae, pauca (plural adj.): few, a few

praeter (prep. + accusative): besides, except, beyond

quī, quae, quod (relative pronoun): who, which, that

rēs pūblica: republic, state

umquam (adv.): ever

Memoranda

Please learn the declension of the relative pronoun *quī, quae, quod,* "who, which, that" (App. §46).

Agenda

i. Create a chart and decline the relative pronoun.

ii. Please translate the following sentences into English.

1. Puella quae puerum pulchrum amat laeta est.

2. Senex cui cibum damus miser est.

3. Hostēs contrā quōs pugnāmus ācrēs sunt.

4. Ager in quō congregant poētae magnus est.

5. Vir cuius filiam laudās, agricola, sevērus est.

6. Est pater puerī quem adōrō.

7. Urbem in quā vīvimus custōdiunt legiōnēs.

8. Colīsne deōs immortālēs dē quibus pontifex maximus vēritātem dīcit?

9. Aeterna est vēritās quam sentīmus.

10. Multōs imperātor dūcit, in quibus est filius meus.

iii. Please translate the following sentences into Latin.

1. Can you (plural) see the star that I see?

2. We hear soldiers of the fierce king by whom the beautiful city is being conquered.

3. The courage of the maidens whom they praise is great.

4. The wine that you (singular) are drinking is most pleasing.

5. The farmer, by whose mother we are being praised, loves his son but he does not have a daughter.

The Relative Pronoun
Lecture 16—Transcript

Salvēte, discipulī discipulaeque linguae Latīnae! Mihi valdē placet vos iterum vidēre et vōs pulchram linguam Latīnam aeternam docēre.

In the last lesson, we looked at third-declension i-stems. This did not require us to memorize much in the way of new forms. All we did was insert a few i's. In this lesson, we will exercise our memories a bit more, but the strain won't be all that great.

The declension of the relative pronoun combines elements of the first, second, and third declensions, as well as forms all its own, so we treat it separately. It does belong to another part of speech, after all. What is a pronoun? What is a relative pronoun? Well, a pronoun takes the place of a noun. *Prō*, in Latin, is a preposition meaning "on behalf of." So a pronoun serves on behalf of a noun." Not only does a relative pronoun take place of a noun, it <u>relates</u> one clause to another, hence the name <u>relative</u>. But none of this may mean much in the abstract. Let me give you an example.

I will begin with two sentences. Sentence number one: Caesar wages war. Sentence number two: He is in Gaul. In the second sentence, the pronoun he served to take the place of the proper noun *Caesar*. Because he serves on behalf of the noun Caesar, he is a pronoun. Now for some magic. Rather than use the *personal* pronoun "he," I shall use a relative pronoun, not only to take the place of Caesar, to serve on his behalf, but also to combine the second sentence with the first as a subordinate clause, thus creating a single complex sentence from my two simple and independent sentences. What will allow me to work this magic? The relative pronoun.

Caesar, *who* is in Gaul, wages war.

This sentence has two clauses, a main clause: Caesar wages war; and a subordinate clause: *who* is in Gaul. The subordinate clause, "who is in Gaul," could not stand as an independent sentence. Unless of course I turned it into a question: Who is in Gaul? But then "who" would become an interrogative pronoun, rather than a relative pronoun, and I'm talking about relative pronouns, not interrogative pronouns, so please don't distract me with these impertinent questions!

Just kidding, of course. These are very good questions. "Who is in Gaul," as a statement, is not a complete sentence. Subordinate clauses cannot generally stand on their own. What is the advantage of having such clauses? Well, we can provide nuance and further information about the main clause and signal that this information is, indeed, subordinate to the main thought. If we take the sentence, "Caesar, who is in Gaul, wages war," and ask ourselves, "What is the main thought?" I think that we would agree that the main thought is that Caesar wages war. So what's the added value of "who is in Gaul?"

The subordinate clause tells us where Caesar wages war. This is interesting, and perhaps even important, but it is not the main focus. Compare this sentence, Caesar, who once again wages war, is in Gaul. In this version of the sentence, the main emphasis is on Caesar's present location. We know that he wages war, and we signal that he is once again waging war, but we point out that, at the moment, he does so in Gaul. We know instinctively, as fluent speakers of English, that the main clause represents the main event. We use subordination in English all the time.

On the other hand, we no longer get carried away with our subordination. Compare 18th century prose to the modern American prose you find in a newspaper. We find we prefer much shorter sentences. Latin, on the other hand, tends to prefer a bit more subordination than we do. At all events, a knowledge of the relative pronoun will unlock the doors to Latin prose. I'm pretty excited. Are you? Let's take a look.

As always, with these charts, there's a lot to take in at first glance. But we'll work through the forms slowly in a moment. Before we start practicing the forms, however, we should explore a bit more thoroughly what they mean. We're not consistent in English in our use of relative pronouns. I'm going to give you some examples in English, all of which mean more or less the same thing.

Example number one: The girl, who you see on the corner, is my daughter. This example made a grammatical error. I used the nominative form "who," when I should have used the accusative form "whom." Here's the same sentence with the grammatical correction. The girl, whom you see on the corner, is my daughter. Either version is perfectly intelligible.

Here is another version: the girl that you see on the corner is my daughter. Personally, this version hurts my pedantic ears, but, alas, probably represents what most Americans would say. We now habitually use the relative "that" to refer to people.

There are two more possibilities: The girl you see on the corner is my daughter. In this version, I omitted the relative pronoun altogether. This is perfectly good English, but would never be allowed in Latin. Latin always expresses the relative pronoun. I can think of one more way to do it, although it would be somewhat strange, at least in modern American English. The girl, which you see on the corner, is my daughter. We no longer use "which" to refer to people. We are, technically, not supposed to use "that" to refer to people either, but most people do. Who am I to argue against King usage? I merely describe what I hear. When I prescribe, I keep to Latin.

So let's review. In English, we have, in reference to people, an array of possible relative pronouns, some better than others, but all intelligible: who, that, which, or nothing at all. And then there are the other forms of "who": I'm talking about "whom" and "whose." "Who, whose, whom"; one of the few words that still declines in English. How exciting for a Latin student! What about in reference to things? We simply eliminate "who" as a possibility.

Example number one: The bicycle that you see on the corner is mine. The bicycle, which you see on the corner, is mine. The bicycle you see on the corner is mine. Unless I'm personifying, the bicycle, whom you see on the corner, is called Fred, "who" does not make much sense.

Armed with this preliminary awareness, let's make our way through the chart. Please repeat after me. We will proceed horizontally. So first, the nominative singular. *Quī, quae, quod.* Again: *Quī, quae, quod.* Masculine *quī,* and feminine *quae* can both mean "who, which, or that." Neuter *quod,* on the other hand, means "which or that." Let's look at the genitive singular line. Please repeat after me: *cuius, cuius, cuius.* Again: *cuius, cuius, cuius.* Masculine, feminine, neuter, they're all identical. Possible translations include "whose or of which." That's how we do the genitive singular of the relative pronoun: *cuius, cuius, cuius.*

Let's try the dative singular. Please repeat after me: *cui, cui, cui.* Again: *cui, cui, cui.* All those datives in i look a bit like the third declension. Possible translations include: "to or for whom, to or for which."

And the accusative singular line. Please repeat after me: *quem, quam, quod.* Again: *quem, quam, quod.* The masculine accusative looks like a third declension accusative in em, the feminine, like a first declension in am. And the neuter? It just looks odd, but it does repeat its nominative form, which was also *quod.* That's always true of neuter forms; the nominative and the accusative are the same. So, again, the accusative singular. Please repeat: *quem, quam, quod.* Possible translations include: "whom, which, that."

And, finally, the ablative singular line. Please repeat: *quō, quā, quō.* Again: *quō, quā, quō.* These ablative singulars, *quō, quā, quō,* look like the first and second declensions. Possible translations include: "by, with, or from whom; by, with, or from which."

Let's move along to the plural. The translations for each case will remain exactly the same as they were for the singular. Why? Because we can't make the relative pronoun plural in English. But in Latin, they've got the forms. Let's have a look at the nominative plural line. Please repeat after me: *quī, quae, quae.* Again: *quī, quae, quae.* We note that the neuter plural does not end in a, but it does look like the feminine singular *quae,* which, of course, looks just like the feminine plural *quae.* Is that confusing? Not to us. In English, we do not distinguish between the singular and plural either.

Possible translations of the nominative plural *quī, quae, quae* include, "who, which, that." The genitive plural looks rather like first and second declensions. Please repeat after me: *quōrum, quārum, quōrum.* Again: *quōrum, quārum, quōrum.* Translations include: "whose, of whom, of which."

With the dative plural line, we return to what looks like the third declension. Please repeat after me: *quibus, quibus, quibus.* We can translate "to or for whom, to or for which." Again, please repeat: *quibus, quibus, quibus.* The accusative plural line goes back to what looks like first and second declension endings for the masculine and feminine and the accusative neuter plural repeats the nominative. Please repeat after me: *quōs, quās, quae.* Again: *quōs, quās, quae.* Translations include: "whom, which, or that."

And finally, the ablative plural line looks just like the dative, and thus looks like the third declension. Please repeat after me: *quibus, quibus, quibus.* "By, with or from whom. By with or from which." And one more time: *Quibus, quibus, quibus.*

And there you have it, the relative pronoun, which, by the way, can also be used as an adjective. But this will become clear enough in a moment. First let us chant, as this is an especially fun paradigm, at least it has been for me over a long career of teaching Latin. Whether it is for you folks at home, in the car, out and about, well, I live in hope.

We shall practice this paradigm horizontally, that is, by case rather than vertically by gender. This is traditional and also practical, as it is useful to observe similarities and differences across the three genders.

Please repeat the nominative singular after me: *quī, quae, quod*

The genitive singular: *cuius, cuius, cuius*

The dative singular: *cui, cui, cui*

The accusative singular: *quem, quam, quod*

The ablative singular: *quō, quā, quō*

The nominative plural: *quī, quae, quae*

The genitive plural: *quōrum, quārum, quōrum*

The dative plural: *quibus, quibus, quibus*

The accusative plural: *quōs, quās, quae*

The ablative plural: *quibus, quibus, quibus*

Okay, now let's do it line by line, but I won't tell you the case and number. Just repeat after me: *quī, quae, quod*

cuius, cuius, cuius

cui, cui, cui

quem, quam, quod

quō, quā, quō

quī, quae, quae

quōrum, quārum, quōrum

quibus, quibus, quibus

quōs, quās, quae

quibus, quibus, quibus

And one more time together, straight through. And, please, again, please feel free to join me:

quī, quae, quod. cuius, cuius, cuius. cui, cui, cui. quem, quam, quod. quō, quā, quō. quī, quae, quae. quōrum, quārum, quōrum. quibus, quibus, quibus. quōs, quās, quae. quibus, quibus, quibus.

Now that's what I call fun, and I encourage you to repeat the exercise on your own. I'm sure you're better singers than I. But I encourage you to repeat the exercise frequently.

What? One more time? Okay, since you begged. Together on the count of three: *ūnus, duo, ūnus, duo, trēs*:

quī, quae, quod. cuius, cuius, cuius. cui, cui, cui. quem, quam, quod. quō, quā, quō. quī, quae, quae. quōrum, quārum, quōrum. quibus, quibus, quibus. quōs, quās, quae. quibus, quibus, quibus.

If you want to do it again, please feel free to rewind. I am at your service. But if you'd like to move along, let's try our hand at some translation.

The historian Sallust was born in 86 B.C.E. and was a partisan of Julius Caesar. One of his surviving works describes a conspiracy that was suppressed during the consulship of Cicero in 63 B.C.E. It's interesting for many reasons, but one of them is that Sallust gives Cicero, who considered himself the hero of the story, a very small role. Instead, in Sallust's account, Julius Caesar and his nemesis, the younger Cato, emerge as the two pole stars of a politically divided society. Sallust's portrait of the conspirator Catiline is compelling. And Sallust uses the relative pronoun. Let's read some Sallust— only slightly adapted—that will allow us to observe the relative pronoun in action, as well as enjoy Sallust's pointed style.

In the following sentence, Sallust describes Aurelia Orestilla. Catiline allegedly murdered his first wife and son so that he could marry this Aurelia, and the relative pronoun will help us understand why.

Catilīna amat Aurēliam Orestillam, cuius praeter formam nihil umquam bonus laudat.

Catiline is a first-declension masculine. *Catilīna, Catilīnae, Catilīnae, Catilīnam, Catilīna.* The verb *amat* is third person singular, and Aurelia Orestilla is a direct object accusative. The beginning of the sentence is, thus, easy to understand. *Catilīna amat Aurīliam Orestillam.* Catiline loves Aurelia Orestilla. But the sentence goes on with a *cuius*, a relative pronoun that binds a subordinate thought to the main clause. *Cuius* is genitive singular, so we may translate it as "whose, of whom, or of which." But the word to which *cuius* refers is the woman Aurelia Orestilla, so we can go with "whose or of whom."

Praeter is a preposition that takes the accusative case. It means "besides, except for." *Forma, formae*, is a feminine noun of the first declension that means "shape or beauty." *Nihil* can mean "nothing," as an adverb; it can mean "not at all." *Umquam* is another adverb that means "ever." *Bonus, -a, -um* is, first and second declension, adjective that means "good." Used by itself, *bonus* can also mean "a good person or good man." And *laudō, laudāre, laudāvī, laudātum*, what's the conjugation? First; it means "to praise." We now have what we need to translate the sentence. "Catiline loves Aurelia Orestilla, (*cuius*) of whom except for the beauty not at all ever a good person praises."

Let's turn it into somewhat better English. First we can start with "not at all ever." The *nihil* and the *umquam* surround *bonus*, but we can combine the two thoughts, and simply say "never." A good person never praises. And for "of whom," let's try "whose." "Except for whose beauty a good person never praises." Proceeding in this way, we can capture some of Sallust's pithiness. Catiline loves Aurelia Orestilla, except for whose beauty a good person never praises. In other words, Aurelia was good looking, but morally bankrupt. A good person could say nothing good about her character, although even a good person could, when speaking truthfully, praise her good looks. Sallust is fun, in no small part, because his rhetoric in phrasing is clever.

Let's look at a more straightforward, albeit less clever, example. Please repeat after me:

Coniūrant paucī contrā rem pūblicam, in quibus Catilīna est.

Coniūrant paucī contrā rem pūblicam, in quibus Catilīna est.

In the sentence, *coniūrō, coniūrāre*, means "to conspire." The verb ends in nt, so can you tell me who conspires? They do. They conspire. How do I know it's not "let them conspire"? First conjugation, so it's "they conspire." We already have a complete thought, and yet the rest of the sentence beckons. The next word *paucī, paucae, pauca*, is a first- and second-declension adjective in the plural; it means "a few" or "a few people." We can now refine our knowledge of the subject. A few people conspire. *Coniūrant paucī*. Onwards. The proposition *contrā* means "against," and it takes the accusative case. A few people conspire against the accusative *rem pūblicam*, which is easy enough to decode as *Republic*.

The thought is complete, and yet a relative pronoun beckons us onward. It joins a thought to the main clause that will make the sum of both clauses greater than each. The preposition "in" can take the ablative case. When "in" takes the ablative case, it frequently means "in, on, or at some place or location." But when that location happens to be a group of people, then we should probably translate "in" as "among," which still describes place where, but is better English. Again and again, we see that prepositions do not map cleanly from one language to another.

At all events: *in quibus*. The relative pronoun *quibus* is in the ablative plural after the preposition "in." We can translate the phrase as "among whom" or "among which." But since the antecedent consists of a group of people, what would you chose? "among whom;" It's "among whom" that we want. A few people conspire against the Republic, among whom Catiline is. Or, in better English: A few people conspire against the Republic, among whom is Catiline.

Now I slipped in the word antecedent. What does antecedent mean? Well, *ante* means "before," and *cedent* derives from a Latin verb that means "to go," so an antecedent is, literally, what goes before the relative pronoun, although we might say that the antecedent is the word to which the relative pronoun refers or the word whose place the relative pronoun takes when it combines the subordinate clause to the main clause. To whom does the "whom" in the phrase "among whom" refer? What is the antecedent of the "whom" in "among whom"? Yes, exactly, "the few," the *paucī*, who conspire.

What is the case, however, of *paucī*? What is the gender? What is the number? *Paucī* is nominative, *paucī* is masculine, and plural. Why is the word *paucī* nominative? Because it's the subject of the verb *coniūrant*, and the nominative is the case of the subject. That explains the antecedent, the word to which the relative pronoun will refer. Now let's parse the relative pronoun. *Quibus* is masculine and plural, so *quibus* may refer to the few who conspire, but it is also ablative. Why? Because the preposition "in" governs the ablative case.

There is an important lesson here. Relative pronouns agree with their antecedents in number and gender, but their case depends on their use in their own clause. Let's go back and check this out for our first example.

Catilīna amat Aurēliam Orestillam, cuius praeter formam nihil umquam bonus laudat.

Catiline loves Aurelia Orestilla, except for whose beauty a good person never praises.

Aurelia Orestilla is in the accusative feminine singular, because she is the direct object of the verb "loves." The relative pronoun *cuius*, however, is in the genitive, because *cuius* shows possession of the *formam*, or beauty. The relative pronoun *cuius* is in the feminine singular, however, because it also refers back to Aurelia Orestilla, but unlike accusative Aurelia Orestilla, *cuius*, again, is in the genitive to show possession. All words, including the relative pronoun, take their case from their use in their own clauses, but pronouns can refer to other words in a sentence through their gender and number.

So remember, relative pronouns agree with their antecedents in number and gender, but they take their case from their use in their own clause. And now, *Et nunc, linguae Latīnae amātōrēs, potestis omnes exire, ut linguam Latīnam discātis. Grātiās vōbis agō et, dōnec nōs iterum vīderimus, curāte, ut valeātis!*

The Imperfect and Future Tenses
Lecture 17

In the last two lectures, we have concentrated on declensions, *i*-stems, and relative pronouns. In this lecture, we'll return to where the action is—to verbs; we will break free of the present tense and look at both the future and the past. Specifically, we'll learn to conjugate and translate the future and imperfect tenses. We've already mastered the present tense in Latin, which is the most challenging; it has four conjugations plus the third *-io*, for a total of five present-tense patterns. The good news is that for the future tense, we have only two patterns to learn, and for the imperfect tense, only one.

The future tense
- The future tense may be translated "I shall verb," "I will verb," or "I am going to verb." In this lesson, we learn the indicative forms of the future. There are no subjunctive forms for the future tense in Latin.

Active endings for future-tense third-conjugation, third *-io*, and fourth-conjugation verbs

	Singular	Plural
1	-am	-ēmus
2	-ēs	-ētis
3	-et	-ent

Passive endings for future-tense third-conjugation, third *-io*, and fourth-conjugation verbs

	Singular	Plural
1	-ar	-ēmur
2	-ēris	-ēminī
3	-ētur	-entur

- To form the future of third-, third -*io*, and fourth-conjugation verbs, we remove the ō from the first principal part and attach the future endings, whether active or passive, to this base.

- Again, the key here is conjugation identification. These endings work only for third-, third -*io*, and fourth-conjugation verbs. We need to know whether a verb belongs to the first, second, third, third -*io*, or fourth conjugation if we want to know what is signified by an -*a*, -*i*, or -*e*.

Future active indicative of third-conjugation *pōnō*

pōnō, pōnere, posuī, positum: put, place

	Singular	Plural
1	pōnam	pōnēmus
2	pōnēs	pōnētis
3	pōnet	pōnent

Future passive indicative of third-conjugation *pōnō*

pōnō, pōnere, posuī, positum: put, place

	Singular	Plural
1	pōnar	pōnēmur
2	pōnēris	pōnēminī
3	pōnētur	pōnentur

Comparison of third- and fourth-conjugation model verbs in the future active and passive

capiō, capere, cēpī, captum: seize, capture

sentiō, sentīre, sēnsī, sēnsum: feel, perceive

Future active indicative conjugation of *capiō* and *sentiō*

		Third -io	Fourth Conjugation
		Singular	
	1	capiam	sentiam
	2	capiēs	sentiēs
	3	capiet	sentiet
		Plural	
	1	capiēmus	sentiēmus
	2	capiētis	sentiētis
	3	capient	sentient

Future passive indicative conjugation of *capiō* and *sentiō*

		Third -io	Fourth Conjugation
		Singular	
	1	capiar	sentiar
	2	capiēris	sentiēris
	3	capiētur	sentiētur
		Plural	
	1	capiēmur	sentiēmur
	2	capiēminī	sentiēminī
	3	capientur	sentientur

Active endings for future-tense first- and second-conjugation verbs

	Singular	Plural
1	-bō	-bimus
2	-bis	-bitis
3	-bit	-bunt

Passive endings for future-tense first- and second-conjugation verbs

	Singular	Plural
1	-bor	-bimur
2	-beris	-biminī
3	-bitur	-buntur

- To form the future of first and second conjugation verbs, we attach the future endings, whether active or passive, to the verb stem, which we obtain by removing the *-re* from the second principal part. This explains why either a long ā (first conjugation) or a long ē (second conjugation) appears before the *b* of the first- and second-conjugation future endings.

- As always, the key is conjugation identification. These future endings work only for first- and second-conjugation verbs.

Future active indicative conjugation of first-conjugation *amō*

amō, amāre, amāvī, amātum: love

	Singular	Plural
1	amābō	amābimus
2	amābis	amābitis
3	amābit	amābunt

Future passive indicative conjugation of first-conjugation *amō*

amō, amāre, amāvī, amātum: love

	Singular	Plural
1	amābor	amābimur
2	amāberis	amābiminī
3	amābitur	amābuntur

Future active indicative conjugation of second-conjugation *videō*

videō, vidēre, vīsī, vīsum: see

	Singular	Plural
1	vidēbō	vidēbimus
2	vidēbis	vidēbitis
3	vidēbit	vidēbunt

Future passive indicative conjugation of second-conjugation *videō*

videō, vidēre, vīsī, vīsum: see

	Singular	Plural
1	vidēbor	vidēbimur
2	vidēberis	vidēbiminī
3	vidēbitur	vidēbuntur

The imperfect tense

- With the imperfect, we complete our overview of the entire present-tense system, which we define as the tenses based on the first two principal parts of the verb. The present-tense system includes the present, the future, and the imperfect.

- To form the imperfect tense, we need just one set of endings for all four conjugations in the indicative and, for the subjunctive, just one simple rule that works for all the conjugations.

- Let's start with the imperfect subjunctive, which can be translated as "I might" plus a verb. To form the imperfect subjunctive of any regular Latin verb, simply add the personal endings, whether active or passive, to the second principal part.

Imperfect active subjunctive of first-conjugation *amō*

amō, amāre, amāvī, amātum: love

	Singular	Plural
1	amārem	amārēmus
2	amārēs	amārētis
3	amāret	amārent

Imperfect active subjunctive of third-conjugation *capiō*

capiō, capere, cēpī, captum: seize, capture

	Singular	Plural
1	caperem	caperēmus
2	caperēs	caperētis
3	caperet	caperent

Imperfect passive subjunctive of fourth-conjugation *sentiō*

sentiō, sentīre, sēnsī, sēnsum: feel, perceive

	Singular	Plural
1	sentīrer	sentīrēmur
2	sentīrēris	sentīrēminī
3	sentīrētur	sentīrentur

The imperfect indicative

- The imperfect tense is used to represent actions in the past that have not yet been completed, are ongoing in the past, are customarily done in the past, or are repeated in the past. In other words, the tense is called "imperfect" because it is used to describe incomplete, customary, or repeated action—in the past.

- In English, we translate the imperfect indicative as "I verbed," "I was verbing," or "I used to verb."

Active endings for the imperfect indicative

	Singular	Plural
1	-bam	-bāmus
2	-bās	-bātis
3	-bat	-bant

Passive endings for the imperfect indicative

	Singular	Plural
1	-bar	-bāmur
2	-bāris	-bāminī
3	-bātur	-bantur

- To form the imperfect indicative tense of first-conjugation verbs, remove the ō from the first principal part and attach the imperect indicative endings to this base, inserting a long ā before the *b* of the imperfect endings.

- To form the imperfect indicative tense of second-conjugation verbs, remove the *eō* from the first principal part and attach the imperfect indicative endings to this base, inserting a long ē before the *b* of the imperfect endings.

- To form the imperfect indicative tense of third-, third -*iō*, and fourth-conjugation verbs, remove the ō from the first principal part and attach the imperfect indicative endings to this base, inserting a long ē before the *b* of the imperfect endings.

Imperfect active indicative of first-conjugation *amō*

amō, amāre, amāvī, amātum: love

	Singular	Plural
1	amābam	amābāmus
2	amābās	amābātis
3	amābat	amābant

Imperfect active indicative of second-conjugation *videō*

videō, vidēre, vīsī, vīsum: see

	Singular	Plural
1	vidēbam	vidēbāmus
2	vidēbās	vidēbātis
3	vidēbat	vidēbant

Imperfect active indicative of third-conjugation *pōnō*

pōnō, pōnere, posuī, positum: put, place

	Singular	Plural
1	pōnēbam	pōnēbāmus
2	pōnēbās	pōnēbātis
3	pōnēbat	pōnēbant

Imperfect active indicative of third -*iō* conjugation *capiō*

capiō, capere, cēpī, captum: seize, capture

	Singular	Plural
1	capiēbam	capiēbāmus
2	capiēbās	capiēbātis
3	capiēbat	capiēbant

Imperfect active indicative of fourth-conjugation *sentiō*

sentiō, sentīre, sēnsī, sēnsum: feel, perceive

	Singular	Plural
1	sentiēbam	sentiēbāmus
2	sentiēbās	sentiēbātis
3	sentiēbat	sentiēbant

Imperfect passive indicative of fourth-conjugation *sentiō*

sentiō, sentīre, sēnsī, sēnsum: feel, perceive

	Singular	Plural
1	sentiēbar	sentiēbāmur
2	sentiēbāris	sentiēbāminī
3	sentiēbātur	sentiēbantur

Basic patterns to remember

- In the future, there are two basic patterns. The third and fourth conjugations use *a/e* before the personal endings, active or passive. The first and second conjugations use *bo/bi/bu* before the personal endings, active or passive.

- The imperfect subjunctive is formed by adding the personal endings, either active or passive, directly to the second principal part.

- The imperfect indicative adds the personal endings to the imperfect marker *bā*, which is then attached to the first principal part minus its ō and with an intervening ā for the first conjugation or ē for the others.

Verba

doleō, dolēre, doluī, dolitūrum: grieve, suffer, hurt

intellegō, intellegere, intellēxī, intellēctum: understand

maneō, manēre, mānsī, mānsum: remain, stay, abide

requīrō, requīrere, requīsīvī, requīsītum: seek, ask for, miss, need, require

rogō, rogāre, rogāvī, rogātum: ask, ask for

Memoranda

Please learn the third-, third *-io*, and fourth-conjugation future active endings; the first- and second-conjugation future active endings; and the imperfect active indicative endings and familiarize yourself with their passive counterparts. Learn the rules for forming the imperfect subjunctive for all conjugations.

Agenda

i. Learn the conjugation of the future tense (active and passive), imperfect indicative (active and passive), and the imperfect subjunctive (active and passive) of the model verbs *amō* (App. §53), *videō* (App. §54), *pōnō* (App. §55), *capiō* (App. §56), and *sentiō* (App. §57).

ii. Please conjugate the following verbs in the tense, voice, and mood indicated.

1. rogō (imperfect, active, indicative)

2. intellegō (future, passive, indicative)

3. requīrō (future, active, indicative)

4. dēcipiō (imperfect, passive, indicative)

5. maneō (future, active, indicative)

6. laudō (future, passive, indicative)

7. cupiō (imperfect, active, indicative)

8. doleō (imperfect, active, subjunctive)

9. intellegō (imperfect, passive, subjunctive)

ii. Translate the following into Latin. (Each answer will be only one word.)

1. I was staying.

2. You (singular) will be missed.

3. They used to ask.

4. She will be understood.

5. You (plural) were grieving.

6. We might grieve.

7. He worshipped.

8. It was being worshipped.

9. You (singular) will be worshipped.

10. We used to protect.

11. They will drink.

12. I will have.

13. He used to have.

14. They will be deceived.

15. She might eat.

16. Were you (plural) fleeing?

17. Is she going to learn?

18. It might cease.

19. They will give.

20. It was being sold.

The Imperfect and Future Tenses
Lecture 17—Transcript

Salvēte, discipulī discipulaeque linguae Latīnae! Mihi valdē placet vōs iterum vidēre et vōs pulchram linguam Latīnam aeternam docēre.

In the last two lessons, we have concentrated on declensions, i-stems and relative pronouns. In this lesson, we return to where the action is—to verbs. It's time to break free of the present tense, and break free we shall. We'll look at the future, and then at the past. More specifically, we learn to conjugate, and translate, the future and the imperfect tenses.

But first, a bit of good news. You've mastered the most challenging tense of all in Latin, the present tense. No other tense offers so much variety. Four conjugations, plus the third -io, for a total of five present tense patterns. These patterns consisted primarily of observing what vowels we used before our personal active endings *o or m, s, t, mus, tis, nt*, and our personal passive endings *r, ris, tur, mur, mini, ntur*.

So what's the good news? For the future tense, you have only two patterns to learn. And for the imperfect tense, only one pattern. And one more piece of good news, there's no subjunctive in the future! And, as long as we're celebrating, just wait till we get to the final three tenses, one set of endings for all four conjugations, plus the third -io. We began with what was most challenging, so if you've made it this far, you'll find that much is familiar. So let's get to it.

How do we express the future in English? Standard answer, I shall verb; you will verb; he, she, or it will verb; we shall verb; you will verb; they will verb. And you will note that I used "shall" for the first person and "will" for the others; that's the most correct in standard English. But, for those who failed to grow up in certain posh districts in and around London, this distinction is lost today, especially on those of us from North America. We can use "will" for all the forms. We can also use "going to," "gonna," "will be verbing," and if you're from the South, "fixing to." We can, in English, even use the present to express the future. Tomorrow I fly to Rome. Latin does not offer such luxurious possibilities, but it does offer, as I've already mentioned, two sets of endings.

Let's begin with some of our first model verbs, beginning with the verb that means to put or place, *pōnō, pōnere, posuī, positum*. To which conjugation does this verb belong? The first principal part ends in ō, the second principal part, in short e-r-e? Yes, good old *pōnō*, third conjugation. Our first set of future-tense endings will work, not just for the third conjugation, but for the third-io and the fourth conjugations as well. So we will also look at our third-io verb to "take," "to grab," or "to capture," our third-io: *capiō, capere, cēpī, captum*, and our fourth conjugation verb "to feel," *sentiō, sentīre, sēnsī, sēnsum*. Just to be clear, the future endings we are about learn work for verbs of the third conjugation, those whose first two principal parts show us o, followed by short e-r-e, the third-io, that's io followed by short e-r-e, and the fourth conjugation, io followed by long ī-r-e.

So what, then, are the future endings, active and passive, for these three verbs? First the active endings. Please repeat in the singular: *am, ēs, et*. And in the plural: *ēmus, ētis, ent*. And again: *am, ēs, et, ēmus, ētis, ent*.

And now the passive endings for the future tense of the third, the third-io, and fourth conjugations. Please repeat in the singular: *ar, ēris, ētur*. And in the plural: *ēmur, ēminī, entur*. And one more time: *ar, ēris, ētur, ēmur, ēminī, entur*.

Let us put these endings first on put or place, *pōnō*. To do so, first, we carefully remove the ō from the first principal part. That gives us the base pōn. Now we attach the endings *am, ēs, et, ēmus, ētis, ent*, and *ar, ēris, ētur, ēmur, ēminī, entur*, directly on the base pōn. Shall we try it? Please join in if you feel comfortable. Ready? Future active:

Ūnus, duo, ūnus duo trēs: *pōnam, pōnēs, pōnet, pōnēmus, pōnētis, pōnent*.

And now let's conjugate *pōnō* in the future passive: I'll provide the English, please provide the Latin equivalent: I shall be placed: *pōnar*. You will be placed: *pōnēris*. He, she, or it will be placed: *pōnētur*. We shall be placed: *pōnēmur*. Y'all will be placed: *pōnēminī*. They will be placed: *pōnentur*.

And now, without the English, let's conjugate *pōnō* in the future passive: *pōnar, pōnēris, pōnētur, pōnēmur, pōnēminī, pōnentur.* If we contemplate our now-familiar personal endings for the Latin verb, both active and passive, what was really new in the future? We changed the vowel before the personal endings. And did you note the pattern? We found the vowel a in the first person, and e, generally a long, in all the other persons. We can summarize simply. To form the future of third and fourth conjugation verbs, we change the theme vowel from the present pattern of o/i/u to a in the first person, and e in the other persons.

Before we move on to the other conjugations with other vowels, please remember that the key, and this bears repeating, as I've mentioned before, and will mention again and again, is conjugation identification. By their conjugations, ye shall know your verbs. We need to know whether a verb belongs to the first, the second, the third, the third -io, or the fourth conjugation if we want to know what is signified by an a, by an i, or by an e. Conjugation identification is our map, our GPS, our verbal tracking device in the big city of Ancient Rome.

Let's look at our third and fourth conjugation model verb in the future active and passive, and by way of experiment, let's conjugate our third -io capiō, capere, in the future active indicative. Please repeat after me, first in the singular: *capiam, capiēs, capiet,* and in the plural: *capiēmus, capiētis, capient.* What lesson do we derive from these forms? What can we say about conjugating third -io verbs in the future? What is different from the future of *pōnō*? There is one difference, and it resides in the i of the third i-o. We keep that i throughout the entire conjugation.

And let's try the fourth conjugation verb "to feel" in the future passive. I'll provide the English. Please try to supply the Latin: I shall be felt: *sentiar.* You will be felt: *sentiēris.* He, she or it will be felt: *sentiētur.* We shall be felt: *sentiēmur.* Y'all are fixin' to be felt: *sentiēminī.* And, finally: They will be felt: *sentientur.* What's the lesson? It's the same lesson. The i before the o in the first principal part of the fourth conjugation, *sentiō,* appears before the future endings in every person in the future.

But time runs apace, and I can sense the excitement. How, *O Molinārī, conjugator noster,* do we conjugate first and second conjugation verbs in the future? Some people say that the first and second conjugation future stinks, but, so long as you mind your conjugations, you, *o conjugatores,* will emerge smelling sweeter than the goddess Venus. And here are the future endings active and passive for the first and second conjugations.

Why do some allege (falsely) that this conjugation stinks? Because they have b-o in the first person singular active. Did you see that? The first person singular active ending is spelled b-o? Sorry. Please repeat the active endings after me: *bō, bis, bit,* and in the plural: *bimus, bitis, bunt.* And one more time: *bō, bis, bit, bimus, bitis, bunt.*

And the passive endings, first the singular: *bor, beris, bitur,* and in the plural: *bimur, biminī, buntur.* Did you notice that the short i in bis changes to a short e in its passive counterpart *beris?* We've seen that vowel weakening before. It's annoying, but we'll just have to live with it. Please repeat these future passive endings: *bor, beris, bitur, bimur, biminī, buntur.*

But how to put these endings on verbs? We chop the re off the second principal part of first and second conjugation verbs, and then add the appropriate set of future endings. Let's try the Latin verb for love, *amō, amāre, amāvī, amātum,* the verb that expresses what we are all feeling in this moment for Latin morphology and inflection. We take *amare,* to love, we remove the re, yielding amā. Let's apply the endings. Let's conjugate "love" in the future active. I shall love: amābō. You will love: *amābis.* He, she, or it's gonna love: *amābit.* We shall love: *amābimus.* Y'all are fixin' to love: *amābitis.* They are going to love: *amābunt.* It's that easy: take the second principal part, chop off the re, and add the endings.

And the passive? The rule is just as simple. Second principal part, chop off the re, add the passive endings *bor, beris, bitur, bimur, biminī, buntur.* Let's give it a try. I shall be loved: *amābor.* You will be loved: *amāberis.* He, she, or it will be loved: *amābitur.* We shall be loved: *amābimur.* You plural will be loved: *amābiminī.* They will be loved: *amābuntur.*

And the second conjugation works in the same way. Have a look the verb "to see," *videō, vidēre, vīdi, vīsum.* And "you will see," or possibly, "you will be seen." We take the second principal part, the infinitive "to see," *vidére,* and we chop of the re. The result? *vidē.* Let's apply the endings and conjugate *videō* in the future active. Please repeat after me: *videbo, videbis, videbit, videbimus, videbitis, videbunt.* And in the passive: *videbor, videberis, videbitur, videbimur, vidēbiminī, videbuntur.*

Now, after all this conjugating, you may wonder why I would consider inflicting the imperfect tense on you in the same lesson. "Have you not flogged us enough, *O Conjugator?*" No. Today is a day of tough love, and if not today, some day you'll thank me. With the imperfect, we complete our overview of the entire present tense system. What, pray tell, is the present tense system? The tenses based on the first two principal parts of the verb, namely, the present tense, the future tense, and the imperfect tense. And compared to the future and present, the imperfect is icing on the cake. To form the imperfect tense, we need just one set of endings for all four conjugations in the indicative and, for the subjunctive, just one simple rule that works for every single conjugation. Seriously. Latin verbs are about to become much more regular. Let's start with the imperfect subjunctive, because it's the easiest to form, and then conclude with the imperfect indicative, because it's more fun and requires just a little bit of attention to conjugation identification.

Okay. To form the imperfect subjunctive of any regular verb, take the second principal part and don't change a single thing, and then, add the personal endings. In the active, we add *m, s, t, mus, tis, nt.* And in the passive, we add *r, ris, tur, mur, minī, ntur.* It's that simple. But what does the imperfect subjunctive mean? Must you know everything? Of course, you must. You're Latin students. We can translate the imperfect subjunctive as "I might verb" and "Might," of course, is the past tense of "may," our go-to helping verb for translating the present subjunctive.

Let's form the imperfect active subjunctive of some model verbs. Please remember the rule: second principal part plus *m, s, t, mus, tis, nt.* And this rule works for all verbs. First verb, first conjugation, to love, *amō, amāre, amāvi, amatum.* What's the second principal part? *amāre,* with a long *āre.*

We're going to add the active endings to *amāre*: I might love: *amārem*. Listen to how we pronounce it, we say, *amārem*. You might love: *amārēs*. He, she or it might love: *amāret*. We might love: *amārēmus*. Y'all might love: *amārētis*. They might love: *amārent*.

Let's try our third -io, to take, *capiō, capere, cēpī, captum.* What is the second principal part of *capiō*? *capere* with a *short* e-r-e. Here we go: I might take: *caperum*, You might take: *caperēs*, He, she, or it might take: *caperet*, We might take: *caperēmus*, Y'all might take: *caperētis*, they might take: *caperent*.

Let's try the imperfect passive subjunctive. The rules are analogous. We take the second principal part and attach the personal passive endings: *r, ris, tur, mur, minī, ntur.* And how do we translate the imperfect subjunctive in the passive? "I might be verbed." Let's do just one, example, because we are running out of time, and we killed the active. Let's conjugate our fourth conjugation verb "to feel," *sentio, sentīre, sēnsī, sēnsum.* We will conjugate it in the imperfect subjunctive passive. I'll provide the English, please provide the Latin. Take *sentīre*, and add the passive endings. I might be felt: *sentīrem.* You might be felt: *sentīrēris.* He she or it might be felt: *sentīrētur.* We might be felt: *sentīrēmur.* Y'all might be felt: *sentīreminī.* They might be felt: *sentīrentur.* And one more time. Please repeat after me: *sentīrer, sentīrēris, sentīrētur, sentīrēmur, sentīrēminī, sentīrentur.*

Catch your breath. We're going to do the imperfect indicative. "But wait!" you protest, "please tell us what the imperfect indicative means!" The imperfect obviously represents events that are not perfect. To do thoroughly or completely in Latin, to finish, *perficiō, perficere, perfēcī, perfectum.* An event represented in the perfect tense is an event that has been completed. The action is viewed as complete, perfect. We'll say more about the perfect tense when we study the perfect tense. We bring it up now only to explain the imperfect, which is used to represent actions in the past that have not yet been perfected, completed, but are, instead, ongoing in the past, customarily done in the past, or repeated in the past. In other words, the tense is called imperfect because it is used to describe incomplete, customary, or repeated action in the past.

But how do we translate the tense in English? I verbed, I was verbing, I used to verb, I habitually verbed. As usual, one tense in Latin can have any number of translations in English. Languages do not map neatly. And that's just part of the fun.

Here are the endings for the imperfect active indicative: *bam, bās, bat bāmus, bātis, bant.* And the endings for the imperfect indicative passive: *bar, bāris, bātur, bāmur, bāminī, bantur.* And what is the sign of the imperfect indicative? Think sheep, ba, or Flintstones, bam, bam, or a place to get a drink: bar. However you care to remember it, the sign is ba plus the personal endings, active or passive. That's it.

But how do we apply these endings to the stems? Good question, *discipulae discipulique.* This is where some theme vowels come into play. For the first conjugation, the theme vowel is? Think *amō, amāre, amāvī, amatum.* Yes, we'll put an a before the b. If we take the first principal part, *amō,* and remove the *ō,* add the theme vowel a, to our base, am-, and then apply the endings, we obtain: *amābam,* I was loving, *amābās,* you were loving. For the second conjugation through fourth conjugations, however, we use the same theme vowel, a long ē. Really, for all of them. This yields *ēbam, ēbās, ēbat, ēbāmus, ēbātis, ēbant.*

But, there are a couple of adjustments, and this is why we begin with the first principal part. Take the first principal part, remove the ō, add theme vowel ē, and then the imperfect indicative endings. Let's try it for *videō, video vidēre*: we remove the ō, we obtain *vide,* but then we don't want two e's in a row, so we get rid that e as well, so we'll only have one e. This yields: I was seeing: *vidēbam.* You used to see: *vidēbās.* He used to see: *vidēbat.* We used to see: *vidēbāmus.* Y'all used to see: *vidēbātis.* They used to see: *vidēbant.*

Third conjugation: *Pōnō, pōnere.* Take *Pōnō,* remove the o. This gives us the base, *Pōn-.* We add a long ē and then the endings. Please repeat after me: *pōnēbam, pōnēbās, pōnēbat, pōnēbāmus, pōnēbātis, pōnēbant.*

Third -io: *capiō, capere.* Take *capiō,* remove the ō. This gives us the stem *capi-,* with an i. This is important. Keep that i. Then add the long ē, and finally the endings. Please repeat after me: *capiēbam, capiēbās, capiēbat, capiēbāmus, capiēbātis, capiēbant.* Lesson? The third -io keeps its i.

And now, you can probably predict how we form the fourth conjugation imperfect indicative active of *sentiō, sentīre,* to feel. We take *sentiō,* we remove the *ō,* giving us *senti-,* with an i. Then we add the ē, and finally, the imperfect endings. Please repeat after me: *sentiēbam, sentiēbās, sentiēbat sentiēbāmus, sentiēbātis, sentiēbant.* Lesson? The fourth conjugation keeps its i.

And let's do the imperfect passive indicative of *sentiō, sentīre.* It's the same process. We take the first principal part, *sentio,* we remove the o, taking care to preserve that i. Now we take *senti,* add the long e, and then apply *bar, bāris, bātur, bāmur, bāminī, bantur.* I'll give you the English. Please give me the Latin. I'll pause, and then provide the correct response.

I was being perceived: *sentiēbar.* You were being perceived: *sentiēbāris.* He, she, or it was being perceived: *sentiēbātur.* We were being perceived: *sentiēbāmur.* Y'all were being perceived: *sentiēbāmini.* They were being perceived. *sentiēbantur.* And one more time. Please repeat after me: *sentiēbar, sentiēbāris, sentiēbātur, sentiēbāmur, sentiēbāmini, sentiēbantur.*

This is all quite simple, easy for me to say, I know, but, please, review and practice, and you will see. All of this can be reduced to a few simple rules. In the future there are two basic patterns. The third and fourth conjugations use the vowels a and e before the personal endings, active or passive. The first and second conjugations use bo, bi, or bu before the personal endings active or passive.

The imperfect subjunctive is formed by adding the personal endings, either active or passive, directly to the second principal part. And the imperfect indicative adds the personal endings to the imperfect marker b-ā, ba, which is then attached to the first principal part minus its ō and with an intervening ē for the second, third, and fourth conjugations, and an ā for the first conjugation. It's that simple. Latin verbs, believe it or not, are among the most regular of all languages. And what will make this clearer? Study.

Chanting. Practice. Practice makes perfect, and in this case, imperfect and future as well. These tenses are yours to enjoy over and over again!

And now, *et nunc, linguae Latīnae amātōrēs,* potestis omnēs exitre, ut *linguam Latīnam discātis, Grātiās vōbis agō et, dōnec nōs iterum vīderimus (id est,* until we meet again), *cūrāte, ut valeātis!*

Building Translation Skills
Lecture 18

In the last lecture, we covered the future and imperfect tenses, active and passive, all four conjugations, and in addition to the indicative, even the subjunctive for the imperfect. In this lecture, we will reap the rewards of this hard work. We will do a bit of review and practice these new tenses by translating some passages from Latin authors and more "modern" Latin: a sentence from the 13ᵗʰ-century Magna Carta.

Practicing with Catullus

- In one of his poems, Catullus uses the future tense to put his love for Lesbia behind him: *Valē, puella, iam Catullus obdūrat, / nec tē requīret nec rogābit invītam. / at tū dolēbis, cum rogāberis nulla.*

- Our translation reads: "Good-bye, girl, now Catullus is being strong / nor will he need you nor will he ask unwilling you. / But you, you will suffer, whenever you will not be asked for, whenever you will not be sought out."

requīrō, requīrere, requīsīvī, requīsītum: **demand, seek after**

Active Indicative		
	Present	**Future**
Singular	requīrō	requīram
	requīris	requīrēs
	requīrit	requīret
Plural	requīrimus	requīrēmus
	requīritis	requīrētis
	requīrunt	requīrent

Present passive indicative

rogō, rogāre, rogāvī, rogātum: ask

	Singular	Plural
1	rogābor	rogābimur
2	rogāberis	rogābiminī
3	rogābitur	rogābuntur

Practicing with Caesar

- In a passage from Caesar, the general claimed to invade Gaul partly in an effort to protect Rome from the Germans. In this sentence, Caesar tells what he was thinking about the people who were the neighbors of the Gauls, the Germans, who in turn, were the neighbors of his province in northern Italy: *[Caesar] intellegēbat magnō cum perīculō prōvinciae futūrum [esse], ut hominēs bellicōsōs, populī Rōmānī inimīcōs, ... finitimōs habēret.*

© Getty Images/Photos.com/Thinkstock.

- Our translation reads: "Caesar understood that there would be great danger for the province, with the result that it, the province, would have warlike people, enemies of the Roman people, as neighbors."

Practicing with other Latin sources

- Here's an authentic medieval Latin sentence from the 13th clause of the Magna Carta pertaining to the *cīvitās* ("city") of London: *Et cīvitās London: habeat*

The Magna Carta, the "Great Charter" granting English liberties, was written in Latin and signed by King John in 1215.

omnēs antīquās lībertātēs. Translated, the sentence reads: "And the city of London: let it have all antique liberties," that is, all its ancient freedoms.

- The *Distichs*, or couplets, of Dionysius Cato, who lived in the 3rd or 4th century A.D., were popular in the Middle Ages and, in fact, remained popular even in Ben Franklin's day. Here's a sample: *Nē timeās illam, quae vītae est ultima fīnis: / Quī mortem metuit, āmittit gaudia vītae*. Translated, Cato's advice reads: "Do not fear that which is life's final end: / He who fears death, misses the joys of life."

- Dionysius Cato also gives us this distich on the wisdom of learning: *Disce aliquid; nam cum subitō fortūna recēdit / Ars remānet vītamque hominis nōn dēserit umquam*, meaning "Learn something, for whenever good fortune suddenly departs, skill remains, and skill does not desert the life of a person ever."

Verba

āmittō, āmittere, āmīsī, āmissum: lose, let go; miss

bellicōsus, bellicōsa, bellicōsum: warlike, relating to war, military

cīvitās, cīvitātis, f.: state, city

dēserō, dēserere, dēseruī, desertum: desert, abandon

ego, meī (personal pronoun; cf. App. §40): I, me

faciō, facere, fēcī, factum: to do, make, bring forth

fīnis, fīnis, m. or f.: end, limit, purpose

fīnitimus, fīnitima, fīnitimum: neighboring, adjoining (used substantively as noun = neighbor) gaudium, gaudiī, n.: joy, delight

homō, hominis: human being, person, man

iam (adv.): now, already, soon

inimīcus, inimīcī, m.: enemy

invītus, invīta, invītum: unwilling

mors, mortis, f.: death

nec (conj.): and not, nor

numquam (adv.): never

obdūrō, obdūrāre, obdūrāvī, obdūrātum: be hard, be unfeeling; endure, persist

perīculum, perīculī, n.: danger, risk

populus, populī, m.: people, nation

prōvincia, prōvinciae, f.: province

recēdō, recēdere, recessī, recessum: depart, go away

timeō, timēre, timuī: fear, be afraid of

tū, tuī (personal pronoun; cf. App. §40): you

ultimus, ultima, ultimum: last, final; extreme

Please review the present, imperfect, and future tenses, both active and passive, of the model verbs *amō* (App. §53), *videō* (App. §54), *pōnō* (App. §55), *capiō* (App. §56), and *sentiō* (App. §57).

i. Conjugate the following verbs in the tense, voice, and mood indicated.

1. recēdō (future active indicative)

2. obdūrō (imperfect active subjunctive)

3. āmittō (imperfect passive indicative)

ii. Decline *warlike state.*

iii. Please translate the following sentences.

1. Fīnem vītae ultimam nōn timēbimus.

2. Dēseretne puella agricolam pulchrum quem iam amābat?

3. Magnā cum virtūte mīlitēs Rōmānī contrā inimīcōs bellicōsōs pugnābant.

4. Tū cum fīliā in cīvitāte manēbis, sed in prōvinciam fīnitimam recēdam ego.

5. Quī mortem timet, gaudium vītae āmittit.

6. Tē numquam dēseret ars linguae Latīnae.

7. Puerum invītum nōn requīram atque dolēbit cum nōn requīrētur.

8. Obdurāte! Perīculum est magnum et paucae sumus, sed cīvitātem custōdīre poterimus.

9. Mēns rēgis bellicōsa dolōrem in populō gignet.

10. Bellum laudāre dēsināmus vīvāmusque et in pāce et magnō cum gaudiō.

Building Translation Skills
Lecture 18—Transcript

Salvēte, discipulī discipulaeque linguae Latīnae! Mihi valdē placet [vōbiscum iterum loquī] et vōs pulchram linguam Latīnam aeternam docēre.

In the last lesson, we were frog-marched through the future and imperfect tenses, active and passive, all four conjugations, and, in addition to the indicative, even the subjunctive for the imperfect. You were very brave, and I'm very proud of you. And in this lesson you reap your rewards. We will do a bit of review and practice these new tenses with some passages from Latin authors.

Let us begin with the future. In this poem, Catullus' love for Lesbia was history. Or at least he was going to try to make it history. And to make it history, Catullus deploys the future tense. Please, repeat after me:

valē, puella, iam Catullus obdūrat,

nec tē requīret nec rogābit invītam.

at tū dolēbis, cum rogāberis nulla.

Let's break this down. Catullus begins with a good-bye: *valē, puella*, "good-bye, girl!" and a resolution: *iam Catullus obdūrat*, "now Catullus *obdūrats*," but what does the first conjugation verb *obdūrō, obdūrāre, obdūrāvī, obdūrātum*, mean? It means to become hardened, more callous, less feeling, more stubborn, hence, our English adjective "obdurate." *iam Catullus obdūrat*, "now Catullus has become and is unfeeling."

nec tē requīret. We can translate *nec* either as "and not" or as "nor," and for *tē*, we need the declension of *tū*, which means "you singular." Please repeat after me: *tū*, you perform a verb in the nominative. *tuī*, of genitive you. *tibi*, to or for dative you. *tē*, someone verbs, accusative you. And finally *tē*, "by, with, or from" ablative you. And please repeat now without the English translations: *tū, tuī, tibi, tē, tē*. And again: *tū, tuī, tibi, tē, tē*.

Our next verb, *requiret*, has the principal parts: *requīrō, requīrere, requīsī, requīsītum*. It means "look for, demand, seek after." To what conjugation does it belong? O followed by short e-r-e? Third. Our English derivative "require" captures only a part of it, although we might translate *nec tē requīret* as "nor will he need you." But did you catch the future? *Obdūrat* was present, but the *requīret* is future. I think we need to compare and contrast *requīrō* in the present and future tenses.

Please repeat after me: *requīrō*, I need; *requīram*, I shall need; *requīris*, you need; *requīrēs*, you will need; *requīrit*, Catullus needs; *requīret*, Catullus will need; *requīrimus*, we need; *requīrēmus*, we shall need; *requīritis*, y'all need; *requīrētis*, y'all will need; *requīrunt*, they need; *requīrent*, they will need. *Nec rogābit invītam*, nor will Catullus *rogābit* you; we have to remember that he said *tē* before we conclude with our *invītam*. But let's return to the verb, our first conjugation verb, *rogō, rogāre, rogāvī, rogātum*, means "ask," and the first and second declension adjective *invītus, a, um*, means "unwilling." So *nec rogābit invītam* means "nor will he ask (pick up the te) you unwilling." Thus Catullus' future behavior. "Nor will he ask you, who are unwilling."

Then he returns to Lesbia and talks directly to her, still in the future: *at tū dolēbis*. *At* means about the same thing in Latin as *sed*, "but." The fact that Catullus actually uses a personal pronoun, tū, is a little unusual, it's highly emphatic, and serves to emphasize the shift: from focus on Catullus to focus on you, Lesbia; YOU will suffer, *dolēbis*. The second conjugation *doleō, dolēre, doluī, dolitum*, means "hurt, suffer." But you, you will suffer! Why do lovers wish pain on each other? Why can't they just remember the good times? Catullus goes on in his spite, and uses *cum* with the indicative, thus indicating repeated action. With the indicative, *cum* means "whenever." *Cum rogāberis*.

Now we just read *rogābit*, which means "he will ask," so what does *rogāberis* mean? What is that ending in *ris*? Yes, *r, ris, tur, mur, minī, ntur*. That's a second person singular passive. Let's conjugate *rogō, rogāre, rogāvī, rogātum* in the future passive. Please repeat after me: *rogābor*, I shall be asked; *rogāberis*, you will be asked; *rogābitur*, she will be asked;

rogābimur, we shall be asked; *rogābiminī*, y'all will be asked; *rogābuntur*, they will be asked.

cum rogāberis nulla. The word *Nullus, a, um* means "not, not anyone," "none," "no one," so literally, the line means "whenever you—not anyone— will be asked out!" Commentators call this nulla a colloquialism for *nōn*, which means not. Catullus personalizes the not by making it agree with Lesbia in case, number, and gender. Whenever you won't be asked! Or, I think we might even treat the line like a "not-joke" *cum rogāberis nulla*: Whenever you will be asked out—not!

So let's put it all together. Please repeat after me:

valē, puella, iam Catullus obdūrat,

Good-bye, girl, now Catullus is being strong; he's a tough guy

nec tē requīret nec rogābit invītam.

nor will he need you nor will he ask unwilling you

at tū dolēbis, cum rogāberis nulla.

But you, you will suffer, whenever you will not be asked for, whenever you will not be asked out.

But enough of the future, at least as Catullus imagined it. Caesar gives us a chance to contemplate the past, and, even more exiting, witness the imperfect in action in Roman history itself. In this passage, Caesar claimed to invade Gaul, partly in an effort to protect Rome from the Germans. "Were the Romans so gullible?" you might ask. "Invade Gaul to protect Rome from Germans?" We know the old argument: "Fight them in Gaul, so we won't have to fight them in Italy! Fight them for the sake of Roman security!" But we're not here for imperfect Roman politics. We're here for the imperfect tense. In the following sentence, Caesar tells what he was thinking about the people who were the neighbors of the Gauls, who were the neighbors of his province in northern Italy. Here's what Caesar said:

[Caesar] intellegēbat magnō cum perīculō prōvinciae futūrum [ESSE], ut hominēs bellicōsōs, populī Rōmānī inimīcōs, ... finitimōs habēret.

Please repeat after me:

[Caesar] *intellegēbat magnō cum perīculō prōvinciae futūrum [ESSE], ut hominēs bellicōsōs, populī Rōmānī inimīcōs, ... finitimōs habēret.* Please repeat after me: [Caesar] *intellegēbat magnō cum perīculō prōvinciae futūrum [ESSE], ut hominēs bellicōsōs, populī Rōmānī inimīcōs, ... finitimōs habēret.*

The third conjugation verb *intellegō, intellegere, intellēxī, intellēctum*, means "to perceive, understand, comprehend," and as Caesar wrote the sentence and made himself subject, we are privy to what he was thinking, *intellegēbat*. Can we parse this verb? Number? Singular. Person? Third— he, she, or it, or Caesar. Tense? Imperfect. Mood? Indicative. Voice? Active. Translation? "Caesar was thinking."

After a verb of thinking, perceiving, feeling, or saying, Latin expresses the thought, feeling or perception with an infinitive construction. We'll discuss indirect statement, which is what we call it, more formally and fully in a later lesson and content ourselves in this lesson with a few preliminary observations. The concept of indirect statement explains why we find the infinitive *futūrum [esse]*, and we supplied the *esse*, by the way, because Roman authors so frequently dropped forms of "to be" as too obvious to put in. What was Caesar perceiving, *quid intellegēbat*? Answer, *magnō cum perīculō prōvinciae futūrum [esse]*. The *magnō* goes with the *perīculō* in the same way that *magnā* goes with *laude* in *magnā cum laude*. But *perīculum, perīculī*, is neuter. It means "danger," so *magnō cum perīculō* means "with great danger."

What is the case of *periculo* after *cum*? Ablative. *Prōvincia, prōvinciae*, means "province," of course, and the genitive in ae. What does that tell us? "Province" belongs to the first declension? We can interpret *prōvinciae* as either nominative plural or dative or genitive singular. The nominative won't work in indirect statement, so we are left with either genitive or dative. Let's reserve judgment.

We conclude the phrase with *futūrum esse*, a future infinitive meaning "to be going to be." We will learn how to form future infinitives in another lesson, but you should be able to recognize esse, which means "to be." The word *futurum* means "going to be." Our own word for future in English derives from this very Latin word. At all events, if we put *futurum*, going to be, together with *esse*, to be, we obtain *futurum esse*, to be going to be.

So what do we have so far? *[Caesar] intellegēbat magnō cum perīculō prōvinciae futūrum [ESSE].* "Caesar perceived, with great danger of, to, or for the province to be going to be." That's obviously not English. You'll need some help. First, "with great danger" is idiomatic. We would use an adjective in English, something like, "very dangerous." The *cum* introduces an ablative of accompaniment. Another way to interpret it might be "a situation accompanied by great danger."

This helps us narrow down prospects for *provinciae*. The dative makes the most sense, a danger "to the province." But what about the infinitive? Latin frequently uses the verb "to be" to express a general situation, that it exists. To express this in English, we generally use the placeholder "there" as the subject. We can try this with the infinitives of "to be" as well. So let's try the sentence again: *[Caesar] intellegēbat magnō cum perīculō prōvinciae futūrum [ESSE].* "Caesar understood there to be going to be a situation accompanied by great danger for the province." Or, in better English: "Caesar understood that there would be great danger for the province."

We have to work our way gradually to more idiomatic English. But it's important also to get a feel for the way that Latin works, as Latin. What was the original and direct thought? Caesar scratched his balding head, and thought, direct quote: "There will be great danger for the Province!" Or, in Latin: *magnō cum perīculō prōvinciae erit!* Then, when Caesar described this as a past thought, he wrote, Caesar most perceptively understood that there would be great danger for the Province. Did you notice how we changed "will be" to "would be"? That's part of adjusting for the sequence of tenses in English. In the past tense, or secondary sequence, we have to shift everything back. In the present, I think that there will be danger. In the past, I thought that there would be danger. But that's English. In Latin, the direct thought *erit* becomes a future infinitive, *futūrum esse*.

At all events, there are other results that follow from this situation, which are introduced to by the conjunction *ut,* with the subjunctive: *ut hominēs bellicōsōs, populī Rōmānī inimīcōs, ... fīnitimōs habēret. Habeō, habēre, habuī, habitum* means "to have." To what conjugation does it belong? eo followed by long e-r-e? Second. If we take the second principal part, and add the personal endings *m, s, t, mus, tis, nt,* we form the imperfect subjunctive. *Habēret* is simply *habēre,* the second principal part, plus the third personal singular ending *t,* so imperfect subjunctive. *ut habēret,* and it, thus, means "with the result that it, the Province, might or would have."

And the rest of the clause presents us with the direct objects, with the result that the Province would have or face: *hominēs bellicōsōs,* war-like men, *populī Rōmānī inimīcōs,* enemies of the Roman people, *fīnitimōs,* neighbors. In Latin, authors can put two nouns next to each other in order to indicate that one noun is as the other noun. This placement is called "apposition." The Romans would have warlike men (*hominēs bellicōsōs*), enemies of the Roman people (*inimīcōs populī Rōmānī*), as neighbors (*fīnitimōs*).

Let's review the whole sentence: [*Caesar*] *intellegēbat,* Caesar was perceiving that, *magnō cum perīculō Prōvinciae futūrum* [*ESSE*] it would be a situation with great danger for the Province, *ut hominēs bellicōsōs, populī Rōmānī inimīcōs, ... fīnitimōs habēret,* with the result that it, the Province, would have war-like people, enemies of the Roman people, as neighbors."

Caesar, who had Gauls as neighbors, had to attack the Gauls to prevent the neighbors of the Gauls, that is, the Germans, from becoming Rome's neighbors. We can't be too careful.

As you can see from these selections, classical Latin still has more mysteries to reveal. But that we can begin to discuss such details indicates just how much you have already achieved. I'd now like to conclude this lesson with some excerpts from more modern Latin, to which you, even as beginning Latin students, likewise begin to have access in the original.

Here's an authentic Mediaeval Latin sentence from the thirteenth clause of the *Magna Carta* pertaining to the *cīvitās* or "city" of London. If I tell you that that *omnēs* means "all," I think that you will be able to figure out the rest, using your knowledge of personal endings and the subjunctive:

Et cīvitās London: habeat omnēs antīquās lībertātēs.

Please repeat after me:

Et cīvitās London: habeat omnēs antīquās lībertātēs.

Tranlsation? And the city of London: let it have all antique liberties, that is, all its ancient freedoms. This particular sentence was formulated in Britain long after Caesar and his successors had left the island, but the English were still, in the thirteenth century, writing in Latin.

But perhaps that was too modern for you. We can go back to late antiquity for some advice from Dionysius Cato, who lived in the third or fourth century A.D. His *distichs*, or couplets, were popular in the Middle Ages, and remained popular even in Ben Franklin's day. Here's a sample:

Nē timeās illam, quae vītae est ultima fīnis:

Quī mortem metuit, āmittit gaudia vītae.

The author uses *nē* plus the subjunctive of the second conjugation verb "to fear," *timeō, timēre, timuī*, there's no fourth principal part, to formulate a negative command. Please repeat: *Nē timeās*. What should you not do? You should not fear. What should you not fear? Can you find a direct object? If you said illam, you were correct. Illam means "that," and you'll note illam is feminine, singular, and accusative, and serves as the antecedent of *quae*, which happens to be feminine and nominative, because *quae* is the subject of the next verb *est*.

Skipping over the *vītae*, can you translate *Nē timeās illam, quae ... est*? "You should not fear that, which is." With this much, we can fill in the blanks up to the colon: *vītae ... ultima fīnis. Fīnis* is a feminine noun of the third declension that means "end," as in "the end." Compare "final." *Ultimus, a, um* is an adjective of the first and second declensions that means "last." The last end. The ultimate conclusion. Redundant? Yes, but pretty emphatic. And *vīta, vītae* is a feminine word of the first declension that means life. The only real possibilities for parsing *vītae* are dative or genitive singular. "Last end for life" or "last end of life"? Personally, I'm going with genitive singular, showing possession of the end.

Let's translate again, but first, let's pronounce it: *Nē timeās illam, quae vītae est ultima fīnis.* You should not fear *Nē timeās* that *illam*, which *quae* is life's final end *vītae est ultima fīnis*. Really? Why not? Read on, my friends. *Quī mortem metuit, āmittit gaudia vītae. Quī* is the masculine singular form of the relative pronoun *quī, quae, quod,* "who." But where is the antecedent? To whom does this "who" refer? We can relax. Latin can begin a sentence with a relative pronoun. We'll find an antecedent eventually, even if it's really a postcedent. *Quī mortem metuit:* "who *metuits mortem."* *metuō, metuere, metuī, metūtum* is a third-conjugation verb that also means "to fear." Authors don't like to keep using the same words. And *mors, mortis,* is a good feminine third-declension noun that means "death." Mortem is, of course, a direct object accusative. Let's translate again: *Quī mortem metuit,* who fears death. And the conclusion: *āmittit gaudia vītae.* He *āmittits* the *gaudia* of life. *Vītae* we just did, so we can translate that much.

The third-conjugation verb *āmittō, āmittere, āmīsī, āmissus* means "away, away from, send it away," *mittō* means "send," *ā* means "away;" so to "send it away," or, literally, "abandon it." And what does this person "send or lose"? Direct object, *gaudia.* And what are *gaudia? Gaudium, gaudiī,* is a neuter word of the second declension that means "joy, pleasure." What form is *gaudia,* ending in that a? If you said—or even just thought—neuter plural accusative, you get extra credit, because you were right. I think we can now handle the whole thought .

Nē timeās illam, quae vītae est ultima fīnis:

Quī mortem metuit, āmittit gaudia vītae.

Do not fear that which is life's final end; he who fears death, misses the joys of life.

So what was the antecedent, after all, of *qui*, which we translated "who"? The unexpressed subject of āmittit, the "he," which you may have noticed I placed in front of the "who" in my translation to make my translation sound more like English. "He who fears death, misses the joys of life." *Quī mortem metuit, āmittit gaudia vītae.*

And we may conclude with one of this late antique Cato's distichs on the wisdom of learning, which, again, you have enough Latin to parse, so enjoy the moment:

> Disce aliquid; nam cum subitō fortūna recēdit
>
> Ars remānet vītamque hominis nōn dēserit umquam.

Didn't understand everything? Well, there's always the issue of vocabulary. It gets us all. Let this be a lesson to you. It's easier to understand a foreign language if you know what the words mean. And there's always help in the form of dictionaries, in print, online, on your phone, and, during this course, from me. You do know what *discō* means? *Discō, discere, didicī, discitūrum* is a third-conjugation verb that means "learn." So what is the form *disce*? What verb form ends in a simple e? The command form; the present second person singular imperative. Learn!

But what? *aliquid; aliquid means* "something." Why? What is the wisdom in learning something? The conjunction *nam* explains, "for." *Cum*, on the other hand, is used not with *subitō*, which, despite its ablative-like appearance, is an adverb that means "suddenly." *Cum*, because the verb *recēdit* is indicative, means "whenever." "Learn something, for whenever fortune suddenly *recēdits*. *Recēdō, recēdere, recessī, recessum,* third conjugation, means "depart, go away," like a dream that recedes from your memory. *nam cum subitō fortūna recēdit,* for whenever fortune suddenly departs, *Ars remānet.* You may remember the word *ars; ars, artis,* third-declension i-stem, means skill, hence our word "art" as in "arts." Skill *remanets,* skill remains, or art abides.

Let's look at the rest of this line: *vītamque hominis nōn dēserit umquam.* Remember that *ars*, "skill," remains our subject. The *que*, on the other hand, on the end of *vītam* means "and." *Vītam* is accusative, so it's the direct object. What about *hominis*? *Homō, hominis,* is a third-declension noun. What's the case? Genitive singular. So whose life? *Vītam hominis,* the life of the person. *Nōn dēserit.* Remember that *ars,* "skill," remains the subject, so *ars,* "skill," does not *dēserit. Dēserō, dēserere, dēseruī, dēsertum,* means, as its fourth principal part *dēsertum* implies, "desert, abandon." Skill does not desert the life of a person a *hominis,* and finally, *umquam,* an adverb that means "ever." Please repeat:

Disce aliquid; nam, cum subitō fortūna recēdit,

Ars remānet, vītamque hominis nōn dēserit umquam.

Learn something, for whenever good fortune suddenly departs, skill remains, and skill does not desert the life of a person, ever. And that *aliquid,* that something, certainly holds true for the Latin language. You've come a long way.

Et nunc, linguae Latīnae amātōrēs, potestis omnes exire, ut linguam Latīnam discātis, Grātiās vōbis agō et, dōnec nōs iterum vīderimus, cūrāte, ut valeātis!

Vocabulary (Verba)

ab (preposition + ablative): by, from (the *b* can be omitted when *ab* is coupled with a word that begins with a consonant: *a Caesare* = by Caesar)

abūtor, abūtī, abūsus sum: abuse, misuse

accipiō, accipere, accēpī, acceptum: hear of, receive, accept

ācer, ācris, ācre: sharp, keen, fierce

acerbus, acerba, acerbum: bitter, harsh

ad (prep. + acc.): to, toward, near

addō, addere, addidī, additum: put or place upon, add

adeō, adīre, adiī, aditum: go to, approach

adōrō, adōrāre, adōrāvī, adōrātum: worship, adore

adsum, adesse, adfuī (compound of *sum*): be present

aestimō, aestimāre, aestimāvī, aestimātum: estimate, value, rate

aetās, aetātis, f.: age, life, time

aeternus, aeterna, aeternum: eternal

ager, agrī, m.: field

agō, agere, ēgī, āctum: do, drive, lead

agricola, agricolae, m.: farmer

alius, alia, aliud: other, another

alter, altera, alterum: another, the other

amīca, amīcae, f.: female friend

amīcus, amīcī, m.: male friend

āmittō, āmittere, āmīsī, āmissum: lose, let go; miss

amō, amāre, amāvī, amātum: love

amor, amōris, m.: love

an (conjunction): or

ancilla, ancillae, f.: maidservant, female slave

angelus, angeli, m.: angel, messenger

anima, animae, f.: spirit, soul

animal, animālis, n.: animal

annuō, annuere, annuī, annūtum: nod, nod to, approve

annus, annī, m.: year

ante (prep. + acc.): before, in front of

antīquus, antīqua, antīquum: ancient

apertē (adv.): openly

apud (prep. + acc.): among, at the house of; with, at, among (compare the French preposition *chez*)

aqua, aquae, f.: water

arbor, arboris, f.: tree

ars, artis, f.: art, skill

asper, aspera, asperum: rough, difficult, harsh

astrum, astrī, n.: star

atque (conjunction): and

audāx, gen. audācis: daring, bold

audeō, audēre, ausus, -a, -um sum (semi-dep.): dare

audiō, audīre, audīvī, audītum: hear, listen to

auris, auris, f.: ear

autem: however, moreover

avārus, avāra, avārum: avaricious, greedy

bāsiō, bāsiāre, bāsiāvī, bāsiātum: kiss

bāsium, bāsiī, n.: kiss

bellicōsus, bellicōsa, bellicōsum: warlike, relating to war, military

bellum, bellī, n.: war

bellus, bella, bellum: beautiful, pretty, handsome

bene (adverb): well

benignissimē, adv.: most kindly

Vocabulary (Verba)

bibō, bibere, bibī, bibitum: drink

bonus, bona, bonum: good

brevis, breve: brief, short

caedō, caedere, cecīdī, caesum: cut, cut down, slay

caelestis, caeleste, third-declension adj.: heavenly

caelum, caelī, n.: sky, heaven

Caesar: Gaius Julius Caesar, politician, author, and conquerer of Gaul, famously assassinated on March 15 (the Ides), 44 B.C.E.

capiō, capere, cēpī, captum: seize, capture

caput, capitis, n.: head

carpō, carpere, carpsī, carptum: seize, harvest, pluck

cārus, cāra, cārum: dear, precious, beloved

causā (ablative form of *causa* when accompanied by a genitive): for the sake/purpose of

celer, celeris, celere: swift, quick

cēna, cēnae, f.: dinner

cēnō, cēnāre, cēnāvī, cēnātum: dine

cernō, cernere, crēvī, crētum: perceive

certus, certa, certum: certain, definite, sure

cēterī, cēterae, cētera: the remaining, the other, the rest

cibum: food

cibus, cibī, m.: food

cīvis, cīvis, m./f.: citizen

cīvitās, cīvitātis, f.: state, city

clādēs, clādis, f.: destruction, defeat, disaster

clārus, clāra, clārum: clear, bright; famous

coepī, coepisse, coeptum: began (defective verb occurring only in the past tense; for present-tense system, use *incipiō*)

cognoscō, cognoscere, cognōvī, cognitum: become acquainted with, know

collum, collī, n.: neck

colō, colere, coluī, cultum: worship

commendō, commendāre, commendāvī, commendātum: commend, approve, recommend

comparō, comparāre, comparāvī, comparātum: prepare, furnish, get ready

compōnō, compōnere, composuī, compositum: arrange, settle

comprobō, comprobāre, comprobāvī, comprobātum: approve, sanction

cōnfīdō, cōnfīdere, cōnfīsus, -a, -um sum (semi-dep.): trust in (takes dative object), have confidence in

cōnfodiō, cōnfodere, cōnfōdī, cōnfossum: stab

congregō, congregāre, congregāvī, congregātum: gather together, assemble

coniūnx, coniugis, m. or f.: spouse

coniūrātī, coniūrātōrum, m.: conspirators

coniūrō, coniūrāre, coniūrāvī, coniūrātum: conspire

cōnsilium, cōnsiliī, n.: counsel, advice, plan, purpose

consuētūdō, consuētūdinis, f.: custom

contrā (prep. + accusative): against

cornū, cornūs, n.: horn

corpus, corporis, n.: body

crās (adv.): tomorrow

crēdō, crēdere, crēdidī, crēditum: believe, trust (takes dative object)

crēscō, crēscere, crēvī, crētum: increase, grow, augment

crūdēlis, crūdēle: cruel

cum (conj.): when, since, although (with subjunctive); whenever (with indicative)

cum (prep. + abl.): with

cupiō, cupere, cupīvī, cupītum: desire, want

cūria, cūriae, f.: senate house

currō, currere, cucurrī, cursum: run, rush

currus, currūs, m.: chariot

custōdiō, custōdīre, custōdīvī, custōdītum: guard, defend, protect

dē (prep. + ablative): about, concerning, from

dea, deae, f.: goddess (dative and ablative plural = *deābus*)

dēbeō, dēbēre, dēbuī, dēbitum: owe, ought (often with infinitive, e.g., *dēbeō dūcere* = I ought to lead)

dēcernō, dēcernere, dēcrēvī, dēcrētum: decide, decree

dēcipiō, dēcipere, dēcēpī, dēceptum: deceive

dēleō, dēlēre, dēlēvī, dēlētum: erase, destroy

dēns, dentis, m.: tooth

dēpōnō, dēpōnere, dēposuī, dēpositum: put down, lay aside

dēserō, dēserere, dēseruī, desertum: desert, abandon

dēsinō, dēsinere, dēsiī: cease, stop

dēspiciō, dēspicere, dēspēxī, dēspectum: despise, look down on

deus, deī, m.: god

dī mānēs: divine spirits (in reference to the ancestral spirits of the deceased), divine spirit (although plural, can also be rendered in the singular to refer to a deceased individual)

dīcō, dīcere, dīxī, dictum: say, speak, tell

diēs, diēī, m. or f.: day

differō, differre, distulī, dīlātum: differ

difficilis, difficile: hard, difficult

dīligō, dīligere, dīlēxī, dīlēctum: esteem, love

dīmittō, dīmittere, dīmīsī, dīmissum: send away, dismiss, abandon

discēdō, discēdere, discessī, discessum: depart, go away

disciplīna, disciplīnae, f.: teaching, instruction

discipulī (m.), discipulae (f.): students

discō, discere, didicī: learn

dīvīnus, dīvīna, dīvīnum: of the gods, divine

dō, dare, dedī, datum: give, offer

doctrīna, doctrīnae, f.: teaching, learning

doleō, dolēre, doluī, dolitūrum: grieve, suffer, hurt

dolor, dolōris, m.: pain, grief

domina, dominae, f.: mistress

dominus, dominī, m.: master, lord

dōnum, dōnī, n.: gift

Druidēs, Druidum, m.: the Druids, the priests of the Celts in Gaul and Britain

dūcō, dūcere, dūxī, ductum: lead; consider, regard

dulcis, dulce: pleasant, sweet, agreeable

dum (conj.): while, as long as, provided that

dummodo (conj.): provided that, as long as

duo: two

dux, ducis: leader, guide, commander

edō, edere, ēdī, ēsum: eat

efferō, efferre, extulī, ēlātum: bring out, expose, publish

ego, meī (personal pronoun; cf. App. §40): I, me

ēiciō,ēicere, ēiēcī, ēiectum: throw out, drive out

enim (conj.): for, indeed

eō, īre, īvī, ītum: go

eō: to that place, thither

epistula, epistulae, f.: letter, epistle

ergō (adv.): therefore

errō, errāre, errāvī, errātum: err, be mistaken, wander

est: is

et: and (et ... et: both ... and)

etiam (adv.): even, also

etsī (conj.): even if, although

ex (prep. + ablative): from, out of

exemplar, exemplāris, n.: example

exeō, exīre, exiī, exitum: go out, exit

exīstimō, exīstimāre, exīstimāvī, exīstimātum: estimate, reckon, consider

exsilium, exsiliī, n.: banishment, exile

extinguō, extinguere, exstīnxī, exstīnctum: extinguish

facilis, facile: easy, agreeable

faciō, facere, fēcī, factum: do, make, cause, bring forth

fāma, fāmae, f.: rumor, report, fame, slander

familia, familiae, f.: family, household (*pater familiās* = father of the household; head of a Roman family)

fās (indeclinable noun), n.: religious law

fās est: it is religiously permissible, it is right, it is lawful

fatīgō, fatīgāre, fatīgāvī, fatīgātum: tire out, weary

fātum, fātī, n.: fate

fēlix, gen. fēlicis: happy, fortunate

fēmina, fēminae, f.: woman

ferō, ferre, tulī, lātum: bear, carry, endure

fidēlis, fidēle: faithful, loyal

fīlia, fīliae, f.: daughter (the dative and ablative plural are *fīliābus* to distinguish the forms from the dative/ablative *fīliīs*, for "sons")

fīlius, fīliī, m.: son

fīnis, fīnis, m. or f.: end, limit, purpose

fīnitimus, fīnitima, fīnitimum: neighboring, adjoining (used substantively as noun = neighbor)

fīō, fierī, factus sum: happen, become; be made, be done; come into existence

flōrēs: flowers

flōs, flōris, m.: flower

flūmen, flūminis, n.: river

fōrma, fōrmae, f.: form, shape, beauty

forsitan (adv.): perhaps

fortis, forte: strong, brave

foveō, fovēre, fōvī, fōtum: cherish, foster, nourish

frāter, frātris, m.: brother

fruor, fruī, fructus sum (+ abl.): enjoy, have the use and enjoyment of

fugiō, fugere, fūgī: flee, run away

Gallia: Gaul (corresponding geographically to modern France)

Gallus, Galla, Gallum: of Gaul, Gallic; pl. as noun: the Gauls, inhabiting Gaul, northern Italy, etc.

gaudeō, gaudēre, gavīsus, -a, -um sum (semi-dep.): rejoice

gaudium, gaudiī, n.: joy, delight

genū, genūs, n.: knee

Germānus, Germāna, Germānum: of Germany, German

gerō, gerere, gessī, gestum: wage, conduct, carry on

gignō, gignere, genuī, genitum: produce, beget, bring forth

grātiā (ablative form of *gratia* when accompanied by a genitive): for the sake/purpose of

grātia, grātiae, f.: favor, charm, grace

grātissimus, grātissima, grātissimum: most pleasing

gravis, grave: severe, serious, heavy, grievous

habeō, habēre, habuī, habitum: have, hold; consider

habitō, habitāre, habitāvī, habitātum: dwell, reside, live; inhabit

herī (adv.): yesterday

hic, haec, hoc (demonstrative adj. and pron.): this, this one

hodiē (adv.): today

homō, hominis, m.: human being, person, man

hōra, hōrae, f.: hour, time

hortor, hortārī, hortātus, -a, -um sum (dep.): urge, encourage

hospes, hospitis, m.: guest, stranger; host

hostis, hostis, m.: enemy

hūmānus, hūmāna, hūmānum: human

iam (adv.): now, already, soon

iānua, iānuae, f.: door

ibi: there

īdem, eadem, idem: the same

ignis, ignis, m.: fire

ille, illa, illud (demonstrative adj. and pron.): that, that one

immortālis, immortāle (adj.): immortal

imperātor, imperātōris, m.: commander, emperor

imperium, imperiī, n.: authority, supreme power, power to command

imperō, imperāre, imperāvī, imperātum: give orders to ; command

in (prep. + ablative): in, on; (prep. + accusative): into

inānis, ināne: empty, vain

incipiō, incipere, incēpī, inceptum: begin, commence

incrēdibilis, incrēdibile: incredible

inde: thence

indignus, indigna, indignum: unworthy

indulgēns, gen. indulgentis: lenient, gentle, kind, indulgent

ineō, inīre, iniī, initum: go in, enter

inimīcus, inimīcī, m.: enemy

iniūria, iniūriae, f.: injury, injustice, wrong

intellegō, intellegere, intellēxī, intellēctum: understand

inter (prep. + acc.): between, among

interficiō, interficere, interfēcī, interfectum: kill, murder

inveniō, invenīre, invēnī, inventum: find, come upon

invidus, invida, invidum: envious

invītus, invīta, invītum: unwilling

invocō, invocāre, invocāvī, invocātum: call upon, invoke

ipse, ipsa, ipsum: myself, yourself, himself, herself, itself, the very

īra, īrae, f.: wrath, anger, ire

is, ea, id (as demonstrative adj.): this, that

is, ea, id (as personal pron.): he, she, it

iste, ista, istud (demonstrative adj. and pron.): that of yours, that (often used disparagingly)

ita (adv.): so, thus

item: likewise

iter, itineris, n.: journey

iubeō, iubēre, iussī, iussum: order, command

iūdex, iūdicis, m.: judge

iūdicium, iūdiciī, n.: judgment, decision, trial

iūs, iūris, n.: law, especially human law (as opposed to *fās*: divine law)

iussum, iussī, n.: order, command, law

iūstus, iūsta, iūstum: just, righteous

iuvō, iuvāre, iūvi, iūtum: help, aid, assist

labor, labōris, m.: labor, work

laetus, laeta, laetum: happy, joyful

Latīnē (adv.): in Latin

laudō, laudāre, laudāvī, laudātum: praise

lēgātus, lēgātī, m.: ambassador

legiō, legiōnis, f.: legion

legō, legere, lēgī, lēctum: read

lēx, lēgis, f.: law

līber, lībera, līberum: free

liber, librī, m.: book

lībertās, lībertātis, f: freedom, liberty

lingua, linguae, f.: language, tongue

linguam Latīnam (direct object form): Latin language (*linguae Latīnae* = of the Latin language)

liquor, liquōris, m.: liquid, fluid

locus, locī, m.: place

longus, longa, longum: long

loquor, loquī, locūtus, -a, -um sum (dep.): talk, speak

lūna, lūnae, f.: moon

lūx, lūcis, f.: light

magis (adv.): more

magister, magistrī, m. (magistra, magistrae, f.): teacher, schoolmaster/schoolmistress

magnus, magna, magnum: big, large, great

maior, maius/maximus, -a, -um: comp./superl. forms of *magnus*

male (adv.): poorly

mālō, mālle, māluī: prefer

malus, mala, malum: bad, wicked, evil

maneō, manēre, mānsī, mānsum: remain, stay, abide

Mānēs, Mānium, m. or f.: departed spirits, the dead

manus, manūs (fourth declension), f.: hand, band, gang

mare, maris, n.: sea

māter, mātris, f.: mother

maximus, maxima, maximum: greatest, chief

melior, melius (comp. of *bonus*): better

memoria, memoriae, f.: memory, recollection

mendācium, mendāciī, n.: lie, falsehood, fiction

mēns, mentis, f.: mind

mēnsis, mēnsis, m.: month

metuō, metuere, metuī, metūtum: fear, dread

meus, mea, meum: my

mīles, mīlitis, m.: soldier

mīrābilis, mīrābile: amazing, marvelous, astonishing

miser, misera, miserum: wretched, unfortunate, miserable

misericors, gen. misericordis: merciful, tenderhearted, compassionate

mittō, mittere, mīsī, missum: send

mordeō, mordēre, momordī, morsus: bite

morior, morī, mortuus sum: die

mors, mortis, f.: death

mortuus, mortua, mortuum: dead

Vocabulary (Verba)

mōs, mōris, m.: custom, habit, manner, practice

mulier, mulieris, f.: woman

multum (adv.): very much

multus, multa, multum: much, many

nam: for, certainly, indeed

nascor, nascī, nātus, -a, -um sum: be born, arise

nāvis, nāvis, f.: ship

-ne (enclitic particle): attaches to the first word in the sentence to indicate that what follows is a question

nē ... quidem: not even, not so much as

nē: used with subjunctive verbs to express negative purpose (so that ... not)

nec (conj.): and not, nor

necesse est/erat/erit: it is/was/will be necessary

negō, negāre, negāvī, negātum: deny (used rather than dīcō ... nōn to introduce a negative indirect statement)

neque (conj.): and not; not even (neque ... neque = neither ... nor)

nequeō, nequīre, nequīvī, nequītum: be unable, not to be able (generally used where we might expect *nōn possum*)

neuter, neutra, neutrum: neither

nihil: nothing, not at all

nisi: if … not, unless

nocturnus, nocturna, nocturnum: nocturnal, by night

nōlō, nōlle, nōluī: not want, be unwilling (*nōlī/nōlīte* + infinitive = negative imperative, e.g., *nōlī amāre* = don't love!)

nōn: not

nōnne: interrogative adverb introducing questions that expect a "yes" answer (*Nōnne mē amās?* = Don't you love me?)

nōs, nostrum (personal pronoun; App. §40): we, us

noster, nostra, nostrum: our, ours

novus, nova, novum: new

nox, noctis, f.: night

nūbēs, nūbis, f.: cloud

nūllus, nūlla, nūllum: no, not any, none

num: interrogative adverb introducing questions that expect a "no" answer

numerus, numerī, m.: number

numquam (adv.): never

nunc: now

obdūrō, obdūrāre, obdūrāvī, obdūrātum: be hard, be unfeeling; endure, persist

obligō, obligāre, obligāvī, obligātum: bind

oboediō, oboedīre, oboedīvī, oboedītum (+ dat.): obey, be subject to

occidō, occidere, occidī, occāsum: fall, fall down, go down, set

oculus, oculī, m.: eye

ōdī, ōdisse (defective verb, with perfect-system forms and present-tense meaning): hate

offerō, offerre, obtulī, oblātum: bring to, present, offer; dedicate

omnis, omne: all, every

opera, operae, f.: work, pains (*dāre operam* = to give attention)

oppugnō, oppugnāre, oppugnāvī, oppugnātum: attack, assault, storm

ops, opis, f.: power, strength, property, assistance

optimus, optima, optimum (superl. of *bonus*): best

ōrdō, ōrdinis, m: order, arrangement, rank

pār, gen. paris: equal

parō, parāre, parāvī, parātum: prepare, provide, obtain

partior, partīrī, partītus, -a, -um sum (dep.): share

parvus, parva, parvum: small, little (comp. = *minor, minus*; superl. = *minimus, -a, -um*)

passus, passūs, m.: step, pace

patefaciō, patefacere, patefēcī, patefactum: make open; disclose, expose

pateō, patēre, patuī: lie open, be open, be accessible, be evident

pater, patris, m.: father

patior, patī, passus, -a, -um sum (dep.): suffer, endure

paucī, paucae, pauca (plural adj.): few, a few

pāx, pācis, f.: peace (not an *i*-stem)

pecūnia, pecūniae, f.: money

peior, peius (comp. of *malus*): worse

per (prep. + acc.): through

peragō, peragere, perēgī, peractus: complete, carry out, accomplish

perīculum, perīculī, n.: danger, risk

perpetuus, perpetua, perpetuum: everlasting, never-ending

perveniō, pervenīre, pervēnī, perventum: arrive, reach

pēs, pedis, m.: foot

pessimus, pessima, pessimum (superl. of *malus*): worst

petō, petere, petīvī, petītum: seek, ask for, beg

plācō, plācāre, plācāvī, plācātum: appease, soothe, calm, placate

poena, poenae, f.: penalty, punishment

poēta, poētae, m.: poet

pōnō, pōnere, posuī, positum: put, place, put aside, put away

pontifex/pontificēs, m.: priest/priests (*pontifex maximus* = chief priest)

Vocabulary (Verba)

populus, populī, m.: people, nation

possum, posse, potuī: be able

post (prep. + acc.): after

potēns, gen. potentis: mighty, powerful, strong

praesidium, praesidiī, n.: fort, defense

praesum, praeesse, praefuī, praefutūrum: be in charge of; be responsible for (takes dative object)

praeter (prep. + accusative): besides, except, beyond

precor, precārī, precātus, -a, -um sum (dep.): pray, beg, entreat

prīncipium, prīncipiī, n.: beginning

prō (prep. + abl.): for, on behalf of, in front of, before

prōcēdō, prōcēdere, prōcessī, prōcessum: go forward, advance, prosper

prōvidentia, prōvidentiae, f.: foresight, providence

prōvincia, prōvinciae, f.: province

puella, puellae, f.: girl

puer, puerī, m.: boy

pugnō, pugnāre, pugnāvī pugnātum: fight

pulcher, pulchra, pulchrum: beautiful

pulsō, pulsāre, pulsāvī, pulsātum: strike, beat

375

pūniō, pūnīre pūnīvī, pūnītum: punish

putō, putāre, putāvī, putātum: think, judge, suppose, imagine

quā: by which route?, where?

quaerō, quaerere, quaesīvī, quaesītum: seek, look for, strive for

quālis, quāle: what sort of?

quam: than (in comparisons); as ... as possible (with superlatives)

quamvīs (conj.): although

quandō: when?

quantus, quanta, quantum: how large?, how great?, how much?, how many?

-que: attaches to a word to indicate "and" (*discipulī discipulaeque* = male students and female students)

queror, querī, questus sum: complain, lament, bewail

quī, quae, quod (interrogative adjective): what?, which?, what kind of? (forms match those of the relative pronoun)

quī, quae, quod (relative pronoun): who, which, that

quia (conj.): since, because

quid: what?

quis, quid (interrogative pronoun): who?, what?, which?

quō: to what place?, whither?

quot: how many?

quotiēns: how often?

rapidus, rapida, rapidum: fast, swift

ratiō, ratiōnis: reckoning, account; reason; method

recēdō, recēdere, recessī, recessum: depart, go away

recipiō, recipere, recēpī, receptum: receive, admit, regain

reddō, reddere, reddidī, redditum: give back, render, restore

relinquō, relinquere, relīquī, relictum: leave, leave behind, abandon

reliquus, reliqua, reliquum: the rest of, the remaining, the other

remissiō, remissiōnis, f: release, letting go; forgiveness

repudium, repudiī, n.: casting off, divorce

requīrō, requīrere, requīsīvī, requīsītum: seek, ask for, miss, need, require

rēs pūblica: republic, state

rēs, reī, f.: thing (any object of imagination or experience), matter, affair; deed; property, wealth

resideō, residēre, resēdī: remain, stay behind; reside, abide

rēx, rēgis, m.: king

rogō, rogāre, rogāvī, rogātum: ask, ask for

Rōma, Rōmae, f.: Rome

rūmor, rūmōris, m.: gossip, report

sacer, sacra, sacrum: sacred, consecrated, devoted

sacrificium, sacrificiī, n.: animal sacrifice

saeculum (or saeclum) saeculī, n.: age, generation; world

salvē (sing.), salvēte (pl.): greetings

sānctus, sāncta, sānctum: holy, sacred

sānus, sāna, sānum: sound, healthy, sane

sapiēns, gen. sapientis: wise, judicious

sapientia, sapientiae, f.: wisdom

scelestus, scelesta, scelestum: wicked, accursed

scientia, scientiae, f.: knowledge, science

scrībō, scrībere, scrīpsī, scrīptum: write, compose

sed (conjunction): but

semper (adv.): always

senātus, senātūs, m. (fourth-declension noun): senate

senex, senis, m.: old man

sentiō, sentīre, sēnsī, sēnsum: feel, perceive

sēparō, sēparāre, sēparāvī, sēparātum: separate, divide

sepeliō, sepelīre, sepelīvī, sepultum: bury

sequor, sequī, secūtus, -a, -um sum (dep.): follow

servō, servāre, servāvī, servātum: save, keep, preserve

servus, servī, m.: slave

sevērissimē, adv.: most severely

sevērus, sevēra, sevērum: stern, severe

sī (conj.): if

silva, silvae, f.: forest, wood

sōl, sōlis, m.: sun

soleō, solēre, solitus, -a, -um sum (semi-dep.): be accustomed

sōlus, sōla, sōlum: only, alone

solvō, solvere, solvī, solūtus: release, loosen, unbind

soror, sorōris, f.: sister

stō, stāre, stetī, statum: stand

studeō, studēre, studuī: be eager for, concentrate on, study (takes dative object)

studium, studiī, n.: study, pursuit, eagerness

stultus, stulta, stultum: foolish, stupid

suādeō, suādēre, suāsī, suāsum: advise, recommend, urge, persuade

sub (prep. + ablative): under

sufferō, sufferre, sustulī, sublātum: hold up, support; endure, suffer

suī (gen.), sibi (dat.), sē, sē (reflexive pronoun): him/her/it/them; himself/herself/itself/themselves (in reference to the main subject)

sum, esse, fuī, futūrum: be

suus, sua, suum (reflexive possessive): his/her/its/their own (in reference to the main subject)

taberna, tabernae, f.: booth, stall, inn, tavern

tālis, tāle: such, of such a sort

tam (adv., often introducing result clause): so, to such a degree

tandem: at length, at last, finally

tantus, tanta, tantum: so large, so great

tellūs, tellūris, f.: earth, globe; ground

tempus, temporis, n.: time

terra, terrae, f.: earth, ground, land

terreō, terrēre, terruī, territum: frighten, terrify

testis, testis, m. or f.: witness

timeō, timēre, timuī: fear, be afraid of

timor, timōris, m.: fear

tōtus, tōta, tōtum: whole, entire

tū, tuī, tibi, tē, tē (personal pronoun; App. §40): you (sing.)

tueor, tuērī, tūtus, -a, -um sum: watch over, guard

tuus, tua, tuum: your, yours (singular)

ubi: where?

ūllus, ūlla, ūllum: any

ultimus, ultima, ultimum: last, final; extreme

ūltiō, ūltiōnis, f.: vengeance, revenge

ultrā (prep. + acc.): beyond

umquam (adv.): ever

unde: from what source?, whence?

ūnus, ūna, ūnum: one

urbs, urbis, f.: city

ūrō, ūrere, ussī, ustum: burn

ut: used with subjunctive verbs to express purpose (so that ...)

uter, utra, utrum: which (of two things), either

utrum ... an: whether ... or

uxor, uxōris, f.: wife

vae tē: woe is you

valē (sing.), valēte (pl.): be well, farewell

valeō, valēre, valuī, valitūrum: be strong, have power, be valid; be well, fare well

-ve (conjunction added to end of word): or

vehemēns, gen. vehementis: furious, violent, harsh, strong

vendō, vendere, vendidī, venditum: sell

venēnum, venēnī, n.: potion, drug, poison

veniō, venīre, vēnī, ventum: come

verberō, verberāre, verberāvī, verberātum: beat, strike, lash

verbum, verbī, n.: word

vereor, verērī, veritus,-a, -um sum (dep.): fear, respect

vēritās, vēritātis, f.: truth

vērō (adv.): in truth, indeed

vester, vestra, vestrum: your, yours (pl.)

via, viae, f.: street, road, way

videō, vidēre, vīdī, vīsum: see, discern

vīlla, vīllae, f.: villa, country house

vincō, vincere, vīcī, victum: conquer

vindicō, vindicāre, vindicāvī, vindicātum: punish, avenge

vīnum, vīnī, n.: wine

vir, virī, m.: man

virgō, virginis, f.: young woman, maiden (*virgō Vestālis* = Vestal priestess)

virtūs, virtūtis, f.: strength, courage

vīta, vītae, f.: life

vitium, vitii, n.: vice

vīvō, vīvere, vīxī, vīctum: live

vocō, vocāre, vocāvi, vocātum: call, summon

volō, velle, voluī: want, wish, be willing

vōx, vōcis, f.: voice (not an *i*-stem)

Vulcānus, Vulcānī, m.: fire (-god)

vulnus, vulneris, n.: wound

Answer Key

Note: Macrons (long marks over vowels) are given for reference. You are encouraged to become familiar with the use of macrons, but your answers do not need to include them.

Lecture 2

I.

	Singular	Plural
1	-ō or -m	-mus
2	-s	-tis
3	-t	-nt

II.

	Singular	Plural
1	agō	agimus
2	agis	agitis
3	agit	agunt

III.

	Singular	Plural
1	pōnō	pōnimus
2	pōnis	pōnitis
3	pōnit	pōnunt

	Singular	Plural
1	bibō	bibimus
2	bibis	bibitis
3	bibit	bibunt

	Singular	Plural
1	vincō	vincimus
2	vincis	vincitis
3	vincit	vincunt

IV.

1. dīcere 2. pōne 3. pōnite 4. bibere 5. edite 6. vendimus 7. agere 8. agit 9. age 10. vincere 11. vincunt 12. bibunt 13. caedimus 14. caedisne 15. editis

V.

1. Caesar says (is saying/does say). 2. We say (are saying/do say). 3. Speak, women! 4. Caesar wages (is waging/does wage) war. 5. Caesar cuts (is cutting/does cut) the flowers. 6. The soldiers cut (are cutting/do cut) the flowers. 7. Put away the flowers, soldiers, and conquer! 8. The soldiers eat (are eating/do eat) the food. 9. The priests drink (are drinking/do drink) the wine. 10. I sell (am selling/do sell) the slave. 11. Conquer, Caesar! 12. Wage war, soldiers! 13. We eat (are eating/do eat) the food and drink (are drinking/do drink) the wine. 14. Are you eating (do you eat) the food? 15. Do you drink (are you drinking) wine?

Note: As indicated in the key for exercise V, the present-tense indicative may be translated "verbs," "is verbing," or "does verb." From this point forward, the answer key will offer only one of these three possibilities, but you may select any of them for your translations of the present-tense indicative.

Lecture 3

I.

	Singular	Plural
1	-ō or -m	-mus
2	-s	-tis
3	-t	-nt

II.

	Singular	Plural
1	vīvō	vīvimus
2	vīvis	vīvitis
3	vīvit	vīvunt

III.

	Singular	Plural
1	vīvam	vīvāmus
2	vīvās	vīvātis
3	vīvat	vīvant

IV.

Note: From this point forward, the answer key will not provide verb charts, but you are encouraged to continue to create your own verb charts, as indicated in the drills, throughout the course.

1. singular: pōnam, pōnās, pōnat/plural: pōnāmus, pōnātis, pōnant

2. dēsinō, dēsinis, dēsinit/dēsinimus, dēsinitis, dēsinunt

3. discō, discis, discit/discimus, discitis, discunt

4. bibam, bibās, bibat/bibāmus, bibātis, bibant

V.

1. we drink 2. let us drink (we may drink/we should drink) 3. they are learning 4. let them learn (they may learn/they should learn) 5. you cease 6. you may cease (you should cease)

Note: As indicated in the key for exercise V, the present-tense subjunctive may be translated "let verb," "may verb," or "should verb." (In actual Latin sentences, context often determines or suggests the best alternative.)

From this point forward, the answer key will offer only one of these three possibilities, but you may select any of them for your translations of the present tense subjunctive.

VI.

1. Mulierēs discunt. 2. Discant mulierēs. 3. Linguam Latīnam discāmus. 4. Dēsine! 5. Dēsinite! 6. Edunt mīlitēs ut vīvant. 7. Edat bibatque mīles. 8. Bibāmus ut vīvāmus. 9. Vincit Caesar. 10. Caesar vincat. 11. Fīat lūx! 12. Salvēte, discipulī discipulaeque!

Note: As indicated in the key for exercise VI, word order in Latin is variable. For example, verbs may come at the beginning, middle, or end of a sentence, and a noun subject may be found anywhere in the sentence—not necessarily at the beginning. As you check your sentence translations against the answer key, focus less on word order and more on noun, adjective, and verb forms and endings. The professor discusses word order at various points in the course.

Lecture 4

I.

legō, legis, legit/legimus, legitis, legunt

II.

sum, es, est/sumus, estis, sunt

III.

1. possum, potes, potest/possumus, potestis, possunt

2. sim, sīs, sit/sīmus, sītis, sint

3. legam, legās, legat/legāmus, legātis, legant

4. possim, possīs, possit/possīmus, possītis, possint

IV.

1. Potest. 2. Possit. 3. Sunt. 4. Sint. 5. Possumus legere. 6. Possīmus legere. 7. Mulierēs discere possunt. 8. Possuntne vincere mīlitēs? 9. Possuntne discipulī discipulaeque linguam Latīnam discere? 10. Estis mīlitēs, sed mīlitēs nōn sumus. 11. Esne mīles? 12. Sit.

V.

1. Caesar can deceive the Roman people. 2. Take care, so that you may be well! 3. We drink and eat so that we may be able to live well. 4. If there is light, we can drink. 5. The soldiers are able to conquer but they do not conquer. 6. Life is short. 7. Art can be long (lasting). 8. To be is to be able. 9. You can read well, (female) students. 10. They are not soldiers.

Lecture 5

I.

1. reddō, reddis, reddit/reddimus, redditis, reddunt

2. prōcēdam, prōcēdās, prōcēdat/prōcēdāmus, prōcēdātis, prōcēdant

3. sum, es, est/sumus, estis, sunt

4. possim, possīs, possit/possīmus, possītis, possint

II.

	Singular	Plural
Nominative	***	-ēs
Genitive	-is	-um
Dative	-ī	-ibus
Accusative	-em	-ēs
Ablative	-e	-ibus

III.

	Singular	Plural
Nominative	mīles	mīlitēs
Genitive	mīlitis	mīlitum
Dative	mīlitī	mīlitibus
Accusative	mīlitem	mīlitēs
Ablative	mīlite	mīlitibus

IV.

	Singular	Plural
Nominative	virtūs	virtūtēs
Genitive	virtūtis	virtūtum
Dative	virtūtī	virtūtibus
Accusative	virtūtem	virtūtēs
Ablative	virtūte	virtūtibus

V.

Note: From this point forward, the answer key will not provide noun charts, but you are encouraged to continue to create your own noun charts, as indicated in the drills, throughout the course.

1. singular: lūx, lūcis, lūcī, lūcem, lūce/plural: lūcēs, lūcum, lūcibus, lūcēs, lūcibus

2. vēritās, vēritātis, vēritātī, vēritātem, vēritāte/vēritātēs, vēritātum, vēritātibus, vēritātēs, vēritātibus

VI.

1. genitive singular, of the truth 2. ablative singular, by/with/from the light 3. nominative plural, the soldiers verb OR accusative plural, verb the soldiers 4. genitive plural, of the soldiers 5. genitive singular, of Caesar 6. dative

plural, to/for the months OR ablative plural, by/with/from the months 7. dative singular, to/for the truth 8. dative singular, to/for Caesar 9. genitive plural, of the lights 10. ablative singular, by/with/from strength

VII.

1. Mīlitēs Caesaris vincunt. 2. Caesar mīlitī dīcit vēritātem. 3. Prōcēdāmus! 4. Sit vēritās lūx mentis. 5. Virtūs mīlitum est magna. 6. Mentis virtūte discit mulier. 7. Caesarī laudem reddite! 8. Reddāmus laudem vēritātī. 9. Caesarem dēcipere mīlitēs nōn possunt. 10. Vēritātem discere nōn possumus.

Lecture 6

I.

1. sum, es, est/sumus, estis, sunt

2. bibō, bibis, bibit/bibimus, bibitis, bibunt

3. possum, potes, potest/possumus, potestis, possunt

II.

1. sim, sīs, sit/sīmus, sītis, sint

2. bibam, bibās, bibat/bibāmus, bibātis, bibant

3. possim, possīs, possit/possīmus, possītis, possint

III.

1. mulier, mulieris, mulierī, mulierem, muliere/mulierēs, mulierum, mulieribus, mulierēs, mulieribus

2. corpus, corporis, corporī, corpus, corpore/corpora, corporum, corporibus, corpora, corporibus

3. flōs, flōris, flōrī, flōrem, flōre/flōrēs, flōrum, flōribus, flōrēs, flōribus

IV.

corpus, corporis, corporī, corpus, corpore/corpora, corporum, corporibus, corpora, corporibus

V.

1. corporibus mīlitum 2. virtūte mulieris 3. hostibus Caesaris 4. lūce mentis 5. Mulierēs liquōrem bibunt. 6. Hostēs cum mīlite pugnant. 7. Salvēte, discipulī discipulaeque linguae Latīnae! 8. Pōnant flōrēs mulierēs. 9. Possumusne flōrēs caedere? 10. Edāmus ut virtūtem reddāmus.

Lecture 7

I.

Case	1st Declension Feminine	2nd Declension Masculine	2nd Declension Neuter
Singular			
Nominative	-a	-us/-er	-um
Genitive	-ae	-ī	-ī
Dative	-ae	-ō	-ō
Accusative	-am	-um	-um
Ablative	-ā	-ō	-ō
Plural			
Nominative	-ae	-ī	-a
Genitive	-ārum	-ōrum	-ōrum
Dative	-īs	-īs	-īs
Accusative	-ās	-ōs	-a
Ablative	-īs	-īs	-īs

II.

	Singular	Plural
Nominative	mīles bonus	mīlitēs bonī
Genitive	mīlitis bonī	mīlitum bōnorum
Dative	mīlitī bonō	mīlitibus bonīs
Accusative	mīlitem bonum	mīlitēs bonōs
Ablative	mīlite bonō	mīlitibus bonīs

III.

1. corpus magnum, corporis magnī, corporī magnō, corpus magnum, corpore magnō/corpora magna, corporum magnōrum, corporibus magnīs, corpora magna, corporibus magnīs

2. mulier pulchra, mulieris pulchrae, mulierī pulchrae, mulierem pulchram, muliere pulchrā/mulierēs pulchrae, mulierum pulchrārum, mulieribus pulchrīs, mulierēs pulchrās, mulieribus pulchrīs

IV.

1. genitive singular, of the good woman 2. ablative singular, by/with/from great strength 3. dative singular, to/for the most pleasing light 4. accusative singular, verb everlasting night 5. nominative plural, beautiful minds verb 6. accusative plural, verb the free soldiers 7. dative plural, to/for the everlasting months OR ablative plural, by/with/from the everlasting months 8. nominative singular, the stern enemy verbs 9. genitive plural, of the beautiful women 10. accusative singular, verb the good old man 11. nominative plural, the large bodies verb OR accusative plural, verb the large bodies 12. nominative plural, the beautiful flowers verb 13. genitive plural, of the great lights 14. dative plural to/for the severe truths OR ablative plural, by/with/from the severe truths 15. dative singular, to/for the good soldier

Lecture 8

I.

1. pontifex maximus, pontificis maximī, pontificī maximō, pontificem maximum, pontifice maximō/pontificēs maximī, pontificum maximōrum, pontificibus maximīs, pontificēs maximōs, pontificibus maximīs

2. astrum aeternum, astrī aeternī, astrō aeternō, astrum aeternum, astrō aeternō/astra aeterna, astrōrum aeternōrum, astrīs aeternīs, astra aeterna, astrīs aeternīs

3. fēmina misera, fēminae miserae, fēminae miserae, fēminam miseram, fēminā miserā/fēminae miserae, fēminārum miserārum, fēminīs miserīs, fēminās miserās, fēminīs miserīs

4. agricola miser, agricolae miserī, agricolae miserō, agricolam miserum, agricolā miserō/agricolae miserī, agricolārum miserōrum, agricolīs miserīs, agricolās miserōs, agricolīs miserīs

II.

1. virginī pulchrae 2. bellō magnō 3. ignis magnī 4. puerōrum bonōrum 5. bāsia grātissima 6. fēminārum līberārum 7. servō sevērō 8. ignibus aeternīs 9. puellās bonās 10. noctis aeternae

III.

1. The women's slaves read well. 2. The wretched boy lives badly. 3. Let the wretched maidens drink. 4. The stern soldiers wage a great war. 5. Let the fire be great. (Let there be a great fire.) 6. Can the good farmers sell (their) food? 7. Let the good old man speak truth to the chief priest. 8. Cut the beautiful flowers!

Lecture 9

I.

-ō (or -m), -s, -t/-mus, -tis, -nt

II.

-r, -ris, -tur/-mur, -mini, -ntur

III.

1. color, coleris, colitur/colimur, colimini, coluntur

2. dēsinar, dēsināris, dēsinātur/dēsināmur, dēsināminī, dēsinantur

3. legam, legās, legat/legāmus, legātis, legant

4. dūcō, dūcis, dūcit/dūcimus, dūcitis, dūcunt

5. mittar, mittāris, mittātur/mittāmur, mittāminī, mittantur

IV.

1. mittor 2. mittar 3. mittimus 4. dūcāmus 5. dūce! 6. dūcantur 7. vendī 8. venditis 9. venditur 10. agiminī! 11. agere 12. agam

V.

The ablative of agent requires a preposition (a/ab); it expresses the person by whom an action is performed. Dūcitur ā Caesarō = ablative of agent.

The ablative of means requires no preposition; it expresses the tool or instrument (generally inanimate) by means of which an action is performed. Dūcitur vēritāte = ablative of means.

VI.

1. Mīlitēs dūcuntur ā Caesare. 2. Potest vēritāte dūcī.

Lecture 10

I.

1. capiō, capis, capit/capimus, capitis, capiunt

2. fugiam, fugiās, fugiat/fugiāmus, fugiātis, fugiant

3. sentiam, sentiās, sentiat/sentiāmus, sentiātis, sentiant

4. veniō, venīs, venit/venīmus, venītis, veniunt

II.

1. Veniant. 2. Venīmus. 3. Fugite! 4. Capiat. 5. Cupere. 6. Ades! 7. Adestis. 8. Custōdīte! 9. Custōdit. 10. Sentiam.

III.

mulier laeta, mulieris laetae, mulierī laetae, mulierem laetam, muliere laetā/ mulierēs laetae, mulierum laetārum, mulieribus laetīs, mulierēs laetās, mulieribus laetīs

IV.

1. They are not able to come to Bethlehem. 2. Are we able to come to Bethlehem? 3. Let them come to Bethlehem. 4. The great legion is able to protect the city. 5. Let the old man guard the truth. 6. Are the severe soldiers able to conquer Caesar's enemies? 7. Let us flee from the city. 8. We are fleeing from the city. 9. The soldiers are coming so that they may guard the city. 10. The students (male or a mixed group) desire to learn the beautiful Latin language so that they may be happy.

Lecture 11

I.

rēx bonus, rēgis bonī, rēgī bonō, rēgem bonum, rēge bonō/rēgēs bonī, rēgum bonōrum, rēgibus bonīs, rēgēs bonōs, rēgibus bonīs

II.

1. -āre 2. -ēre 3. -ere 4. -ere 5. -īre

III.

1. audiō, audīs, audit/audīmus, audītis, audiunt

2. amō, amās, amat/amāmus, amātis, amant

3. habeam, habeās, habeat/habeāmus, habeātis, habeant

4. videō, vidēs, videt/vidēmus, vidētis, vident

5. adōrem, adōrēs, adōret/adōrēmus, adōrētis, adōrent

IV.

1. Dominum magnum adōrāmus. 2. Adōret rēgem bonum. 3. Vidē rēgem angelōrum! 4. Legiōnēs rēgis audīre potest. 5. Amāsne mīlitem pulchrum? 6. Virtūtem mulieris magnae laudētis. 7. Vēritātem laudant. 8. Vēritātem amā, Caesar! 9. Laeta nōn est, et populum Rōmānum dēcipit. 10. Rēgem magnum nōn vidēmus, sed virtūtem mīlitum sentīre possumus. 11. Dominum sevērum amāre nōn possumus. 12. Legat dominus librōs bonōs, ut vēritātem amet. 13. Virtūtem mentis nōn habet. 14. Habeāmus cibum vīnumque! 15. Veniunt in Bethlehem, ut rēgem adōrent.

Lecture 12

I.

1. vīvō, vīvis, vīvit/vīvimus, vīvitis, vīvunt

2. amem, amēs, amet/amēmus, amētis, ament

3. aestimem, aestimēs, aestimet/aestimēmus, aestimētis, aestiment

4. amo, amās, amāt/amāmus, amātis, amant

5. vīvam, vīvās, vīvat/vīvāmus, vīvātis, vīvant

II.

1. sum, es, est/sumus, estis, sunt

2. possim, possīs, possit/possīmus, possītis, possint

III.

1. disce, discite: Learn! 2. adōrā, adōrāte: Adore! 3. habē, habēte: Have! 4. potes, poteste: Be able! 5. audī, audīte: Hear!

IV.

lūx perpetua, lūcis perpetuae, lūcī perpetuae, lūcem perpetuam, lūce perpetuā/lūcēs perpetuae, lūcum perpetuārum, lūcibus perpetuīs, lūcēs perpetuās, lūcibus perpetuīs

V.

1. Vīvāmus. 2. Ament. 3. Amant. 4. Senem audiāmus. 5. Vēritātem senex audit. 6. Vīnum dominī laudat. 7. Rēgem meum audīte! 8. Occīdit sōl. 9. Amāsne fēminam alteram? 10. Lūcem legiōnēs miserī nōn vident.

Lecture 13

I.

1. laudō, laudās, laudat/laudāmus, laudātis, laudant

2. videar, videāris, videātur/videāmur, videāminī, videantur

3. sentior, sentīris, sentītur/sentīmur, sentīminī, sentiuntur

4. congregem, congregēs, congreget/congregēmus, congregētis, congregent

5. habeō, habēs, habet/habēmus, habētis, habent

6. audiar, audiāris, audiātur/audiāmur, audiāminī, audiantur

II.

1. Puella ūnum puerum amat. 2. Multae puellae ā puerō amantur. 3. Puerum pulchrum virgo misera amāre dēsinat. 4. Senēs bonī ā Caesare audiantur. 5. Caesar ā mīlitibus nōn audītur. 6. Agricolae laetī in urbe congregant. 7. Congregāte, servī! 8. Sub magnā ulmō congregāmur. 9. Urbēs ā legiōnibus imperātōris custōdiantur. 10. Vidērisne ā fēminā? 11. Vidētisne puerum alterum in aquā? 12. Possuntne hostēs capī? 13. Ā discipulīs audīrī nōn possum. 14. Deī laudentur! 15. Lūx vēritātis ā rēge nōn vidētur.

Lecture 14

I.

1. poēta audāx, poētae audācis, poētae audācī, poētam audācem, poētā audācī/poētae audācēs, poētārum audācium, poētis audācibus, poētās audācēs, poētis audācibus

2. vir fortis, virī fortis, virō fortī, virum fortem, virō fortī/virī fortēs, virōrum fortium, virīs fortibus, virōs fortēs, virīs fortibus

3. vulnus ācre, vulneris ācris, vulnerī acrī, vulnus ācre, vulnere ācrī/vulnera ācria, vulnerum ācrium, vulneribus ācribus, vulnera ācria, vulneribus ācribus

II.

1. linguae facilis 2. legiōnibus ācribus 3. sub caelō pulchrō 4. in magnō dolōre 5. corporibus fortibus 6. puellārum audācium 7. mēnsēs brevēs 8. mente fortī 9. bella facilia 10. in ācrem hostis urbem

III.

1. The wound causes pain for the soldier. 2. Let us praise the courage of the brave women. 3. The truth can be learned from bitter grief(s). 4. Students of the Latin language have keen minds. 5. Beautiful flowers are brought forth by the sun's light. 6. Strong, good men are being killed in the fierce war. 7. The (female) slaves of the fierce master are being gathered into the wretched place. 8. Be strong, boys and girls! 9. Let us worship the eternal God, not brief life. 10. It is not easy to discern the truth.

Lecture 15

I.

1. mare magnum, maris magnī, marī magnō, mare magnum, marī magnō/ maria magna, marium magnōrum, maribus magnīs, maria magna, maribus magnīs

2. urbs magna, urbis magnae, urbī magnae, urbem magnam, urbe magnā/ urbēs magnae, urbium magnārum, urbibus magnīs, urbēs magnās, urbibus magnīs

II.

1. The city's women desire peace. 2. The enemies are coming in (or by) ships across the sea in order to wage a great war. 3. The truth cannot be perceived by the wretched men. 4. There are fierce animals in the forest but at night

I am protected by Caesar's soldier. 5. Let us overcome the grief of (these) never-ending nights! 6. Rumors are not heard by a good king.

III.

1. Virginis artem poēta magnus laudat. 2. Bellum agere dēsinat et in pāce vivāmus laetī. 3. Multa animālia ab alterō agricolā venduntur. 4. Vōcem dominī audīre nōn potest senex. 5. Servī magnīs in nāvibus ā legiōnum imperātōre congregantur.

Lecture 16

I.

Please see the chart in the lecture summary for the correct forms of the relative pronoun. It may also be found in App. §46.

B

1. The girl who loves the beautiful boy is happy. 2. The old man to whom we are giving food is wretched. 3. The enemies against whom we fight are fierce. 4. The field in which the poets are assembling is large. 5. The man whose daughter you praise, O farmer, is stern. 6. He is the father of the boy whom I adore. 7. The legions are guarding the city in which we live. 8. Do you worship the immortal gods about whom the chief priest is telling the truth? 9. The truth that we discern is eternal. 10. The commander leads many (men), among whom is my son.

b

1. Potestisne astrum vidēre quod videō? 2. Rēgis ācris mīlitēs audīmus, ā quō urbs pulchra vincitur. 3. Virginum virtus quās laudant magna est. 4. Vīnum quod bibis grātissimum est. 5. Agricola ā cuius mātre laudāmur fīlium amat, sed fīliam nōn habet.

Lecture 17

I.

1. rogābam, rogābās, rogābat/rogābāmus, rogābātis, rogābant 2. intellegar, intellegēris, intellegētur/intellegēmur, intellegēminī, intellegentur 3. requīram, requīrēs, requīret/requīrēmus, requīrētis, requīrent 4. dēcipiēbar, dēcipiēbāris, dēcipiēbātur/dēcipiēbāmur, dēcipiēbāminī, dēcipiēbantur 5. manēbō, manēbis, manēbit/manēbimus, manēbitis, manēbunt 6. laudābor, laudāberis, laudābitur/laudābimur, laudābiminī, laudābuntur 7. cupiēbam, cupiēbās, cupiēbat/cupiēbāmus, cupiēbātis, cupiēbant 8. dolērem, dolērēs, dolēret/dolērēmus, dolērētis, dolērent 9. intellegerer, intellegerēris, intellegerētur/intellegerēmur, intellegerēminī, intellegerentur

II.

1. manēbam 2. requīrēris 3. rogābant 4. intellegētur 5. dolēbātis 6. dolērēmus 7. colēbat 8. colēbātur 9. colēris 10. custōdiēbāmus 11. bibent 12. habēbō 13. habēbat 14. dēcipientur 15. ederet 16. Fugiēbātisne? 17. Discetne? 18. dēsineret 19. dābunt 20. vendēbātur

Lecture 18

I.

1. recēdam, recēdēs, recēdet/recēdēmus, recēdētis, recēdent 2. obdūrārem, obdūrārēs, obdūrāret/obdūrārēmus, obdūrārētis, obdūrārent 3. āmittēbar, āmittēbāris, āmittēbātur/ āmittēbāmur, āmittēbāminī, āmittēbantur

II.

cīvitās bellicōsa, cīvitātis bellicōsae, cīvitātī bellicōsae, cīvitātem bellicōsam, cīvitāte bellicōsā/cīvitātēs bellicōsae, cīvitātum bellicōsārum, cīvitātibus bellicōsīs, cīvitātēs bellicōsās, cīvitātibus bellicōsīs

III.

1. We will not fear the ultimate end of life. 2. Will the girl desert the handsome farmer whom she now (recently) used to love? 3. The Roman soldiers were fighting against (their) warlike enemies with great courage. 4. You will remain in the city with (your) daughter but I will go away into a neighboring province. 5. One who fears death misses the joy of life. 6. Skill (art) in (of) the Latin language will never abandon you. 7. I will not pursue the unwilling boy and he will grieve when he is not pursued. 8. Persist (be hard)! The danger is great and we women are few, but we will be able to protect the city. 9. The warlike mind of the king will bring forth grief among the people. 10. Let us stop praising war and let us live both in peace and with great joy.

Appendix

This appendix represents an adaptation of pp. 424–465 of Arthur Tappan Walker's *Caesar's Gallic War with Introduction, Notes, Vocabulary and Grammatical Appendix* (Chicago and New York: Scott Foresman and Company, 1907).

PRONUNCIATION

LENGTH OF VOWELS

1. A vowel is usually short:

    a. Before another vowel or before h; as in eō, nihil.

    b. Before nd and nt; as in laudandus, laudant.

    c. In words with more than one syllable before any final consonant other than s, as in laudem, laudat. (But compare laudās.)

2. A vowel is long:

    a. Before nf, ns, nx, and nct, as in īnferō, cōnsul, iūnxī, iūnctum.

    b. When it results from contraction, as in īsset, from iisset.

3. A vowel is usually long:

    a. In one syllable words (monosyllables) not ending in b, d, l, m, or t, as in mē, hīc (but compare ab and ad where the vowels are short).

PRONUNCIATION OF VOWELS

4. In classical Latin pronunciation, long vowels, whether they were accented or not, were supposed to receive twice the time given to the

pronunciation of short vowels. This rule matters more in reading poetry metrically than it does in reading prose.

a = a in tuba	ā = a in father
e = e in net	ē = e in they
i = i in pin	ī = i in machine
o = o in for (not as in hot)	ō = o in pony
u = oo in foot	ū = oo in food

y = French u or German ü; but this sound rarely occurs.

SOUNDS OF DIPHTHONGS

5. Diphthongs are the sounds produced by two vowels when the first slides into the second so quickly that it seems as if both are pronounced simultaneously. A diphthong thus produces only one, not two, syllables. The following diphthongs are those that appear in classical Latin:

ae = ai in aisle

oe = oi in oil

au = ow in how

eu has no English equivalent. Run together in one syllable the sounds eh'-oo.

ui has no English equivalent. Run together in one syllable the sounds oo'-ee. This diphthong appears in cui, huic, cuius, and huius.

a. When the consonant i (= j in older classical editions) appears between two vowels, as in maior, eius, Troia, and cuius, though i was written only once it was pronounced twice, as if the spelling were maiior, eiius, Troiia, and cuiius. The second i is the consonant, pronounced like y in yet. The first i is a vowel, which makes a

404

diphthong with the vowel that precedes it according to the rules indicated above in number 5.

SOUNDS OF CONSONANTS

6. The consonants are generally pronounced as they are in English, but the following points should be noted:

c and g are always hard, as in can and go

i (the consonant, which is sometimes printed j) = y in yet

n before c, g, q, and x = ng in sing

r should always be pronounced

s should always be pronounced as in this, never as in these

t as in tin, never as in nation

v = w

x = ks

z = dz

ch, ph, th = c, p, t

bs, bt = ps, pt

qu = qu in quart

ngu = ngu in anguish

su = sw as in suādeō.

a. When consonants are doubled, as in mittō and annus, both consonants should be pronounced, as they are in out-take and pen-knife. We pronounce only one consonant in kitty and penny.

7. We generally consider i a consonant when it occurs between vowels and when it appears at the beginning of a word in front of another vowel. In compounds of iaciō (throw), we find the form iciō. We believe that in these words the consonant i was pronounced, even though it was not written, before vowel i. If we adopt this rule, dēiciō is pronounced as if it were spelled dēiiciō and abiciō as if it were spelled abiiciō.

SYLLABLES

8. Every Latin word has as many syllables as it has vowels or diphthongs.

a. When a single consonant appears between two vowels, it is pronounced with the vowel that follows it, as in fe-rō, a-gō, mo-nē.

a. Some consonants can be pronounced indefinitely. They "flow" and are thus called "liquids." Other consonants fall silent immediately after they are pronounced. Such consonants are called "mutes." When liquids (l or r) follow mutes (b, c, d, g, p, t, ch, ph, or th), the resulting combination is often pronounced like a single consonant together with the following vowel, as in pa-tris and a-grī.

b. Any other combination of two or more consonants is divided before the last consonant or before the "mute-liquid" combination described above (§8.b), as we find in mit-tō, dic-tus, magis-ter, and magis-trī.

LENGTH OF SYLLABLES

9. A syllable is long:

a. If it contains a long vowel or a diphthong, as in both syllables of lau-dās and the first syllable of ēius (§5.a).

b. If its vowel is followed by any two consonants (except the combination of a mute and a liquid [see §8.c]) or by one of the double consonants x (= ks) and z (= dz). The quantity of a short vowel is not changed by its position: est is pronounced est, not ēst. The syllable, not the vowel, becomes long. The time taken to pronounce a consonant at the end of a syllable before the consonant at the beginning of the next syllable (§8.c) lengthens that syllable. You will perceive this if you pronounce each of the consonants that are supposed to be pronounced distinctly in mit-tō (see §6.a), an-nus, dic-tus, par-tōs, and nos-ter.

ACCENT

10. Words with two syllables are accented on the first syllable, as in Caesar.

11. Words with more than two syllables are accented on the penult (second-to-last syllable), if that syllable is long, as in dīvī́sa and appel'lō. If the penult is short, the antepenult (i.e., the syllable third from the end) receives the accent, as in per'tinent.

12. When an enclitic (a word that attaches to the end of another word) is joined to another word, the accent falls on the syllable immediately preceding the enclitic, as in Gallia'que.

INFLECTION

NOUNS

THE GENERAL RULES OF GENDER

13. Latin nouns are classified as masculine, feminine, or neuter. For most nouns, gender is grammatical rather than biological. Often, the gender of nouns can be determined from the nominative ending. In other instances, it must be learned for individual words. The following rules should prove helpful.

a. The names of male beings (human, animal, divine), as well as rivers, winds, and months, are masculine.

a. The names of female beings (human, animal, divine), as well as countries, towns, islands, plants, trees, and most abstract qualities, are feminine.

b. Indeclinable nouns and infinitives, phrases, and clauses used as nouns are neuter.

DECLENSIONS

14. There are five declensions of Latin nouns. They are distinguished from each other by the final letter of the stem and the ending of the genitive singular.

DECLENSION	FINAL LETTER OF STEM	ENDING OF GEN. SING.
I. First	ā	-ae
II. Second	o	-ī
III. Third	consonant or i	-is
IV. Fourth	u	-ūs
V. Fifth	ē	-ēī or -eī

a. In a linguistically precise world, we would form cases by adding case endings to the stem. But the stems of Latin nouns combine with the vowels of case endings in odd ways. It is thus much more convenient (because this method works in practice) to say that the cases are formed by adding case endings to the base. We find the base of a noun by dropping the ending of the genitive singular.

FIRST DECLENSION

15. The stem ends in -ā; the nominative in -a; (and the base ends in whatever remains after removing the genitive singular; see §14.a). The gender is usually feminine.

puella, f., girl

	SINGULAR		ENDINGS
Nominative	puella	the girl ("verbs" as subject)	-a
Genitive	puellae	of the girl, the girl's	-ae
Dative	puellae	to or for the girl	-ae
Accusative	puellam	the girl (as object)	-am
Ablative	puellā	by, from, in, or with the girl	-ā

	PLURAL		ENDINGS
Nominative	puellae	the girls ("verb" as subjects)	-ae
Genitive	puellārum	of the girls, the girls'	-ārum
Dative	puellīs	to or for the girls	-īs
Accusative	puellās	the girls (as objects)	-ās
Ablative	puellīs	by, from, in, or with the girls	-īs

a. Exceptions in gender are generally revealed by the meanings of words (see §13), as in Belgae, m., the Belgae (because groups of people are considered masculine); Matrona, m., the (river) Marne (because rivers are masculine). Others must be learned, as in agricola, m., farmer.

b. The "locative" singular is a way to indicate "place where," i.e., "location." It ends in -ae, such as Romae, at Rome.

c. The "vocative" case is identical with the nominative singular and plural: Puella! O girl! and Puellae! O girls!

SECOND DECLENSION

16. The stem ends in -o; the nominative masculine in -us, -er, or -ir; the nominative neuter in -um; and the base will be found by removing the genitive singular ending (see §14.a).

	servus, m., slave Base serv-	puer, m., boy Base puer-	ager, m., field Base agr-	bellum, n., war Base bell-
SINGULAR				
Nom.	servus	puer	ager	bellum
Gen.	servī	puerī	agrī	bellī
Dat.	servō	puerō	agrō	bellō
Acc.	servum	puerum	agrum	bellum
Abl.	servō	puerō	agrō	bellō
PLURAL				
Nom.	servī	puerī	agrī	bella
Gen.	servōrum	puerōrum	agrōrum	bellōrum
Dat.	servīs	puerīs	agrīs	bellīs
Acc.	servōs	puerōs	agrōs	bella
Abl.	servīs	puerīs	agrīs	bellīs

a. Exceptions in gender are revealed by the meanings of the words (see §13). Fraxinus, ash tree, is feminine; vulgus, crowd, is usually neuter. Locus, m., place, has the plural loca, n., places.

b. The "locative" singular is a way to indicate "place where" or "location." It ends in -ī, such as Agedincī, at Agedincum.

c. In classical Latin, nouns ending in -ius regularly form the genitive and vocative singular with -ī, instead of with -ii, and nouns ending in -ium form the genitive with -ī. The words are accented as if the longer form were used; e.g., consi´lī (from consilium) of advice. In later Latin, genitives in -ii became increasingly common, and many modern editions prefer -ii.

d. The "vocative" case is identical with the nominative except in the nominative singular for second-declension nouns that end in -us or -ius. Nominative -us changes to vocative -e and -ius to vocative -ī; e.g., Serve! O slave! and Molinārī! O Molinarius!

THIRD DECLENSION

17. Third-declension stems end in a consonant or in -i. The nominative case ending for masculines and feminines is an -s or no ending at all; for neuters, none. Because the nominative is so varied, it is convenient to think of it as a "blank." The more useful base may be found by removing the genitive ending (see §14.a). The vocative case is identical with the nominative.

A. CONSONANT STEMS

	lux, f., light Base luc-		mīles, m., soldier Base mīlit-		corpus, n., body Base corpor-	
	SING.	PLURAL	SING.	PLURAL	SING.	PLURAL
Nom.	lux	lucēs	mīles	mīlitēs	corpus	corpora
Gen.	lucis	lucum	mīlitis	mīlitum	corporis	corporum
Dat.	lucī	lucibus	mīlitī	mīlitibus	corporī	corporibus
Acc.	lucem	lucēs	mīlitem	mīlitēs	corpus	corpora
Abl.	luce	lucibus	mīlite	mīlitibus	corpore	corporibus

B. I-STEMS

18. Third-declension nouns are *i*-stems, if (1) they are masculine and feminine nouns ending in -is or -ēs and they have the same number of syllables in the genitive as in the nominative or if (2) they are neuter nouns that end in -e, -al, or -ar.

19. Because this declension became confused with the regular third declension, the i does not appear consistently, and no absolute rule can be given for the endings. Masculine and feminine nouns usually have accusative -em, ablative, -e, accusative plurals either in -ēs or -īs. (Most,

but not all, texts regularize the accusative plural as -ēs; nevertheless, one occasionally encounters the alternative accusative plural that we offer below in our chart of hostis.) Neuters have ablative -ī.

	hostis, m., enemy (Stem hosti-) Base host-	animal, n., animal (Stem animāli-) Base animāl-
SINGULAR		
Nom.	hostis	animal
Gen.	hostis	animālis
Dat.	hostī	animālī
Acc.	hostem	animal
Abl.	hoste	animālī
PLURAL		
Nom.	hostēs	animālia
Gen.	hostium	animālium
Dat.	hostibus	animālibus
Acc.	hostēs or hostīs	animālia
Abl.	hostibus	animālibus

a. Feminine *i*-stem nouns of the third declension decline according to the pattern of hostis, hostis, m., enemy.

C. IRREGULAR NOUNS

20. Some common nouns of the third declension are irregular:

	senex, m., old man Base sen-	vīs, f., force Base v-	bōs, m., f., cow Base bov-	Iuppiter, m., Jupiter Base Iov-
SINGULAR				
Nom.	senex	vīs	bōs	Iuppiter
Gen.	senis	vīs	bovis	Iovis
Dat.	senī	vī	bovī	Iovī
Acc.	senem	vim	bovem	Iovem
Abl.	sene	vī	bove	Iove

Appendix

PLURAL			
Nom.	senēs	vīrēs	bovēs
Gen.	senum	vīrium	bovum or boum
Dat.	senibus	vīribus	bovibus or būbus
Acc.	senēs	vīrēs	bovēs
Abl.	senibus	vīribus	bovibus or būbus

FOURTH DECLENSION

21. The stem of fourth-declension nouns ends in -u; the nominative masculine ends in -us, the nominative neuter in -ū. The base may be found by removing the genitive singular ending (see §14.a).

	manus, f., hand Base man-		cornū, n., horn Base corn-	
	SING.	PLURAL	SING.	PLURAL
Nom.	manus	manūs	cornū	cornua
Gen.	manūs	manuum	cornūs	cornuum
Dat.	manuī	manibus	cornū	cornibus
Acc.	manum	manūs	cornū	cornua
Abl.	manū	manibus	cornū	cornibus

a. Masculine nouns of the fourth declension decline like manus, f., hand.

b. The dative singular of nouns in -us sometimes ends in -ū.

c. The dative and ablative plural of a few nouns sometimes end in -ubus.

d. The vocative is identical to the nominative.

e. Domus, f., house, base dom-, has some second-declension forms. The forms in general use are:

	SING.	PLURAL
Nom.	domus	domūs
Gen.	domūs	domuum
Dat.	domuī or domō	domibus
Acc.	domum	domōs
Abl.	domō or domū	domibus
Locative	domī (at home)	domibus (at or in their homes)

FIFTH DECLENSION

22. Fifth-declension nouns have a stem that ends in -ē and a nominative in -ēs. They are usually feminine.

	rēs, f., thing Base r-		diēs, m., day Base di-	
	SING.	PLURAL	SING.	PLURAL
Nom.	rēs	rēs	diēs	diēs
Gen.	reī	rērum	diēī	diērum
Dat.	reī	rēbus	diēī	diēbus
Acc.	rem	rēs	diem	diēs
Abl.	rē	rēbus	diē	diēbus

a. In the singular, diēs is either masculine or feminine (the feminine is usually used in the sense of an appointed day or for a long space of time); in the plural, diēs is masculine. Its compounds are also masculine.

b. The ending of the genitive and dative singular of fifth-declension nouns is -ēī after a vowel, -eī after a consonant. Sometimes the ending -ē is used instead of either.

c. The vocative is identical to the nominative.

ADJECTIVES

22. FIRST- AND SECOND-DECLENSION ADJECTIVES

magnus, magna, magnum, large

	SINGULAR			PLURAL		
	Masc.	Fem.	Neuter	Masc.	Fem.	Neuter
Nom.	magnus	magna	magnum	magnī	magnae	magna
Gen.	magnī	magnae	magnī	magnōrum	magnārum	magnōrum
Dat.	magnō	magnae	magnō	magnīs	magnīs	magnīs
Acc.	magnum	magnam	magnum	magnōs	magnās	magna
Abl.	magnō	magnā	magnō	magnīs	magnīs	magnīs

līber, lībera, līberum, free

	SINGULAR			PLURAL		
	Masc.	Fem.	Neuter	Masc.	Fem.	Neuter
Nom.	līber	lībera	līberum	līberī	līberae	lībera
Gen.	līberī	līberae	līberī	līberōrum	līberārum	līberōrum
Dat.	līberō	līberae	līberō	līberīs	līberīs	līberīs
Acc.	līberum	līberam	līberum	līberōs	līberās	lībera
Abl.	līberō	līberā	līberō	līberīs	līberīs	līberīs

pulcher, pulchra, pulchrum, beautiful

	SINGULAR			PLURAL		
	Masc.	Fem.	Neuter	Masc.	Fem.	Neuter
Nom.	pulcher	pulchra	pulchrum	pulchrī	pulchrae	pulchra
Gen.	pulchrī	pulchrae	pulchrī	pulchrōrum	pulchrārum	pulchrōrum
Dat.	pulchrō	pulchrae	pulchrō	pulchrīs	pulchrīs	pulchrīs
Acc.	pulchrum	pulchram	pulchrum	pulchrōs	pulchrās	pulchra
Abl.	pulchrō	pulchrā	pulchrō	pulchrīs	pulchrīs	pulchrīs

a. The vocative ending is -e for second-declension masculine singular adjectives ending in -us; e.g., Magne! O great one! (from magnus). For second-declension masculine singular adjectives ending in -ius, the vocative ending is -ī; e.g., Alī! O other one! (from alius). Elsewhere, the vocative is identical with the nominative. Compare second-declension nouns in §16.d.

ADJECTIVES WITH GENITIVE IN -īus.

24. Nine adjectives of the first and second declensions have a genitive singular that ends in -īus (the genitive of alter is usually -ius) and a dative singular that ends in -ī in all genders. These nine adjectives are alius, another; sōlus, only; tōtus, whole; ūllus, any; nūllus, no; ūnus, one; alter, the other; uter, which (of two); and neuter, neither. In the plural, the case endings of these adjectives are exactly the same as they are for magnus. Note also the ending -ud in the neuter of alius.

	SINGULAR			PLURAL		
	Masc.	Fem.	Neuter	Masc.	Fem.	Neuter
Nom.	alius	alia	aliud	aliī	aliae	alia
Gen.	alīus	alīus	alīus	aliōrum	aliārum	aliōrum
Dat.	aliī	aliī	aliī	aliīs	aliīs	aliīs
Acc.	alium	aliam	aliud	aliōs	aliās	alia
Abl.	aliō	aliā	aliō	aliīs	aliīs	aliīs

	SINGULAR			SINGULAR		
	Masc.	Fem.	Neuter	Masc.	Fem.	Neuter
Nom.	ūnus	ūna	ūnum	tōtus	tōta	tōtum
Gen.	ūnīus	ūnīus	ūnīus	tōtīus	tōtīus	tōtīus
Dat.	ūnī	ūnī	ūnī	tōtī	tōtī	tōtī
Acc.	ūnum	ūnam	ūnum	tōtum	tōtam	tōtum
Abl.	ūnō	ūnā	ūnō	tōtō	tōtā	tōtō

THIRD-DECLENSION ADJECTIVES

25. Adjectives of the third declension include both consonant stems and *i*-stems. Third-declension adjectives with three endings have a different form in the nominative singular for each gender. Third-declension adjectives with two endings have one form in the nominative singular for the masculine and feminine and another for the neuter. Third-declension adjectives with one ending have the same form in the nominative singular for all three genders. Except comparatives (which have short -e), all third-declension adjectives with two or three endings always have -ī in the ablative singular.

26. Three endings.

ācer, ācris, ācre, sharp

	SINGULAR			PLURAL		
	Masc.	Fem.	Neuter	Masc.	Fem.	Neuter
Nom.	ācer	ācris	ācre	ācrēs	ācrēs	ācria
Gen.	ācris	ācris	ācris	ācrium	ācrium	ācrium
Dat.	ācrī	ācrī	ācrī	ācribus	ācribus	ācribus
Acc.	ācrem	ācrem	ācre	ācrēs (or ācrīs)	ācrēs (or ācrīs)	ācria
Abl.	ācrī	ācrī	ācrī	ācribus	ācribus	ācribus

27. Two endings.

a. All third-declension adjectives of two endings follow this pattern (except comparatives, for which see next, i.e., §27.b.).

fortis, forte brave

	SINGULAR		PLURAL	
	Masc. & Fem.	Neuter	Masc. & Fem.	Neuter
Nom.	fortis	forte	fortēs	fortia
Gen.	fortis	fortis	fortium	fortium

Dat.	fortī	fortī	fortibus	fortibus
Acc.	fortem	forte	fortēs (or fortīs)	fortia
Abl.	fortī	fortī	fortibus	fortibus

b. The comparative degree of the adjective (see §30) does not follow the regular third-declension adjective paradigm. Note especially the ablative in -e (not -ī), the genitive plural in -um (not -ium), and the neuter nominative and accusative plurals in -a (not -ia).

fortior, fortius, braver

	SINGULAR		PLURAL	
	Masc. & Fem.	Neuter	Masc. & Fem.	Neuter
Nom.	fortior	fortius	fortiōrēs	fortiōra
Gen.	fortiōris	fortiōris	fortiōrum	fortiōrum
Dat.	fortiōrī	fortiōrī	fortiōribus	fortiōribus
Acc.	fortiōrem	fortius	fortiōrēs	fortiōra
Abl.	fortiōre	fortiōre	fortiōribus	fortiōribus

28. One ending.

audāx, gen. audācis, bold

	SINGULAR		PLURAL	
	Masc. & Fem.	Neuter	Masc. & Fem.	Neuter
Nom.	audāx	audāx	audācēs	audācia
Gen.	audācis	audācis	audācium	audācium
Dat.	audācī	audācī	audācibus	audācibus
Acc.	audācem	audāx	audācēs (or audācīs)	audācia
Abl.	audācī	audācī	audācibus	audācibus

29. Present active participle.

amans, loving

	SINGULAR		PLURAL	
	Masc. & Fem.	Neuter	Masc. & Fem.	Neuter
Nom.	amans	amans	amantēs	amantia
Gen.	amantis	amantis	amantium	amantium
Dat.	amantī	amantī	amantibus	amantibus
Acc.	amantem	amans	amantēs (or amantīs)	amantia
Abl.	amante or -ī	amante or -ī	amantibus	amantibus

a. Participles usually have an ablative singular that ends in -ī when they are used as adjectives and in -e when they are used as participles or nouns.

COMPARISON OF ADJECTIVES

30. The regular comparative endings are the third-declension adjective endings -ior (m. & f.), -ius (n.). (See above, §27.b, for the declension of the comparative.) The superlative, -issimus, -a, -um, uses first- and second-declension adjective endings. They are added to the base of the positive form of the adjective (which is found by removing the case ending from the genitive singular). Examples: altus, -a, -um, high; altior, -ius, higher; altissimus, -a, -um, highest; fortis, brave; fortior, braver; fortissimus, bravest.

31. Adjectives in -er form the comparative regularly but form the superlative by adding -rimus to the nominative of the positive. Example: ācer, sharp (base, ācr-), ācrior, ācerrimus.

32. Most adjectives in -ilis form the comparative and superlative regularly. Six adjectives, however, although they form the comparative regularly, form the superlative by adding -limus to the base of the positive. These six are facilis, easy; difficilis, difficult; similis, like; dissimilis, unlike; humilis, low; gracilis, slender. Example: facilis, facilior, facillimus.

IRREGULAR COMPARISON OF ADJECTIVES

33. bonus, melior, optimus, good, better, best

malus, peior, pessimus, bad, worse, worst

magnus, maior, maximus, big, bigger, biggest

parvus, minor, minimus, small, less, least

multus, plūs, plūrimus, much, more, most

dexter, dexterior, dextimus, on the right, favorable (because good omens appeared on the right)

COMPARISON OF ADJECTIVES WITH ADVERBS

34. When an adjective ends in a -us that is preceded by a vowel, it generally forms the comparative and superlative by using the adverbs magis, more, and maximē, most. Many other adjectives employ this method, as well. Example: idōneus, suitable; magis idōneus, more suitable; maximē idōneus, most suitable.

COMPARISON OF ADVERBS

35. Most adverbs are formed from adjectives in all the degrees of comparison.

   a. The positive form of the adverb is formed from adjectives of the first and second declensions by adding -ē to the base, such as lātus, wide, lātē, widely. Adjectives of the third declension add -ter or -iter to the base, except third-declension adjectives whose base ends in nt, which instead add only -er; some examples include: audāx, audācis, bold, audacter, boldly; fortis, brave, fortiter, bravely; prūdēns, prūdentis, prudent, prūdenter, prudently. The neuter accusative singular of adjectives of all declensions may also be used adverbially, such as multum, much; facile, easily.

   a. The comparative form of the adverb is identical with accusative singular neuter of the comparative form of the adjective; such as lātius, more widely; audācius, more boldly; fortius, more bravely; prūdentius, more prudently; plūs, more; facilius, more easily.

b. The superlative form of the adverb is formed by adding -e to the base of the superlative form of the adjective or, less often, its accusative singular neuter, such as lātissimē, most widely; audācissimē, most boldly; fortissimē, most bravely; prūdentissimē, most prudently; plūrimum, most; facillime, most easily.

ROMAN NUMERALS

36. Numeral adjectives include cardinals, which answer the question how many (one, two, three, etc.) and ordinals, which answer the question in what order (first, second, third).

Roman Numerals	Cardinal Numbers	Ordinal Numbers
I.	ūnus, -a, -um	prīmus,-a, -um
II.	duo, -ae, -a	secundus, -a, -um or alter, -a, -um
III.	trēs, tria	tertius, -a, um
IV.	quattuor	quārtus, -a, um
V.	quīnque	quīntus, -a, um
VI.	sex	sextus, -a, um
VII.	septem	septimus, -a, um
VIII.	octo	octāvus, -a, um
IX.	novem	nōnus, -a, um
X.	decem	decimus, -a, um
XI.	ūndecim	ūndecimus, -a, um
XII.	duodecim	duodecimus, -a, um
XIII.	tredecim	tertius decimus tertia decima tertium decimum
XIV.	quattuordecim	quārtus decimus, -a -a, -um -um
XV.	quīndecim	quīntus decimus, -a -a, -um -um
XVI.	sēdecim	sextus decimus, -a -a, -um -um
XVII.	septendecim	septimus decimus, -a -a, -um -um
XVIII.	duodēvīgintī	duodēvīcēsimus, -a, um
XIX.	ūndēvīgintī	ūndēvīcēsimus, -a, um
XX.	vīgintī	vīcēsimus, -a, um

XXI.	ūnus et vīgintī (vīgintī ūnus)	vīcēsimus prīmus, -a -a, -um -um
XXVIII	duodētrīgintā	duodētrīcēsimus, -a, um
XXIX	ūndētrīgintā	ūndētrīcēsimus, -a, um
XXX.	trīgintā	trīcēsimus, -a, um
XL.	quadrāgintā	quadrāgēsimus, -a, um
L	quīnquāgintā	quīnquāgēsimus, -a, um
LX.	sexāgintā	sexāgēsimus, -a, um
LXX.	septuāgintā	septuāgēsimus, -a, um
LXXX.	octōgintā	octōgēsimus, -a, um
XC.	nōnāgintā	nōnāgēsimus, -a, um
C.	centum	centēsimus, -a, um
CI.	centum (et) ūnus	centēsimus (et) prīmus, -a -a, -um -um
CC.	ducentī, -ae, -a	ducentēsimus, -a, um
CCC.	trecentī	trecentēsimus, -a, um
CCCC.	quadringentī	quadringentēsimus, -a, um
D.	quīngentī	quīngentēsimus, -a, um
DC.	sescentī	sescentēsimus, -a, um
DCC.	septingentī	septingentēsimus, -a, um
DCCC.	octingentī	octingentēsimus, -a, um
DCCCC.	nōngentī	nōngentēsimus, -a, um
M.	mīlle	mīllēsimus, -a, um
MM.	duo mīlia	bis mīllēsimus, -a, um

a. The ending -ēnsimus is often used for -ēsimus.

37. The cardinal numbers, ūnus, duo, and trēs are declined; cardinals from quattuor to centum are indeclinable; cardinals from ducentī to nōnāgentī are declined like the plural of magnus (§23); mīlle, when used as an adjective, is indeclinable, but when used as a substantive, it is declined like the plural of animal (§19) and generally spelled mīlia. Ordinal numbers are declined like magnus (§23).

38. For the declension of ūnus, see §24. Its plural usually means only or alone. Duo and trēs are declined as follows:

	duo, two			trēs, three	
	Masc.	Fem.	Neut.	Masc. & Fem.	Neut.
Nom.	duo	duae	duo	trēs	tria
Gen.	duōrum	duārum	duōrum	trium	trium
Dat.	duōbus	duābus	duōbus	tribus	tribus
Acc.	duōs, duo	duās	duo	trēs, trīs	tria
Abl.	duōbus	duābus	duōbus	tribus	tribus

39. The numbers that would fall between the numbers provided in the table in §36 may be produced as follows: In a combination of tens and units, the units may precede the tens, followed by et, as in trēs et quadrāgintā, three and forty = forty-three; or the tens may precede the units but without an et, as in quadrāgintā trēs, forty-three. In other combinations of two numbers, the higher number precedes the lower number, with or without et, as in ducentī (et) vīgintī, two hundred (and) twenty. In combinations of three or more numbers, the order is as in English without et, as in duo mīlia sescentī vīgintī sex, two thousand six hundred twenty six.

PRONOUNS

40. PERSONAL PRONOUNS

	First person: ego, I; nōs, we		Second person: tū, you (thou); vōs, you (y'all, you guys, ye)	
	SING.	PLURAL	SING.	PLURAL
Nom.	ego	nōs	tū	vōs
Gen.	meī	nostrum or nostrī	tuī	vestrum or vestrī
Dat.	mihi	nōbīs	tibi	vōbīs
Acc.	mē	nōs	tē	vōs
Abl.	mē	nōbīs	tē	vōbīs

a. There is no personal pronoun for the third person. A demonstrative pronoun generally serves in its place, often is, he; ea, she; id, it (§45), although other demonstrative pronouns may be used, as well.

b. The preposition cum is enclitic with personal pronouns (i.e., it attaches to the personal pronoun), as in vōbīscum, with y'all.

REFLEXIVE PRONOUNS

41. There is no nominative form of reflexive pronouns because they cannot be the subjects of finite verbs (infinitives have accusative subjects), and they cannot agree with the subject of finite verbs. For the first and second persons, the personal pronouns are also used as reflexives. For the third person, however, there is a special pronoun.

	First person, meī, of myself; nostrum, of ourselves		Second person, tuī, of yourself; vestrum, of yourselves		Third person, suī, of himself, of herself, of itself, of themselves	
	SING.	PLURAL	SING.	PLURAL	SING.	PLURAL
Gen.	meī	nostrum or nostrī	tuī	vestrum or vestrī	suī	suī
Dat.	mihi	nōbīs	tibi	vōbīs	sibi	sibi
Acc.	mē	nōs	tē	vōs	sē	sē
Abl.	mē	nōbīs	tē	vōbīs	sē	sē

a. The preposition cum is enclitic with reflexive pronouns (i.e., it attaches to the reflexive pronoun), as in sēcum, with himself.

42. POSSESSIVE ADJECTIVES AND PRONOUNS

	SINGULAR	PLURAL
1st person	meus, -a, -um, my	noster, -tra, -trum, our
2nd person	tuus, -a, -um, your	vester, -tra, -trum, your
3rd person	eius (gen. sing. of is), his, her, its (when not referring to the subject)	eōrum, eārum, eōrum (gen. sing. of is), their (when not referring to the subject)
3rd person reflexive	suus, -a, -um, his, her, its (when referring to the subject)	suus, -a, -um, their (when referring to the subject)

DEMONSTRATIVE PRONOUNS

43. hīc, haec, hoc (near the speaker), this, these.

	SINGULAR			PLURAL		
	Masc.	Fem.	Neut.	Masc.	Fem.	Neut.
Nom.	hīc	haec	hoc	hī	haec	haec
Gen.	huius	huius	huius	hōrum	hārum	hōrum
Dat.	huic	huic	huic	hīs	hīs	hīs
Acc.	hunc	hanc	hoc	hōs	hās	haec
Abl.	hōc	hāc	hōc	hīs	hīs	hīs

44. ille, illa, illud (something more remote), that, those.

	SINGULAR			PLURAL		
	Masc.	Fem.	Neut.	Masc.	Fem.	Neut.
Nom.	ille	illa	illud	illī	illae	illa
Gen.	illīus	illīus	illīus	illōrum	illārum	illōrum
Dat.	illī	illī	illī	illīs	illīs	illīs
Acc.	illum	illam	illud	illōs	illās	illa
Abl.	illō	illā	illō	illīs	illīs	illīs

45. is, ea, id (unemphatic) this, that, he, she, it; plural: these, those, they

	SINGULAR			PLURAL		
	Masc.	Fem.	Neut.	Masc.	Fem.	Neut.
Nom.	is	ea	id	eī (or īī)	eae	ea
Gen.	eius	eius	eius	eōrum	eārum	eōrum
Dat.	eī	eī	eī	eīs (or īīs)	eīs (or īīs)	eīs (or īīs)
Acc.	eum	eam	id	eōs	eās	ea
Abl.	eō	eā	eō	eīs (or īīs)	eīs (or īīs)	eīs (or īīs)

46. THE RELATIVE PRONOUN

qui, who, which, that

	SINGULAR			PLURAL		
	Masc.	Fem.	Neut.	Masc.	Fem.	Neut.
Nom.	quī	quae	quod	quī	quae	quae
Gen.	cuius	cuius	cuius	quōrum	quārum	quōrum
Dat.	cui	cui	cui	quibus	quibus	quibus
Acc.	quem	quam	quod	quōs	quās	quae
Abl.	quō	quā	quō	quibus	quibus	quibus

a. Quīcumque, whoever, is a generalizing relative. The quī of quīcumque is declined regularly (i.e., decline quī and add cumque).

b. The preposition cum is usually enclitic with (i.e., it attaches to) the relative pronoun, as in quibuscum, with whom.

47. INTERROGATIVE PRONOUNS AND ADJECTIVES

The interrogative adjective quī, quae, quod, what, is declined like the relative pronoun (§46). The interrogative pronoun quis, quid, who, what, is used in the singular.

quis, who? what?

	SINGULAR	
	Masc. & Fem.	Neut.
Nom.	quis	quid
Gen.	cuius	cuius
Dat.	cui	cui
Acc.	quem	quid
Abl.	quō	quō

a. The enclitic -nam is sometimes added to an interrogative to strengthen it; quisnam, who (in the world)?

b. Cum is usually enclitic with (i.e., it attaches to) the interrogative pronoun, as in quōcum, with whom?

48. INDEFINITE PRONOUNS AND ADJECTIVES

The indefinite pronouns are quis, quī and compounds formed with quis, quī as their base. Quis and quī in this sense are generally declined like the interrogatives.

PRONOUN	ADJECTIVE
quis, quid, any one	quī, quae, quod, any
aliquis, aliquid, some one	aliquī, aliquae, aliquod, some
quispiam, quidpiam, some one	quispiam, quaepiam, quodpiam, some
quīvīs, quaevīs, quidvīs or quīlibet, quaelibet, quidlibet any one (you like)	quīvīs, quaevīs, quodvīs or quīlibet, quaelibet, quodlibet any you like
quīdam, quaedam, quiddam, a certain one	quīdam, quaedam, quoddam, a certain
quisque, quidque, each	quisque, quaeque, quodque, each

VERBS

49. There are four conjugations of Latin verbs. They are distinguished from one another by the final vowel of the stem, which can be seen most clearly in the present infinitive.

CONJUGATION	FINAL VOWEL OF STEM	PRESENT INFINITIVE ENDING
I.	ā	-āre
II.	ē	-ēre
III. & III.-io	ĕ (ĭ, ŭ)	-ĕre
IV.	ī	-īre

50. All verb forms can be produced on the basis on one of three stems, which we derive from a verb's "principal parts" (see §51): the present stem (which we derive from the first and second principal parts), the perfect stem (from the third principal part), and the supine stem (from the fourth principal part). In regular verbs, the perfect and supine stems are based on the present stem, but in some irregular verbs, they are formed on distinct roots.

a. Verb forms based on the present stem (derived from the first and second principal parts) include in both the active and passive: the

429

present, imperfect, and future indicative; the present and imperfect subjunctive; the imperative; and the present infinitive. Additional verb forms include in the active only: the present participle and gerund; and in the passive only: the gerundive.

b. Verb forms based on the perfect stem (found in the third principal part) include in the active voice only: the perfect, pluperfect, and future perfect indicative; the perfect and pluperfect subjunctive; and the perfect infinitive.

c. Verb forms based on the supine stem (found in the fourth principal part) include in both the active and passive: the future infinitive; in the active only: the future participle and supine; and in the passive only: the perfect, pluperfect, and future perfect indicative; the perfect and pluperfect subjunctive; the perfect infinitive; and the perfect participle.

51. The principal parts of a verb are those forms commonly listed by grammars and dictionaries to reveal a verb's conjugation, as well as its various stems. These parts are, in the active: (1) the first-person singular present indicative (as the first principal part), (2) the present infinitive (to indicate the conjugation and give the present stem), (3) the first-person singular perfect indicative (to give the perfect stem), (4) the supine (to give the supine or perfect passive stem).

For example, the principal parts of amō are:

amō, amāre (present stem, amā-).

amāvī (perfect stem, amāv-).

amātum (supine stem, amāt-).

Not all verbs have supines. Nor do all verbs have perfect passive participles. Rather than the supine, some textbooks supply the perfect passive participle as a fourth principal part; for example, amātus rather than amātum. In such instances, one finds the supine stem by removing an us rather than an um. At all events, because there is no one form that can be supplied for all verbs, the supine is commonly used for the sake of convenience. And if we translate the fourth principal part as a perfect passive participle (with which it is identical in form), it is because it is more useful to know how to translate a perfect passive participle. Supines occur relatively infrequently, whereas perfect passive participles are ubiquitous.

52. CONJUGATION OF SUM (irregular verb)

Principal parts: sum, esse, fuī, futūrus, be

a. Because there is no supine, we use the future active participle as the fourth principal part for forms based on the supine stem.

N.B.: Translations of the subjunctive are provided by way of example, and are not exhaustive.

INDICATIVE		SUBJUNCTIVE	
SING.	PLURAL	SING.	PLURAL
Present		**Present**	
sum I am	sumus	sim I may be, let me be, I am	sīmus
es	estis	sīs	sītis
est	sunt	sit	sint
Imperfect		**Imperfect**	
eram I was	erāmus	essem (or forem) I might be, I was	essēmus (or forēmus)
erās	erātis	essētis (or forētis)	essētis (or forētis)
erat	erant	esset (or foret)	essent (or forent)

431

Future			
erō I will be	erimus		
eris	eritis		
erit	erunt		
Perfect		Perfect	
fuī I have been, I was	fuīmus	fuerim I may have been, I have been, I was	fuerīmus
fuistī	fuistis	fuerīs	fuerītis
fuit	fuerunt (or fuēre)	fuerit	fuerint
Pluperfect		Pluperfect	
fueram I had been	fuerāmus	fuissem I might have been, I had been	fuissēmus
fuerās	fuerātis	fuissēs	fuissētis
fuerat	fuerant	fuisset	fuissent
Future Perfect			
fuerō I will have been	fuerimus		
fueris	fueritis		
fuerit	fuerint		

SINGULAR		
Masc.	Fem.	Neuter
alterus	altera	alterum
alterius	alterius	alterius
alterī	alterī	alterī
alterum	alteram	alterum
alterō	alterā	alterō

IMPERATIVE		PARTICIPLE
Present		Fut. futūrus, -a, -um going to be
2nd pers. es be!	este be!	INFINITIVE
Present		Pres. esse to be
2nd pers. estō thou shalt be!	estōte ye shall be!	Perf. fuisse to have been
3rd pers. estō he, she, or it shall be!	sunto they shall be!	Fut. futūrus, -a, -um esse or fore to be going to be, to be about to be

53. FIRST CONJUGATION

Active principal parts: amō, amāre, amāvi, amātum, love

Passive principal parts: amor, amārī, amātus sum, be loved

N.B.: Translations of the subjunctive are provided by way of example and are not exhaustive.

	ACTIVE VOICE		PASSIVE VOICE	
	INDICATIVE	SUBJUNCTIVE	INDICATIVE	SUBJUNCTIVE
	Present		Present	
Sing.	amō I love, I am loving, I do love	amem I may love, let me love, I love, etc.	amor I am loved, I am being loved	amer I may be loved, let me be loved, I am loved, etc.
	amās	amēs	amāris or -re	amēris or -re
	amat	amet	amātur	amētur
Plural	amāmus	amēmus	amāmur	amēmur
	amātis	amētis	amāminī	amēminī
	amant	ament	amantur	amentur
	Imperfect		Imperfect	
Sing.	amābam I loved, I was loving, I used to love	amārem I might love, I loved, etc.	amābar I was loved, I was being loved, I used to be loved	amārer I might be loved, I was loved, etc.
	amābās	amārēs	amābāris or -re	amārēris or -re
	amābat	amāret	amābātur	amārētur
Plural	amābāmus	amārēmus	amābāmur	amārēmur
	amābātis	amārētis	amābāminī	amārēminī
	amābant	amārent	amābantur	amārentur
	Future		Future	

Sing.	amābō I will love		amābor I will be loved	
	amābis		amāberis or -re	
	amābit		amābitur	
Plural	amābimus		amābimur	
	amābitis		amābiminī	
	amābunt		amābuntur	
	Perfect		**Perfect**	
Sing.	amāvī I have loved, I loved	amāverim I may have loved, I have loved, I loved	amātus, -a, -um sum I have been loved, I was loved	amātus, -a, -um sīm I may have been loved, I have been loved, I was loved
	amāvistī	amāverīs	amātus, -a, -um es	amātus, -a, -um sīs
	amāvit	amāverit	amātus, -a, -um est	amātus, -a, -um sit
Plural	amāvimus	amāverīmus	amātī, -ae, -a sumus	amātī, -ae, -a sīmus
	amāvistis	amāverītis	amātī, -ae, -a estis	amātī, -ae, -a sītis
	amāvērunt or -ēre	amāverint	amātī, -ae, -a sunt	amātī, -ae, -a sint
	Pluperfect		**Pluperfect**	
Sing.	amāveram I had loved	amāvissem I might have loved, I had loved	amātus, -a, -um eram I had been loved	amātus, -a, -um essem I might have been loved, I had been loved
	amāverās	amāvissēs	amātus, -a, -um erās	amātus, -a, -um essētis
	amāverat	amāvisset	amātus, -a, -um erat	amātus, -a, -um esset

	amāverāmus	amāvissēmus	amātī, -ae, -a erāmus	amātī, -ae, -a essēmus	
Plural	amāverātis	amāvissētis	amātī, -ae, -a erātis	amātī, -ae, -a essētis	
	amāverant	amāvissent	amātī, -ae, -a erant	amātī, -ae, -a essent	

Future Perfect	Future Perfect

Sing.	amāverō I will have loved		amātus, -a, -um erō I will have been loved	
	amāveris		amātus, -a, -um eris	
	amāverit		amātus, -a, -um erit	
Plural	amāverimus		amātī, -ae, -a erimus	
	amāveritis		amātī, -ae, -a eritis	
	amāverint		amātī, -ae, -a erunt	

IMPERATIVE

ACTIVE VOICE		PASSIVE VOICE	
SING.	PLURAL	SING.	PLURAL
Present		Present	
2nd pers. amā love!	amāte love!	amāre be loved!	amāminī be loved!
Future		Future	
2nd pers. amātō thou shalt love!	amātōte ye shall love!	amātor thou shalt be loved!	
3rd pers. amātō he, she, or it shall love!	amantō they shall love!	amātor he, she, or it shall be loved!	amantor they shall be loved!

INFINITIVE		
	ACTIVE VOICE	PASSIVE VOICE
Present	amāre to love	amārī to be loved
Perfect	amāvisse to have loved	amātus, -a, um esse to have been loved
Future	amātūrus, -a, um esse to be going to love	amātum īrī to be going to be loved

PARTICIPLE		
	ACTIVE VOICE	PASSIVE VOICE
Present	amāns loving	—
Perfect	—	amātus, -a, -um loved, having been loved
Future	amātūrus, -a, -um going to love, about to love	amāndus, -a, -um, necessary to be loved, must be loved

SUPINE (Active Voice)	
Accusative	amātum (for the purpose of) loving, in order to love, etc.
Ablative	amātū in loving, by the loving, to love, etc.

GERUND (Active Voice)	
Genitive	amandī of loving

Dative	amandō to or for loving
Accusative	amandum loving
Ablative	amandō by, with, or from loving

54. SECOND CONJUGATION

Active principal parts: videō, vidēre, vīdī, vīsum, see

Passive principal parts: videor, vidērī, vīsus sum, be seen, seem

N.B.: For sample translations of each tense, infinitives, participles, etc., see amō (§53).

	ACTIVE VOICE		PASSIVE VOICE	
	INDICATIVE	SUBJUNCTIVE	INDICATIVE	SUBJUNCTIVE
	Present		**Present**	
Sing.	videō	videam	videor	videar
	vidēs	videās	vidēris or -re	videāris or -re
	videt	videat	vidētur	videātur
Plural	vidēmus	videāmus	vidēmur	videāmur
	vidētis	videātis	vidēminī	videāminī
	vident	videant	videntur	videantur
	Imperfect		**Imperfect**	
Sing.	vidēbam	vidērem	vidēbar	vidērer
	vidēbās	vidērēs	vidēbāris or -re	vidērēris or -re
	vidēbat	vidēret	vidēbātur	vidērētur
Plural	vidēbāmus	vidērēmus	vidēbāmur	vidērēmur
	vidēbātis	vidērētis	vidēbāminī	vidērēminī
	vidēbant	vidērent	vidēbantur	vidērentur
	Future		**Future**	
Sing.	vidēbō		vidēbor	
	vidēbis		vidēberis or -re	
	vidēbit		vidēbitur	
Plural	vidēbimus		vidēbimur	
	vidēbitis		vidēbiminī	
	vidēbunt		vidēbuntur	
	Perfect		**Perfect**	
Sing.	vīdī	vīderim	vīsus sum	vīsus sīm
	vīdistī	vīderīs	vīsus es	vīsus sīs
	vīdit	vīderit	vīsus est	vīsus sit
Plural	vīdimus	vīderīmus	vīsī sumus	vīsī sīmus
	vīdistis	vīderītis	vīsī estis	vīsī sītis
	vīdērunt or -ēre	vīderint	vīsī sunt	vīsī sint

	Pluperfect		Pluperfect	
Sing.	vīderam	vīdissem	vīsus eram	vīsus essem
	vīderās	vīdissēs	vīsus erās	vīsus essētis
	vīderat	vīdisset	vīsus erat	vīsus esset
Plural	vīderāmus	vīdissēmus	vīsī erāmus	vīsī essēmus
	vīderātis	vīdissētis	vīsī erātis	vīsī essētis
	vīderant	vīdissent	vīsī erant	vīsī essent
	Future Perfect		Future Perfect	
Sing.	vīderō		vīsus erō	
	vīderis		vīsus eris	
	vīderit		vīsus erit	
Plural	vīderimus		vīsī erimus	
	vīderitis		vīsī eritis	
	vīderint		vīsī erunt	

IMPERATIVE				
ACTIVE VOICE		PASSIVE VOICE		
SING.	PLURAL	SING.	PLURAL	
Present		Present		
2nd pers. vidē	vidēte	vidēre	vidēminī	
Future		Future		
2nd pers. vidētō	vidētōte	vidētor		
3rd pers. vidētō	videntō	vidētor	videntor	

INFINITIVE		
	ACTIVE VOICE	PASSIVE VOICE
Present	vidēre	vidērī
Perfect	vīdisse	vīsus esse
Future	vīsūrus esse	vīsum īrī

Appendix

440

PARTICIPLE		
	ACTIVE VOICE	**PASSIVE VOICE**
Present	vidēns	—
Perfect	—	vīsus, -a, um
Future	vīsūrus, -a, um	vidēndus, -a, um

SUPINE (Active Voice)	
Accusative	vīsum
Ablative	vīsū

GERUND (Active Voice)	
Genitive	videndī
Dative	videndō
Accusative	videndum
Ablative	videndō

55. THIRD CONJUGATION

Active principal parts: pōnō, pōnere, posuī, positum, put, place

Passive principal parts: pōnor, pōnī, positus sum, be put, be placed

N.B.: For sample translations of each tense, infinitives, participles, etc., see amō (§53).

		ACTIVE VOICE		PASSIVE VOICE	
		INDICATIVE	**SUBJUNCTIVE**	**INDICATIVE**	**SUBJUNCTIVE**
		Present		**Present**	
Sing.		pōnō	pōnam	pōnor	pōnar
		pōnis	pōnās	pōneris or -re	pōnāris or -re
		pōnit	pōnat	pōnitur	pōnātur

Plural	pōnimus	pōnāmus	pōnimur	pōnāmur
	pōnitis	pōnātis	pōniminī	pōnāminī
	pōnunt	pōnant	pōnuntur	pōnantur

	Imperfect		Imperfect	
Sing.	pōnēbam	pōnerem	pōnēbar	pōnerer
	pōnēbās	pōnerēs	pōnēbāris or -re	pōnerēris or -re
	pōnēbat	pōneret	pōnēbātur	pōnerētur
Plural	pōnēbāmus	pōnerēmus	pōnēbāmur	pōnerēmur
	pōnēbātis	pōnerētis	pōnēbāminī	pōnerēminī
	pōnēbant	pōnerent	pōnēbantur	pōnerentur

	Future		Future	
Sing.	pōnam		pōnar	
	pōnēs		pōnēris or -re	
	pōnet		pōnētur	
Plural	pōnēmus		pōnēmur	
	pōnētis		pōnminī	
	pōnent		pōnentur	

	Perfect		Perfect	
Sing.	posuī	posuerim	positus sum	positus sīm
	posuistī	posuerīs	positus es	positus sīs
	posuit	posuerit	positus est	positus sit
Plural	posuimus	posuerīmus	positī sumus	positī sīmus
	posuistis	posuerītis	positī estis	positī sītis
	posuērunt or -ēre	posuerint	positī sunt	positī sint

	Pluperfect		Pluperfect	
Sing.	posueram	posuissem	positus eram	positus essem
	posuerās	posuissēs	positus erās	positus essētis
	posuerat	posuisset	positus erat	positus esset
Plural	posuerāmus	posuissēmus	positī erāmus	positī essēmus
	posuerātis	posuissētis	positī erātis	positī essētis
	posuerant	posuissent	positī erant	positī essent

Appendix

	Future Perfect		Future Perfect	
Sing.	posuerō		positus erō	
	posueris		positus eris	
	posuerit		positus erit	
Plural	posuerimus		positī erimus	
	posueritis		positī eritis	
	posuerint		positī erunt	

IMPERATIVE

ACTIVE VOICE		PASSIVE VOICE	
SING.	PLURAL	SING.	PLURAL
Present		**Present**	
pōne	pōnite	pōnere	pōniminī
Future		**Future**	
2nd pers. pōnitō	pōnitōte	pōnitor	
3rd pers. pōnitō	pōnuntō	pōnitor	pōnuntor

INFINITIVE

	ACTIVE VOICE	PASSIVE VOICE
Present	pōnere	pōnī
Perfect	posuisse	positus esse
Future	positūrus esse	positum īrī

PARTICIPLE

	ACTIVE VOICE	PASSIVE VOICE
Present	pōnens	—
Perfect	—	positus, -a, um
Future	positūrus, -a, um	pōnendus, -a, um

SUPINE (Active Voice)

Accusative	positum
Ablative	positū

GERUND (Active Voice)	
Genitive	pōnendī
Dative	pōnendō
Accusative	pōnendum
Ablative	pōnendō

56. THIRD-IŌ CONJUGATION

Active principal parts: capiō, capere, cēpī, captum, take

Passive principal parts: capior, capī, captus sum, be taken

N.B.: For sample translations of each tense, infinitives, participles, etc., see amō (§53).

		ACTIVE VOICE		PASSIVE VOICE	
		INDICATIVE	SUBJUNCTIVE	INDICATIVE	SUBJUNCTIVE
		Present		Present	
Sing.		capiō	capiam	capior	capiar
		capis	capiās	caperis or -re	capiāris or -re
		capit	capiat	capitur	capiātur
Plural		capimus	capiāmus	capimur	capiāmur
		capitis	capiātis	capiminī	capiāminī
		capiunt	capiant	capiuntur	capiantur
		Imperfect		Imperfect	
Sing.		capiēbam	caperem	capiēbar	capierer
		capiēbās	caperēs	capiēbāris or -re	capierēris or -re
		capiēbat	caperet	capiēbātur	capierētur

	capiēbāmus	caperēmus	capiēbāmur	capierēmur
Plural	capiēbātis	caperētis	capiēbāminī	capierēminī
	capiēbant	caperent	capiēbantur	capierentur
	Future		**Future**	
	capiam		capiar	
Sing.	capiēs		capiēris or -re	
	capiet		capiētur	
	capiēmus		capiēmur	
Plural	capiētis		capiminī	
	capient		capientur	
	Perfect		**Perfect**	
	cēpī	cēperim	captus sum	captus sīm
Sing.	cēpistī	cēperīs	captus es	captus sīs
	cēpit	cēperit	captus est	captus sit
	cēpimus	cēperīmus	captī sumus	captī sīmus
Plural	cēpistis	cēperītis	captī estis	captī sītis
	cēpērunt or -ēre	cēperint	captī sunt	captī sint
	Pluperfect		**Pluperfect**	
	cēperam	cēpissem	captus eram	captus essem
Sing.	cēperās	cēpissēs	captus erās	captus essētis
	cēperat	cēpisset	captus erat	captus esset
	cēperāmus	cēpissēmus	captī erāmus	captī essēmus
Plural	cēperātis	cēpissētis	captī erātis	captī essētis
	cēperant	cēpissent	captī erant	captī essent
	Future Perfect		**Future Perfect**	
	cēperō		captus erō	
Sing.	cēperis		captus eris	
	cēperit		captus erit	
	cēperimus		captī erimus	
Plural	cēperitis		captī eritis	
	cēperint		captī erunt	

IMPERATIVE			
ACTIVE VOICE		**PASSIVE VOICE**	
SING.	PLURAL	SING.	PLURAL
Present		**Present**	
2nd pers. cape	capite	capere	capiminī
Future		**Future**	
2nd pers. capitō	capitōte	capitor	
3rd pers. capitō	capiuntō	capitor	capiuntor

INFINITIVE		
	ACTIVE VOICE	**PASSIVE VOICE**
Present	capere	capī
Perfect	cēpisse	captus esse
Future	captūrus esse	captum īrī

PARTICIPLE		
	ACTIVE VOICE	**PASSIVE VOICE**
Present	capiens	—
Perfect	—	captus, -a, -um
Future	captūrus, -a, -um	capiendus, -a, -um

SUPINE (Active Voice)	
Accusative	captum
Ablative	captū

GERUND (Active Voice)	
Genitive	capiendī
Dative	capiendō
Accusative	capiendum
Ablative	capiendō

57. FOURTH CONJUGATION

Active rincipal parts: sentiō, sentīre, sēnsī, sēnsum, feel, perceive

Passive principal parts: sentior, sentīrī, sēnsus sum, be felt, be perceived

N.B.: For sample translations of each tense, infinitives, participles, etc., see amō (§53).

	ACTIVE VOICE		PASSIVE VOICE	
	INDICATIVE	SUBJUNCTIVE	INDICATIVE	SUBJUNCTIVE
	Present		**Present**	
Sing.	sentiō	sentiam	sentior	sentiar
	sentīs	sentiās	sentīris or -re	sentiāris or -re
	sentit	sentiat	sentītur	sentiātur
Plural	sentīmus	sentiāmus	sentīmur	sentiāmur
	sentītis	sentiātis	sentīminī	sentiāminī
	sentiunt	sentiant	sentiuntur	sentiantur
	Imperfect		**Imperfect**	
Sing.	sentiēbam	sentīrem	sentiēbar	sentīrer
	sentiēbās	sentīrēs	sentiēbāris or -re	sentīrēris or -re
	sentiēbat	sentīret	sentiēbātur	sentīrētur
Plural	sentiēbāmus	sentīrēmus	sentiēbāmur	sentīrēmur
	sentiēbātis	sentīrētis	sentiēbāminī	sentīrēminī
	sentiēbant	sentīrent	sentiēbantur	sentīrentur

	Future		Future	
Sing.	sentiam		sentiar	
	sentiēs		sentiēris or -re	
	sentiet		sentiētur	
Plural	sentiēmus		sentiēmur	
	sentiētis		sentiēminī	
	sentient		sentientur	
	Perfect		**Perfect**	
Sing.	sēnsī	sēnserim	sēnsus sum	sēnsus sīm
	sēnsistī	sēnserīs	sēnsus es	sēnsus sīs
	sēnsit	sēnserit	sēnsus est	sēnsus sit
Plural	sēnsimus	sēnserīmus	sēnsī sumus	sēnsī sīmus
	sēnsistis	sēnserītis	sēnsī estis	sēnsī sītis
	sēnsērunt or -ēre	sēnserint	sēnsī sunt	sēnsī sint
	Pluperfect		**Pluperfect**	
Sing.	sēnseram	sēnsissem	sēnsus eram	sēnsus essem
	sēnserās	sēnsissēs	sēnsus erās	sēnsus essētis
	sēnserat	sēnsisset	sēnsus erat	sēnsus esset
Plural	sēnserāmus	sēnsissēmus	sēnsī erāmus	sēnsī essēmus
	sēnserātis	sēnsissētis	sēnsī erātis	sēnsī essētis
	sēnserant	sēnsissent	sēnsī erant	sēnsī essent
	Future Perfect		**Future Perfect**	
Sing.	sēnserō		sēnsus erō	
	sēnseris		sēnsus eris	
	sēnserit		sēnsus erit	
Plural	sēnserimus		sēnsī erimus	
	sēnseritis		sēnsī eritis	
	sēnserint		sēnsī erunt	

IMPERATIVE			
ACTIVE VOICE		PASSIVE VOICE	
SING.	PLURAL	SING.	PLURAL
Present		Present	
2nd pers. sentī	sentīte	sentīre	sentīminī
Future		Future	
2nd pers. sentītō	sentītōte	sentītor	
3rd pers. sentītō	sentiuntō	sentītor	sentiuntor

INFINITIVE		
	ACTIVE VOICE	PASSIVE VOICE
Present	sentīre	sentīrī
Perfect	sēnsisse	sēnsus esse
Future	sēnsūrus esse	sēnsum īrī

PARTICIPLE		
	ACTIVE VOICE	PASSIVE VOICE
Present	sentiens	—
Perfect	—	sēnsus, -a, -um
Future	sēnsūrus, -a, -um	sentiendus, -a, -um

SUPINE (Active Voice)	
Accusative	sēnsum
Ablative	sēnsū

GERUND (Active Voice)	
Genitive	sentiendī
Dative	sentiendō
Accusative	sentiendum
Ablative	sentiendō

CONTRACTED FORMS

58. When the perfect stem ends in v, the v is sometimes dropped, and usually the two vowels brought together as a result contract. Such forms are sometimes called "syncopated."

    a. Perfects in -āvī, -ēvī, and -ōvī and other tenses based on the same stem sometimes (seem to) drop ve, vē, or vi before r or s.

    Examples: amāsti for amāvistī; amāsse for amāvisse; delērunt for delēvērunt.

    a. Perfects in -īvī and other tenses based on the same stem sometimes drop v in all forms. When the combination of vowels resulting from this is iis, it usually contracts to īs.

    Examples: audiī for audīvī; audieram for audīveram; audisse for audīvisse.

DEPONENT VERBS

59. Deponent verbs have passive forms with active meanings. But the future passive participle remains passive in meaning, and the perfect participle is sometimes passive in meaning. On the other hand, they have the following active forms: future infinitive, present and future participles, gerund, supine.

In the indicative, the subjunctive, and the imperative, the following verbs have the same forms that the verbs in their corresponding conjugation outlined above (§§53–57) have in the passive voice.

	hortor, hortārī, hortātus sum, urge	vereor, verērī, veritus sum, fear	sequor, sequī, secutus sum, follow	patior, patī, passus sum, suffer	partior, partīrī, partītus sum, share
	1st (§53)	2nd (§54)	3rd (§55)	3rd-iō (§56)	4th (§57)
INFINITIVE					

Present	hortārī	verērī	sequī	patī	partīrī
Perfect	hortātus esse	veritus esse	secutus esse	passus esse	partītus esse
Future	hortātūrus esse	veritūrus esse	secutūrus esse	passūrus esse	partītūrus esse
PARTICIPLE					
Present	hortāns	verēns	sequens	patiens	partiens
Perfect	hortātus	veritus	secutus	passus	partītus
Future	hortātūrus	veritūrus	secutūrus	passūrus	partītūrus
Future passive	hortandus	verendus	sequendus	patiendus	partiendus
GERUND					
	hortandī, -ō etc.	verendī, -ō etc.	sequendī, -ō etc.	patiendī, -ō etc.	partiendī, -ō etc.
SUPINE					
	hortātum, -ū	veritum, -ū	secutum, -ū	passum, -ū	partītum, -ū

60. SEMI-DEPONENT VERBS

Semi-deponent verbs have active forms for the tenses based on the present stem and passive forms for the tenses based on the perfect stem.

audeō, audēre, ausus sum, dare

gaudeō, gaudēre, gavīsus sum, rejoice

soleō, solēre, solitus sum, be accustomed

fīdō, fīdere, fīsus sum, trust

PERIPHRASTIC CONSTRUCTIONS

61. Active periphrastic constructions express thoughts about future or intended action. They are formed by combining the future active participle with the verb sum:

Present: amātūrus sum, I am about to love, I intend to love

Imperfect: amātūrus eram, I was about to love, I intended to love, etc.

62. Passive periphrastic constructions express obligation or necessity. They are formed by combining the future passive participle with the verb sum:

Present: amandus sum, I am to be loved, I must be loved, I have to be loved

Imperfect: amandus eram, I was to be loved, I had to be loved, etc.

    a. The agent is generally expressed in the dative case; e.g., Bellum Caesarī agendum erat. The war had to be waged by Caesar.

IRREGULAR VERBS

SUM AND ITS COMPOUNDS

63. For the conjugation of sum, see §52. Sum is conjugated in the same way when combined in compounds with the prepositions ad, dē, in, inter, ob, prae, sub, and super. Praesum has a present participle: praesēns.

64. In the compound absum, sum is conjugated in the same way, but ā is used instead of ab before f, which yields āfuī, āfutūrus, etc. There is a present participle: absēns.

65. In the compound prōsum, sum is conjugated in the same way, but the preposition prō has its original form prōd before all forms of sum beginning with e, as in prōdesse and prōderam. The present tense is: prōsum, prōdes, prōdest; prōsumus, prōdestis, prōsunt.

66. Possum, be able, can, is a compound of pot- and sum.

Principal parts: possum, posse, potuī, be able, can

	INDICATIVE	SUBJUNCTIVE
Present	possum, potes, potest possumus, potestis, possunt	possim, possīs, possit possīmus, possītis, possint
Imperfect	poteram	possem
Future	poterō	
Perfect	potuī	potuerim
Pluperfect	potueram	potuissem
Future Perfect	potuerō	
	INFINITIVE	**PARTICIPLE**
Present	posse	potēns
Perfect	potuisse	—

67. ferō, ferre, tulī, lātum, carry

ACTIVE VOICE

	INDICATIVE	SUBJUNCTIVE
Present	ferō, fers, fert ferimus, fertis, ferunt	feram, ferās, ferat ferāmus, ferātis, ferant
Imperfect	ferēbam, ferēbās, ferēbat ferēbāmus, ferēbātis, ferēbant	ferrem, ferrēs, ferret ferrēmus, ferrētis, ferrent
Future	feram, ferēs, feret ferēmus, ferētis, ferent	
Perfect	tulī	tulerim
Pluperfect	tuleram	tulissem
Future Perfect	tulerō	

PASSIVE VOICE

	INDICATIVE	SUBJUNCTIVE
Present	feror, ferris, fertur ferimur, feriminī, feruntur	ferar, ferāris, ferātur ferāmur, ferāminī, ferantur
Imperfect	ferēbar, ferēbāris, ferēbātur ferēbāmur, ferēbāminī, ferēbantur	ferrer, ferrēris, ferrētur ferrēmur, ferrēminī, ferrentur
Future	ferar, ferēris, ferētur ferēmur, ferēminī, ferentur	
Perfect	lātus sum	lātus sim
Pluperfect	lātus eram	lātus essem
Future Perfect	lātus erō	

	ACTIVE		PASSIVE	
IMPERATIVE				
Present	fer	ferte	ferre	feriminī
Future	fertō	fertōte	fertor	
	fertō	fertuntō	fertor	feruntor
INFINITIVE				
Present	ferre		ferrī	
Perfect	tulisse		lātus esse	
Future	lātūrus esse		lātum īrī	
PARTICIPLE				
Present	ferēns		–	
Perfect	—		lātus, -a, -um	
Future	lātūrus, -a, um		ferendus, -a, um	

68.

volō, velle, voluī, be willing

nōlō, nolle, nōluī, be unwilling

mālō, mālle, māluī, prefer

INDICATIVE

Present	volō	nōlō	mālō
	vīs	nōn vīs	māvīs
	vult	nōn vult	māvult
	volumus	nōlumus	mālumus
	vultis	nōn vultis	māvultis
	volunt	nōlunt	mālunt
Imperfect	volēbam	nōlēbam	mālēbam
Future	volam	nōlam	mālam
Perfect	voluī	nōluī	māluī
Pluperfect	volueram	nōlueram	mālueram
Future Perfect	voluerō	nōluerō	māluerō

SUBJUNCTIVE

Present	velim, velīs, velit velīmus, velītis, velint	nōlim, nōlīs, nōlit nōlīmus, nōlītis, nōlint	mālim, mālīs, mālit mālīmus, mālītis, mālint
Imperfect	vellem, vellēs, vellet vellēmus, vellētis, vellent	nollem, nollēs, nollet nollēmus, nollētis, nollent	mallem, mallēs, mallet mallēmus, mallētis, mallent
Perfect	voluerim	nōluerim	māluerim
Pluperfect	voluissem	nōluissem	māluissem

IMPERATIVE

Present		nōlī nōlīte	

Future		nōlītō	nōlītōte	
		nōlītō	nōluntō	
INFINITIVE				
Present	velle	nōlle	mālle	
Perfect	voluisse	nōluisse	māluisse	
PARTICIPLE				
Present	volēns	nōlēns		

69. Fīō, be made, be done, become, happen, supplies the irregular passive of faciō, make. The vowel ī appears before all vowels except before the vowel e when e appears in the combination -er. In this case, ī becomes ĭ.

Principal parts: fīō, fierī, factus sum

	INDICATIVE	SUBJUNCTIVE
Present	fīō, fīs, fit fīmus, fītis, fīunt	fīam, fīās, fīat fīāmus, fīātis, fīant
Imperfect	fīēbam, fīēbās, fīēbat fīēbāmus, fīēbātis, fīēbant	fierem, fierēs, fieret fierēmus, fierētis, fierent
Future	fīam, fīēs, fīet fīēmus, fīētis, fīent	
Perfect	factus sum	factus sim
Pluperfect	factus eram	factus essem
Future Perfect	factus erō	
IMPERATIVE	**INFINITIVE**	**PARTICIPLE**
Pres. fī, fīte	Pres. fierī	
	Perf. factus esse	Perf. factus, -a, -um

70. eō, īre, iī, itum, go

	INDICATIVE	SUBJUNCTIVE
Present	eō, īs, it īmus, ītis, eunt	eam, eās, eat eāmus, eātis, eant
Imperfect	ībam, ībās, ībat ībāmus, ībātis, ībant	īrem, īrēs, īret īrēmus, īrētis, īrent
Future	ībō, ībis, ībit ībimus, ībitis, ībunt	
Perfect	iī (for īvī)	ierim
Pluperfect	ieram	iissem or īssem
Future Perfect	ierō	

IMPERATIVE	INFINITIVE Active unless marked passive	PARTICIPLE
Pres. ī, īte	Pres.: īre Pres. passive: īrī	Pres. iēns (Gen. euntis)
Fut. ītō ītōte ītō euntō	Perf. iisse or īsse	
	Fut. itūrus esse	Fut. itūrus, -a, -um
GERUND		SUPINE
eundī, etc.		itum, -ū

a. In the tenses based on the perfect stem, ii usually contracts to ī before s.

Resources for Further Study

Basic grammar and syntax review

For self-study, revision, and review, *Wheelock's Latin* is excellent. "Wheelock," as the work is universally known among Latin students, combines concise explanations with thorough coverage of Latin morphology and syntax. Another helpful feature of this text is that it includes extra practice exercises with an answer key. This feature allows self-study students to check their work. Supplementary workbooks and readers, as well as a dedicated website, offer additional practice and study opportunities.

Wheelock's Latin, by Frederic M. Wheelock, 7th ed. rev. by Richard A. LaFleur, New York: Collins Reference, 2011. ISBN: 9780061997228.

More information is available at the official "Wheelock's Latin" website: http://www.wheelockslatin.com.

Vocabulary building

Anyone with a computer, smart phone, or tablet can find sites and apps for studying Latin vocabulary, but a highly effective low-tech option is still available. Vis-Ed produces a box of 1,000 flash cards that cover basic Latin vocabulary. These cards include essential morphological information, including the principal parts of verbs, the genitives and genders of nouns, the nominative forms of adjectives, and of course, English meanings, all in a handy format that allows students to build vocabulary at whatever pace suits them. Additional information is available at http://www.vis-ed.com/.

Latin Vocabulary Cards, by the Visual Education Association, Springfield, OH: Vis-Ed, 1997. ISBN: 9781556370113.

Roman authors in Latin: First readings

The student who wishes to read Latin authors in the original has almost countless choices. The following selections are offered with an eye to easing the transition from guided reading to reading on one's own.

Jerome's translation of the Bible is always a good choice. Jerome translated the Bible for an audience who would have had trouble with the classical Latin of Caesar's and Cicero's day, and for this reason, the Vulgate (as it's commonly called) is an especially good transitional text. Jerome's translations aims to facilitate understanding, and if you already know the stories, so much the better; you will read more Latin more quickly, thus acquiring a feel for Latin syntax, as well as a larger vocabulary.

Biblia Sacra (Vulgate: Bible in Latin), ed. by Robert Weber, 5th ed. rev. by Roger Gryson et al. Stuttgart: Deutsche Bibelgesellschaft, 2007 [1969]. ISBN: 9783438053039.

For the student who wishes to read classical Latin authors, the best first step is a transitional reader. Bolchazy-Carducci offers six authors in the *Legamus* ("Let's Read!") series: Caesar, Catullus, Cicero, Horace, Ovid, and Vergil. These readers feature grammar and syntax review, practice exercises, background essays, and extensive notes and vocabulary that help students make the transition to reading classical Roman authors in the original and unadapted Latin. Self-study students should also consider acquiring the *Teacher's Guide*, which provides answers to the practice exercises, translations, and extra guidance. Of special interest to students of this course may be:

Catullus: A Legamus Transitional Reader, by Sean Smith, Wauconda, IL: Bolchazy-Carducci Publishers, 2006. ISBN: 9780865166349.

Caesar: A Legamus Transitional Reader, by Rose Williams and Hans-Friedrich Mueller, Wauconda, IL: Bolchazy Carducci Publishers, 2013. ISBN: 9780865167339.

Caesar: Legamus Transitional Reader: Teacher's Guide, by Rose Williams and Hans-Friedrich Mueller, Wauconda, IL: Bolchazy Carducci Publishers, 2013. ISBN: 9780865167360.

Additional information about the authors in the *Legamus* series is available at http://www.bolchazy.com/.

And for those interested in inscriptions, a rewarding place to begin is Tyler Lansford's "walking guide" to the inscriptions of Rome. He includes transcriptions of the Latin text, along with English translations and discussion. As a bonus, after you have finished the book, you can book a flight to Rome to view and read the inscriptions *in sitū*:

The Latin Inscriptions of Rome: A Walking Guide, by Tyler Lansford, Baltimore: The Johns Hopkins Press, 2009.

Bilingual editions of Roman authors

For students with an interest in a particular author, it is always helpful to consult a translation. Close translations of most major Latin authors may be found in the bilingual editions of the Loeb Classical Library, published by Harvard University Press. The original Latin appears on the left-hand page, and the corresponding English translation on the right-hand page. This is very helpful, but please bear in mind that these editions do not provide any additional help. They do not provide vocabulary or extensive commentary. More information is available at http://www.hup.harvard.edu/.

Latin literature online

The *Perseus Digital Library*, edited by Gregory R. Crane, Tufts University, offers the works of most major Roman authors through a freely accessible website. These texts are hyperlinked, so that readers may click on individual words for help in parsing. Additional links bring access to dictionary entries, translations, and commentaries. It would be difficult to exaggerate how helpful *Perseus* can be for readers trying to make their way through a Latin text. More information is available at http://www.perseus.tufts.edu.

Also worthy of mention is *Lacus Curius*, a site that offers a short introduction to Latin inscriptions in three levels: 13 "easy" inscriptions, 10 inscriptions of "medium" difficulty, and 5 classified as "hard." Each inscription includes a photograph, a transcription, and an answer key. *Lacus Curtius* also provides a wealth of information about ancient Rome more generally. The short introduction to epigraphy (the study of inscriptions) may be found here: http://penelope.uchicago.edu/Thayer/E/Roman/Texts/Inscriptions/home.html.

Basic reference works

Despite the easy access we now enjoy to electronic resources, it is also sometimes nice to have a good dictionary and a reference grammar. A good dictionary can help explain an unusual meaning, and a good reference grammar can explain an odd form, a mood, or an unusual turn of phrase. And both can supply endlessly fascinating information if one cares to explore vocabulary or syntax in depth.

There is really only one smaller dictionary worth purchasing, and that is William Smith's *Chambers Murray Latin-English Dictionary*. It provides good coverage beyond a wide range of Latin authors and, despite its compact size, a surprising range of examples of Latin usage. Most smaller Latin dictionaries are mere word lists. This dictionary delivers much more in a small format and at a reasonable price:

Chambers Murray Latin-English Dictionary, by William Smith and John Lockwood, Edinburgh & London: Chambers & Murray Publishers, 1994 [1933]. ISBN: 9780550190031.

For those who want a large dictionary with excellent coverage of both classical and Christian Latin, then Lewis and Short's *Latin Dictionary* is an excellent choice. The even larger *Oxford Latin Dictionary* does not include Christian Latin (although it is now the standard authority in English on pre-Christian Latin). Lewis and Short has entered the public domain. It may be accessed online and downloaded without charge from: http://athirdway.com/glossa/. Lewis and Short is also still available in print:

A Latin Dictionary: Founded on Andrews' Edition of Freund's Latin Dictionary, by Charlton T. Lewis and Charles Short, Oxford: Clarendon Press, 1956 [1879]. ISBN: 9780198642015.

There are various reference grammars available, and Latin teachers are often partisans of one or another. Many advocate Gildersleeve's *Latin Grammar* on the grounds that Gildersleeve is the most thorough. I would agree with that assessment, and I prefer using Gildersleeve myself. However, unless one already knows Latin fairly well, I would not recommend Gildersleeve as a first stop. I generally recommend that students in search of more detailed information about Latin syntax begin with Allen and Greenough's *New Latin Grammar* and that they reserve Gildersleeve for deeper inquiries after they have consulted Allen and Greenough.

Allen and Greenough's New Latin Grammar, by James B. Greenough and J. H. Allen, rev. by G. L. Kittredge et al. Mineola, NY: Dover Publications, 2006 [1903]. ISBN: 9780486448060.

Gildersleeve's Latin Grammar, by B. L. Gildersleeve and G. Lodge, Mineola, NY: Dover Publications, 2009 [1894]. ISBN: 9780486469126.

Notes

Notes

Notes

Notes